OHIO OUR STATE

By **Robert T. Howe**

Roblen Publishing Company
Cincinnati, Ohio

OHIO OUR STATE

Author: Robert T. Howe
Professor Emeritus, University of Cincinnati

Executive Editor: Lyn McLean

Assistant: Aerin Csigny

Design and Artwork: Slaughter & Slaughter, Inc.

Printing & Binding: C. J. Krehbiel Company

Library of Congress 91-67205

10   9   8   7   6   5   4   3   2   1

ISSN: 0-9631313-0-3

Roblen Publishing Company
1516 Northview Ave.
Cincinnati, Ohio 45223

Supplementary materials:
Teacher's Handbook

Roblen Publishing Company

Acknowledgments and Credits

Copy Editor: Helen Cooper Howe
>Retired teacher of history, Walnut Hills High School
>Cincinnati, Ohio

Assistant Copy Editor: Elizabeth Bookser Barkley
>Instructor in Humanities, College of Mount St. Joseph
>Cincinnati, Ohio

Critique of First Draft: Jan Derry Catherwood
>Teacher of English and Ohio History, Shelby Junior High School
>Shelby, Ohio

Critique of First Draft: Andy Mitchel
>8th-grade student, Shelby Junior High School

Critique of First Draft: Andrew Bishop
>7th-grade student, Turpin Junior High School, Cincinnati

Critique of Revised Draft: George W. Knepper
>Distinguished Professor of History, University of Akron
>Akron, Ohio

Critique of Revised Draft: Ed Stober
>Chairperson of Social Studies, Porter Junior High School
>Cincinnati, Ohio

Graphic Design and Artwork: Susan and James Slaughter
>Graphic Design, Book Design, and Typographic Instructors
>Xavier University, Cincinnati Art Academy, Northern Kentucky University, and NIOSH

Table of Contents

Education
Women
Religion
Recreation
Creative and Performing Arts

Map List

CHAPTER 1

What's it all about?

Be ready to learn...

- where Ohio is in the world.

- why Ohio is an interesting place to live.

- how Ohio and its counties got their names.

- how to learn about our state.

- about our state symbols.

As you study the State of Ohio, you will discover how it became the state we know today as well as what may happen in the years to come. You will learn about the history, geography, government, and economics of our state. You will also learn how the county in which you live relates to the rest of Ohio. Most important, you will learn how people of the past made decisions that affect your life today.

State symbol used on all official documents

Where is Ohio?

Try to find Ohio on this map of the world below. It is such a small speck there is no room for an identification label! Ohio looks much bigger on the map of the United States mainland on the next page.

People from different parts of the United States look at this second map and see Ohio in a variety of ways. To people in Maine, New Jersey or Maryland, Ohio is "out west." To people living in California, Oregon, or

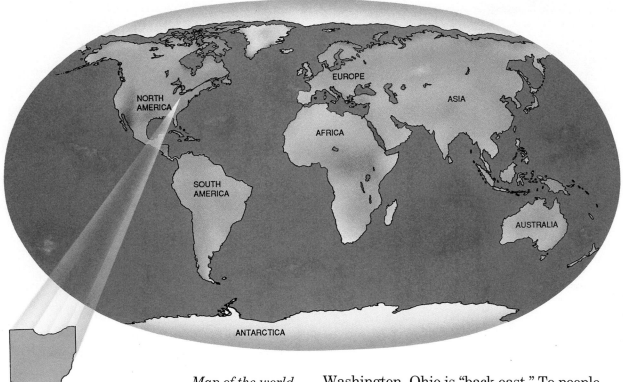

Map of the world adapted from a satellite photo.

Washington, Ohio is "back east." To people in Florida and Louisiana, we are "Northerners." To people in Michigan or Minnesota, we are "Southerners."

We Ohioans usually call ourselves "Midwesterners." But people living in Kansas or Colorado may also think of themselves in that same way.

How was Ohio named?

Ohio takes its name from the river which forms its southern and eastern boundaries. Long before anyone thought of creating a state, this river was well-traveled by the Iroquois people. They lived in what is now New York State. When European explorers asked the Iroquois the name of the river, they spoke a word that sounded like "Ohio."

The Europeans soon began to call the area to the north and west of this river the "Ohio Country." When the United States of America came into existence in 1776, this area was called the "**Territory** Northwest of the Ohio River." When the first state was formed out of the Northwest Territory in 1803, it was named "Ohio."

State flag of Ohio

Map of the continental United States. Alaska and Hawaii are not shown.

3

How would you describe Ohio?

Of the 50 states of the United States, Ohio is 35th in size. If you travel across our state from east to west at its greatest width, you will go about 200 miles (320 kilometers[1]). If you cross the state from north to south, you will travel about the same distance.

The distinctive shape of Ohio is created by Lake Erie and the Ohio River. The Ohio marks our southern border with Kentucky and our eastern border with West Virginia. The boundaries with our other neighbors: Pennsylvania to the east, Indiana to the west, and Michigan to the north are straight lines.

In order to keep government convenient for all citizens, the states of the United States are divided into **counties**.[2] Ohio's 88 counties are shown on the map below. You can find the year in which your county was organized, its size in square miles, and the origin of its name in Appendix A on page 383.

Ohio has been divided into two quite different regions by the forces of nature. Notice the dividing line drawn from the southwest corner of Ohio (in Hamilton County) to the northeast corner of Ohio (in Ashtabula County).

If you live to the northwest of this **diagonal**, you may think that Ohio is very

Map of Ohio. North of the diagonal line the state is flat; south it is hilly. Within the diagonal band the state is urban; outside it is rural.

4

flat. If you live to the southeast, you may think our state is very hilly. (You will learn what caused this "line" in Chapter 2.)

We can use this diagonal to describe Ohio in another way. If you live within about 25 miles (40 km) to either side of it — in the shaded area — you may think that Ohio is **urban** — just one city after another. If you live outside this band, you may think Ohio is a **rural** state.

Why is Ohio Important?

The 17th State

When the thirteen original colonies signed the Declaration of Independence in 1776, they agreed to cooperate with each other under the Articles of Confederation. These Articles established a system for governing the unsettled regions in the West. The Ohio Country, or the Territory Northwest of the Ohio, was part of this unsettled area.

The United States Constitution, adopted in 1787, said that additional states could be added to the United States of America. Vermont joined the original thirteen states in 1791, Kentucky in 1792, Tennessee in 1796, and Ohio in 1803.

Population

From 1840 through 1880, Ohio had the third largest population of the existing states. Only New York and Pennsylvania had more people.

During the 1880s, Chicago grew into a very large city. By 1890, therefore, Illinois had more people than Ohio. That made Ohio the fourth largest state in terms of population.

The 'Buckeye State'

Early explorers traveling in the Ohio Country found many trees with unusual fruits. Once the prickly outer shell was removed, the inner nut reminded them of the eye of a deer.

They called these nuts "buckeyes." (A buck is a male deer.) Soon the trees were called "**buckeyes**" as well.

The scientific name for the Ohio buckeye tree is *Aesculus globra*. It is closely related to the horse chestnut tree, but the buckeye has *five* leaflets — which look something like the spread-out fingers of

your hand. The horse chestnut has *seven*. In the spring, flowers appear after the buckeye leaves are out.

President William Henry Harrison, who lived most of his adult life in Ohio, used a buckeye tree as the symbol for his election campaign in 1840. After that, people everywhere began to refer to Ohio as "the buckeye state." The Ohio General Assembly made the buckeye the official state tree in 1953.

State animal: deer
(proposed but not yet
officially adopted)

State fossil: trilobite

The Symbols of Ohio

All human beings take pride in the groups to which they belong. Ancient peoples used marks, signs, and words to identify themselves as members of a particular tribe or group. Even today, organizations of all kinds use special symbols, handshakes, and rituals that set them apart from other groups.

The State of Ohio has adopted special symbols to mark our state's identity. These symbols are shown on pages 1 - 9.

Following World War II, many Americans chose to move to what we now call the "sun belt." This includes California, Arizona, Texas, and Florida. As a result, by 1990 Ohio ranked seventh in population.

Important Cities

In the 1850s, Cincinnati was the fourth largest city in the United States with a population of 100,000. Only New York, Philadelphia, and New Orleans were larger.

By 1950, Ohio was the only state to have eight cities of more than 100,000 people. Cleveland, in Cuyahoga County near the northeast end of the diagonal, was by far the largest city. Cincinnati, in Hamilton County at the southwest end of the diagonal, was the second largest. Columbus, in Franklin County near the middle of the diagonal, was third. By 1980, Columbus was larger than either Cleveland or Cincinnati.

Industrial Heartland

For almost 100 years, from 1860 to 1960, Ohio was part of the "industrial heartland" of America. Between 1910 and 1950, you could travel anywhere in the United States and find heavy construction equipment made in the Ohio cities of Euclid, Galion, and Marion; machine tools made in Cincinnati or Cleveland; locomotives made in Lima; glass made in Toledo; and tires made in Akron.

But as the population of the United States shifted after World War II, industries also moved to the South and West. During the 1970s, Ohio and its neighboring states were often referred to as the "rust belt." During the 1980s, the people of Ohio worked hard to regain the great industrial reputation our state once had. A new state slogan was adopted to capture this new spirit: "Ohio: The Heart of It All." This slogan can now be seen on Ohio's automobile license plates.

State bird: cardinal

How will we study our state?

We will begin our study of Ohio by looking at the events that have shaped its development. We will begin about 500 million years ago when the oldest rocks were formed. We will end the study by considering the challenges we face in the future.

This book is divided into three parts: Part One covers events up to the time Ohio became a state in 1803. Part Two looks at the 19th century (1801-1900). Part Three focuses on the 20th century (1901-2000).

Much of this book will talk about counties because every Ohioan lives in a county. Each of us also lives in a township, a village, or a city. We will also study these units of government because they affect our lives in many ways every day. Appendix A will tell you when your county was formed, its seat, and why it was given its name.

Almost everything you know today you have learned from others. You have listened to them speak. You have read what they wrote. You have watched their actions. As you study Ohio from this textbook, you will be encouraged to go out into your own neighborhood and study the things that are all around you. This is another important way to learn.

You may want to learn more about someone in your own family, community, or county or about some of the most famous people in the world who have lived in Ohio.

Stop and Think!

Perhaps you have lived in Ohio all of your life. Perhaps you have just moved into the "Buckeye State." In either case, you cannot appreciate our state today unless you understand the events that have shaped the present. In this book we will examine how and why changes took place over the centuries in order to understand what is likely to happen in the future.

While learning the particular history, geography, government, and economics of Ohio, you will also be learning how to study history, how to use geography, how to analyze government, and how to understand economics. These are important skills for the rest of your life — no matter where you live!

State mineral: flint

Footnotes

1. All present measurements will be given in both English and metric form. Historic measurements will be given only in English units.

2. Words in boldface are explained in the glossary.

State insect: ladybug

'Beautiful Ohio'

The following words to the state song were written by Ballard MacDonald. The music was composed by Mary Earl.

Long, long ago, someone I know
Had a little red canoe
In it room for only two
Love found its start,
Then in my heart
And like a flower grew.

Chorus:

Drifting with the current down a
    moonlit stream
While above the Heavens in their
    glory gleam
And the stars on high
Twinkle in the sky
Seeming in a Paradise of love divine
Dreaming of a pair of eyes that
looked in mine
Beautiful Ohio, in dreams again I see
Visions of what used to be.

This song tells about a love story that took place on the Ohio River, and was adopted as the state song in 1969.

It really says nothing about our state. From time to time people have suggested alternative words to the beautiful music.

Review the Chapter!

Building vocabulary...

buckeye
county
diagonal
rural
scale (of a map)
territory
urban

State flower: scarlet carnation

Meeting new people...

William Henry Harrison

Testing yourself...

Do you know...

1. how many counties Ohio has?
2. the county in which you live?
3. What is unusual about the geography of Ohio?
4. our state tree?
5. what bodies of water give Ohio its unusual shape?
6. what states surround Ohio?

True or false...

1. Ohio is the fifth-largest state based on population.
2. Columbus is the largest city in Ohio.
3. "Ohio" is a Cherokee name.
4. Ohio was the 17th state to join the United States.
5. Cincinnati is the county seat of Cuyahoga County.

Learning by doing...

1. Locate your county on the map of Ohio on page 4. Is it hilly or flat? Is it urban or rural?
2. Use Appendix A to learn how your county was named. How did your township, village, or city get its name?
3. Practice until you can draw a reasonably accurate outline map of Ohio. Label each boundary line and adjacent state.

Keeping a scrapbook...

Begin a scrapbook of information about Ohio. Divide it into chapters to match those in this book.

Clip and save articles from your daily newspaper about the people, places, and events of your local community, your county, and the state as a whole. If you live in a rural area, get a copy of the Sunday edition of the newspaper in the nearest large city.

Gather brochures about tourist attractions in Ohio from your local library, historical society, or a nearby hotel or motel.

Read *Timeline* (the magazine of the Ohio Historical Society) *and Ohio Magazine.* Both are excellent sources of information about Ohio.

State beverage: tomato juice

Working with maps...

Every chapter includes map work. You will need four maps:

— A map of your county

— A highway map of Ohio

— A map of the United States

— A map of the world

It is important to have your own maps so you can mark on them as you tackle problems like these:

1. Each map has a **scale** along either its top or bottom edge. This scale shows how the distance you measure on the map in inches or centimeters relates to the actual distance on the ground in miles or kilometers. Write on a piece of notebook paper the scale of each of the four maps listed above.
2. Learn the scale of your Ohio map. Draw two lines on your paper. Make one represent 100 miles to scale. Make the other 100 kilometers. Label the left end of each line "0" and the right end "100."
3. Compare the scale of your map of the United States with the scale of your Ohio map. Beginning at the left end of each line you have drawn in #2, measure and mark off 100 miles and 100 kilometers according to the U.S. map scale. Label these points.
4. Compare the scale of the map of the world to the scale of the other maps. Using the world map scale, plot similar points along your two lines.
5. Compare the scale of the map of your county to all the other maps, Measure points at 10 miles and 10 kilometers along the two lines.
6. Why do these four maps have such different scales?

Part One:

What is **history**? History is the record of human activity, primarily in *written* form. The essays you wrote and the grades you received in school last year are now part of the history of your life and of the school you attended.

The world's oldest historic records are the writings found on clay tablets in the Middle East and on walls of Egyptian tombs. These date back to about 3000 BC.

The ability to write and keep records is essential to our understanding of history. **Prehistoric** peoples are those who have no written language. Some people in our world today, such as the aborigines in Australia, are "prehistoric" by this definition.

The native peoples of North America did not write. We therefore call the time before the arrival of Europeans, the "prehistoric period." In Ohio that means anything before about 1700 when the first European explorers began to write about their experiences in this area.

One way to learn about prehistoric people is from the physical remains of their lives. Broken pottery, bones, fragments of weapons — these can last for thousands of years. **Archaeologists** study such things to learn how people lived long ago.

Another way to learn about prehistoric events is to examine the structure of the earth. By studying rocks and glacier movements, **Geologists** can learn much about prehistoric times.

In Part One of this book, we shall explore all kinds of information — both prehistoric and historic — that help us understand what Ohio was like over the many thousands of years before it became a state in 1803.

Bringing History to Life

Many people have studied the history, and prehistory, of Ohio, but few have written such interesting stories about it as James Alexander Thom. He tells the story of how the first white settlers and Ohio's native peoples struggled to get along with one another.

Before Mr. Thom began to write, he gathered together all of the historical information available on the subject. Then he traveled the area where the events occurred. He writes as though reporting on Ohio events as they actually happened.

His book *Long Knife* deals with the life of George Rogers Clark, whom you will meet in Chapter 4. *Panther in The Sky* is the life story of Tecumseh, whom you will learn about in Chapters 4, 5 and 6.

CHAPTER 2

How did nature shape Ohio?

Be ready to learn...

- what geology tells us about geography.

- how glaciers shaped Ohio as we know it today.

- about the rocks and soils of Ohio.

- how forces of nature change the landscape.

- about the raw materials of our state.

Geologists now believe that our Earth has existed for somewhere between four and five billion years. Fortunately for those of us studying Ohio history, the oldest rocks in our state were formed only about 500 million years ago. That's important to know, because these rocks help us understand our state.

Learning From Geologists

Bedrock — How It All Began

Bedrock is the solid rock below the layer of soil. If you live in southeastern Ohio, you can see bedrock exposed in the hills around you. If you live in northwestern Ohio, the bedrock may be far below the surface of the ground.

All of the bedrock in Ohio is made up of sandstone, shale, and limestone. These are all forms of **sedimentary** rock — and that tells us a lot about what Ohio used to be like!

The land on which you now live was at the bottom of a saltwater sea several times during the past billion years. (So was almost every other square inch of the Earth's surface.) The sedimentary bedrock all over Ohio was created as small bits (sediments) of sand, clay, and calcium settled to the ocean bottom and became cemented together.

This sedimentary rock eventually covered almost all of the older **igneous** rock which makes up the earth's core. (Igneous means rocks "made by fire.") The map on page 13 shows the layers of rock under our state.

Limestone was made from the remains of billions of small creatures that once lived in saltwater. When they died, their bones and shells, made of calcium, dropped to the bottom of the ocean and lay there for thousands of years. Eventually this sediment formed some of the bedrock of Ohio. When you go to a beach and pick up shells or pieces of coral, you are handling the raw material of limestone.

Ohio limestone is used as a building material. You can see limestone quarries and cliffs in central Ohio. The marble window sills in your home or school are one form of limestone.

Right: The geology of Ohio affects our lives everyday.
Below: Sandstone under Lorain County has been used for buildings for more than 100 years.

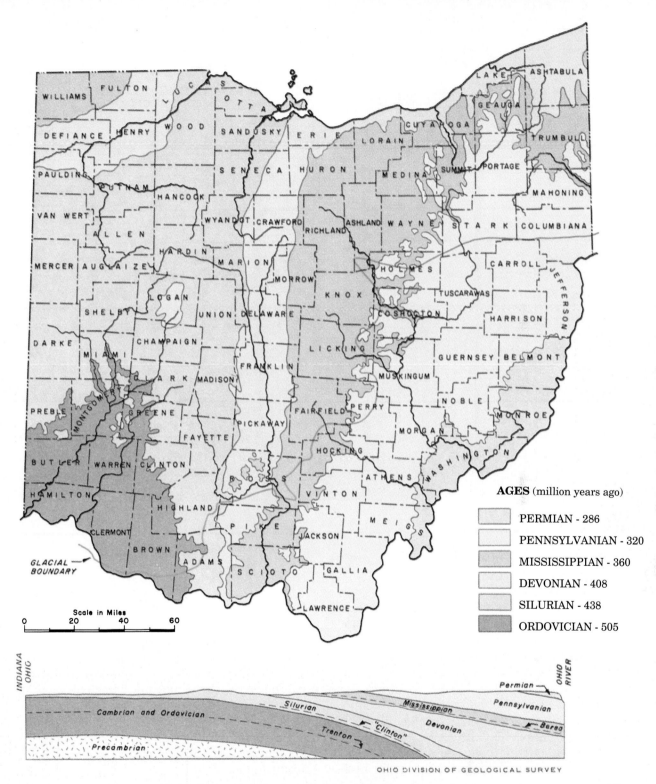

Scale in Miles
0   20   40   60

GLACIAL
BOUNDARY

AGES (million years ago)

PERMIAN - 286
PENNSYLVANIAN - 320
MISSISSIPPIAN - 360
DEVONIAN - 408
SILURIAN - 438
ORDOVICIAN - 505

INDIANA
OHIO

OHIO RIVER

Permian
Pennsylvanian
Mississippian
Berea
Silurian
Devonian
"Clinton"
Cambrian and Ordovician
Trenton
Precambrian

OHIO DIVISION OF GEOLOGICAL SURVEY

13

Geological Timeline

	Snails	Trilobites	Clams	Lungfish	Sharks	Spiders	Insects	Dinosaurs	Turtles
Age (million years ago)									

EPOCHS

Pleistocene - 1.8	
Pliocene - 5	
Miocene - 24	
Oligocene - 37	
Eocene - 58	
Paleocene - 66	

PERIODS

Cretaceous - 144	
Jurassic - 208	
Triassic - 245	
Permian - 286	
Pennsylvanian - 320	
Mississippian - 360	
Devonian - 408	
Silurian - 438	
Ordovician - 505	
Cambrian - 570	

When you play on a sandy beach, you are playing with the raw material of **sandstone**. In some cities you can see houses built of sandstone; these are often called "brownstones." Blocks of sandstone are cut from the century-old **sandstone quarry** in Lorain County, shown on page 12.

The weakest form of bedrock found in Ohio is **shale**. Shale was formed from clay at the bottom of the prehistoric ocean. You may have blackboards in your school made from a form of shale called slate. Slate is formed when shale is submitted to great heat and pressure by the forces of nature.

The map on page 13 shows that the oldest rocks in Ohio (the dark pink Ordovician) are in the southwest corner of the state. These are limestone and shale. It also shows that the youngest rocks (the orange Permian) are in the southeast corner. These are sandstone and shale.

Limestone breaks down to produce good soil for agriculture. Sandstone and shale produce poor soil.

14

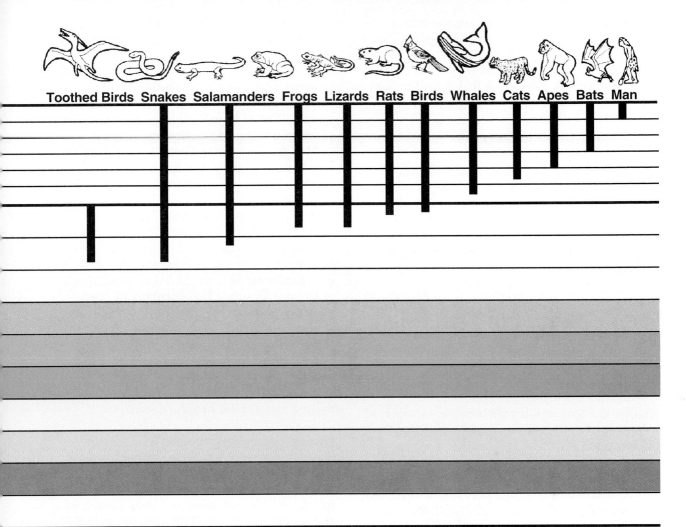

Toothed Birds **Snakes** **Salamanders** **Frogs** **Lizards** **Rats** **Birds** **Whales** **Cats** **Apes** **Bats** **Man**

The rocks of Ohio contain fossils of creatures that lived millions of years ago.

The **cross section** of Ohio on the geological map at the bottom of page 13 shows that the layers of rock under Ohio are curved. Millions of years ago the Precambrian (or igneous) rocks heaved upward and broke the layers of sedimentary rocks above. During the next long, long period of time, the forces of **weathering** and **erosion** weakened and removed the broken pieces of rock that resulted from the upheaval.

Geological Time

The diagram above shows how geologists divide time over the past 570 million years. The artist has divided the lower part of the diagram in what looks like 10 equal bands representing geological *periods*. If you subtract the numbers shown with the periods, you find that the Silurian was the shortest (30 million years) and the Cretaceous was longest (78 million years). You will also see that the artist divided the upper part, which is called the *Tertiary*

15

period, into 6 equal bands representing geological **epochs**. The total length of the Tertiary period was 66 million years. The lengths of the epochs vary from 18 million for the Paleocene to 1.8 million for the Pleistocene.

Fossils — Clues to Early Life

Have you ever looked for **fossils** in the rocks of Ohio? Fossils are "remnants in stone" of animals and plants that lived millions of years ago. The diagram on pages 14 and 15 shows the kinds of creatures that lived when the various layers of rocks were being formed.

For example, trilobites, our state fossil, lived during the millions of years that the rocks under Ohio were being created. They are not found in older rocks, nor in younger rocks. The oldest fossils of dinosaurs appear in Triassic rocks, which were created after trilobites disappeared. There are no dinosaur fossils after the Cretaceous period. Fossils of spiders first appeared in the Devonian period.

To the right of this diagram you can see that the oldest remains of humans found so far are of people who lived less than two million years ago — during the Pliocene Epoch. (An **epoch** is a very long period of time.) But the oldest records of human activity in Ohio dates back to about 12,000 BC.

A Changing Landscape

When the temperature and humidity go up, we become uncomfortable. When the weather turns cold, we protect ourselves by wearing warm clothing and by building fires to heat the space around us. Rain is essential for growing food, but it can interfere with our work or play. These ordinary weather events can have tremendous effects on the land surfaces.

The strongest of rocks can be destroyed by heating and cooling, by wetting and drying, by freezing and thawing. Granite, one of the hardest forms of rock, can be destroyed in a place like the Arizona desert where it is heated by the sun to about 130^0 Fahrenheit (50^0 Celsius) every day and then cooled to about 70^0 F (21^0 C) every night.

If you leave a piece of wood in water for a week and then put it out in the sun for several days to dry, and repeat the operation for many cycles, you will eventually be able to take the wood apart with your fingers. The potholes in our streets are good example of how freezing and thawing can break down hard materials such as concrete and asphalt. When the natural processes of heating and cooling, wetting and drying, freezing and thawing go on for thousands of years, whole mountains can be broken down.

Caves, or caverns, are one example of change at work. A cave is an open space in underground rock. It is formed when acid surface water moves down through cracks in a layer of sandstone and then dissolves the limestone below. The map on page 17 shows the names and locations of the most important caves in Ohio open to visitors.

Ash Cave and Old Man's Cave in Hocking Hills State Park are interesting geological features, but they are not really caves! These above-ground indentations in rock were formed by erosion, the process by which the earth's surface is worn away or moved by the force of wind, water, or glacial ice. You see the power of erosion at work when you turn a stream of water from a garden hose against a pile of dirt or sand.

LAKE ERIE
CAVES

CRYSTAL ROCK CAVE
SENECA CAVERNS
INDIAN TRAIL CAVERNS

ZANE CAVERNS
OHIO • OLENTANGY CAVERNS
CAVERNS

SEVEN CAVES

You can visit these caves in our state.

Flooded streams can carry away large rocks, and high waves can erode shore lines.

Wind can also erode. Have you ever seen a "whirlwind" form behind a tractor as a farmer plows a field? A strong wind blowing across a bare field picks up fine particles of soil. When the flying particles hit a hard object, they cause erosion. The most dramatic examples of wind erosion near Ohio are the rock arches at Natural Bridge State Park in Kentucky.

Studying Ohio's Glaciers

Many people who live in northwest Ohio never see the bedrock on the geological map. It is covered by layers of **glacial drift**, the soil and rock left behind by the glaciers that once covered that part of Ohio.

Glaciers are huge sheets of ice that moved over Ohio, as well as other parts of North America and the world, four times. These glaciers have had a tremendous influence on life in Ohio.

17

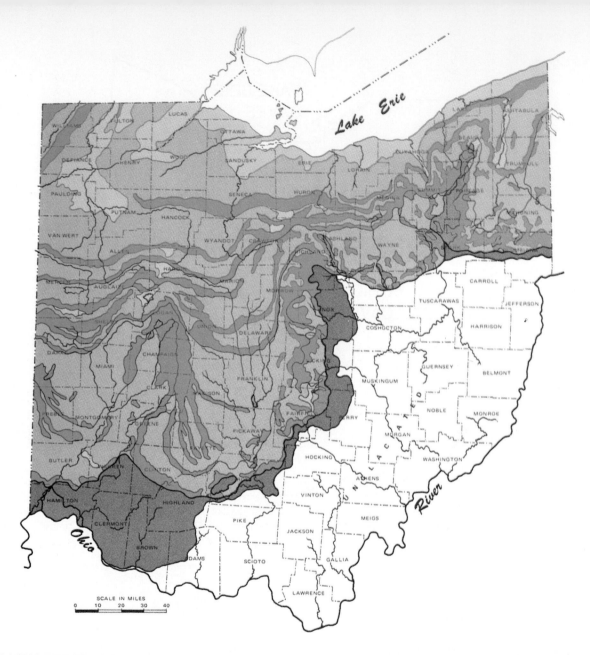

GLACIAL DEPOSITS OF OHIO

Many years ago, the land we call Ohio was covered by great sheets of ice.

WISCONSINAN

- KAMES AND ESKERS
- LAKE DEPOSITS
- GROUND MORAINE
- END MORAINE

ILLINOIAN

- UNDIFFERENTIATED

KANSAN

- GROUND MORAINE

No one really knows what caused glaciers to move in and out of Ohio, but there are several good guesses. Perhaps weather patterns changed and the Earth became so much colder that the polar ice caps extended farther south into the northern hemisphere. Or perhaps thin pieces of the Earth's crust shifted so that the area we now call Ohio was much closer to the North Pole.

These glacial movements took place from one million to 15,000 years ago. Each glacial period in the United States is named after the state in which it was first studied. From the earliest to the most recent, they are: the *Nebraskan Ice Age*, the *Kansan Ice Age*, the *Illinoian Ice Age*, and the *Wisconsin Ice Age*.

The remains of the last three glacial periods in Ohio are shown on page 18. All of the Nebraskan glacial material was covered or eroded away by the later glaciers.

The Lay of the Land

What is the thickest layer of ice you have ever seen? In northern Ohio today you can sometimes see ice on ponds or lakes as much as three feet (one meter) thick. If you live in southern Ohio, you can go ice-skating when the pond ice becomes six inches (15 centimeters) thick.

Geologists tell us that the glaciers in Ohio were 10,000 feet (3,000 meters) thick! Of course the southern edges of the glaciers were not so thick because ice "flows" very, very slowly. But, still, that's some "ice cube!"

The glaciers did not cover the southeast third of our state. But water from melting glacial ice caused great erosion there. In

the northwestern part of the state, the glaciers changed the entire countryside. Beginning far north in Canada, the glaciers acted like huge bulldozers pushing soil and broken rock to the south into Ohio. They also leveled whatever hills were in front of them.

In some places where the ground was soft, a glacier scooped out the soil to make a huge pit. When the ice later melted, the pit was filled with water. Five such "pits" are the Great Lakes: Lake Ontario, Lake Erie, Lake Huron, Lake Michigan, and Lake Superior. (See the map on page 53.)

The soil and rock scraped loose by an advancing glacier froze into the mass of ice and moved southward with the slowly moving glacier. When the front edge of a glacier reached a warmer climate, the glacier stopped advancing and the ice began to melt. In that process of melting, the glacier dropped the soil and rocks it had picked up while moving south.

The last glacial period ended about 15,000 years ago. At that time the ice melted back to about where we find the Arctic ice cap today. Visitors to Alaska or the Rocky Mountains of Canada can still see glaciers in action!

A New Drainage System

Geologists know that most of the rivers of Ohio once flowed to the north. As the glaciers blocked these streams, the water had to cut new paths. The most dramatic examples of this new stream-cutting can be found along the southern border of our state. Here the Ohio River now flows through the "notches" it cut in the bedrock. The artist's sketch of travel on the Ohio in the early 1800's, on page 21, shows such a "notch" in the background where steep hillsides rise on both side of the river.

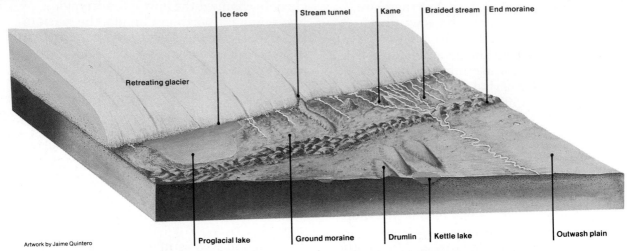

| Ice face | Stream tunnel | Kame | Braided stream | End moraine |

Retreating glacier

| Proglacial lake | Ground moraine | Drumlin | Kettle lake | Outwash plain |

Artwork by Jaime Quintero

As the glaciers melted they left behind the land forms we live with today.

Since the last glacier disappeared, the path of Ohio's main streams are as shown on page 22. The **divide** traces the highest land across the state. Water that falls to the north of the divide flows to the Atlantic Ocean by way of Lake Erie, Lake Ontario, and the St. Lawrence River. Water that falls to the south of the divide flows to the Gulf of Mexico by way of the Ohio and Mississippi Rivers.

In southeastern Ohio you can easily see divides as distinct lines. In northwestern Ohio you may need surveying instruments to find them.

Distinctive Soils.

More than one-half of the soils of Ohio are directly related to the actions of the glaciers. The Wisconsin glacier had the greatest influence on present-day Ohio, as shown on the map on page 18. The diagram above shows glacial features you can see today.

All the yellow and green areas on the map are **moraines**, or the soil left behind by the melting Wisconsin glacier. There are two types of moraines, depending on whether the deposits were left behind when the glacier was melting slowing or rapidly.

The yellow areas on the map are "ground moraines." The landscape in these areas is almost flat because the soils and rocks trapped in the ice dropped straight down as the ice melted slowly. Most of this soil is very good for agriculture.

The green bands represent "end moraines." These are long ridges of sand and gravel that dropped when the glacier was melting so rapidly that the fine soil particles were carried away by erosion. End moraines are seldom good for agriculture, but they are sources of sand and gravel for construction projects.

20

The Ohio River flows between steep hills.

Almost all the hills you see in northwest Ohio are actually end moraines. The city of Moraine in Montgomery County includes an end moraine within its boundaries.

The small dark pink areas on the map represent **eskers** and **kames**. Eskers are rather similar to end moraines, but smaller. Kames are mounds of sand and gravel. Some prehistoric people used kames as burial places for their dead.

The blue area on the map represents soil created on a lake bottom. As the Wisconsin glacier melted back to the north, tremendous volumes of water were created,

including what we call the Great Lakes. Twelve thousand years ago these lakes were much larger than they are now. In fact, Lake Erie once included all the blue area at the top of the map. When soil eroded by the melting glacier reached the still water of the lake, it settled out. Later, when the lake shrunk, large areas of excellent soil were exposed.

When white settlers entered northern Ohio about 1800, the area shown in blue was covered with shallow water and dense vegetation. For this reason they call it the Black Swamp. In Chapter 10 you will learn

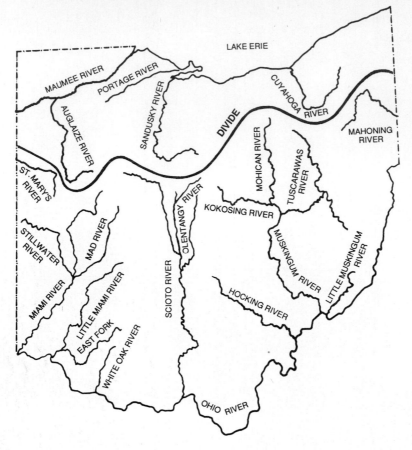

Our state is drained by a complicated pattern of rivers.

how this area was eventually changed into some of the best farm land in Ohio.

The Illinoian glacier deposits are shown in light pink. All the types of deposits we talked about above in connection with the Wisconsin glacier are also found in this area. But this map does not show the individual ground formations for lack of space.

Remains of the Kansan glacier can be seen today only in a portion of Hamilton County. See the one small area of brown on the map.

The best soils in southeast Ohio (the white area on the map) are along the streams. Where glacial melt water washed soils into the valleys, the valleys are broad. In all other places, however, the valleys are quite narrow.

The hills of this region are made up of sandstone and shale. The soil produced when these rocks break down is poor for agriculture. Because of the combination of steep slopes and poor soil, the principal crop in this region is grass for grazing cows and sheep. A typical scene of the hills and forests of this region is shown on page 23.

Southeastern Ohio has many forests and beautiful scenes.

▼ PETROLEUM
● COAL

Coal and petroleum are important raw materials in these counties of Ohio.

Raw Materials of Ohio

A **raw material** is something found in nature that can be changed into something of value. The raw materials that are important to life in Ohio today include rocks, trees, salt, coal, and petroleum. Iron Ore was once very important, but was all used by 1900.

Rock

Quarries are sources of bedrock that can be cut into usable shapes for building purposes, or crushed into granular material.

The sandstone quarry in northeastern Ohio pictured on page 12 has been used for more than 100 years.

Ohio does not have any of the very hard rocks, such as granite, or any of the decorative rocks, such as marble. But some Ohio limestone and sandstone is of such high quality that it can be used as **cut stone** — that is, as trim on buildings or for tombstones.

Granular materials, such as sand and gravel, are very important raw materials for highway construction and for making concrete. Areas of Ohio that do not have

24

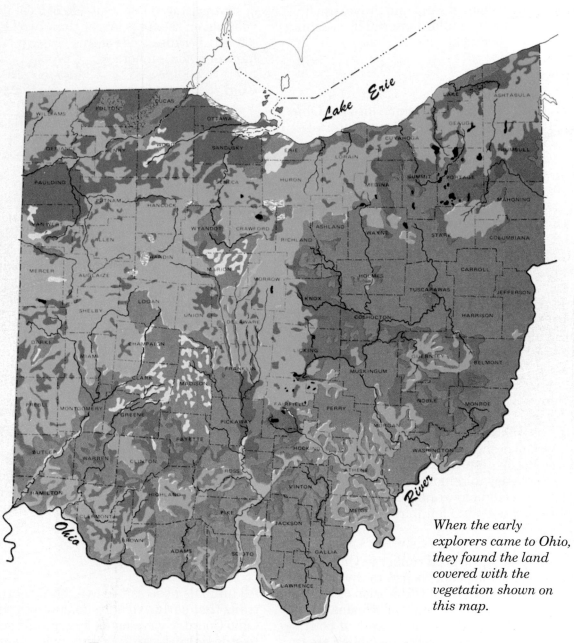

When the early explorers came to Ohio, they found the land covered with the vegetation shown on this map.

	BEECH FORESTS		PRAIRIE GRASSLANDS
	MIXED OAK FORESTS		OAK SAVANNAS
	OAK - SUGAR MAPLE FORESTS		MARSHES AND FENS
	ELM - ASH SWAMP FORESTS		SPHAGNUM PEAT BOGS
	MIXED MESOPHYTIC FORESTS		BOTTOMLAND HARDWOOD FORESTS

natural deposits of sand and gravel must manufacture granular material by crushing limestone bedrock.

Timber

When the early settlers came into the Ohio country, the most plentiful raw material was trees! Almost the entire area was covered by trees, some as large as seven feet (two meters) in diameter. See the vegetation map on page 25.

These forests were mixed blessings to the settlers. Trees provided fuel for heating and cooking as well as wood for building houses, barns, fences, and furniture. But settlers had to cut down thousands of trees to clear the land for farming.

During the 1800's, many of the trees felled to clear the Ohio land for farming were sold to sawmills. These trees provided the lumber used to build the cities of the United States.

It was relatively easy to cut down the trees. It was also easy enough to drag the logs over frozen ground to the sawmills. But it was not easy to remove the stumps so that farmers could plow and plant seeds. These stumps were often left to rot over a period of years.

After most of the good timber in Ohio had been cut, some people began to worry about the loss of woodlands, the erosion of hillsides, and the clogging of streams. These **conservationists** began to work at both state and national levels to establish areas where forests could grow again under protection of the law.

Today there are state-owned forests and parks scattered across Ohio. Wayne National Forest covers many square miles

of southeastern Ohio. Outside of local parks you seldom see trees larger than two feet (60 cm), because trees of this size are harvested for lumber.

Coal

Coal is a black material that looks like rock, but it will break easily if hit with a hammer. It is one of the most useful raw materials found in Ohio.

Beds of coal were created from the trees and other plants that fell into swamps millions of years ago. When the surface of the Earth later dropped below sea level, all this dead vegetation, or **organic matter**, was buried under the shells, sand, and clay that settled to the bottom of the sea. The great weight of the water and the sediments pressed the organic matter into the form of soft rock that we call coal.

Today coal is mined in several counties of eastern Ohio as shown on the map on page 24. Unfortunately, most of the coal found in Ohio contains sulfur. When sulfur burns, it creates sulfur dioxide, and when this chemical mixes with moisture in the atmosphere it makes sulfuric acids. The resulting **acid rain** is the source of many environmental problems for people living in places to the northeast of our state.

Salt

All animals need salt to live. Many of the trails that early explorers followed in the Ohio Country were made by animals going to **salt licks**. Licking County was given its name because its salt deposits were used for hundreds of years by Native Americans, animals and, later, white settlers.

Buckeye Furnace

When the canals of Ohio were created during the 19th century, salt was one of the most important items carried in the canal boats. In the days before refrigeration, there were only three ways to preserve meat: dry it, smoke it, or pack it in barrels with salt. Northeastern Ohio still produces a large amount of salt.

Iron

Iron is so important to civilization that the entire span of time from about 2000 BC to about 1800 AD is called the Iron Age. When European explorers reached America, the native people were still living in the Stone Age. That means they had no ability to work with metals. Even today there are people living in remote parts of the world under Stone Age conditions.

During the last half of the 19th century, Ohio was one of the most important sources of iron in the United States. In fact, Ohio's Hanging Rock Iron Region was one of the leading iron-producing centers of the world. This area extended more than a hundred miles from Logan, Ohio, to Mt. Savage, Kentucky, and contained all the materials necessary to produce high-grade iron.

Sixty nine charcoal iron furnaces like the one shown on page 27 operated in Ohio. The region was named for the small community of Hanging Rock on U.S. 52 in Lawrence County. Twenty-three of these furnaces were located in Lawrence County. No wonder the county seat was named Ironton!

Scioto County also had many furnaces. You will find small communities in that area named Scioto Furnace, Franklin Furnace, and Ohio Furnace.

As you travel along the older roads of Ohio, you can find roadside markers that tell about local history. The following words appear on a historical marker on Buckeye Furnace Road in Jackson County, a short distance southeast of Wellston:

Buckeye Furnace (1851-1874)

One of 69 charcoal iron furnaces in the famous Hanging Rock Iron Region. Extending more than 100 miles from Logan, Ohio, to Mt. Savage, Kentucky, this area contained all materials necessary to produce high grade iron. The industry flourished for over 50 years in the mid 19th century during which time the area was one of the leading iron producing centers in the world. The charcoal iron industry was responsible for the rapid development of southern Ohio, and the romance of the Hanging Rock Region forms a brilliant chapter in the industrial chapter of the Buckeye State.

Almost 100 years after it closed, the Ohio Historical Society gained control of the Buckeye Furnace and repaired the buildings as shown on page 27.

Petroleum

Petroleum is the source of gasoline, diesel fuel, and lubricating oils. Almost one half of the petroleum used in the United States today comes from foreign countries. But in 1890, about one half of the petroleum used in the United States came from Ohio!

You can see oil wells like this in some parts of our state.

The map on page 24 shows the places in Ohio where natural gas and oil are obtained today. As you ride along a highway in these areas, you can see small petroleum pumps similar to the one shown on page 29. You will often see one, two, or three small storage tanks nearby. These pumps are raising petroleum from 3,000 to 5,000 feet below the surface of the ground. You will learn more about Ohio's petroleum industry in Chapters 10 and 14.

Stop and Think!

One of the greatest gifts we have is the ability to study nature and to use the Earth's resources creatively.

The greatest single event of nature to affect life in Ohio was the glacial period between one million and 15,000 years ago. During this time four great sheets of ice covered large parts of our state.

The glaciers created the good farm land in northwest Ohio. The fact that they did not reach into southeast Ohio left that area with poor land for agriculture. The rivers, streams, and lakes of Ohio were also shaped by the glaciers.

Ohio has some natural resources that are plentiful and some that are scarce. During the 19th century, so much iron was taken out of Ohio that no more is available today.

In 1900 Ohio produced one half of all the petroleum used in the United States, but today we do not produce nearly enough for our own use. Ohio still has large deposits of coal, but sulfur in the coal creates problems of acid rain. One Ohio resource that is renewable is our trees, and lumbering continues to be an important industry.

Conservationists are now trying to work in harmony with nature so that future citizens of Ohio will be able to enjoy the natural resources we enjoy today. In all of the remaining chapters of this book, we will see how these natural resources have influenced the development of Ohio — and how Ohioans have used these resources to pursue the good life.

Review the Chapter!

Building vocabulary...

acid rain
archaeologists
cave/cavern
cross section
cut stone
conservationist
divide
epoch
erosion
esker
fossil
geologist
glacial drift
glacier
history
igneous
kame
limestone
moraine
organic matter
petroleum
prehistoric
quarry

raw material
salt lick
sandstone
sedimentary
shale
soil
weathering

Testing yourself...

Match...

1. geologist
2. epoch
3. igneous
4. limestone
5. natural resource
6. shale
7. conservation
8. meteorologist
9. salt
10. erosion

...with these.

a. fire stone
b. preservative for food
c. studies the weather
d. learns from rocks
e. formed from shells and bones
f. period of time
g. formed from clay
h. water acting on rock
i. protection of natural resources
j. nature's gift to Ohio

Name...

1. one place where you could mine salt.
2. two types of erosion.
3. three ages of glaciers.
4. four kinds of rock.
5. five natural resources.
6. six counties that produce oil or gas.
7. seven counties that were covered by glaciers.
8. eight forms of life in Ohio before the explorers.
9. nine Ohio streams (four flowing north and five south).
10. ten kinds of trees found in Ohio.

Which would you prefer and why?

1. To work in a coal mine or a salt mine?
2. To live in a forest or on a prairie?
3. To own a petroleum well or a stand of timber?
4. To have a home of stone or of wood?
5. To live in historic times or in prehistory?

Learning by doing...

1. Use PLAY-DOH® and sand to demonstrate how the glaciers affected Ohio.

2. Run water through a piece of plastic tubing into a container of sand to demonstrate erosion.

3. Find objects around your home or neighborhood that show the effects of weathering. Explain how the weathering took place.

4. Fossils occur naturally in only a few places in Ohio. If you can't find one in nature, locate one in a museum.

5. Prepare a display of the natural resources of Ohio. Explain how each of these is important to your county.

6. Perform some science experiments on a piece of Ohio coal.

PLAY-DOH® is a trademark of Kenner Products

Thinking it through...

What would happen if...

1. The Earth's crust shifted so that Ohio moved much further north?

2. We used up all of our natural resources?

3. Foreign petroleum producers stopped selling to us?

4. A drought hit the entire United States for two years? For four years?

5. A blight hit all of the trees of Ohio and they began to die?

Working with maps...

1. Locate the caves (caverns) of Ohio shown on page 17 on your state map. Scale the distance from your home to the nearest cave. Calculate the distance in miles and kilometers.

2. Use your map of the United States and your imagination to sketch the parts of Indiana, Michigan, Pennsylvania, West Virginia and Kentucky that you think might have been covered by one or more glaciers.

3. On your map of the United States, find Nebraska, Kansas, Illinois, and Wisconsin. In which state was the most recent glacier studied? After which state was the oldest glacier named?

4. Using the map on page 24, name 10 counties where you can expect to find coal as well as oil and natural gas.

5. Use the map on page 25 to determine what kinds of trees covered your county in 1800. What kinds of trees grow in your community today?

CHAPTER 3

Who lived in Ohio before 1600?

Be ready to learn...

• when and how people first came to Ohio.

• how we learn about prehistoric people.

• where and how the earliest Ohioans lived.

• why some prehistoric Ohio people are called mound builders.

Our state was named after the river that forms its southern boundary. When European explorers and settlers began to move westward from the Atlantic Coast in the early 1700s, they called this area the Ohio Country.

The earliest explorers from Europe found strange mounds of earth scattered over the Ohio Country, especially in the southern half. The native people living in the region had not built these mounds, and they had no **legends**, or stories about where they came from. We now know that these mounds were built by highly skilled people who lived here between 1000 BC and 600 AD. For the next 1000 years, people of lesser skills lived in the area.

Chapter 2 surveyed the geography and the natural resources which the early Europeans found in the Ohio country. Now we will focus on the people who lived here long before the arrival of the white traders.

Earliest People of the Ohio Country

Indians — that is how almost every book written before 1970 refers to the people who lived in North America before Europeans arrived. But we use the same name for people who live in the country of India. Why the same name for such very different people?

When Columbus sailed the ocean blue in 1492, the educated people of Europe knew about the wonders of the *Indies* — their name for the lands in the **Far East** we now call India, Indonesia, Thailand, Vietnam, and China. These **exotic** (foreign) lands produced spices, herbs, silk, and works of art not available in 15th-century Europe. Wealthy Europeans were eager to have such treasures.

Because Christopher Columbus believed the Earth was round, he decided he could reach the Far East by sailing west. He had no idea that the continents of North America and South America existed. When Columbus reached the island in the Caribbean Sea which he named San Salvador, he was convinced he must be in the Indies. In a letter he wrote in February of 1493, he referred to the dark-skinned native people as "Indios."

The explorers who followed Columbus called all the native peoples of North and South America "Indians." Today, many of the descendants of these so-called American Indians prefer to be called "Native Americans."

Where did these Native Americans come from? Few experts accept the idea that people may always have lived in the

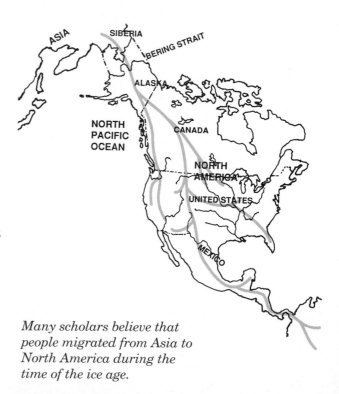

Many scholars believe that people migrated from Asia to North America during the time of the ice age.

Prehistoric People in Ohio

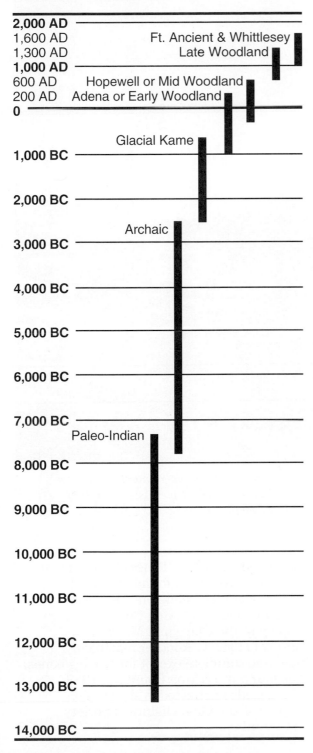

2,000 AD	
1,600 AD	Ft. Ancient & Whittlesey
1,300 AD	Late Woodland
1,000 AD	
600 AD	Hopewell or Mid Woodland
200 AD	Adena or Early Woodland
0	
	Glacial Kame
1,000 BC	
2,000 BC	
	Archaic
3,000 BC	
4,000 BC	
5,000 BC	
6,000 BC	
7,000 BC	
	Paleo-Indian
8,000 BC	
9,000 BC	
10,000 BC	
11,000 BC	
12,000 BC	
13,000 BC	
14,000 BC	

Americas. The oldest human remains date to the end of the last glacial period, about 13,0000 BC.

Anthropologists (scientists who study prehistoric people) have long known that Native Americans have physical features resembling the people of China, Japan, and Korea. For this reason, they decided that the earliest people of North America must have been able to travel by land from Asia to the area we call Alaska. The Bering Sea has covered this land since the last glacier retreated. The map on page 34 shows how they might have moved across North America over a period of several thousands of years.

Learning About Prehistoric Ohioans

People who do not know how to work with metals, such as bronze or iron, are said to live in the *Stone Age*. Most Stone Age people have no written language so they are also prehistoric. The people who lived in the Ohio Country before 1600 lived under Stone Age conditions.

Although these early inhabitants left no written records, we have ways of learning about their lives. Ever since Ohio became a state, farmers plowing their fields and construction workers digging foundations for buildings have found bones, arrowheads, and other **relics** (remains) which provide clues to how these people lived. Even today, archeologists from the colleges of Ohio receive calls from people who uncover ancient artifacts.

The chart on this page shows a timeline of the various prehistoric groups that called Ohio home.

Two complete skeletons of mastodons have been found in Ohio. Scientists think they looked like this.

Paleo-Indians

The Greek word *palaio* means ancient. All English words that begin with "paleo" refer to things that are very old. The earliest people who lived in North America are called *Paleo-Indians*. Some of them entered Ohio about 13,000 BC. Paleo-Indians hunted ice-age animals, and gathered nuts and berries for food. The largest animal they hunted in Ohio was the **mastodon**, an animal similar to an elephant. An artist's idea of a mastodon is shown above.

Fossilized (rock-like) bones of these huge creatures have been found in Ohio. In 1926, a complete skeleton was uncovered at Johnstown in Licking County. It is on display in the Cleveland Museum of Natural History. Another mastodon skeleton, complete except for two leg bones, was found in Licking County in 1989. There is also a mastodon skeleton on display at the Ohio Historical Society in Columbus.

Flint, a rock that has very sharp edges when broken, was the most important tool of the Paleo-Indians. The people used flint weapons to kill mastodons, and flint knives to skin the animals.

Flint Ridge, in Licking County, was an important source of flint for prehistoric people living over a very large area. Tools and weapons made from Flint Ridge stone have been found all over the eastern half of the United States. This is why it is our state mineral.

This material was so important to the Stone Age people that all tribes agreed that flint workers would never be attacked while traveling to or from Flint Ridge — or while working there. Today you can visit Flint Ridge State Memorial and stand in places where Paleo-Indians once worked.

Archaic Indians

Archaeological evidence tells us that about 7,000 BC more skilled people entered the area we know as Ohio. **Archaic** also means "very old", and these newcomers are called *Archaic Indians*. As you can see from the timeline on page 35, these people occupied the Ohio Country for almost 4000 years, but we know very little about them.

We know that the Archaic people used fire because charcoal has been found at their campsites. Charcoal can last for thousands of years, and scientists can accurately calculate its age.

Between 2000 BC and 1000 BC, some Archaic Indians found a use for the glacial kames we discussed in Chapter 2. They dug shallow holes in these mounds of sand and gravel to bury their dead. These people are called the *Glacial Kame* Indians.

Woodland Indians

Great changes in life-styles came to the eastern parts of the United States about 1000 BC. This date marked the beginning of the *Woodland* period. The centuries between 1000 BC and about 1200 AD are divided into the Early, Middle, and Late Woodland Periods.

In Ohio the early period is called **Adena** and the middle period **Hopewell**. Together these periods are called the time of the Mound Builders.

Why "Adena?"
Why "Hopewell?"

When Ohio became a state in 1803, Thomas Worthington, a man you will learn more about in Chapter 6, lived in Ross County, north of Chillicothe. Mr. Worthington called his home *Adena*, a Hebrew word that means "beautiful place." The Great Seal of the State of Ohio, shown in Chapter 1, includes the view from Adena.

When archeologists began to explore the mounds on his property, they called the people who had lived there, many years before, the Adena people.

Other explorations were made on the farm of Mr. M.C. Hopewell in Ross County. Since the remains of the people on this site were quite different from those at the Adena site, they were named the Hopewell people.

During the late 1830s, a group of people interested in archaeology hired two citizens of Ross County, Ohio, to study and map almost 300 prehistoric mounds east of the Mississippi River.

Ephriam G. Squier and Dr. Edwin H. Davis hired skilled workers, and proceeded to make the first scientific explorations of Adena and Hopewell mounds. Their work was completed in 1847, and published under the title *Ancient Monuments of The Mississippi Valley: Comprising the Results of Extensive Original Surveys and Explorations.*

When early explorers and settlers came into the area of southern Ohio, they found mounds of many sizes and shapes. Most of these were rather small, perhaps 6 feet (2 meters) high and 20 feet (7 meters) in diameter. Some, however, were very high, very long, or in complicated patterns. Many of the smaller mounds were destroyed as farmers and builders went about their business, but many of the largest mounds are still visible today.

Ohio Mounds

Forty-one Adena and Hopewell mounds have been studied in the southern half of Ohio and nearby parts of Indiana,

Serpent Mound, in Adams County, was the most unusual mound mapped by Squier and Davis in 1846.

You must see the Serpent Mound from the air to appreciate this prehistoric work of art.

Kentucky, and West Virginia. You can visit the places shown on the map below and see these mounds. Several of the sites have small museums that display **artifacts** (objects) found in the mounds.

The two highest mounds are at Miamisburg, in Montgomery County, and just across the Ohio River from Belmont County, in Moundsville, West Virginia. Each of these is more than 60 feet (20 meters) high, and more than 200 feet (70 meters) in diameter.

The city of Circleville, in Pickaway County, was established inside two large rings of mounds. Some of the original streets were laid out in circular form to fit the mounds.

Serpent Mound

The most unusual Ohio mound is the Serpent Mound in the northeast corner of Adams County. Five feet (1 1/2 meters) high and almost 1,350 feet (415 meters) long, it is a clear representation of a snake swallowing an egg. Squier and Davis made the map shown on page 38 but you must climb an observation tower to appreciate this prehistoric work of art.

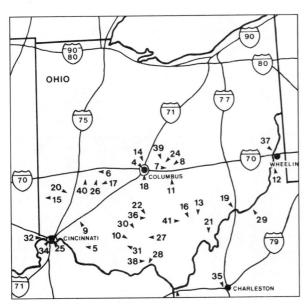

You can visit prehistoric mounds at these places in Ohio and neighboring states.

4. *Campbell Mound*
5. *Elk Lick Road Mound*
6. *Enon Mound*
7. *Fairmount Mound*
8. *Flint Ridge State Memorial*

9. *Fort Ancient State Memorial*
10. *Fort Hill State Memorial*
11. *Glenford Fort*
13. *Hartman Mound and Wolfe's Plains Group*
14. *Highbanks Park Mound and Earthworks*
15. *Hueston Woods Campground Mound*
16. *Indian Mound Campground*
17. *Indian Mound Park*
18. *Indian Mounds Park*
19. *Marietta Earthworks*
20. *Miamisburg Mound*
21. *Mound Cemetery*
22. *Mound City Group National Monument*
24. *Newark Earthworks*
25. *Norwood Mound*
26. *Orator's Mound*
27. *Piketon Mound Cemetery*
28. *Portsmounth Mound Park*
30. *Seip Mound State Memorial*
31. *Serpent Mound State Memorial*
32. *Shawnee Lookout Park*
34. *Shorts Woods Park Mound*
36. *Story Mound*
37. *Titonsville Cemetery Mound*
38. *Tremper Mound*
39. *Williams Mound*
40. *Wright Brothers Memorial Mound Group*
41. *Zaleski State Forest Mound*

Ross County Mounds

When you visit the Mound City Group National Monument in Ross County today, you can imagine that you are seeing the large Hopewell burial ground that early explorers found. What you are actually seeing are reconstructed mounds.

During World War I, the United States Army built a huge military camp in this area, and leveled all the ancient earthworks. Some of the artifacts are on display in the museum on the site.

Newark Earthworks

Newark, the county seat of Licking County, was established on the site of the most complex system of mounds found in Ohio. Many of the mounds were destroyed as the city grew, but two remain under the protection of the Ohio Historical Society. The large circular mound in the south-center of the map is used as a park. The large octagonal mound in the northwest is part of a golf course. This may be the only golf course in the world where flags are placed on prehistoric mounds to show golfers the way to the next hole.

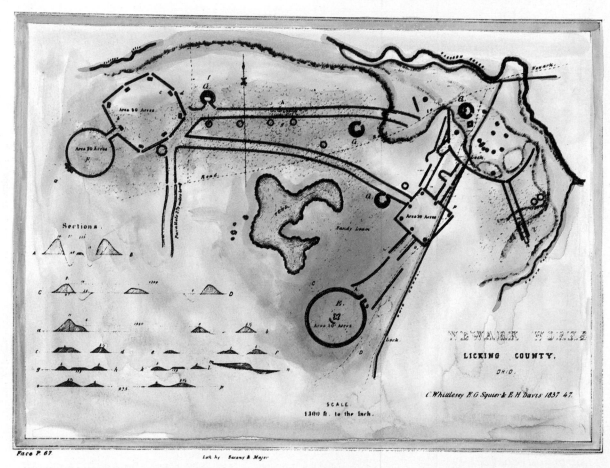

Many of the mounds Squier and Davis found in Licking County were removed as Newark grew.

40

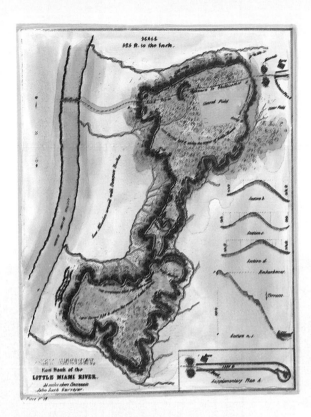

The longest mound mapped by Squier and Davis was at Fort Ancient in Warren County.

Fort Ancient

Fort Ancient, in the east-central part of Warren County, was built by the Hopewell people. It is the largest prehistoric construction project found in the United States. The mounds and walls are more than 3-1/2 miles (5 1/2 km) in length, and they enclose an area of about 100 acres (40 hectares). Squier and Davis made the map of this site shown above.

Today you can visit a museum at Fort Ancient and see artifacts of the Hopewell people. At the same time you can learn about the *Fort Ancient* people who lived in the area long after the Hopewells had disappeared.

Why did the Hopewells build this large project? Thus far no one really knows the answer to this question, but some people believe strongly that prehistoric people used it to make observations on the movement of the sun.

Later Prehistoric People

No evidence of the Hopewell people has been found that can be dated later than about 600 AD. The people who lived in the Ohio Country after that date were more primitive than the Hopewells.

The timeline on page 35 shows Whittlesey people living at the same time as the Fort Ancient people. They were named for Charles Whittlesey, a geologist and archaeologist who studied prehistoric sites in northern Ohio during the 19th century. He found that people living in that area between about 1000 AD and 1600 AD had skills similar to those of the Fort Ancient people in southern Ohio. When the earliest European explorers came, they found almost no one living in the Ohio Country.

Hopewell burial ceremony

Life in Prehistoric Ohio

Prehistoric people lived in harmony with nature, and they gave little thought to trying to change their surroundings. If conditions in one location became too difficult, they moved to a more favorable place and adapted their lives as necessary. It seems safe to say that life in the Ohio Country changed less between 13,000 BC and 1600 AD than it did between 1800 and 2000 AD.

Since we have the most information about the Adena and Hopewell people, we will limit our discussion of life-styles to these two groups.

Houses

These early people lived together in small villages. Several Adena families lived together in large houses.

Archaeologists can determine the size and shape of the houses by studying the holes in the ground which held the wall posts. The walls were made by weaving branches or twigs through the wall posts and filling the spaces with mud.

The Hopewells lived in circular or oval-shaped wigwams. Small holes two feet apart outlined the shape of the building. Young trees or large branches were set into these holes. The tops of the poles were bent inward and tied together to form simple arches. The sides were then covered with large pieces of tree bark, hide, or woven mats. The roofs were either covered with bark or with bundles of reeds tied together. Below you will see a typical building called a *wigwam*, or more properly a **wigewa**. There are primitive people living in houses like this in some countries of the world today.

Many ancient people made houses like these wigwams, or wigaweas.

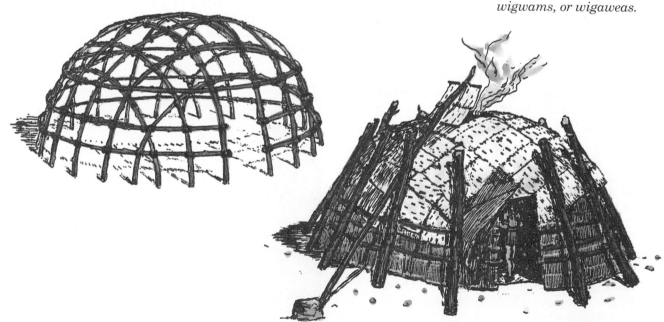

Food

The Adena and Hopewell people were primarily hunters and food-gatherers. We know from bones found in waste pits near prehistoric villages that they ate a variety of meat, including deer, fish, and small animals. We assume that they gathered nuts and berries because these are widely used by people who live close to nature.

But these people also made an important change in their life-style. After early Adena women gathered seeds from wild plants, they found that they could drop these seeds into the earth the next spring and the seeds would produce new plants. This discovery led to plant cultivation which produced a dependable food supply year after year. As a result of this discovery, the Adena and Hopewell people established permanent villages where they could grow their crops. Later the Fort Ancient peoples learned how to plant **maize** (what we call corn), beans, squash, and pumpkins.

The increase in food supply had several important results, including an increase in population, the establishment of larger towns, and more leisure time to make a variety of items earlier people did not have.

Handcrafts

The Adena and Hopewell people learned to make pottery by the coil method. They formed moist clay into rope-like coils and built these coils up to form large jars. These jars were heated until the clay became hard. Pottery jars were used to store foods from the time they were harvested until needed.

Pottery is one of the most useful items for studying prehistoric people. First, pottery lasts for thousands of years. Of course most of it is found broken, but the pieces can often be reassembled. Second, each group of people developed its own styles of making and decorating pottery. This helps archaeologists identify how people from various places related to one another.

Perhaps the most interesting handcraft of the Hopewell people was the artistic *bowls* they made for smoking tobacco, like the ones shown below. These bowls were made from what is called **Ohio pipe stone**, a soft stone found in the Scioto River valley that can be easily carved, and then baked to form pottery. Hopewell pipes have been found in many places in the eastern half of the United States.

Hopewell craftsmen made many kinds of pipes from Ohio pipe stone.

43

Tools

The most important tools required for survival in a forest were knives, axes, and drills. With these sharp-edged tools, the natives were able to cut small trees and to strip bark from large ones for building houses and canoes. They hunted with sharp pieces of flint tied to short sticks to make arrows, and to long sticks to make spears.

Sharpened pieces of deer antler were used to scrape flesh from the skins of animals to make clothing. Pointed pieces of bone were used to drill holes in skins or bark. Bone needles threaded with fibers were used to sew the material together. They used small boulders — brought into Ohio by the glaciers — as **pounders** to grind grain and as we use hammers.

Transportation

Walking was the most important form of transportation before the white explorers brought horses to America. The natives also traveled along rivers and lakes in canoes. Frames for canoes can be made from young trees, or branches, tied together. Covers were made from a variety of forms of tree bark, and the seams were filled with resin from pine trees.

Canoes are very useful vehicles because they can carry heavy loads over water. At the same time they are light enough in weight that they can be carried from one stream or lake to another over a **portage** path.

Trade

The Hopewells engaged in a broad network of trade because objects from great distances have been found in their burial sites — **obsidian** from the Rocky Mountains, shells from the Atlantic and Gulf coasts, copper from the Lake Superior region, alligator teeth from Florida, and **mica** from the Carolinas. As you learned earlier, Hopewell pipes have been found in all these places.

Obsidian is a form of glass created by volcanos. It is pretty to look at, and has very hard and sharp edges when broken. Pure copper is a soft metal that can be beaten into a variety of shapes. Mica is a very thin flat mineral that has a shiny surface that could be used as a mirror. The pictures on page 43 show objects found in Ross County.

Wampum

Since the natives of North America could not read or write, they created permanent records of important events by stringing together different colors, sizes, and patterns of shell beads. A simple **wampum** was a single string, perhaps 10 inches (25 cm) long, that told the owner's name and tribe. A wampum recording a treaty agreement between two tribes might be made up of 50 or more simple strings. Each string would be a kind of "sentence" representing an idea.

Wampum was very important in the lives of native Ohioans. Agreements made with wampum were considered sacred. Unfortunately, few Europeans understood the importance of wampum. The word wampum comes from New England, where the native people used the word wampumpeag for a "white string of shell beads." An example of a wampum belt can be seen on the next page.

John Kahiones Fadden, a 20th century Iroquois artist, made this drawing of a wampum belt.

Stop and Think!

Scholars (people who study a subject carefully) know that people moved into the Ohio Country shortly after the last glacier melted back. Most scholars believe that the ancestors of these people came from Asia across a land bridge where the Bering Sea now exists.

From 1000 BC to 600 AD, the Adena and the Hopewell people lived in the Ohio Country and built mounds. Some mounds were burial places for their dead, but we do not know why the others were built. From their burial places and from their waste areas, we know that these people were very skillful, and that they traded with people who lived far away from the Ohio Country.

From 600 AD to about 1300 AD, the less skillful Fort Ancient and Whittlesey people lived in the Ohio country. For some unknown reason, very few people lived here after about 1600.

Prehistoric people lived in Ohio for over 15,000 years. They used the resources they found here, but each generation left the land to those that followed pretty much as they found it. Aside from the Adena and Hopewell mounds, little changed in the appearance of the Ohio country.

Review the Chapter!

Building vocabulary...

AD
Adena
anthropologist
archaic
artifact
BC
boulder
exotic
Far East
flint
Hopewell
Indians
legend
maize
mastodon
mica
obsidian
Ohio pipe stone
origin

paleo
portage
pounder
relic
scholar
Stone Age
wampum
wigewa

Testing yourself...

Which came first...

1. the Adenas or the Paleo-Indians?
2. the Hopewells or the Fort Ancients?
3. hunting or planting?
4. corn or seeds and berries?
5. walking or canoes?

Where was/is...

1. the Bering Sea land bridge?
2. Moundsville?
3. Circleville?
4. Serpent Mound?
5. Fort Ancient?
6. San Salvador?
7. Flint Ridge?
8. Adena (the Worthington home)?
9. Newark?
10. Chillicothe?

Complete this thought...

1. Columbus was looking for a route to...
2. Prehistoric Ohioans used mounds for...
3. Native people used flint for
   tools because...
4. Natives used shell beads to make...
5. Facial features of Native
   Americans resemble...
6. Animals were important to early
   Ohioans who used them for...
7. Many ancient artifacts have been
   lost because...

8. We know that some prehistoric people
   farmed because...

Thinking it through...

1. Why do archaeologists believe that
   Hopewell people traveled hundreds of
   miles to trade goods? Using a map of the
   United States and an encyclopedia,
   write a short report on one possible
   trade route these people may
   have followed.

2. Pretend that you can return to the
   neighborhood where you now live in the
   year 2500 AD. Write a newspaper
   account about what you might find left
   from your earlier life.

Working with maps...

1. Between 1983 and 1987 Steve Newman,
   a young man from Bethel in Clermont
   County, walked around the world. Look
   at your world map and make a list of
   the countries, provinces and states you
   would have to travel through to walk
   from your home to China.

2. Using your United States map, make a
   list of the present states that the
   Hopewell and Adena people might have
   traveled through to obtain the obsidian,
   mica, and copper that they used in Ross
   County, Ohio.

CHAPTER 4

What happened to the natives when Europeans came?

Be ready to learn...

• where the Native Americans lived in 1700.

• how people from Europe affected the natives.

• why several tribes moved into the Ohio Country.

• about the French and Indian War in the Ohio Country.

• about the Revolutionary War in the Ohio Country.

The course of history for the natives of the Western Hemisphere changed drastically in the year 1492! As word about Columbus's discovery of land across the Atlantic Ocean moved through Europe, the rulers and wealthy merchants of every sea-going nation began to plot how they could get rich from the resources of what they thought was a new route to the Far East. In this chapter you will learn what happened to the natives who lived in the eastern part of North America when the Europeans came.

Post-Contact Period

Time after time over a period of about a hundred years, from 1600 to 1700, the natives were willing to *share* their lands, but the Europeans wanted to control the land. The natives did not understand the idea of *ownership* of land. For example, the Pilgrims could not have survived in New England without help from the natives, but a few years later the natives were driven westward. For the rest of this chapter we shall refer to these invaders and the people who followed them as the *whites*, because almost all were **Caucasian** (the technical word for the "white race") from several nations of Europe.

Almost all of the people who left Europe for the *New World*, as they called America, were seeking better lives for themselves. Some dreamed of gaining the right to worship God as they chose, while others wanted to own land and acquire wealth.

The natives believed that life was to be lived in close harmony with the forces of Nature. On the other hand, many whites believed that they could use knowledge and energy to overcome the forces of Nature. The whites had iron tools and gunpowder; they could read, write, and calculate. Because

they thought that they worshipped God in the *right* way, they looked upon the natives as **heathens** (people who do not believe in God).

Native Tribes in The 17th Century

No one knows how many Native Americans lived in what are now the United States in 1600, but estimates run from 200,000 to 500,000. The map on the next page shows where the tribes important to the history of Ohio were living during the 17th century. As you learn more about the geography of the United States, you will find that there are places named for almost every one of the tribes shown on this map.

Each tribe had its own language, but **linguists** (people who study languages) now agree that the natives of the area shown were all members of one or the other of two language groups — Iroquoian and Algonquin. The Iroquoian-speaking people on the map were the Mohawk, Oneida, Onondaga, Cayuga, and Seneca tribes shown in present New York State; the Erie, Huron, Neutral, and Tobacco tribes shown in present Ontario, Canada, and the Tuscarora tribe shown in present North Carolina. The Algonquin-speaking people, included the Delawares who lived in present New Jersey, and the Shawnees in present Maryland, Virginia, and West Virginia.

The five tribes of Iroquois people shown in present New York were very warlike. They fought with each other for many years

Estimated population of American colonies 1630 to 1780. (in thousands)									
Year	1630	1650	1670	1690	1700	1720	1740	1750	1770	1780
Pop.	5	50	112	210	251	466	906	1171	2148	2780

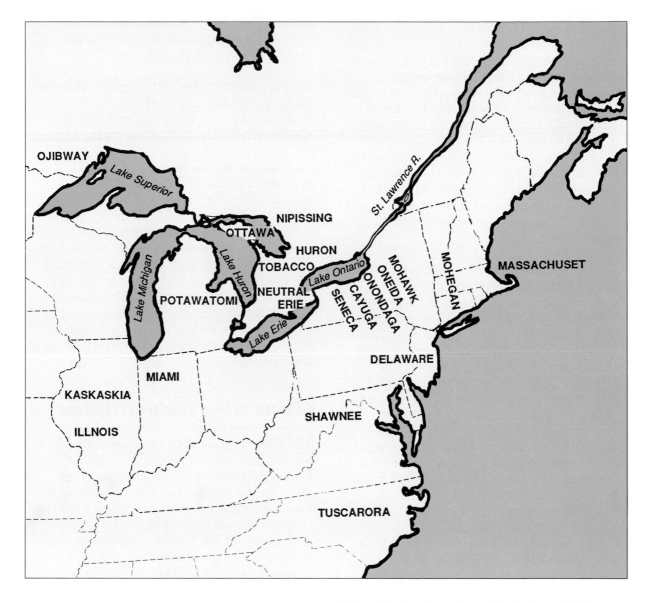

Where Native Americans lived about 1600.

until they realized that they would be better off if they cooperated. When they worked together, they became the most powerful group in the region, and the whites called them the *Iroquois League*, or the *Five Nations*. After the Tuscaroras moved north, the League became known as the *Six Nations*.

This map does not show any natives living in present Ohio or Kentucky in 1700. But most of the tribes mentioned above played an important role in the history of Ohio, and some places in Ohio are named for some of them.

French Fur Traders

In 1534 Jacques Cartier, a French explorer who was looking for the **Northwest Passage** (a sea route across the north coast of North America to reach the Far East), discovered a large river which he named for St. Lawrence, see the map on page 49. He sailed up the river until he reached the great falls where the city of Montreal was later established. Cartier met with many natives, and discovered that the region was filled with animals whose fur would be valuable in Europe.

In 1603 Samuel de Champlain led a group of Frenchmen to the mouth of the St. Lawrence River to establish trading posts where they could exchange European goods for the furs gathered by the natives. The French traders, who were known as **voyageurs** (from the French word for "traveler"), offered the natives guns and gunpowder to use in place of their bows and arrows, iron hatchets to use in place of their stone tomahawks, colorful blankets to use in place of skins to keep warm, glass beads to use in place of shells for making wampum, and alcohol to use for "fun." The lives of the natives began to change dramatically!

In 1669 Rene Robert Cavalier Sieur de la Salle, a French nobleman, came to the St. Lawrence Valley in a ship similar to that shown on page 51. He later explored and laid claim to the region of the Great Lakes for the King of France. In 1681 La Salle led another group of explorers through the Great Lakes to the south end of Lake Michigan. By rivers and portages, they found their way to the Mississippi River. They followed the Mississippi southward to its mouth, and then made their way back to Quebec. On March 14, 1682, La Salle held a formal ceremony at a native town on the Mississippi River and declared that the valleys of the Mississippi and Ohio Rivers belonged to the King of France.

By the middle of the 18th century, **British** traders (people from England, Scotland, Wales, and North Ireland) competed with the French for the furs of the Ohio Country.

The map on the on page 53 shows important places about 1760. In 1749 a French official in Canada, Pierre Joseph Celeron de Blainville, led an army of 250 soldiers to establish more firmly the French claim. They planted lead plates in the right bank of the Allegheny and Ohio Rivers at the mouth of every important **tributary** (side river) between present Franklin, Pennsylvania, and the southwest corner of Ohio. On page 56 you can see a picture of one of these plates and read a translation of the message.

Effects of Fur Trade on Natives

The Five Nations of the Iroquois quickly learned how valuable furs were to the European traders. With the guns given them by the whites, the Iroquois began to expand their area of influence. In 1649 the Iroquois moved into what is now Canada, and drove out the *Hurons*, who were also trading furs with the French. The Iroquois went on to destroy the *Neutrals*, the *Tobaccos* , and the *Eries*, all of whom disappeared as tribes.

Ships used by LaSalle to cross the Atlantic Ocean

Inscription Rock, on Kelley's Island, is an unsolved mystery.

The picture on this page shows *Inscription Rock,* a prehistoric **pictograph** (line drawings on a rock) on Kelley's Island in Erie County. In the 19th century, some scholars thought that these pictures were made to tell the story of the Erie tribe during this difficult period. Modern scholars doubt this interpretation, but they do not know who made the inscriptions or what they mean. You can see these inscriptions today, but they are not nearly so clear as they appear in the picture.

British Settlers

As the British established permanent settlements along the East Coast of North America, they forced the natives to move westward. No one knows how many people lived in the British Colonies in North America, but the numbers in the chart on page 48 are reasonable estimates. From this table, you can guess how trouble developed for the natives as more and more whites claimed the land. The tribes that lived in the colonies of New Jersey, Connecticut, and Massachusetts faced the greatest pressures because the largest numbers of whites came to these colonies.

52

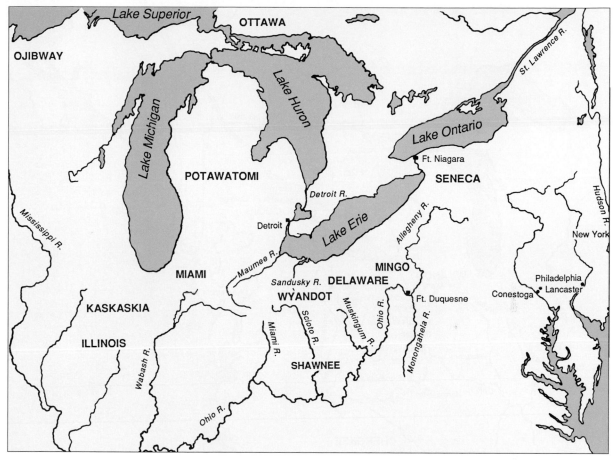

Native areas and White towns around 1760.

Natives Who Moved to the Ohio Country

Delawares

The map on page 49 shows the natives who once lived in the area we call New Jersey and Delaware. They called themselves the *Lenape*, with the first three letters meaning *ordinary*, *real*, or *original*, and the last three meaning *person*.

When William Penn established his first settlement, and named it *Philadelphia* (which means *brotherly love*), he chose a site very close to the principal town of the Lenape. Penn and his fellow members of the *Society of Friends* (Christians whom we often call "Quakers") were among the few settlers who tried to live in "brotherly love" with the natives. Unfortunately the growing numbers of Friends helped to crowd the natives out of their home land. By 1751 some of the Lenape were living in the Ohio Country where they were known as *Delawares*.

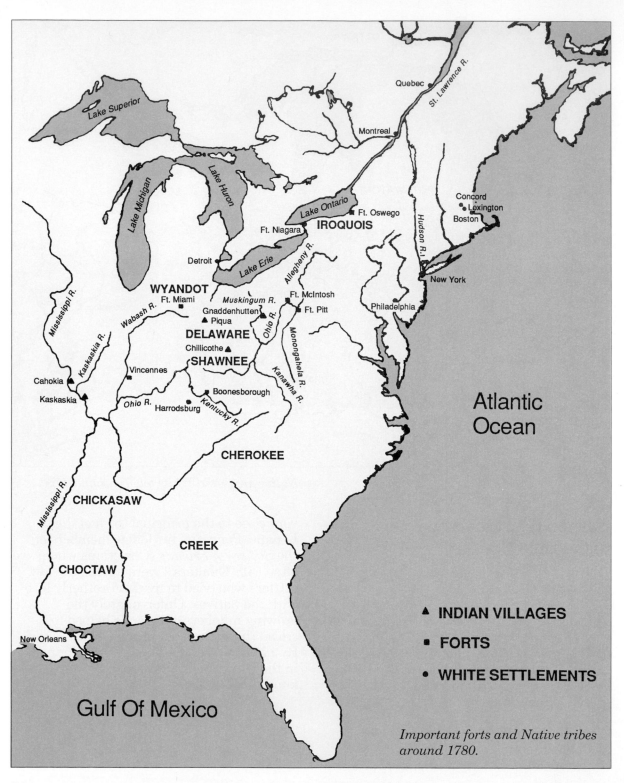

Lake Superior

Lake Michigan

Lake Huron

Quebec

St. Lawrence R.

Montreal

Lake Ontario   Ft. Oswego

Ft. Niagara   IROQUOIS

Concord
Loxington
Boston

Hudson R.

Detroit   Lake Erie

Allegheny R.

New York

WYANDOT
Ft. Miami   *Muskingum R.*   Ft. McIntosh
Gnaddenhutten   Ft. Pitt
Piqua   *Ohio R.*

Philadelphia

Mississippi R.

Wabash R.

Kaskaskia R.

DELAWARE
Chillicothe
SHAWNEE

Monongahela R.

Kanawha R.

Vincennes

Cahokia

Kaskaskia

Ohio R.   Harrodsburg   *Kentucky R.*

Boonesborough

CHEROKEE

Atlantic
Ocean

CHICKASAW

Mississippi R.

CREEK

CHOCTAW

New Orleans

Gulf Of Mexico

▲ INDIAN VILLAGES

▪ FORTS

● WHITE SETTLEMENTS

Important forts and Native tribes
around 1780.

Shawnees

The *Shawnees* (meaning *people of the south*) lived in present Maryland, Pennsylvania, and Virginia early in the 18th century. They met in a council with the whites at Lancaster, Pennsylvania (see the map on the page 53) in July, 1748, to sign a treaty in which the whites agreed not to move west across the Allegheny Mountains. After signing the treaty, the Shawnees moved westward into present West Virginia and southern Ohio.

The natives considered the present state of Kentucky to be a sacred hunting area: all tribes could hunt in it, but none could live there. For this reason the area was very attractive to white settlers, and by 1770 there were almost 15,000 whites living in the part of Virginia west of the mountains. The Shawnees greatly **resented** (did not like) having settlers in their sacred hunting area, so they raided the settlements frequently. When whites began to move into the region north of the *Spay-lay-wi-theepi* (the Shawnee name for the Ohio River), the Shawnees resisted strongly.

The Shawnee people were divided into five major groups, called **septs**. The septs cooperated with each other in many ways, but they were not as closely united as the Iroquois Nation. The central meeting place of the septs was on the bank of the Little Miami River in present Greene County. The natives called this place, and all their villages, *chillicothe*. In 1768 the leaders of the Shawnee septs met to decide how to deal with the ever-growing stream of whites crossing the Appalachian Mountains: some leaders wanted to fight, while others felt that their weapons could not compete with the guns of the whites.

During this meeting Methotasa, the wife of Chief Pucksinwah, gave birth to a baby boy. The passage of a comet, or "shooting star" across the sky that night helped the parents decide upon a name for their son. They named him *Tecumseh*, which in their language meant *Panther passing across*. Twenty years later this boy became one of the greatest leaders of the Native Americans in their fight against the whites.[1]

Blue Jacket

A aseventeen year-old white boy, named Marmaduke Van Swearington, had been captured in western Virginia by hunters from Tecumseh's tribe. The boy actually knew some Shawnee words, and wanted to be adopted by the tribe. In order to prove that he was worthy of adoption, *Duke*, as his friends in Virginia knew him, had to run a **gauntlet** (long, double line of natives armed with sticks and whips who would beat upon his bare body). *Duke* was badly hurt as he ran the entire length of the line,

LAN 1749 DV REGNE DE LOVIS XV ROY DE
FRANCE NOVS CELORON COMMANDANT DVN DE
TACHEMENT ENVOIE PAR MONSIEVR LE Mis DE LA
GALISSONIERE COMMANDANT GENERAL DE LA
NOVVELLE FRANCE POVR RETABLIR LA TRANQVILLITE
DANS QVELQVES VILLAGES SAUVAGES DE CES CANTONS
AVONS ENTERRÉ CETTE PLAQVE A LENTREE DE LA
RIVIERE CHINODAHICHETHA LE 18 AOUST
PRES DE LA RIVIERE OYO AUTREMENT BELLE
RIVIERE POVR MONVMENT DV RENOVVELLEMENT DE
POSSESSION QVE NOVS AVONS PRIS DE LA DITTE
RIVIERE OYO ET DE TOVTES CELLES QVI Y TOMBNT
ET DE TOVES LES TERRES DES DEVX COTES IVSQVE
AVX SOVRCES DES DITTES RIVIES VINSI QVEN ONT
IOVY OV DV IOVIR LES PRECEDENTS ROYS DE FRANCE
ET QVILS SISONT MAINTENVS PAR LES ARMES ET
PAR LES TRAITTES SPECIALEMENT PAR CEVX DE
RISVVICK DVTRCHT ET DAIX LA CHPELLE

In the year 1749 of the reign of Louis XV, King of France, our celebrated commandant of a detachment [group of soldiers], sent by Monsieur Le Mis de La Galissoniere, Commandant General of New France, to restore tranquility in some savage villages of these districts having buried a plate at the entrance of the Yenangue River, otherwise Beautiful [Ohio] River, for a monument of the renewing of the possession that we have taken of the said Ohio River, and all those who come there, and of all the lands of the two sides as far as the source of said rivers that they have the joy of being in possession on it as well as the former Kings of France, and that they be maintained by arms and treaties, especially by those of Risnuick of Utrecht and Aix La Chapelle

but he proved his courage, and was adopted by the tribe. Because he was wearing a blue jacket when he was captured, the natives called him *Wey-yah-pih-ehr-sehn-wah*, which meant *Blue Jacket*. The four-year old Tecumseh was part of this gauntlet line.

Other Tribes

As whites moved into lands controlled by the Iroquois Nations, some of the weaker groups, including Senecas, Cayugas, and Tuscaroras, were pushed into the Ohio Country. The Delawares and whites called these people *Mingos*. Some of the Hurons who escaped the Iroquois by fleeing to the north later moved to the area around present Sandusky Bay in Ohio, where they became known as *Wyandots*.

The Miami and Potawatomi tribes, shown on the maps on pages 49 & 53, traded with the French for many years. Their lives became disrupted as natives from the east coast moved into the Ohio Country.

Indian Agents

The British government and many of the colonies appointed **Indian Agents** to communicate with the natives. Two agents who influenced developments in Ohio were Conrad Weiser and George Croghan.

Conrad Weiser

The parents of Conrad Weiser moved from Germany to what is now New York State early in the 18th century, while Conrad was quite young. At the age of seventeen, he went to live with a Mohawk tribe for several years. He learned the language and customs of the Six Nations, and became a friend of the Iroquois. He was a very talented young man who kept a **journal** (diary) of his activities.

For several years, beginning in 1743, Weiser led naturalists and map-makers in exploring the Ohio Country. In 1748 he began to work with George Croghan. These two men met with leaders of many tribes at Logstown, on the Ohio River near present East Liverpool, Ohio. There they **negotiated** (reached agreement on) a treaty that kept the western natives from joining the French in the war you will learn about later in this chapter.

George Croghan

George Croghan, an Irishman, was an outstanding trader on the western frontier of Pennsylvania. By 1744 he had established a trading post at Logstown. From there he sent traders as far west as the Mississippi River. In 1748 he built a **palisaded** (walled) fort at the Miami village at Pickawillany, in present Miami County, Ohio.

George Croghan traveled throughout the Ohio Country, and encouraged the Miami tribes to attend annual meetings at Logstown. Much of what we know about the natives of Ohio during the middle of the 18th century is based on Croghan's official reports and diaries.

Wars

The kings of England and France were at war with each other for hundreds of years. Each wanted to control the fur trade in North America. The battles between French and British interests in the Ohio Country were small but bloody and decisive. As you learn more about them, and as you visit battle sites in the future, you will be surprised that these small events could have been so important.

French and Indian War 1754 - 1763

In 1754 the ongoing war between England and France led to the *French and Indian War* in North America. The French controlled the fur trade in the St. Lawrence River Valley and the upper Great Lakes region, while British settlers were taking land from the Iroquois people in present New York State.

The French and the British traders all needed the help of the natives to get the furs they wanted. But the French traders were more honest in their dealings, and did not try to seize control of the land. Therefore, when the war came, a majority of the natives decided to support the French. The French rewarded the natives for each enemy soldier they killed. Evidence of a killing was the **scalp** (skin and hair from top of head) of the victim.

Although the war ended in North America in 1760 when the British conquered the great French city of Montreal, it went on in Europe for several more years. When the peace treaty was signed in Europe in 1763, the French gave up all claims to North America.

During this period, French people living in this region continued to encourage the natives to fight the British by giving them guns and ammunition.

Pontiac's Rebellion in 1763

Pontiac, an Ottawa war chief, lived near Lake Huron. About 1761 he set out to unite the tribes in the area of the Great Lakes to drive the British from this region (look at map on page 53).

For almost two years, Pontiac worked on a plan to attack Fort Detroit. The warriors were to set up camps around the fort for a council meeting. Some of the chiefs, with guns hidden under their blankets, were to enter the fort to negotiate with the commander. At a given signal, all the warriors were to attack and overwhelm the British soldiers. Unfortunately for the natives, the commander learned of the plan. The natives did keep the fort surrounded for five months, and almost starved the British into surrender.

While Pontiac was urging the natives to continue fighting, he received word that the French had surrendered all of their claims in North America to the British. Without French help, Pontiac had to stop fighting.

In August of 1765, George Croghan met with Pontiac and negotiated a peace plan. The British encouraged the natives to settle near Detroit, but Pontiac did not want this. The box contains what Croghan wrote in his diary about this meeting.

American Revolution 1776 - 1783

War came again in 1776. As you can see in the table on page 48 there were more than 2,000,000 people living in the thirteen British colonies at that time. Between 1770 and 1776, the population of Fincastle County, Virginia — which included the present states of West Virginia and Kentucky — jumped from about 15,000 to 45,000. The only whites in the Ohio Country at that time lived in scattered trading posts, and in the Moravian settlements along the Tuscarawas River that you will learn about later. The map on page 54 shows important places in the war.

At the beginning of the war, both the Americans and the British tried to enlist the help of the natives. The natives did not trust the British, but the British offered them guns and ammunition, and money for each American scalp. In fact, the British commander at Fort Detroit, General Henry Hamilton, was known as the "Hair Buyer."

The Two Simons

Two good friends named *Simon* played important roles in the Ohio Country during the American Revolution. In 1756 Simon Girty was fifteen years old when Native Americans raided his home in central Pennsylvania. They carried him and his brothers into captivity. At the end of the French and Indian War, Girty was freed by the natives and soon became an interpreter for the British Agent at Fort Pitt.

Simon Kenton was born in the western part of Virginia in 1755. At the age of fifteen he had a fight and almost killed a man. In fright, he changed his name to *Simon Butler*, and moved to the wilds of what became known as *Kain-tuck-ee* to begin a lifetime of exploring. The Shawnees feared

Artist's idea of George Rogers Clark march on Vincennes.

and respected him, and he respected them. When he later learned that his opponent had not died, he again used his family name.

The two Simons met each other and became close friends. When the American Revolution reached the western frontier in 1778, Girty decided that his loyalty belonged to the British, while Kenton decided to work for the American cause.

In September, 1778, while traveling through the Ohio Country to spy on Fort Detroit, Simon Kenton was captured by

natives who were fighting for the British. As he was about to be tortured to death, a leader of the Shawnees came forward and asked the natives to **spare** (save) the life of this brave opponent. The leader was Simon Girty! Kenton's life was saved, but in a short time he escaped from the British to continue fighting for American freedom.

At the close of the Revolution, Simon Girty fled to Canada. The British government gave him land in payment for his services, and he died in 1818. He was considered a traitor to the American cause, but he was a hero in the eyes of the British.

George Rogers Clark

When the treaty ending the French and Indian War was signed in 1763, the British gained control of all former French forts, including the three at Vincennes on the Wabash River, and at Kaskaskia and Cahokia on the Mississippi River shown on the map on page 54.

In 1774 George Rogers Clark moved from his boyhood home near Williamsburg, Virginia, to *Kentucky County*, which had been created from the western part of Fincastle County. Shortly before the Declaration of Independence was signed, Clark was appointed to the rank of major and placed in command of the Kentucky **militia** (citizens who become soldiers in times of danger).

In June, 1777 Major Clark sent spies to examine the forts at Kaskaskia and Cahokia on the Mississippi River. Near the end of August, the spies returned to Clark's headquarters with information that made Clark decide he could capture these places if he had 350 soldiers.

By June, 1778 Major Clark had gathered an "army" of only 178 frontiersmen, including Simon Kenton. Many of these men had lost family and friends to the natives who sold scalps to the *Hair Buyer* at Fort Detroit. For several days they camped at the falls of the Ohio, at present Louisville, Kentucky. Then they moved down the Ohio River, and across the southern tip of Illinois to a point near Kaskaskia, without being discovered by the British. On July 4, 1778, Clark's army so surprised the defenders of the fort at Kaskaskia that they surrendered without firing a shot.

The people of Kaskaskia sent word to their friends at Cahokia, a few miles to the north, that Clark's army had done them no harm. A few weeks later when Clark and his followers rode to Cahokia, the people of that town also surrendered without firing a shot. Clark then persuaded the natives living in the area to support the American cause.

When General Hamilton, at Fort Detroit, learned about the loss of the forts at Cahokia and Kaskaskia, he moved part of his army to Vincennes. There he hoped to enlist hundreds of natives to join the British in recapturing Kaskaskia and Cahokia during the Spring of 1779.

George Rogers Clark learned of this plan and decided that his best defense was to attack. On the rainy day of February 5, 1779, he set out with about a hundred Americans and thirty French settlers of the area to conquer the fort at Vincennes. One of Clark's assistants, Captain John Bowman, kept a diary of the trip, including the entries shown in the box on the page 62.

On the night of February 22, the temperature dropped below freezing and the wet soldiers had no protection. The next day French people living in the village around the fort welcomed Clark and his army with food, blankets, and ammunition, and the **siege** of Vincennes began.

Colonel Clark arranged his men around the fort and instructed them to fire their rifles in such a way that the British in the fort would feel that they were surrounded and outnumbered. On February 24, the British surrendered to Clark and were dumbfounded to learn how a few weary men had fooled them. Not one of the men who marched from Kaskaskia was lost! The picture on page 60 is an artist's idea of Clark's difficult trip.

Clark was promoted to the rank of
Brigadier General in the Army of Virginia,
and led troops in several battles in what is
now Ohio. Clark County was named in his
honor, and you can visit George Rogers
Clark Park to the west of Springfield, Ohio.
But neither Virginia nor the United States
ever repaid him for all of his personal
resources he gave to his "army." In 1813 he
died, penniless and bitterly disappointed, at
Louisville, Kentucky.

Simon Kenton

After the Revolutionary War, Simon
Kenton became even more important in the
development of Ohio. In 1785 he led a

*In the last years of his life,
Simon Kenton dressed like this.*

group of soldiers, under command of Major
Benjamin Stites, into southwest Ohio to
recapture some horses stolen by a band of
Shawnees. When the group entered what
is now Hamilton County, Stites was very
impressed by the quality of the land. In

Chapter 5 you will learn how Stites later led the first group of settlers in southwest Ohio.

In 1801 Kenton became the founder of the town of Springfield, in Clark County. A few years later he moved his family to the new town of Urbana, in Champaign County. From his picture on page 62 you might guess that he was a rather successful person. Actually Simon Kenton was a failure in every business venture he tried. In 1810 he was sentenced to jail at Urbana because he could not pay his debts. His friends in the town immediately elected him to the position of county jailer so that he could live at the jail without being in a cell.

Simon Kenton may have done more than anyone else to make the Ohio Country safe for white settlers, but his name is almost unknown today. The city of Kenton, in Hardin County, is named for him, and there is a Kenton County in Kentucky, directly opposite Hamilton County, Ohio. You can visit Simon Kenton's grave in Urbana.

Fort McIntosh and Fort Laurens

Early in the Revolution, General George Washington decided that the Americans needed a line of forts between Fort Pitt and Fort Detroit. In the autumn of 1778, General Lachlan McIntosh led a group of men from Fort Pitt to begin construction. They built the first fort near Logstown, on the Ohio River, and called it Fort McIntosh. The soldiers next built a fort on the Tuscarawas River near the northern boundary of present Tuscarawas County, and named it Fort Laurens (French for Lawrence).

Unfortunately, Fort Laurens was so far from Fort Pitt, and the American army in the area was so small, that the natives were able to steal almost all the supplies sent to it. In February 1779, the natives under the leadership of Simon Girty, laid siege to Fort Laurens, and very nearly starved the defenders. With his men reduced to trying to survive by eating their moccasins and the skins of animals, the commanding officer decided on a brilliant scheme. Under a flag of truce, he gave the natives a barrel of flour to make them think that there was more than enough food in the fort. The siege was lifted and the troops in the fort survived.

Fort Laurens was abandoned, and so was Washington's plan for a line of forts. Today the site of Fort Laurens is a state memorial.

The Mission at Gnadenhutten

David Zeisberger was a minister of a Christian group called *United Brethren*. A large group of Brethren migrated to North America in 1734 from *Moravia* in eastern Germany. The *Moravians*, as they were generally known, tried to live peacefully and wanted to share their Christian faith with the natives.

In 1772 a group of Delawares was forced to leave their temporary living area in central Pennsylvania. Zeisberger and his friend, John Heckewelder, together with their wives and children, led these Delawares into what is now Tuscarawas County, Ohio. The Moravians helped the Delawares build a village, which they named *Schoenbrunn*, meaning "beautiful springs." They built a church and established the first school in the Ohio Country. Zeisberger wrote books for the natives in their language. Schoenbrunn was so successful that the

Moravians soon created two more towns along the Tuscarawas River: *Gnadenhutten*, meaning "tents of grace", and *Salem*, meaning "peace."

In 1781 the British army and its native allies forced the Moravian Delawares to move to the Sandusky River to share the land of the Wyandot people. The Christian Delawares called their new home *Captivetown*. David Zeisberger, his family and co-workers, were taken to Fort Detroit to be tried as spies for the American rebels.

Although the Americans defeated the British at Yorktown, Virginia, in October 1781, fighting continued in the Ohio Country. During the winter of 1782, there was not enough food at Upper Sandusky for both the Wyandots and the Christian Delawares. The British allowed about 150 of the Delaware captives to return to their villages along the Tuscarawas River to gather corn, beans, and squash from their former fields.

Early in March, 1782 David Williamson, a young American officer in command of a hundred men, set out from Ft. Pitt to punish natives who were attacking white settlers in western Pennsylvania. Williamson led his men into the Ohio Country. On March 8 they found a hundred peaceful Delawares gathering food at Gnadenhutten.

Because the Christian Delawares had learned to trust the Americans, they agreed to hand over their weapons when Williamson asked for them. The soldiers then forced the natives to kneel in their church building, smashed their heads, and burned the building over them. Only two boys managed to escape to warn the other

fifty Delawares at Schoenbrunn and Salem. Today you can visit a reconstruction of the village of Schoenbrunn, just outside the city of New Philadelphia, in Tuscarawas County. You can also visit a museum at the site of Gnadenhutten and learn more about the peaceful Delawares who died there.

Colonel William Crawford

When the natives around Sandusky learned of the **massacre** (mass killing) at Gnadenhutten, they began attacking white settlements in the Ohio Country and western Pennsylvania. The British at Detroit did all that they could to encourage these attacks. By May, 1782 the militia at Fort Pitt were demanding that the Delawares be punished for their reactions to the massacre at Gnadenhutten. In an election between Colonels Williamson and Crawford, William Crawford was chosen to lead an attack on the native villages around Upper Sandusky, in present Wyandot County. Colonel Crawford thought that the idea was a mistake, but the soldiers insisted on acting as fast as possible. Several hundred men set out on horseback directly for Gnadenhutten, and then on toward Upper Sandusky.

Early in June, as the Americans were approaching Upper Sandusky, they came face to face with a large group of very angry Delawares. Both sides camped for the night and built large bonfires. During the night, Simon Girty came forward from the native side with a white flag of truce. He called for Colonel Crawford to come forward to talk. Girty told Crawford that the Delawares were in the process of surrounding the Americans, but that they had one chance to escape through a swampy area.

The Americans did escape the trap, but could not agree on what to do next. By the end of the second day many of the Americans were dead. On June 13, 1782 William Crawford was captured and tortured to death by fire. Crawford County is named in his honor.

The Americans finally won their independence from Great Britain in 1783. They soon forgot about the tribes that had fought to support their cause, and treated all of the natives as enemies who had helped the British.

Stop and Think!

The natives of North America had well-established life styles long before the people of Europe knew they existed. They did not have the educational and cultural advantages enjoyed by some Europeans, but they lived in harmony with nature, and they worshipped the Great Spirit of life.

The British, the French, and later the Americans, did not hesitate to use the natives to their own advantage. When the natives rebelled, the whites set out to remove them. As you will learn in the next chapter, shortly after the United States of America became a nation, our government adopted a policy of eliminating the Native Problem. In the process of doing this, the culture of the natives was almost destroyed.

Footnotes

1. Thom: *Panther in the Sky*, pp. 18-19
2. Thom: *Panther in The Sky* pp. 37-52

Review the Chapter!

Building vocabulary...

British
Caucasian
fatigue
fording
gauntlet
heathen
Indian Agent
journal
linguist
massacre
negotiate
notwithstanding
militia
Northwest Passage
palisade
provisions (food)
resent
siege
spare (save)
scalp
sept
tributary
voyageurs

Meeting new people...

Tecumseh
Chief Pontiac
David Zeisberger
Conrad Weiser
George Croghan
Blue Jacket
Simon Girty
Colonel William Crawford
Simon Kenton
George Rogers Clark
Colonel David Williamson

Where is it?

(Locate the following places on a map of Ohio.)

Cincinnati
Schoenbrunn
Urbana
East Liverpool
Tuscarawas River
Gnadenhutten
Springfield
Xenia
Kenton

Match them up and tell the page where you found the answer ...

1. Caucasian	a. lead plates
2. Clark	b. Vincennes
3. La Salle	c. Gnadenhutten
4. Celeron	d. 6 nations
5. Croghan	e. Springfield
6. Kenton	f. white
7. Pontiac	g. Delawares
8. Zeisberger	h. Ottawa war chief
9. Col. Crawford	i. Indian agent
10. Girty	j. Mississippi River

Thinking it through...

1. Explain why the Ohio Historical Society recreated Schoenbrunn, and why a monument was built at Gnadenhutten.

2. Arrange a debate about the patriotism and loyalty of Simon Kenton and Simon Girty to decide which one took the "right" side during the Revolutionary War.

3. Review the discussion and picture of Inscription Rock. Draw a pictograph of a recent event in your life, and let a friend try to interpret it.

4. Summarize the conflict between the natives of Ohio and the whites who came into this area. Who was "right" and who was "wrong" about this conflict?

5. What would life in Ohio be like today if the "other side" in the several conflicts had won?

6. Why do people like George Rogers Clark and Simon Kenton act as they do? Should they receive more rewards for their efforts? What kinds of rewards?

7. Organize a debate on the topic: The massacre at Gnadenhutten should NOT be taught in a course on Ohio History.

Working with maps...

1. On the map of Ohio, locate the counties named for the Delaware, Erie, Huron, Miami, Ottawa, Seneca, and Wyandot tribes. Why is each name suitable for the county? How many cities in Ohio have these names? Which cities are in counties of the same name?

2. On the map of the United States, locate as many places as you can that are shown on the map on page 54.

3. On the map of the United States, try to draw the route that La Salle followed from Quebec to the mouth of the Mississippi River.

How did the Americans displace the natives?

Be ready to learn...

- that poor land descriptions lead to quarrels.

- how the American Colonies paid Revolutionary War soldiers.

- how the Public Land Act influenced the geography of the U.S.

- how the Northwest Territory Act influenced the Ohio Country.

- how the natives resisted settlers in Ohio.

- how the Treaty of GreeneVille influenced development of Ohio.

When the representatives of the thirteen colonies along the Atlantic Coast declared their independence from Great Britain, they were forced to assume many new responsibilities. Their first difficult challenge was to learn to work with each other. The representatives labored for more than a year to create a plan of cooperation that all the colonies could accept. On November 15, 1777, they signed the *Articles of Confederation* (agreement), but the Articles had no power until 1781 when the last of the thirteen colonies agreed to obey them. One of the biggest problems the new Congress (from the Latin word *congredi*, "to meet") faced was control of the lands to the west of the Appalachian Mountains.

Colonial Land Claims

Who owned Ohio in 1776? As you learned in Chapter 4, the Native Americans believed that the Great Spirit had created the land for them to use and enjoy. The French once said that it belonged to them because of the claims made by La Salle and Celeron. The British claimed it because they had

defeated the French. In addition, several of the American Colonies said that various kings of England had granted sections of the Ohio Country to them.

Virginia, for example, claimed that its **charter** (grant of land) included the present states of West Virginia, Kentucky, Ohio, Indiana, Illinois, Michigan, and Wisconsin, and parts of Minnesota. Connecticut and Massachusetts also claimed ownership of some of the same land. Perhaps the hardest problem the representatives to the Congress faced was to decide exactly the boundaries of each colony.

The "wiggly" solid lines you see on the map on the next page are rivers. Rivers seem to be exact boundaries, but they can change their courses in times of flooding. The

Latitude and Longitude

The only exact way to describe the geographic position of a point on the surface of the Earth is to give its latitude and longitude. The diagram shows that **latitude** is the angular position north or south of the equator, and that **longitude** is the angular position east or west of the **meridian** (true north-south line) through Greenwich, England. The Figure shows the latitude of Columbus, Ohio, as 40° North, and the longitude as 83° West.

Lines of latitude and longitude are not visible on the surface of the Earth unless a **surveyor** (a person who makes measurements on the Earth) sets **monuments** (permanent markers) to mark the lines.

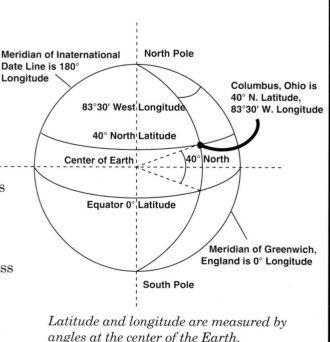

Latitude and longitude are measured by angles at the center of the Earth.

THE UNITED STATES
1783
SHOWING WESTERN LAND CLAIMS

SCALE OF MILES
0   50   100   200   300   400

The Thirteen Colonies claimed land westward to the Mississippi River.

69

dashed lines you see represent boundaries that are easy to draw, but may be very difficult to find on the ground. For example, if the boundary is supposed to be a mountain ridge, how do you make certain that everyone agrees which ridge is the correct one? Many of the straight dashed lines you see are lines of latitude and longitude. The north-south lines, labelled 75 to 85, are lines of longitude: the east-west lines labelled 25 to 50 are lines of latitude.

The representatives to the Congress finally agreed that each state had to give up its claim to lands west of the Appalachian Mountains. Since more than 15,000 people already lived in the area we call West Virginia and Kentucky (see maps on pages 69 and page 3), it was agreed that Virginia should keep control of that area until it could be made into a state.

Descriptions of Land Parcels

In order to claim ownership of a **parcel** (area) of land, you must be able to describe the parcel exactly. During the colonial period, several kings of England gave individuals small grants of land, but no one kept accurate records of how the grants fitted together. As a result, there were many quarrels about who owned particular pieces of land.

The delegates to the Congress had many experiences with the problems of describing land parcels. They knew that they did not want their inaccurate system of parcel descriptions used in the vast lands west of the Appalachian Mountains. Even before the end of the Revolution, Thomas Jefferson and others were trying to decide how to describe land parcels in the West.

When the American Colonies declared war on Great Britain, they had no money, and no power of taxation to raise money. The only thing they owned was land in the west. Therefore, they issued land **warrants** (claims) to their soldiers as "pay." Each warrant said that the named soldier was entitled to a certain number of acres of land, but it did not describe a particular parcel.

Public Land Act of 1785

As early as 1778, the representatives to the Congress agreed that their conflicting claims to lands in the West could be solved only by **ceding** (giving up) these claims to the Congress. In 1785 they adopted the *Public Land Act* in order to protect the ownership of land in the Ohio Country.

The diagram on the next page shows the final plan for laying out townships, ranges, and sections, but only a few areas in our state have exactly this system. The idea behind the Public Land Act was to establish easily-described parcels of land, as nearly square in shape as possible, on the round surface of the Earth. Parts of Ohio surveyed before 1820 have a variety of patterns — in fact Ohio has more different public land surveys than any other state.

If you live in a rural area you, or your parents, probably know the township and section in which you live. If you live in a large city, the legal description of the parcel of land on which you live is also related to a township and section. This pattern of subdivision also had great influence on the location of highways in our state.

In Chapter 11 you will learn how every county of Ohio is divided into *political townships*. Some of these political townships are 6-miles by 6-miles in size, as shown on the next page, but many others are irregular in shape.

Division of Land Into Tracts 24 miles Square

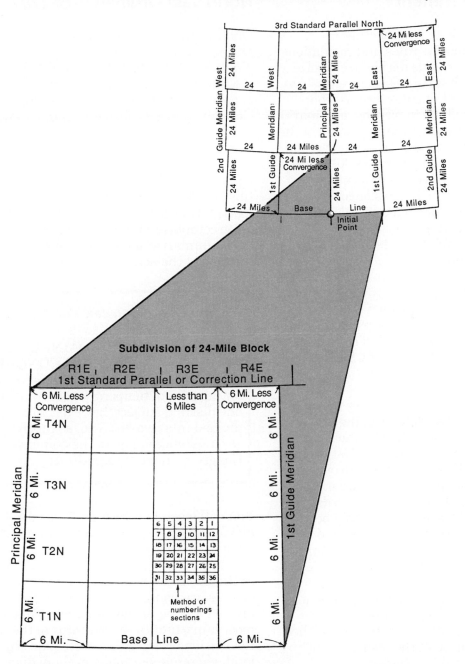

Subdivision of 24-Mile Block

Showing the Division Of Land Into Townships

The Public Land Survey created square tracts of land on the round surface of the Earth.

71

Role of Government

In order for people to live together in groups, there must be rules and regulations. If you and some friends decide to organize a club, one of the first things you are likely to do is agree on a set of rules for the group. These rules should be in writing, and may be called the **bylaws** or **constitution** of the group. If you want to join an existing group, you must agree to obey its rules. After you have joined a group, you may want to change the rules. The bylaws or constitution should have "rules" for making changes. *Government* is the form of rules and regulations a group of people adopts to live together in harmony.

The three basic purposes of government in a free society are: 1. to provide a situation free of **turmoil** (trouble), 2. to keep records of all important events in the lives of citizens, and 3. to raise money (**taxes**) to pay for the first two services.

Turmoil may arise from outsiders trying to break in, or from people within the organization refusing to live by the rules and regulations. One of the greatest desires of people in the United States is to own property, and the most important form of property is land. Without good records of land ownership, there will certainly be turmoil. Records relating to individual lives are important so that the government knows who has the rights of citizenship. If the government cannot raise money to operate a military system to keep outsiders from breaking in, the government will be destroyed. If it cannot raise money to police its citizens and protect the ownership of property, there will be **chaos** (utter confusion and loss of personal rights).

Northwest Ordinance of 1787

On July 13, 1787, the Congress adopted *An Ordinance for the Government of the Territory of the United States Northwest of the River Ohio*. This law described the form of government to be used in the Ohio Country, and established a plan for creating new states. It also required that all land be surveyed under the Public Land Act.

Ohio was the first state to be formed under this law. As you can see from the **excerpt** (portion) of the Ordinance, the wording is quite complicated. For this reason, we will only summarize some of the most important sections of the act.

Excerpt from Northwest Ordinance

SECTION 1: BE IT ORDAINED BY THE UNITED STATES IN CONGRESS ASSEMBLED, That the said territory, for purpose of temporary government, be one district, subject, however, to be divided into two districts, as future circumstances may, in the opinion of Congress, make it **expedient**.

You will learn how Section 1 was used to divide the Ohio Country into two counties later in this chapter.

Section 2: If the holder of a land warrant died before using it, his claim would be divided among his descendants. This was most important to the veterans of the Revolution because they were paid with land warrants, but many of them died before they could claim their "pay."

Section 3: Congress would appoint governors for the territory until there were enough people living in the west to elect their political leaders.

Section 4: Congress would appoint a secretary of the territory who would keep all legal records, and send copies of these records to the Congress. Congress would also appoint three judges to settle disputes between residents in the territory.

Section 5: The governor and judges together would adopt all laws necessary for operation of the territory until there were enough people to elect a **legislature** (law-making body) within the region.

Section 6: The governor would be the commander-in-chief of the militia.

Section 7: The governor would appoint people to serve as police officers, or sheriffs, in order to protect citizens from turmoil.

Section 8: Whenever Indian titles to land were ended, the governor would arrange to have the land surveyed on the Public Land Survey system.

Section 9 through 13 gave instructions about how the territory would be governed until various portions of it had enough people to form new states.

Section 14 outlined the steps required for a portion of the territory to become a state. This section was divided into six *Articles*.

Article I said that no law-abiding person would be injured because of religious ideas. Article II said that every person would have certain rights in every court. Article III is quoted in the box.

Article III of Section 14 of Northwest Ordinance

"Religion, morality, and knowledge being necessary to good government and the happiness of mankind, schools and the means of education shall forever be encouraged. The utmost of good faith shall always be observed towards the Indians; their lands and property shall never be taken from them without their consent; and in their property, rights, and liberty they shall never be invaded or disturbed, unless in just and lawful wars authorized by Congress; but laws founded in justice and humanity shall from time to time be made for preventing wrongs being done to them, and for preserving peace and friendship with them.

Article IV provided for relationships between newly formed states and the Congress. It also said, "The **navigable** waters leading to the Mississippi and Saint Lawrence, and the carrying places (portages) between the same, shall be common highways and forever free ... without any tax, impost, or duty therefor."

Article V provided for formation of not fewer than three, nor more than five, states within the territory northwest of the Ohio River.

Article VI prohibited slavery within the territory.

You will learn more about certain parts of this ordinance later.

Sale and Subdivision of Ohio Lands

As you have learned, at the end of the Revolutionary War, many people living along the Atlantic Coast were eager to move west and begin new lives. We will now look at how these desires influenced the development of Ohio.

Virginia Military District

Because Virginia had the strongest claim for the largest area northwest of the Ohio River, it was allowed to keep all of the land between the Little Miami River on the west, the Ohio River on the south, and the Scioto River on the east and north, as shown in the southwest quarter of the map on the next page. Today we know this area as the *Virginia Military District*. Because this area was not surveyed under the Public Land Act, the people living in it have had many problems describing the land they own.

The Old Seven Ranges

Along the east side of the map on the page 75, you can see an area labeled *The Seven Ranges*, the first part of the United States surveyed under the Public Land Act of 1785. The subdivision of this area could not begin until Thomas Hutchins, the Surveyor General of the United States, had established the line of longitude — approximately 80° 31' West — that defined the west boundary of Pennsylvania. Today Hutchins' line is the boundary between Pennsylvania and West Virginia. The northern part of this line — the boundary between Pennsylvania and Ohio — was surveyed later. One of the assistants to Hutchins was a young man named Israel Ludlow, whom you will learn more about later in this chapter.

The starting point for the survey of the Seven Ranges is on the north shore of the Ohio River on the Ohio-Pennsylvania border.

Rufus Putnam and The Ohio Company

Shortly after the end of the Revolution, a group of New England soldiers and officers met in a tavern in Boston, Massachusetts, to plan new lives for themselves in the Ohio Country. They formed *The Ohio Company of Associates*, and took steps to purchase land along the Ohio River.

Congress sold almost one million acres to this company just southwest of the Seven Ranges. The price was about ten cents per acre. Later the Ohio Company bought a smaller tract as shown in the southeast corner of the map on page 75.

The Ohio Company was very well organized, as you can see from the following account of its journey to the Ohio Country.

The picture on the page 76 shows the first group leaving Massachusetts.

THE MICHIGAN SURVEY 1836

1792

1786

CONGRESS LANDS 1820-21

THE FIRE LANDS

THE CONNECTICUT WESTERN RESERVE

CONGRESS LANDS 1819

CONGRESS LANDS 1799-1804

CONGRESS LANDS 1798-1801

CONGRESS LANDS 1802-05

U.S. MILITARY DISTRICT 1796-1802

THE SEVEN RANGES

1786

THE VIRGINIA MILITARY DISTRICT

CONGRESS LANDS 1795-1802

SECOND PURCHASE

THE OHIO COMPANY

THE OHIO COMPANY FIRST PURCHASE 1787

THE REFUGEE TRACT 1798

THE DONATION TRACT 1792

SYMMES PURCHASE 1794

HAMILTON

1784

1792

The French Grants 1795 – 98

WILLIAMS, FULTON, DEFIANCE, HENRY, WOOD, OTTAWA, LUCAS, SANDUSKY, ERIE, LORAIN, CUYAHOGA, LAKE, GEAUGA, ASHTABULA, TRUMBULL, PAULDING, PUTNAM, HANCOCK, SENECA, HURON, MEDINA, SUMMIT, PORTAGE, MAHONING, VAN WERT, ALLEN, WYANDOT, CRAWFORD, RICHLAND, ASHLAND, WAYNE, STARK, COLUMBIANA, MERCER, AUGLAIZE, HARDIN, MARION, MORROW, KNOX, HOLMES, TUSCARAWAS, CARROLL, JEFFERSON, HARRISON, SHELBY, LOGAN, UNION, DELAWARE, COSHOCTON, GUERNSEY, DARKE, CHAMPAIGN, FRANKLIN, LICKING, MUSKINGUM, BELMONT, MIAMI, CLARK, MADISON, NOBLE, MONROE, MONTGOMERY, GREENE, FAIRFIELD, PREBLE, PICKAWAY, PERRY, MORGAN, WASHINGTON, BUTLER, WARREN, CLINTON, ROSS, HOCKING, ATHENS, CLERMONT, HIGHLAND, VINTON, MEIGS, BROWN, PIKE, JACKSON, GALLIA, ADAMS, SCIOTO, LAWRENCE

Ohio has more forms of the Public Land Survey than any other state.

75

How The Ohio Company Settlers Moved to Ohio

In exact **compliance** with this order a company of twenty-two men, including Jonathan Devoll, a master-shipbuilder, and his assistants, assembled at the house of Dr. Manasseh Cutler, in Ipswich, Mass., on December 3, 1787. About the dawn of day they paraded in front of the house, and, after a short address from him, three **volleys** were fired, and the party went forward, cheered heartily by the bystanders ...

Capt. Ezra Putnam ... had prepared a large and well-built wagon for their use, covered with black canvas ... on which ... [was] ... painted ... in large white letters, "FOR THE OHIO COUNTRY." After a **tedious** journey on foot of nearly eight weeks, they arrived at Sumrill's ferry, on the Youghiogheny river (now West Newton, Westmoreland county, Pa.), January 23, 1788, where they were to build the boats to float down the [Youghiogheny, Monongahela and Ohio] rivers to the Muskingum [River].
From: Howe: vol. 2, page 798

An artist's idea of The Ohio Company leaving Massachusetts.

On April 7, 1788 forty-eight men, plus women and children, of the Ohio Company arrived at the mouth of the Muskingum River and founded the town of Marietta. This was the first permanent settlement in the Ohio Country. It was named for the Queen of France, Marie Antoinette, to show appreciation for the aid France gave to the Americans during the Revolutionary War.

The settlers built the log fort shown below, and gave it the Latin name *Campus Martius,* meaning "A Field of War." Today you can visit the Campus Martius Museum at Marietta, and see a part of Rufus Putnam's family home — the only part of the fort shown on this page that has been **preserved** (saved).

Before the settlers could move away from the fort to build homes and farms for themselves, the land had to be surveyed in accord with the Public Land Act. The United States appointed Rufus Putnam as the surveyor in charge of this work. Because the land was very hilly, the surveying was not nearly as accurate as the straight lines shown in the diagram on page 71.

The Symmes Purchase

The earliest settlements in southwest Ohio were made in the autumn and winter of 1788-9. In Chapter 4 you learned how Simon Kenton led Benjamin Stites into present Hamilton County in 1786. After returning to his home in New Jersey, Stites talked to his congressman, John Cleves

Campus Martius, at Marietta, was the first permanent white settlement in Ohio.

Symmes, about the rich land between the Great and Little Miami Rivers. Symmes traveled west to visit the area, and decided to organize a company to buy the land.

Symmes and several friends wanted to buy a million acres of land at "two-thirds dollars per acre." They hoped to sell it to settlers for $2.00 per acre. Eventually they were able to purchase about 330,000 acres, extending from the Ohio River northward to a line through present Lebanon, in Warren County, as shown on page 75.

Benjamin Stites was the first to buy land from Symmes. In October 1788, he led a group of twenty-six men, and their wives and children, to establish a settlement near the mouth of the Little Miami River. This land later became part of Cincinnati.

In 1788 Symmes led a party of settlers down the Ohio River to establish a settlement on the land between the Miami Rivers. When they stopped to rest at Marietta, Symmes persuaded Israel Ludlow to move west with him. In January 1789 the Symmes party established the town of North Bend near the mouth of the Great Miami River. North Bend still exists as a village of about 600 people.

Symmes put Israel Ludlow in charge of laying out the section lines in the land between the Miami Rivers. The system of numbering the sections and townships they established is different from any other part of Ohio, or the United States, but the pattern was later extended into the area labeled "Congress Lands 1802-05" on the map on page 75. Ludlow also laid out several of the towns in the region, and you can find streets named for him in these towns.

A third settlement was made in the Symmes Purchase by three land developers from Lexington, Kentucky. These men bought a tract opposite the mouth of the Licking River, and laid out a street system for a town. On December 28, 1788, Robert Patterson, one of the partners, led eleven families plus twenty-four single men to the planned town of *Losantiville*.

What Does Losantiville Mean?

You must divide Losantiville into parts and read them right to left. *Ville* is French for village. *Anti* is Latin for opposite. *Os* is Greek for mouth. And L stands for Licking River.

A few years later, Robert Patterson and his family moved about fifty miles north to establish a town in Montgomery County. It was named to honor Jonathan Dayton, one of Symmes' partners. There is no record that Mr. Dayton ever came to the Ohio Country.

War with The Natives

At the end of the Revolution, the British controlled all of the St. Lawrence River Valley and most of the Great Lakes area. They gladly supplied guns and ammunition to the natives, and encouraged them to attack the American settlers. In 1789 the settlers at Losantiville persuaded Congress to send soldiers to protect them. The soldiers built a fort and named it Fort Washington.

*Charles Willson Peale, an
American painter of the late
18th century, painted portraits
of 250 Americal leaders,
including this picture of
Arthur St. Clair.*

Arthur St. Clair

During the Revolution Arthur St. Clair rose to the rank of General, and became a good friend of George Washington. Congress appointed him to be the first governor of the Northwest Territory. St. Clair moved to Marietta to begin his new duties. In July 1788, he took the lead in dividing the Northwest Territory into two parts. The entire eastern half of what is now Ohio was named Washington County, and all the remainder of the territory was named Hamilton County.

In December 1789, Arthur St. Clair moved the seat of government of the Northwest Territory to Fort Washington. Because he did not like the name *Losantiville*, he named the town *Cincinnati*. He chose this name because he was a member of the *Society of the Cincinnati*, an organization of American officers of the Revolution. You can see a picture of him on page 79.

In the autumn of 1790, St. Clair sent General Josiah Harmar north from Fort Washington, with an army of about 1,450 men, to punish the natives who were attacking the new settlements. Several hundred women and children walked along behind the army as **camp followers**. This poorly-trained army marched up the valley of the Great Miami River and moved across the divide of the Wabash River to a point near present Fort Wayne, Indiana, as shown on the map on the next page. A surprise attack (**ambush**) by the Miamis, under Chief Little Turtle, killed many of the Americans and forced the rest to flee back to Fort Washington.

In the autumn of 1791 St. Clair himself led a group of 2,700 poorly-trained men, plus many camp followers, northward to fight the natives. He built a small fort in present Darke County, and named it Fort Jefferson, as shown on page 81.

By the time his army reached a point just west of present Mercer County, Ohio, almost one-half of the men had deserted. The Miamis and their allies, under Little Turtle, attacked again. They surrounded the remaining American troops and killed 613 and injured another 237. Many camp followers were also killed or wounded. Unfortunately for the natives, every victory they achieved made the whites more determined to crush them.

Anthony Wayne

In 1792 the United States Government sent General Anthony Wayne, a very skillful military leader, to Fort Washington to crush the natives. Because of his daring acts during the Revolutionary War, Wayne was often called *Mad Anthony*. Wayne spent eighteen months training an army. In the autumn of 1793, he led his men and the camp followers northward from Fort Washington into present Darke County, where he built Fort GreeneVille to protect his line of supplies. After Wayne moved on to the site of St. Clair's defeat and built Fort Recovery, he decided to spend the winter at the location of present Greenville. Simon Kenton, who was serving as a scout, urged Wayne to continue moving north so that he could attack the natives immediately, but Wayne did not want to take the risk.

*Military campaigns against the natives in Ohio
after the Revolutionary War.*

Battle of Fallen Timbers

In the spring of 1794, Wayne moved his army northward, and built Fort Defiance where the Auglaize River empties into the Maumee, as shown on the map on the previous page. The natives watched everything that the Americans were doing, and reported to the British at Fort Detroit. The British, concerned that Wayne might attack Detroit, sent troops to build Fort Miami on the Maumee River in the present city of Maumee.

When the natives asked Little Turtle to lead them again, he advised the other chiefs that the Americans were so strong that the natives should not try to resist. When they refused his advice, Little Turtle said that he would stay with his people and fight, but could not be the leader of the battle. The native leaders, including Tecumseh, named Blue Jacket, whom you learned about in Chapter 4, to be their leader.

About the middle of August 1794, Wayne's army moved northeastward along the Maumee River. At a point near the southern edge of present Lucas County, there was a large area that had once been covered by tall trees. A great wind had blown down many of these trees, and the natives hid among the fallen trees awaiting Wayne's attack. Wayne tricked the natives into leaving their shelter and defeated them in the open fields nearby. As some of the natives fled to the north, the British closed the gates of Fort Miami to prevent the escaping warriors from seeking protection. The natives bitterly resented this action by the British who had always encouraged them to fight the Americans.

William Henry Harrison

An ambitious young man named William Henry Harrison served as General Wayne's assistant throughout the campaign and at the Treaty of GreeneVille. Harrison was born in 1773 at Berkeley Plantation, near Petersboro, Virginia, which you can visit today. He began to study medicine, as his father wanted him to do. But at the age of twenty-one years, he joined the United States Army and was assigned to Fort Washington in Cincinnati. After the signing of the Treaty of GreeneVille, Harrison returned to Fort Washington. You will learn more about him in Chapter 6.

Treaty of GreeneVille

In the autumn of 1794, Wayne sent messages to twelve tribes of natives, living in Ohio, Indiana, and Michigan, demanding that they appear at Fort GreeneVille in June of 1795 to sign a treaty of peace. Blue Jacket and Tecumseh felt that they could not continue to fight after the British refused to help them at the Battle of Fallen Timbers. Most of the native leaders called to appear at GreeneVille agreed to go, but Tecumseh told them that he would not sign a treaty with the whites.

By the end of July a total of 1,130 natives had gathered at the assigned place. Wayne wanted to be certain that every chief knew both what the Americans wanted from them and what they would be given in payment. In order to identify the native leaders, Wayne had an artist make a colored drawing of each leader, showing every possible detail that could be used to

Howard Chandler Christy's painting of The Treaty of GreeneVille.

distinguish him. The picture on this page is the best-known painting of the signing of the treaty. This painting, hanging in the Garst Museum in Greenville, was created in 1922 by Howard Chandler Christy, a native of Ohio. In 1945 the General Assembly asked Mr. Christy to make a very large copy of this painting, which you can see in the stairway above the High Street entrance to the State Capitol.

The Treaty of GreeneVille described a new boundary between lands that the Americans could occupy and lands reserved for the natives. The line described in the box is shown on the map on the next page.

In return for giving up more than two-thirds of present Ohio, the natives were promised that the United States would give each of the twelve tribes $1,666 in trade goods plus $825 in cash once every year. Wayne closed the meeting with the words in the box on page 85.

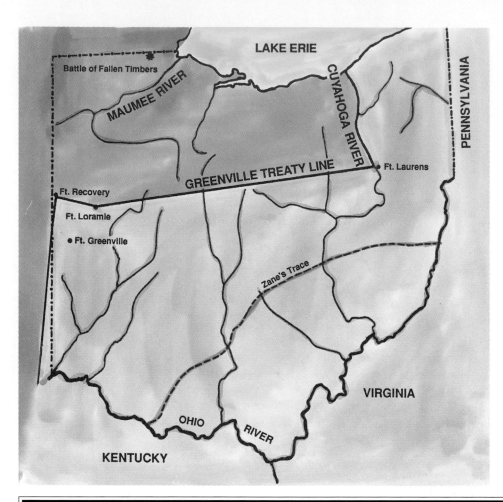

LAKE ERIE

Battle of Fallen Timbers

MAUMEE RIVER

CUYAHOGA RIVER

PENNSYLVANIA

GREENVILLE TREATY LINE

• Ft. Laurens

• Ft. Recovery

• Ft. Loramie

• Ft. Greenville

Zane's Trace

VIRGINIA

OHIO

RIVER

KENTUCKY

The Treaty of GreeneVille line was suposed to separate Natives and Whites forever.

Treaty of GreeneVille Boundary

The general boundary line between the lands of the United States and the lands of the said Indian tribes shall begin at the mouth of the Cuyahoga River and run **thence** up the same to the Portage between the Tuscarawas branch of the Muskingum, thence down that branch to the crossing place above Fort Laurens, thence westwardly to a fork of that branch of the Great Miami running into the Ohio, at or near which stood Loramie's Store and where commenced the portage between the Miami of the Ohio and St. Mary's River, which runs into Lake Erie [Maumee River]; thence a westerly course to Fort Recovery, which stands on a branch of the Wabash; thence southerly in a direct line to the Ohio, so as to intersect that river (in present Indiana) opposite the mouth of the Kentucke or Cuttawa River.

Words of General Anthony Wayne at GreeneVille

"I now **fervently** pray to the Great Spirit that the peace now established may be permanent and that it now holds us together in bonds of friendship until time shall be no more.

I also pray that the Great Spirit above may enlighten your minds and open your eyes to your true happiness, that your children may learn to **cultivate** the earth and enjoy the fruits of peace and industry."

Historic Sites

Today you can see monuments marking the locations of Ft. Washington, Ft. Jefferson, Ft. St.Clair, Ft. Recovery, Ft. Defiance, and Fallen Timbers. You can visit the partially reconstructed fort in Greenville. In the village of Ft. Loramie, you can visit a reconstruction of the house-store built in 1769 by Peter Loramie, a French-Canadian trader.

Connecticut Western Reserve

The royal grant given to the founders of Connecticut was a narrow strip of land extending from the Atlantic Ocean to the Mississippi River, as shown on the map on page 69. Although this grant overlapped New York and Pennsylvania, there were no actual conflicts. In 1780 Connecticut offered to give up its claim except for the land extending 120 miles westward from the west boundary of Pennsylvania. This tract became known as the *Western Reserve of Connecticut*, but today it is usually called the *Western Reserve*.

The map on page 84 shows that the lands claimed by Connecticut to the west of the Cuyahoga River were assigned to the natives in the Treaty of GreeneVille. The Delaware, Wyandot, Ottawa, and Chippewa tribes lived to the west of the Cuyahoga River, and they intended to protect their land from the settlers. (The Chippewas were a part of the Ojibway tribe, which is shown on page 49 as living to the north of Lake Superior.) A few weeks after the Treaty of GreeneVille was signed, the State of Connecticut sold three million acres of this land, as shown on page 75, to the *Connecticut Land Company* for $1,200,000.

The *Connecticut Land Company* was made up of about fifty men, one of whom was General Moses Cleaveland. Cleaveland graduated from Yale College in 1777, and served in both the Connecticut legislature and militia during the Revolution. In the spring of 1796, the Company sent Cleaveland into the Western Reserve to survey the land for settlement, including a town at the mouth of the Cuyahoga River. The pattern of subdivision they used was based on tracts of land five miles on each side, and they did not subdivide these into one-mile sections of the Public Land Survey.

Cleaveland and his helpers made great progress with the surveying during the summer and autumn months. He then returned to Connecticut and never again traveled west. By the end of 1797 all of the land east of the Cuyahoga had been surveyed, and was being sold to settlers. The city of Cleveland, in Cuyahoga

County, was named for Moses Cleaveland, but for some reason, the spelling was changed.

The Fire Lands

You will notice that the west end of the Connecticut Reserve on the map is labeled *The Fire Lands*. During the Revolution, several towns in Connecticut were destroyed by fires set by British raiders, and the people living in these towns suffered greatly. In 1792 Connecticut decided to give 500,000 acres in the west end of its Reserve to those who had lost their homes. Today this area is known as *the Fire Lands*, and the pattern of land subdivision in Erie and Huron Counties is unlike any other.

Other Subdivisions of Ohio

As you can see from the map on page 75, the surveys you have learned about thus far covered about one-half of the present area of Ohio. This same figure shows all of the other surveys of large areas that were completed by 1822.

The map also shows some of the small areas that were given by the Congress of the United States to a wide variety of people. For example, near the center of it, you can see an east-west strip of land labeled The Refugee Tract. It has this name because Congress gave the area to residents of Canada who supported the Americans during the Revolutionary War. After the war, these people were despised by the British who continued to control Canada. Refugee Road in Columbus takes its name from this tract.

In 1803 President Thomas Jefferson appointed Jared Mansfield to the position of Surveyor General, and he was in charge of subdividing many of the parts of Ohio we have not discussed. Mansfield was very well qualified for surveying, and the later Public Land Surveys were made very accurately. The city of Mansfield, the county seat of Richland County, was named for him.

Effects on Native Americans

There was great rejoicing throughout Ohio and the eastern states when the Treaty of GreeneVille was signed, because settlers thought that it would now be safe to live in the Northwest Territory. On the other hand, the natives were suffering because the whites were ignoring Article III, Section 14, of the Northwest Ordinance, that you read earlier. Tecumseh had refused to sign the Treaty of GreeneVille because he felt that what Wayne called "bonds of friendship" would last only as long as it was convenient for the whites. He wanted to be able to resist them without breaking the pledge of peace required by the treaty.

In 1795 the Americans told the natives that the Cuyahoga River would be the boundary between their lands forever. In 1805 Congress forced them to give up their rights to all lands within 120 miles of the Pennsylvania border.

A few years later Congress decided that the natives should live as white farmers. In the next chapter you will learn how the natives again turned to the British for help in resisting the Americans who were taking their lands in northern Ohio.

Stop and Think!

In a period of about thirty years, from 1776 to 1805, the United States of America defeated the forces of Great Britain and began the development of one of the greatest nations in the world. There were very few whites living in the Ohio Country during the Revolutionary War, but people from the original States began moving west immediately after the war.

The Ohio Country was the laboratory for developing many of the tools of government, such as the Public Land Survey of 1785 and the Northwest Ordinance of 1787. These tools were very important as the United States grew from a population of about three million in 1776 to more than 250 million by the end of the 20th century.

The Native Americans tried to resist the expansion of whites into the Ohio Country. They won some battles, but learned that they could not prevent the white settlers from taking their lands.

Review the Chapter!

Building vocabulary...

ambush	legislature
by-laws	longitude
camp follower	meridian
chaos	monument
charter	navigable
compliance	ordained
confederation	ordinance
constitution	parcel
cultivate	preserved
excerpt	refugee
expedient	tedious

fervently	thence
general assembly	turmoil
surveyor	volley
taxes	warrant (land)

Meeting New People ...

Little Turtle	Rufus Putnam
Arthur St.Clair	Benjamin Stites
Anthony Wayne	William Henry
Israel Ludlow	Harrison
John Cleves Symmes	Moses Cleaveland

Testing yourself...

Why it true or false?

1. All of the Ohio Country belonged to Kentucky at one time.
2. Manasseh Cutler led the Ohio Company people to Ohio.
3. Cleveland, Ohio, was surveyed by Israel Ludlow.
4. The Campus Martius Museum is in Marietta, Ohio.
5. Anthony Wayne was an outstanding American general.
6. Blue Jacket replaced Little Turtle as leader of the natives.
7. The United States paid soldiers in land rather than in money.
8. Ohio was the first state to be divided into townships and sections.
9. At the end of the Revolutionary War, the British cooperated with the newly formed government of the United States.
10. Tecumseh was the first native to sign the Treaty of GreeneVille.

Complete this thought ...

1. The first permanent white settlement in Ohio was ....
2. The Miami chieftain who decided that it was futile to fight the whites was ....

3. The original name of Blue Jacket was
....

4. The correct name for what some people
called the "rectangular system" is
....

5. Large areas of the land in Ohio were
given to veterans of the ....

6. The Northwest Ordinance was adopted
by Congress in ....

7. Jared Mansfield came to Ohio after he
was appointed ....

8. William Henry Harrison came to the
Northwest Territory in ....

9. The people who settled Marietta came
from ....

10. The first settlers in the Western
Reserve came from............

Debate the issue ...

Arrange teams with 3 or 4 pupils on each
side. Pick one of the following topics, and
stage an informal debate. People not
debating should take notes, question the
speakers, and vote on which side "wins."

1. The white settlers and Native Americans
could have gotten along peacefully if
matters had been handled differently.

2. The United States Government was fair
in its treatment of the natives of Ohio.

Thinking it through...

1. Look at the map on page 75 and decide
which of the surveys covers the area in
which you live. If your parents own your
home, look at the deed to see what it says
about the survey in which you live.

2. Pretend that you are a tribal chief in the
Ohio Country between 1770 and 1805.
How would you advise your people to
deal with the settlers?

3. Imagine that you are the leader of an
early settlement in Ohio. How would
you advise your followers to treat
the natives?

4. Imagine that you are living in the Ohio
Country 200 years ago, and you are
captured by a native war party. How
would you behave?

Working with maps...

1. Look at a globe of the world, and
determine the latitude and longitude
of Columbus, Ohio.

2. Call the airport nearest you home,
and ask for the latitude and longitude
of the control tower. Calculate how
many degrees of latitude and longitude
the control tower is from Columbus,
as shown in the diagram on page 68.

3. On the map of the world find the point on
the opposite side of the world from the
airport nearest your home. This point
will be at 180 degrees of longitude from
the airport, and as many degrees south of
the equator as the airport is north.

4. On the map of Ohio, look at the county
lines and list ten lines that seem to be
related to the Public Land Survey.

5. On the map of the United States, list the
names of states that seem to have at
least two boundaries related to the Public
Land Survey.

CHAPTER 6

What happened during the earliest years of Ohio?

Be ready to learn...

- about the role of women in government.

- about the role of slavery.

- how government developed in the Ohio Country.

- how Ohio became a state.

- the role of Ohio in the War of 1812.

By the year 1800 almost everyone in the United States knew about the Ohio Country. Thousands of people had moved, were in the process of moving, or were dreaming of moving into what they considered to be the "Promised Land." Since the Northwest Territory was owned by the United States of America, we must first look at two of the many problems facing the leaders of the new nation. We shall then look at the steps taken to create the State of Ohio. Finally, we shall look at the role of Ohio in the War of 1812.

Role of Women

In 1776 almost all the nations of Europe were ruled by men, who had the titles of "king," "prince," or "emperor." A few places were ruled by women, who had the title of "queen" or "princess." Many of these rulers claimed to govern by **Divine Right**, which means that they believed they were appointed to rule by God. During the 18th century, some European scholars wrote books about a philosophy of government in which the people would rule themselves. The leaders of the American colonies included some of these ideas in the *Declaration of Independence*. But no nation had ever tried to use the theories to form a government.

The Native Americans were one of the few groups of people in the world who ruled themselves in 1776. Between 1776 and 1787, representatives of the Congress of the United States met many times with leaders of the Iroquois and Lenape (Delaware) tribes. They learned how tribes selected their chiefs, how they decided where to live or whom to fight, how those who disobeyed were punished. They learned how representatives of several tribes met together to make decisions affecting their common welfare, and how these decisions were recorded in *wampum*. One of the most important things the representatives of Congress learned was that women made many important decisions for the tribes! The chiefs of the Iroquois tribes were always men, but they were chosen by, and served with the consent of councils made up of women!

Abigail Smith Adams

In Chapter 11 you will learn how the women of the late 19th century struggled to gain human and political rights. In Chapter 15 you will learn how women of the late 20th century are struggling to achieve "equal rights." During the last years of the 18th century, Abigail Smith Adams was a leader in seeking equal rights for women.

Abigail Smith was born in Weymouth, Massachusetts, near Boston in 1744. Although she had very little formal schooling, she was a "quick learner" and achieved a good education — partly by studying what her brothers were being taught. At the age of eighteen, she was introduced to John Adams, a twenty-seven-year-old lawyer who had graduated from Harvard College. Abigail and John were married in 1764.

John Adams and his cousin, Samuel Adams, were leaders in resisting the attempts of England to control life in Massachusetts and the other colonies. Over a period of twenty years, John represented Massachusetts on almost every committee that met in the various colonies to decide how they might gain freedom from Great Britain and govern themselves.

When George Washington was elected President of the United States in 1788, John Adams was elected Vice President. When Washington completed his second term as President, John Adams became our second president. Adams County, Ohio was named for him.

Abigail and John exchanged many letters over the years, and these have become the bases for several books. In the Spring of 1776, while John was helping to write the Declaration of Independence, Abigail wrote what has come to be called the *Remember the Ladies* letter.

Excerpt from Abigail Adams' "Remember the Ladies" Letter

I long to hear that you have declared an independency — and by the way in the new Code of Laws which I suppose it will be necessary for you to make I desire you would Remember the Ladies, and be more generous and favourable to them than your ancesters. Do not put such unlimited power into the hands of the Husbands. Remember all Men would be **tyrants** if they could. If perticular care and attention is not paid to the Ladies we are determined to **foment** a Rebellion, and will not hold ourselves bound by any Laws in which we have no voice, or Representation....
From: Phyllis Lee Levin, *Abigail Adams*, p. 83.

Abigail's letter influenced John's thinking, but he could not change the ideas of the men who wrote the Declaration of Independence, the Northwest Ordinance, and the Constitution. They adopted many ideas from the Native Americans, but gave women no role in the new government.

Role of Slaves

One of the most difficult **issues** (problems) facing the founders of our nation was the question of slavery. People in the North had very different views on this subject than people in the South.

Most African-American slaves were in the South, but there were some in New England and other northern colonies.

African-American

In this book Black Americans will be called *African-Americans*, except in direct quotations, because of the following reasoning: "... Black people wherever they are, come from the land called Africa. We have been called by many different names — colored, Negro, Black, etc. Most people are known by the land which they or their ancestors lived in or come from. Germans are called Germans because there is a land named Germany. ... Now look at a map. Is there a land called Colorland? Negroland? Blackland? No. There is a land named Africa, which is where we came from. So in our book we shall refer to ourselves as ... Africans in America."
From *Preface to Lessons in History — A Celebration of Blackness* (Elementary Edition), by Jawanza Kunjufu, African-American Images, Chicago, Illinois

---

In 1770 the people of Boston were protesting against British soldiers staying in their city. One day five African-Americans were walking toward a

British guardpost when the soldiers shot at them. Crispus Attucks, one of the five, was killed immediately, and the others died within a few days. The newspapers called this event *The Boston Massacre*, and news of it traveled throughout the colonies.

A short time later a group of slaves sent word to the governor of Massachusetts that they would be willing to fight for the cause of the colony, if they were given weapons AND their freedom when the fighting ended. Abigail Adams wrote to John about her views on this subject.

Abigail Adams'
Views on Slavery

You know my mind upon this Subject, I wish most sincerely there was not a slave in the **province**. It allways appeared a most **iniquitous** Scheme to me — fight ourselves for what we are daily robbing and **plundering** from those who have as good a right to freedom as we have.
From: Levin, p. 82

What do people do when they know that they must cooperate with each other in order to live, but cannot agree on a very important issue? They must **compromise** (reach an agreement both sides can live with).

The compromise our Founding Fathers worked out had three parts:
(1) Each state could decide the slavery question for itself.
(2) If a slave escaped to a free state, the owner could recapture the person in any other state.

(3) There would be no slavery in the Northwest Territory. Here is the full statement of Section 14, Article VI, of the Northwest Ordinance that was briefly mentioned in Chapter 5.

Article VI of Northwest Ordinance
Concerning Slavery

There shall be neither slavery nor involuntary servitude in the said territory, otherwise than in the punishment of crimes, whereof the party shall have been duly convicted: PROVIDED ALWAYS, That any person escaping into the same [Northwest Territory] from whom labor or service is lawfully claimed in any one of the original States, such fugitive [slave] may be lawfully claimed, and conveyed to the person claiming his or her labor or service aforesaid.

Steps in Ohio Becoming A State

As you learned in Chapter 5, the Northwest Ordinance laid out a series of steps to be taken in establishing local government in the territory. Section 9 of the Northwest Ordinance said:

General Assembly: So soon as there shall be five thousand free male **inhabitants** ... in the district ... they shall receive authority .. [to form a] .. general assembly. Section 12 said: "as soon as the legislature shall be formed .. [it] shall have authority ... to elect a **delegate** to Congress, who shall have ... a right of debating, but not voting..."

You also learned that Arthur St. Clair was appointed governor of the territory. In 1798 William Henry Harrison gave up his role as a soldier to become secretary of the territory, and in 1799 he was appointed to be the first representative of the Northwest Territory to Congress. When Congress created the *Indiana Territory* in 1800, all of the present Indiana, Illinois, Michigan, and Wisconsin, it appointed Harrison to be the Territory governor-general of this region.

Population Growth

The first step toward forming a state was to have enough people living in the area. Article V said that a new state could be formed when at least 60,000 lived in the area. The United States Census of 1800 found 45,365 people living in the area now called Ohio, including 337 African-Americans. The census did not include Native Americans because they were not taxed by the government.

As the growing population spread through the Ohio Country, additional counties were formed out of the original Washington County and Hamilton County. By 1802 there were seventeen counties, and one "unorganized" area in what was called "the eastern region of the Northwest Territory," as shown on the map below. If you look back to the map on page 84, you can see how some of these counties related to the Treaty of GreeneVille.

When Ohio became a state in 1803, there were seventeen counties.

Ordinance of 1802

Early in 1802 Thomas Worthington and Michael Baldwin were appointed to take a request for statehood to Congress. On April 30, Congress set the boundaries of the proposed state and gave the assembly permission to write a constitution. You can read the **preamble** (introduction) to this law in the box.

Preamble to The Ordinance of 1802

CHAP. 300 (XL.) An act to enable the people of the eastern division of the territory northwest of the river Ohio, to form a constitution and state government, and for the admission of such state into the union, on an equal footing with the original states, and for other purposes.

In addition to describing the boundaries of the new state, which you will learn about below, the ordinance included the following points:

1. The residents of the seventeen counties would elect representatives to meet in Chillicothe, in Ross County, to choose a name for the new state and prepare a constitution.
2. Section 16 of every township of the Public Land Survey would be set aside for the support of education. You can find Section 16 on the diagram on page 71, and you will learn more about this in Chapter 11.
3. Congress would give to the new state ownership of the salt springs in what we know as Licking County.
4. The part of Michigan previously included in the "eastern division" would become part of the Indiana Territory.

Boundaries of Ohio

Section 2 of the ordinance of 1802 said that the new state would be:

"bounded on the east by the Pennsylvania line, on the south by the Ohio river, to the mouth of the Great Miami river, on the west by the line drawn **due north** (a line of longitude) from the mouth of the Great Miami ... and on the north by an east and west line drawn through the southerly extreme of Lake Michigan ... and thence ... through Lake Erie, to the Pennsylvania line ..."

Although this description of Ohio sounds simple, there were several problems in it.

The description of the north line almost led to war between the citizens of Ohio and their neighbors to the north when Michigan became a state in 1837. The people of Ohio wanted the mouth of the Maumee River to be in their state. No one knew whether this point was north or south of the south end of Lake Michigan. You can look back to the map on page 81 to see how the north lines of Indiana and Ohio were finally drawn to solve the problem.

During the last half of the 20th century, a problem arose over the southern boundary of our state. As you have read, the Ordinance of 1802 said that the southern boundary of Ohio would be the Ohio River. As you will learn in Chapter 7, rivers were the most important form of inland transportation during the 18th century. When Virginia gave up its claim to lands northwest of the Ohio River, it gave up the land but kept ownership of the entire width of the river. This means that Virginia owned all the waters of the Ohio River except during times of flooding. Almost everywhere in the world where a river

This building in Chillicothe was the first capitol of Ohio.

forms a boundary, the center of the stream is the boundary line. When the western part of Virginia became the state of Kentucky, the ownership of the Ohio River passed to the new state. This arrangement caused no serious problems until new locks and dams were built on the Ohio River during the 1960s and 1970s to make it deeper. When the water became deeper, it also became wider, which meant that Kentucky and West Virginia had claim to land — under water — that had long been part of Ohio, Indiana, and Illinois. These three states petitioned Federal Courts to make their southern boundaries where they were originally, and Congress made this change in 1982.

Constitutional Convention

During the summer of 1802, the voters living in the seventeen counties elected delegates to the Constitutional Convention, and these men met in Chillicothe in November. The picture on the previous page shows the building in which they met.

The General Assembly met in this same building from 1803 until 1810, and from 1812 to 1816.

Within a few weeks the delegates drew up a proposed Constitution and sent a copy of it to Congress, which was meeting in Philadelphia at that time. The following excerpts from this Constitution give some idea of life in Ohio two hundred years ago.

Excerpts from
First Constitution of Ohio

We the people of the eastern division of the territory of the United States northwest of the river Ohio, having the right of admission into the general government as a member of the Union, consistent with ... the law of Congress entitled "An act to enable the people of the eastern division of the territory of the United States northwest of the river Ohio to form a Constitution and state government, ... in order to establish justice, promote the welfare and secure the blessings of liberty to ourselves and our **posterity**, do ordain and establish the following Constitution or form of government; and do mutually agree with each other to form ourselves into a free and independent State, by the name of the STATE OF OHIO.

ARTICLE I -Section 1. The legislative authority of this State shall be **vested** in a General Assembly, which shall consist of a Senate and House of Representatives, both to be elected by the people.

ARTICLE II - Section 1. The **supreme** executive power of this State shall be vested in a Governor.

ARTICLE III - Section 1. The judicial power of this State ... shall be vested in a Supreme Court, in Courts of Common Pleas for each County, [and] in Justices of the Peace (town and township courts).

ARTICLE IV - Section 1. In all elections, all white male inhabitants above the age of twenty-one years ... shall enjoy the right of an **elector** ...

ARTICLE VI - Section 1. There shall be elected in each County one **Sheriff** (Chief of Police) and one **Coroner** (person who determines cause of death in questionable cases)...

ARTICLE VII - Section 3 dealt with formation of new counties.

Section 4. Chillicothe shall be the seat of government until the year one thousand eight hundred and eight ...

ARTICLE VIII was the *Bill of Rights* of the citizens of the state.

Congress Admits Ohio to the United States

Thomas Worthington immediately carried the proposed constitution of the State of Ohio to the Congress of the United States, and delivered it a few days before Christmas. On February 19, 1803, Congress adopted, and President Thomas Jefferson signed: *AN ACT TO PROVIDE FOR THE DUE EXECUTION OF THE LAWS OF THE UNITED STATES WITHIN THE STATE OF OHIO*. This act said:

Whereas, the people of the Eastern division of the territory northwest of the river Ohio did ... form for themselves a Constitution and state government, and did give to the said state the name of the "State of Ohio," in [accord with] an act of Congress ... whereby the said state has become one of the United States of America ...

In this same act, Congress established a Federal Court, and court officers, to enforce federal laws in the new state.

Early Leaders of Ohio

Four men who worked hard to create the State of Ohio also served as the first four governors of our state. Without strong support from their wives, they could not have been so effective.

Edward and Mary Worthington Tiffin

In 1789 Edward Tiffin, a physician, married Mary Worthington in Virginia. They moved to Chillicothe in Ross County. In 1798, Mary was the sister of Thomas Worthington, whom you will learn more about later. Edward Tiffin was very active on the committee that wrote the first constitution for Ohio, and he was elected to

be the first governor of the new state. He served two terms as governor, and in 1807 he was elected to represent Ohio in the Senate of the United States. The Tiffins had no children, and when Mary died in 1808, Edward grieved so much that he resigned from the Senate the following year. The county seat of Seneca County is named for Edward Tiffin.

Samuel and Hannah Huntington Huntington

In 1791 Samuel Huntington married his distant cousin, Hannah Huntington, in Connecticut. After graduating from Yale College, Samuel became a lawyer. In 1801 the Huntingtons and their six children moved to a 300-acre farm in the Western Reserve, where downtown Cleveland is now located. Samuel represented Trumbull County (see map on page 93) in writing the constitution for Ohio. He was then elected to the Ohio Senate, and later to the Supreme Court of the state. Samuel Huntington served as governor of our state from 1808 to 1810.

Since Chillicothe was more than 150 miles from Cleveland, and transportation was very poor, Hannah stayed at home to manage the farm and care for the children.

Return J. and Sophia Wright Meigs

Return J. Meigs, Jr. and Sophia Wright were married in Connecticut in 1788. That same year they moved to Marietta with The Ohio Company of Associates. Their first home was part of the Campus Martius fortification. Their one child, Mary, was born in that house in 1793. In 1808 they built a large house on Front Street in Marietta that you can visit today.

Return Meigs served as governor of Ohio from 1810 to 1814 — a critical period that you will learn about later in this chapter. Meigs County, created in 1819 from the north part of Gallia County (look at the map on page 93), was named for him.

Thomas and
Eleanor Swearington Worthington

Eleanor Swearington inherited a large estate in Virginia before she married Thomas Worthington in 1796. Shortly after their marriage, they decided to move to the Ohio Country with the Tiffins. The Worthingtons first lived in a small log house in Chillicothe, and then in a larger one just to the north of town. In 1807 they built a stone mansion on the hillside just north of Chillicothe, and named it Adena. (You first learned about Adena in Chapters 1 and 3.) The picture on page 99 shows Adena as it looks today. If you visit this house, and stand at a certain place, you can view the scene shown on the Great Seal of Ohio. (Look back to page 2 (Great Seal of Ohio).)

Thomas Worthington helped to write the constitution of Ohio. He served as the first United States Senator from Ohio, from 1803 to 1807, and again from 1811 to 1814. In 1814 he was elected Governor of Ohio and served in this office until 1818. In the early 1820s he served in the Ohio General Assembly where he worked hard to improve the transportation system of our state. The city of Worthington in Franklin County is named for him.

Eleanor Worthington gave birth to ten children. She had to manage the home estate while her husband served in the various political offices. She entertained many national leaders at Adena, including Presidents James Madison and James Monroe, New York Governor DeWitt Clinton, and Senators Henry Clay and Daniel Webster. She also welcomed Tecumseh, the great Shawnee leader, to her home.

You will find more information about the early governors of Ohio in Appendix C.

Resistance from Native Americans

The census of 1810 found 228,861 whites and 1,899 African-Americans living in Ohio. What were the Native Americans doing in Ohio while the "invaders" were increasing so fast? They were becoming more bitter because some Americans were ignoring the boundary established by the Treaty of GreeneVille.

In the peace treaty of 1783 that officially ended the Revolutionary War, the British gave up control of the colonies along the Atlantic coast, including their claims to land westward to the Mississippi River. But the British kept control of the St. Lawrence River and the Great Lakes. British traders continued to roam throughout the Northwest Territory, and encouraged the natives to fight the American settlers who were moving into the Ohio Country.

Adena was the home of Thomas and Eleanor Worthington.

Tecumseh's Plan

Tecumseh did not like the British, but he disliked the Americans even more because of the way they seized control of land. He especially disliked William Henry Harrison who was appointed Governor of the Territory of Indiana in 1800. Harrison set up his headquarters at Vincennes, on the Wabash River (see the map on page 54), and built a new home there, which he also used as his office. He named the house Grouseland, and you can visit it today. Between 1800 and 1810, Harrison forced the natives to sign one treaty after another in which they turned over more and more of their "homeland" to white settlers in the area we know as the State of Indiana.

Today we would say that Tecumseh had **psychic** powers because he had ways of gaining knowledge that are hidden from most people. He did not like to show this hidden power, and often had his brother speak for him. In order to drive the whites out of the region, Tecumseh developed a plan that might be called a *United Nations* of the tribes living west of the Appalachian

Mountains. For more than two years, he traveled from tribe to tribe throughout the states we know as Ohio, Michigan, Indiana, Illinois, and Wisconsin encouraging all the natives to unite against the whites. He also encouraged these tribes to move to a new town on the west bank of the Wabash River just upstream from the mouth of the Tippecanoe River.

Tecumseh's last trip began in May, 1811 with a visit to General Harrison at Vincennes. For the next six moons, as the natives measured what we call months, Tecumseh traveled through the area we know as the states of Kentucky, Tennessee, Mississippi, and Alabama, encouraging the tribes to unite in one big uprising against the whites. The chief of each tribe was given a bundle of sticks, and told to break one stick on the night of each full moon. When the last stick was broken, they were to watch for a great sign from Moneto (the Shawnee name for God), which would be the signal for them to attack the white settlements near each tribe.

The Prophet

Tecumseh's younger brother was born in 1772 and given the name Lalawethika, meaning He-Makes-A-Loud-Noise. He lost an eye in an accident when young, and he was very **self-conscious** about this loss. He also became an alcoholic, and he was generally a weak character. In 1805 "Loud Noise" told the people that he had received a vision of the future. This experience led him to give up alcohol and to change his name to Tenskwatawa, meaning He-Opens-The-Door. Each time Tecumseh traveled, he left Tenskwatawa in charge of the growing village at the mouth of the Tippecanoe River. The whites called Tenskwatawa, *The Prophet*, and the village, *Prophet's Town*.

100

Tecumseh allowed only one white artist to paint his picture. This was made from the original

The New Madrid Earthquake

By the end of November, 1811 every chief who had agreed to help Tecumseh threw away his last stick. On December 6, all of the region within more than 500 miles of the small town of New Madrid, in the southeast corner of the state of Missouri, began to shake violently: even some buildings in Ohio were destroyed. The course of the Mississippi River near New Madrid shifted by several miles, and a block of earth sank in Western Tennessee to create *Reelfoot Lake*. This was the greatest earthquake on record in North America. If

Wm. Henry Harrison, and other war leaders were often honored by statues of them on horseback.

the natives had taken arms and attacked the white settlers on that day, they might have changed the course of history of the United States!

Tippecanoe

Tenskwatawa became very vain as he saw more and more of Tecumseh's prophecies come true. Time after time, Tecumseh warned him that the natives must wait for the great sign before attacking Harrison's headquarters at Vincennes. He also told Tenskwatawa to lead the people away to safety if Harrison should threaten to attack their town.

Traders and scouts told William Henry Harrison about the natives gathering at Tippecanoe. He decided to lead a large army to a place near Prophet's Town, and then try to trick the natives into attacking before Tecumseh returned from his travels.

On November 5, 1811, Harrison ordered his army to make camp on a high flat area on the west side of the Wabash River, just south of the Tippecanoe River. No fortifications were built, but the soldiers were told to sleep in their uniforms, with their loaded rifles beside them. Guards were posted all around the camp. On that same day, Tenskwatawa sought help from *Moneto*

Fort Meigs was important during the War of 1812. It has been reconstructed in Perrysburg, Ohio.

by going into a trance-like state. In this state, he had a vision of a bone-handled knife going through Harrison's heart and killing him.

The war chiefs gathered around Tenskwatawa to decide what to do. Some urged that they should follow the instructions Tecumseh had given and move

The original painting of Perry's victory at Put In Bay hangs in the Ohio State Capitol.

away from Prophet's Town. Others wanted to attack Harrison's army in the night. Tenskwatawa decided to send representatives to Harrison to ask for a meeting to discuss the situation. The Prophet's men met with Harrison, looked over his camp, and returned to their council.

Of course, the only people who really know what happened in the Prophet's Town that night are long gone. But we do know that before dawn on November 7, 1811, the natives attacked what they thought was Harrison's sleeping army. A soldier guarding the camp fired one shot that

awakened his armed companions. In the fighting that followed, the natives suffered severe losses, and had to move their women and children as quickly as possible to the north and west. Harrison's troops destroyed the village, but did not pursue the fleeing natives.

Tecumseh returned to the banks of the Wabash River a short time later. When he learned what happened, he was furious about what his brother had done. On December 6, Tecumseh and a few friends were standing near the spot where *Loud*

103

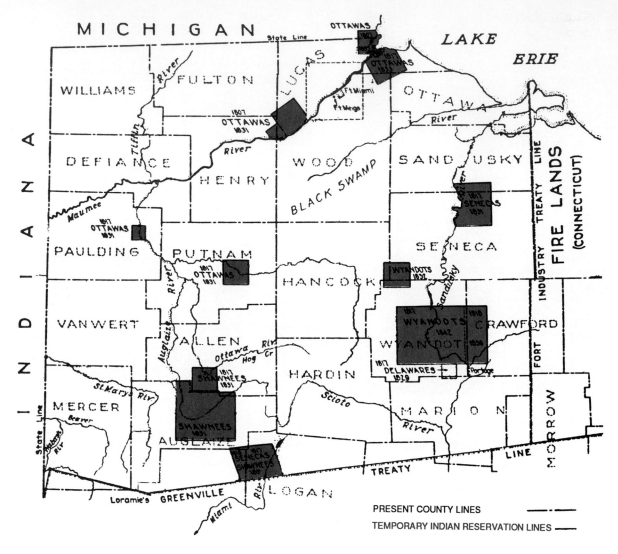

During the 1830's Native Americans were assigned to live in these reservations in northwest Ohio.

Noise had stood during the attack on Harrison when they were knocked off their feet by the shaking of the ground during the great earthquake. A short time later, Tecumseh and the natives who remained loyal to him moved across the Detroit River to Canada to gain the protection of the British army stationed there.

The War of 1812

During the 18th century, the British navy gained control of the Atlantic Ocean and most of the seas of the world. By 1810

British ships were attacking merchant ships of the United States. At the same time, British officers in Canada were encouraging the natives to attack the Americans. On June 18, 1812 the United States declared war on Great Britain, and William Henry Harrison was appointed commander of American troops in the West.

The British and their native allies, under the leadership of Tecumseh, quickly moved across the Detroit River and captured Fort Detroit. To meet this threat, General Harrison ordered the construction of a new fort on the south side of the rapids of the Maumee River: he named it *Fort Meigs* in honor of the Governor of Ohio, Return J. Meigs, Jr. The British bombarded the new fort heavily, while the warriors under Tecumseh surrounded it and cut off all supplies, but they could not capture it. On page 102 you can see a picture of the reconstructed Fort Meigs that you can visit at Perrysburg in Wood County.

Battle of Lake Erie

Commodore Oliver Hazard Perry of the United States Navy was given orders to build a small fleet of ships on Lake Erie to protect the communities of northern Ohio. On September 10, 1813, Perry's ships defeated the British fleet at Put-in Bay of South Bass Island, and this ended British control of the Great Lakes. Perry notified General Harrison of his victory by writing a letter on the back of an old envelope:

Dear General: We have met the enemy and they are ours — two ships, two brigs, one schooner and a sloop.
Yours with great respect and esteem,
Oliver Hazard Perry

In 1857 the General Assembly offered William H. Powell, an Ohio artist, $5000 to create a large painting to honor Perry's victory. The picture on page 103 shows the painting that hangs in the Ohio Capitol. Congress then asked Powell to make a second painting, which you can see in Washington, D.C.

Battle of the Thames

With the British Navy driven from Lake Erie, the Americans took control of Fort Detroit. On October 4, 1813, General Harrison's troops prepared to attack the British base on the Thames River in Canada, as shown on page 81. The frightened British commander decided to retreat, and ordered Tecumseh and his warriors to stand between his troops and the advancing Americans. Tecumseh predicted to his friends that he would die in the battle that was to come. The Americans attacked on October 5 and quickly defeated the native warriors. The picture on page 100 was made from the most accurate **portrait** (painted image) of Tecumseh because he permitted only one white artist to create a picture of him.

Tecumseh was killed in the first round of fighting. According to Shawnee legend, Tecumseh was wearing a disguise so that the Americans could not recognize him and **mutilate** (destroy) his body. The same legend tells that during the very early morning of October 6, Shawnee warriors crept onto the battlefield to find Tecumseh's body. They carried it away and buried it with great honor in a place they would long remember, but the whites could not find.

On December 24, 1814 the British signed the Treaty of Ghent in Belgium. On January 2, 1815, the natives signed another treaty with the government of the United States at St. Louis, Missouri. As part of this treaty, the Native Americans who wanted to continue living in Ohio agreed to stay on the reservations shown on the page 104. The people of Ohio and the United States were ready for a long period of tremendous growth.

Stop and Think!

This chapter has covered a period of about thirty years, from the close of the Revolutionary War in 1783 to the close of the War of 1812. During that short period, a small new nation, called the United States of America, accomplished many things. It adopted a system for surveying and governing the western lands, which were at least twice as large as the total areas of the original states. It adopted a Constitution, that has been changed fewer than thirty times, and it added the states of Vermont, Kentucky, Tennessee, and Ohio to the original thirteen.

By 1800 more than 45,000 men, women and children had moved into the Ohio Country. By following the many steps required by the Northwest Ordinance and the Constitution of the United States, Ohio became a state in 1803. Dedicated men and women worked hard to make Ohio a good place in which to live. The success of their efforts can be measured by the fact that the population of Ohio increased almost five-fold between 1800 and 1810.

Each success for the whites meant another defeat for the Native Americans. In the hope of driving the whites out of Ohio, the natives supported the British during the War of 1812 and lost again. By 1840 a few hundred individual families lived in northwest Ohio, but there were no tribal groups.

Review The Chapter !

Building vocabulary...

amend
compromise
coroner
delegate
divine right
due north
elector
foment
inhabitant
iniquitious
issues
mutilate
plunder
portrait
posterity
preamble
province
psychic
self-conscious
sheriff
supreme
supplementary
tyrant
vested interest

Meeting new people...

Abigail Adams
Return J. and Sophia Meigs
Edward and Mary Tiffin
Thomas and Eleanor Worthington
Samuel and Hannah Huntington
Tenskwatawa
Oliver Hazard Perry

Fill in the blanks ...

1. Ohio became a state in ....
2. Tenskwatawa was known to the whites as ....
3. The first governor of Ohio was ....

4. When the United States was formed, there were .... states.
5. The capital of Ohio was first located at ....
6. The government of the Ohio Country was established by a law called ....
7. The Shawnees, under leadership of Tecumseh, fought on the side of the .... in the War of 1812.
8. The greatest earthquake ever to occur in the United States was centered at .... in the year ....
9. Tecumseh urged many tribes to attack white settlements at a sign from a great ....
10. Tecumseh died at the Battle of the ....

Why is it true or false?

1. The natives lived peacefully in the Ohio country after the end of the Revolutionary War.
2. Tecumseh had psychic powers so that he could foresee coming events.
3. American troops under General Harrison won the Battle of the Thames.
4. The Battle of the Thames was fought in Lucas County.
5. The War of 1812 was fought because of slavery in the south.
6. The Prophet and Tecumseh were brothers.
7. The Ordinance of 1787 and the Northwest Ordinance are the same.
8. The center of the Ohio River has always been the boundary of Ohio.
9. Slavery has never been legal in Ohio.
10. Tecumseh's plan could have changed the history of the United States if it had been successful.

Thinking it through...

1. Why did Tecumseh want to unite the natives of the western lands? How did he go about his plan? Why did the plan fail?

2. Why was the Northwest Ordinance so important for people living in the Ohio Country?

3. Why could John Adams not get the representatives of the other colonies to "Remember the Ladies?"

Working with maps...

1. On the map of Ohio, draw the counties shown on the map on page 93. In 1803, which county included the land where you now live?

2. If he could travel five miles per hour on horseback, how long did it take Samuel Huntington to travel from his home to Chillicothe in good weather?

3. On the map of the United States, lay out a route that Thomas Worthington might have traveled between Chillicothe and Philadelphia.

4. Locate New Madrid, Missouri, on the map of the United States. Draw a circle with a radius of 500 miles (800 km.) and New Madrid as the center. Estimate the fraction of the area of Ohio within this distance of New Madrid.

Life in Ohio During the 19th Century

In Part One you learned about the natural resources and the native people of the Ohio Country. In 1800 a few thousand white settlers lived in the wilderness that had existed for thousands of years.

During the 19th century, 4 million people moved into the area we call Ohio. The earliest settlers cut down the forests, planted, and built a simple road system. As more and more people came, they created new industries and new cities. As they moved about, they created the demand for better transportation systems. As more and more people lived closer together, they adopted new laws to protect the rights of all citizens.

In Part Two you will learn about the events that took place in the Ohio Country during the 19th century that had the greatest influence on our lives today.

Bringing History to Life

In this part of the book you will read several passages and see pictures created by Henry Howe (who is not related to the author of this book). Mr. Howe was a native of New England. In 1846, at the age of thirty, he decided to write a history of Ohio. He spent one year traveling on horseback through 79 counties of Ohio, collecting information, and making sketches of objects, scenes, and people. He published this book in 1847. In 1886, at the age of seventy, he decided to bring his 1847 history up to date. He traveled by railroad in all of the 88 counties, and published *Historical Collections of Ohio* in 1889.

If you want to experience life in Ohio during the 19th century, you may want to read portions of "... *And Ladies of The Club*", by Helen Hooven Santmyer. The book is very long (almost 1200 pages), but it gives the "flavor" of life in a small Ohio city from 1868 to 1932.

Ms. Santmyer was born in Cincinnati, Ohio, in 1895, but lived most of her life in Greene County. When she died in Xenia, Ohio in 1986 she was the oldest writer of a best-selling book. Ms. Santmyer was the daughter of an owner of the Hooven and Allison Company in Xenia. While working as a teacher and a librarian, she used her spare time over many years to write this book.

CHAPTER 7

How did transportation influence the development of Ohio?

- the importance of transportation to life.

- several principles about human behavior.

- about the earliest roads in Ohio.

- about travel by highways, waterways, and railways.

All of the human activities we have discussed so far have depended on the two most elementary forms of transportation: either some form of walking over land — by humans or animals — or some form of boat moving over water. How often do you use these forms of movement today?

To help you appreciate the importance of transportation, make a list of the things you have done and expect to do this week. What do you need to accomplish many of the items on your lists? Your answer is almost certain to be related to *transportation*!

Basic Principles Relating to Transportation

Before we look at the various forms of transportation used during the 19th century, we must learn about some theories of human activity that are closely related to movement.

A Theory of Optimization of Human Behavior

What do you think of this statement? "Every person attempts, at all times and in every way, to **optimize** (make the best of) his/her position to the best of her/his ability, within the limitations of the environment."[1]

As you study the history of Ohio, or of any other place, you will often ask yourself, "Why did they do that?" There are only a few basic answers to this question. Perhaps existing conditions were so bad that people were willing to do anything — to the point of risking their lives — to change them. On the other hand, the stories about another place may have seemed so wonderful — like *Alice in Wonderland*, or *The Wizard of Oz*, or "Thar's gold in them thar hills" — that the people were willing to leave comfortable places in hope of finding something even better.

Almost all of the people who came to America, except the slaves from Africa, came for a combination of reasons. Perhaps conditions in the "old country" were

difficult, and stories of the "new world" sounded "too good to be true." In short, they moved in order to *optimize* their situation.

Efficiency is an example of optimization. In almost every human activity you can do something "the hard way" — like an amateur — or "the easy way" — like a professional. But if there is something that has to be done over and over for a long time, you should try to find a way to do it with the least effort, or in the most efficient way.

Central Place Theory

About 1900, geographers tried to explain why cities of all sizes developed as they did in any given state or nation. The answer they found was related to how individuals and families satisfy their needs.

For example, almost every family that moved to the Ohio Country had to produce most of its own food — as you will learn about in Chapter 8. Grains, such as wheat, corn, and oats, are much easier to use as food if they are first ground into fine flour or "meal." Grain can be ground by hand, as the Native Americans did, or by a simple device like that shown on the next page, but it is more efficient if it can be ground in a water-powered mill. Settlements that had mills became *central places*. As farmers began to grow more grain than they needed for their families, the owners of some mills built **silos** (storage buildings for grain).

Every pioneer family needed some iron goods — such as nails, pots, hinges, and knives — but only **blacksmiths** (people with the tools and ability to work with iron) could make such products. For this reason, settlements that had blacksmiths became "central places" for ironware. Farmers could then sell their **surplus** (extra) grain to the

The boy is using a simple tool to grind grain.

larger mills for cash, and purchase ironware, or other goods they could not produce. As methods of transportation were improved, food materials from many small farms and storage places could be brought together for processing at large efficient mills. This made the larger mills more important central places.

Other settlements became central places for government. Even though the county seat had a small population, people from all over the county had to travel to it to pay taxes, record land sales, and settle law suits.

Right-of-Way

Have you ever walked over land owned by someone you did not know? Did you have permission from the owners to travel across the land? If not, did the owner try to stop you? In legal terms, permission for people to move across land owned by someone else is called **right-of-way**, and every form of land transportation depends on such permission.

Theory of Accessibility

In order for land to be useful, it must be **accessible**. Land has no value if there is no right-of-way leading to it. Of course today you can go to the most remote place on the planet Earth by airplane and/or helicopter, but even these vehicles must have the right to land.

In general, the easier it is to get to a piece of land, the more valuable is the land. Roads that lead to larger central places carry more people than roads leading to smaller places. The greater the number of people going to a place, the more valuable the location is for business. As more businesses try to operate in a given area, the cost of land increases.

Before 1960, the **Central Business District** (downtown area), or CBD, of every town was the most desirable location for business. The land was used **intensively**, which means the buildings were built tall and close together. During the 1950s, as shopping centers, or *malls*, were built in outlying areas, they became central places. Today many malls are more important business areas than the old CBDs.

Economics of Transportation

Every time you move between two points, you need a means of movement — such as walking, riding, flying, or sailing — and a route to move over or place to land — such as a trail, street, railroad, airport, or harbor. If you have a clear, smooth route, movement will require less energy, or be more efficient.

For example, pretend you are living in 1850, and you want to travel from your home to our state capital in Columbus. You might have to walk, ride horseback, or ride in a wagon over dirt roads. If you live along the Ohio and Erie Canal — you will learn about this later in the chapter — you can ride in a canal boat.

If we move ahead thirty years to 1880, you may be able to travel by railroad. This is much faster and more pleasant because energy has been invested to create tracks and trains. Today, of course, you can make the trip by private automobile or by intercity bus over well-paved highways that cost millions of dollars to build.

Earliest Highways

When you think of a *highway* today, you probably think of something like Interstate 70, 71, 75, 77, 80, or 90, all of which you can travel on in Ohio. The basic meaning of the word is a right-of-way over which the public may travel. Today *highways* are usually called *roads* in rural areas and *streets* in urban areas.

Walking

Throughout history, walking has been the most important form of transportation. Walking requires a large amount of personal energy that you get from the food you eat. The route for walking requires almost no energy for preparation, because you can walk through a dense forest, around large rocks, up and down hills, and across many streams.

You can use animal energy to save some of your personal energy, if you can afford to buy an animal, feed it, and provide shelter. Wagons and sleds pulled by animals can carry heavy loads of people and goods, but there must be a right-of-way wide enough, smooth enough, and firm enough to permit movement.

Wherever possible, the earliest trails or roads in the Ohio Country followed trails the Native Americans or wild animals had used. New routes often followed streams or ridge lines. After the lines of the Public Land Survey were established on the ground, many roads were created along the section and township lines. But very few of the rural highways of Ohio were paved before 1920.

Zane's Trace

The first "road" in Ohio paid for by the Congress of the United States was created by Ebenezer Zane in 1797. *Zane's Trace* — as this road was called — became part of an overland transportation system linking Pittsburgh, Pennsylvania, with New Orleans, Louisiana (see below).

During the first half of the 19th century, most goods were floated downstream on the Ohio River on rafts or **flatboats** like the

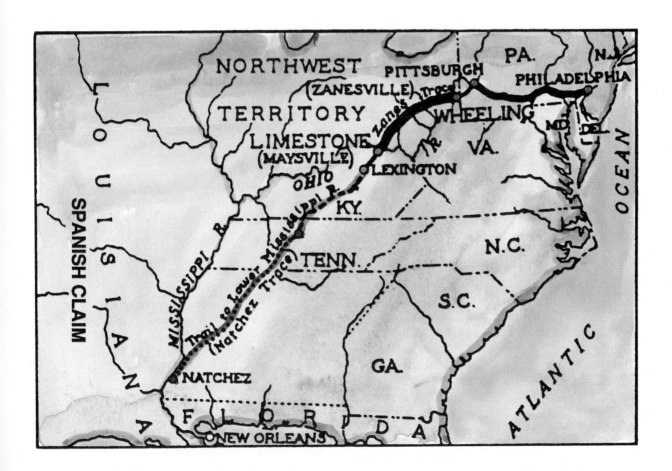

Zane's Trace and the Natchez Trace formed a walking route between New Orleans and Pittsburgh.

113

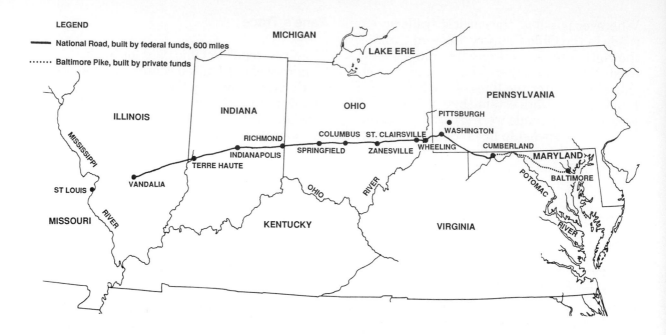

The National Road was built from Cumberland, Maryland to Vandalia, Illinois.

one on page 21. These simple water vehicles could not move upstream against the current, so they were sold at their **destination** (end of the trip), taken apart, and the lumber used for other purposes.

When goods were moved all the way from Pittsburgh to New Orleans, the boatmen had to walk hundreds of miles back to their homes. The map on page 113 shows that the most important trail to the north, the *Natchez Trace*, reached the Ohio River at Maysville, Kentucky, directly across the Ohio River from Aberdeen, Ohio. Zane's Trace connected Aberdeen to what is now Bridgeport, in Belmont County, opposite Wheeling, West Virginia.

Zane and his helpers cut a path through the forest wide enough for a person to travel on horseback. They built ferries to help travelers cross the Scioto, Muskingum, and

Hocking Rivers. In payment for their labor, the workers were given tracts of land. Zane chose for himself land in Muskingum County where the city of Zanesville now stands.

The National Road

In 1806 under the leadership of President Thomas Jefferson, Congress authorized the Federal Government to build a road from the Potomac River to the Ohio River at present Wheeling, West Virginia (see above). Five years passed before construction started, and the road did not reach Wheeling until 1818. By that time Indiana and Illinois were states. Congress decided that the *National Road* — as it was called — should be extended through these new states to the Mississippi River. In 1840 the road reached Vandalia, Illinois. No further work was done on the project.

Before 1920 almost all rural roads looked like this in the Spring.

In 1925 the *National Road* was identified as U.S. Route 40. During the 1940s, long stretches of U.S. 40 were widened into four-lane divided highways. But you can still travel on two-lane sections of the original right-of-way in Muskingum County, Guernsey County, and Belmont County.

Today Interstate Highway 70 carries almost all the traffic that once used U.S. 40. The National Road / Zane Grey Museum, near the Norwich interchange of I-70 in Muskingum County, explains the interesting history of Zane's Trace and the National Road.

Toll Roads

The total population of Ohio jumped from 581,434 to 937,903 between 1820 and 1830. Many new central places developed, older central places grew larger, and the demand for transportation increased greatly.

Many roads were **opened** — which means that rights-of-way were created — but almost all had dirt surfaces. The picture above shows how bad roads were in 1891: they were just as bad thirty years later in many rural areas.

115

The cost of moving over the dirt roads became so great that private companies were formed to **pave** (build a hard surface) public rights-of-way to reduce the cost of moving over them. In exchange for improving the roads, **turnpike** companies were given permission to charge travelers **tolls** (fees) to use the roads.

During the 1890s, the General Assembly authorized each county to buy the toll roads within its boundaries. In many counties today there are roads that older people call "pikes." For example, there is a "Wooster Pike" in Hamilton County and "Wooster Pike" in Cuyahoga County.

Why We Call A Toll Road A Turnpike

The word "turnpike" became associated with toll roads in England. The company that paved a road had the right to build gates across the pavement at intervals of one to two miles. In some cases the "gate" was just a long pole, which reminded Englishmen of the 'pikes,' or lances, that medieval knights had used for fighting. When a traveler paid the required toll, the gate keeper would open the gate, or turn the "pike."

Freight Wagons

Goods and heavy objects were moved in freight wagons pulled by animals as shown in the picture on page 76. Horses, mules, and oxen were the most widely used sources of power. As many as eight or ten animals might be used to pull a wagon. Because very good freight wagons were built in the town of Conestoga, in southeastern Pennsylvania, many freight wagons were called Conestogas.

Stage Coaches

The picture on the next page shows a typical vehicle used to move people, packages, and mail between settlements. After 1816, stage coach companies offered regularly-scheduled service between the state capital at Columbus and the towns of Ohio. Taverns were built along the stage routes to provide food and shelter for the passengers and for the horses that pulled the coaches. You can still dine at the old taverns listed on the next page, and even sleep in two of them.

Travel by Water

Throughout history people have known that the easiest way to move a heavy load from one point to another is to float it on water. Early explorers and traders in the Ohio Country used canoes like those made by the Native Americans. These canoes could be used to carry heavy loads over water. When necessary, the canoes could be carried easily from one waterway to another over a portage path.

Many of the earliest settlers in southern Ohio moved down the Ohio River on flatboats. Such boats were as large as twenty feet wide by sixty feet long, and were steered by means of a crude rudder. Sometimes a sail was used to speed movement downstream.

Keelboats were more complicated to build than flatboats, but they were easier to steer, and could be moved upstream by pulling or by using poles.

Stage coaches were the intercity "busses" of the 19th century.

19th century stage coach stops in Ohio that serve travelers today.

Year Established	County	Location	Name	Restaurant	Rooms
1803	Warren	Lebanon	Golden Lamb	Yes	Yes
1804	Adams	West Union	Olde Wayside Inn	Yes	No
1804	Montgomery	Germantown	Florentine Hotel	Yes	No
1812	Licking	Granville	Buxton Inn	Yes	Yes
1820	Richland	Mansfield	Malabar Inn	Yes	No
1828	Lucas	Waterville	Columbian House	Yes	No
1840's	Geauga	E. of Welshfield	Welshfield Inn	Yes	No

The Ohio River at Portsmouth about 1886.

Many of the settlers in northern Ohio traveled across Lake Erie on sailing ships. Boats operating on open water, such as Lake Erie, need **harbors** where they can be safely tied during storms or freezing weather. The only good natural harbors in Ohio are Sandusky Bay and Maumee Bay. All other harbors have been man made.

Steamboats

In 1807 Robert Fulton lived in New York when he developed the first successful steam-powered boat in America. A few years later, he moved to Pittsburgh. In 1811 he and a partner built the *New Orleans*, the first steamboat to operate on the Ohio River. This marvelous invention made it possible to carry from five to ten times as much cargo as the largest flatboat; in addition, it could move upstream against the current of the river.

The *New Orleans* passed Cincinnati on October 27, 1811 on its way to New Orleans. It arrived in the vicinity of New Madrid, Missouri close to the time of the great earthquake you learned about in Chapter 5. Each year after 1811 steamboats became more important, while flatboats and keelboats gradually disappeared.

Henry Howe's drawing above shows a view of the waterfront at Portsmouth, in Scioto County, in 1886. You will notice that the closest boat carried United States mail. There is also a large raft in the picture. By 1820 steamboats were operating on Lake Erie.

Canals

While there are many advantages to travel by water, such travel also presents several problems. Large lakes, especially those as large as Lake Erie, are very dangerous when winds create high waves. In the winter, ice prevents movement.

Rivers present many more problems because they can be dangerous when the water is very high, and impassable when it is very low. While the early steamboats needed water only two or three feet deep to operate, there were times every summer when the Ohio River was almost dry.

When Ohio became a state, it was a frontier wilderness compared to the established countries of Europe. Nevertheless, few of the roads in Europe were better than those in Ohio. During the last half of the 18th century, the people of England, France, and Germany began to build waterways — called **canals** — to improve their transportation systems. Shortly after the close of the War of 1812, this form of transportation became popular in the United States.

The Erie Canal

Between 1800 and 1820, the population of the United States jumped from a little more than 5,000,000 to almost 10,000,000, and thousands of immigrants wanted to move to the west. In 1817 the state of New York began work on a canal to connect the Hudson River, near Albany, to Lake Erie at Buffalo. When it was finished, people could travel by water from New York City to Lake Erie. For this reason, the Erie Canal had a tremendous effect on the development of northern Ohio.

Canals in Ohio

When Thomas Worthington — whom you learned about in Chapter 6 — was governor of Ohio (1814-1818) he worked hard to promote *internal improvements* for our state. While internal improvements might mean many things, during the early 19th century, this term was widely used to mean *better transportation*.

Before construction could begin, three major problems had to be solved:
1. How to pay for the improvements.
2. How to find engineers to design the canals.
3. Where to build the canals.

The first problem was solved by borrowing money from wealthy people living in the eastern states and in Europe. The second was solved by hiring people who had worked on the canals of Europe or on the Erie Canal. Because people of every county of our state were demanding improvements, the most difficult problem was to decide where to build.

The General Assembly finally decided to build two canals. The first would run from the mouth of the Scioto River, at Portsmouth, to the mouth of the Cuyahoga River, at Cleveland. The second would run from Cincinnati, in Hamilton County, to Dayton, in Montgomery County. The map on page 120 shows these two canals, and all the others finally built in Ohio.

Many miles of canals were built in Ohio between 1825 and 1850.

Technical Problems

The canals were much more difficult to build than the National Road. A road can go up and down hills, but a canal must be almost level. Since there are very few places in Ohio that are level, **locks** (a form of "steps") had to be built. The diagram on page 123 shows how locks were — and still are — used to raise or lower boats. The lock chambers were about 20-feet wide and 100-feet long. This means that every boat had to be small enough to fit into the locks. The water of the main canals was 40-feet wide and 4-feet deep. Boats were pulled by horses or mules walking along a 10-foot wide **towpath**.

Because water runs downhill, no canal could be built until the engineers were certain that there would be enough water available at the **summit** (the highest elevation) of the canal to float the boats. This problem could only be solved by building **reservoirs** (lakes) along the summit sections of the canals.

The Ohio and Erie Canal

On July 4, 1825 Governor Jeremiah Morrow of Ohio dug the first spadeful of earth for the Ohio and Erie Canal at a point near the town of Heath in Licking County. If you visit this site on State Route 79 today, you can see the remains of Lock #1. This section of the canal is called the Licking Summit. Buckeye Lake in Fairfield County was created to provide water for this high stretch of the canal. The high land in Summit County created a more difficult problem. Reservoirs were built at the Portage Lakes to provide water for this summit.

By 1830 you could travel from Lake Erie to the Licking Summit, by 1831 to Chillicothe in Ross County, and by 1834 to the Ohio River at Portsmouth in Scioto County.

The Miami and Erie Canal

Later in the summer of 1825, work also began on the Miami and Erie Canal at a point just south of Middletown. In November, 1827 the first boat moved from Middletown to the edge of downtown Cincinnati. By 1834 you could travel on the canal from Cincinnati to the heart of Dayton, in Montgomery County.

In 1837 work was begun to extend the Miami and Erie Canal to Lake Erie at Toledo, in Lucas County. The biggest problem on this section was the high ground in Shelby and Auglaize Counties. Lake Loramie was built in Shelby County, Indian Lake in Logan County, and Grand Lake St. Marys in Auglaize and Mercer Counties to supply water to the canal.

As you can see on page 120, several small canals were built as "feeders" to the two large ones. These were important to local communities, but within a few years they were replaced by railroads.

Operations on the Canals

Three kinds of canal boats were used on the canals: passenger boats, freight boats, and combination freight and passenger boats. Some boats were owned by families that lived on them, as shown on page 124.

The following verse from a canal song gives an idea of how people felt about the canals.

Verse from A Canal Song

There's a little silver ribbon runs
    across the Buckeye State,
'Tis the dearest place of all the earth
    to me, For upon its **placid**
    surface I was born some
    years ago
And its beauty, grandeur, always do
    I see. Cleveland is the northern
    end and Portsmouth is the south,
While its **sidecuts** they are many,
    many, Pal
And where e'er we went we took
    along our Home Sweet, Home,
    you know,
In those balmy days upon the old
    canal.
From: Pearl R. Nye papers of
Ohio Historical Society

Importance of Canals to Ohio

No one knows how our state would have developed without the canals. We can only say that the canals made it possible for people to move inland from the Ohio River and Lake Erie so that larger areas could be developed. In addition, the canals made it possible for inland farmers to send their surplus grain and animals to the large cities of the United States.

Every lock also provided a fall of water that could be used to operate a mill. Several of the large industries of Ohio, especially paper-making factories, were established to use the water power at the locks. You can still see some of the old mills, but they are no longer powered by water.

The last sections of the canals were abandoned for transportation in 1913. In fact, there was almost no traffic on the canals after 1890 because of development of the railroads you will learn about later.

The Canals Today

You may be surprised to find how many miles of the old canals you can see today! In fact you can take canal boat rides in Miami County north of Piqua, in Coshocton County at Roscoe Village, and in Stark County at Canal Fulton. You can see water in several miles of the Ohio Canal in the Cuyahoga National Recreation Area, in Cuyahoga, and Summit Counties.

In the central places that developed along the canals you will find towns with the word *port* or *canal* in their names. You will find city streets and rural roads named *Canal* and *Lock* in places where the canal itself is no longer visible.

Today State Route 104 runs over and along the Ohio and Erie Canal from a point north of the Ohio River to the south line of Franklin County. State Route 16 is over and along the canal between Newark and Coshocton. In Akron a whole series of locks was removed to build Interstate 77. In Cuyahoga County, Canal Road runs along several miles of water in the old canal.

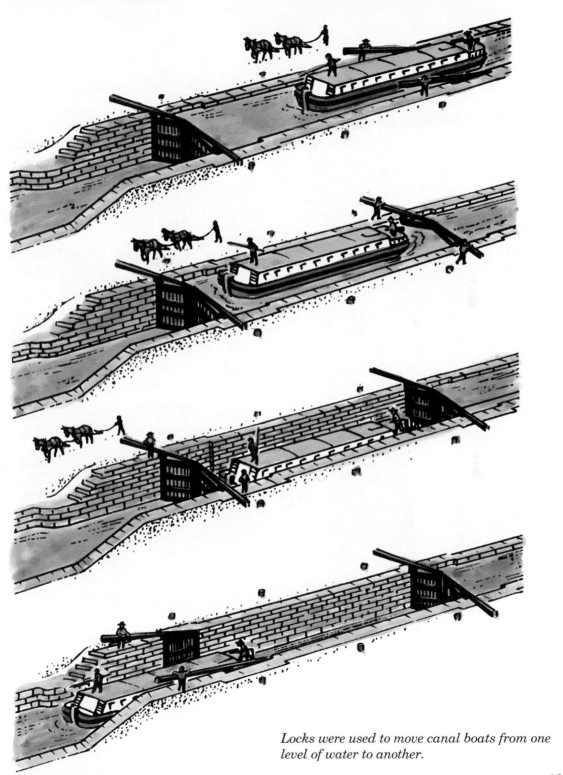

Locks were used to move canal boats from one level of water to another.

Some families lived on canal boats.

Railroads

Shortly after steamboats began to operate, inventors experimented with using steam to drive vehicles over land. Because the roads were in such poor condition, inventors concentrated on creating steam-powered vehicles that could move over iron rails.

The earliest rail passenger cars looked very much like stage coaches.

In 1828 the Baltimore & Ohio Railroad operated the first passenger train in America over a few miles of track at Baltimore, Maryland. By 1845 when the last canal in Ohio was completed, several short railroads were in operation in our state, and people with vision knew that the canals would soon lose business to the railroads.

Technical Problems of Railroads

Railroads have a great advantage over canals because they can operate on gentle slopes or hills. All of the early railroads were operated by steam created by boiling water on the **locomotive** (self-propelled machine). In the earliest days the fuel was wood, which could be cut in forests along the track. Later coal was found to be a more efficient fuel. Water was obtained from creeks or ponds along the route. The first train to operate in Ohio, in 1835, on the Erie & Kalamazoo (Michigan) Railroad is shown above.

Early Railroads in Ohio

By 1833 citizens living in places not served by the canals were begging for railroads. The General Assembly of Ohio decided to give **franchises** (legal permits to provide public services) to private companies to build railroads.

More than 2000 miles of railroad were built between 1851 and 1861.

Any company with a franchise could try to raise money to pay for construction. By the end of 1838 there were fifteen miles of railroad leading southwest from the Lake Erie port city of Sandusky in Erie County. By 1851 there were 788 miles of track in Ohio, and by 1861 there were more than 3,000 miles. The map above shows how the situation changed in these ten years. By 1871 there were about 54,000 miles of railroads in the United States. A person living in Ohio could travel by railroad to the East Coast, the West Coast, the Gulf Coast, or the Canadian border of the United States. Today you can see the first engine to operate on the Cincinnati, Hamilton & Dayton Railroad in the museum at Carillon Park in Dayton.

126

Raising Money to Build Railroads

The railroad companies had to raise money to pay for construction of tracks, to build stations, and to buy engines, cars, and fuel. They raised this money by two methods which private companies still use today: they sold **bonds** and they issued **stock**.

When you buy a bond you are lending money to the company that issues the bond. When you buy stock, you are buying a share of ownership of the company. If the company earns money, the bond holders get their money back with interest, while shareholders are given part of the profit. If a company becomes prosperous, the shareholders may become wealthy. If the company loses money, both bond holders and shareholders may lose their **investments** (money used to buy bonds or stock).

The biggest cost in building a railroad could have been buying the right-of-way. But many land owners were so anxious to have better transportation that they *gave* the right-of-way — plus rights to cut wood and take water for the engines. Cities and towns gave rights-of-way for building tracks in streets and land for stations. Individual people bought stocks and bonds, and cities issued bonds to raise money to "bribe" railroad companies to serve their communities.

How Railroads Affected Ohio

By the 1840s the railroad tracks were built strong and straight enough, and engines and cars were built well enough, that passenger trains could operate at ten miles per hour. During the 1850s so many technical improvements were made that passenger trains could operate at more than twenty miles per hour — which some people thought was too fast for the human body to endure. Freight trains always operated at slower speeds, but they were much faster than ox carts moving over dirt roads.

Interurban Railroads

By 1890 **entrepreneurs** (people who take risks in business) were building electric-powered **interurban** (meaning "between cities") rail lines between the cities of Ohio. This new form of transportation could move people more quickly and conveniently than the steam railroads. During the three years from 1898 to 1901, our state issued permits for construction of more than sixty electric

railway lines. By 1910 there were almost 2,800 miles of interurban lines in Ohio. The last interurban line went out of business in 1935. You can still see some of the rights-of-way of these lines if you know where to look.

Stop and Think!

When Ohio became a state in 1803, people were traveling from place to place in ways that had been used for thousands of years They walked or used animals to travel over land, and they sailed, rowed, or floated to travel over water. Throughout the 19th century, very few miles of roads were useable in all kinds of weather.

The development of steam-powered boats improved transportation for people living along Lake Erie and the Ohio River. Steamboats made it possible for some farmers to ship food products to market faster, but river travel had certain disadvantages. Between 1825 and 1845, transportation improved greatly for the citizens of Ohio who lived near one of the new canals.

The development of steam engines that could move from place to place led to construction of railroads that could operate in all kinds of weather at speeds much faster than any other method of transportation. By the year 1900 the people of Ohio could use one of the biggest and best railroad systems available in the United States. These rail lines greatly influenced the development of the cities and industries of our state.

During the last few years of the 19th century, a form of transportation was invented that changed everything about the way people move from place to place — *automobiles* were created!

127

Building vocabulary...

accessible	opened (road)
blacksmith	optimize
bond (finance)	pave
canal	placid
Central Business District	raft
efficiency	reservoir
entrepreneur	right-of-way
flatboat	sidecut
franchise	silo
harbor	stock (finance)
intensively	surplus
interurban	summit
investment	toll
lock (canal)	tow path
locomotive	turnpike

Meeting new people...

Ebenezer Zane
Robert Fulton

Explain why you would rather....?

1. Travel by land or water in early Ohio?
2. Travel on a toll road or a free road in 1880?
3. Help build a canal or help create Zane's Trace? What hardships might you meet on either job?
4. Work on a flatboat or a canal boat?

Fill in the blanks ....

1. Different levels of land along the path of a canal make it necessary to build ....
2. Canal boats were moved by .... or ....
3. The people who benefitted most from construction of the canals were ....
4. The President of the United States who encourage construction of the National Road was ....
5. Lake Erie is not always useful for transportation because of .... and ....
6. The most common form of transportation in early Ohio was ....

Thinking it through...

1. What means of transportation did early settlers in your county use to come to Ohio? Give reasons for your answer.
2. How were canals related to several lakes in Ohio?
3. How did the canals help the economy of Ohio?
4. Explain some of the problems the builders of the early highways and canals had to solve.
5. In your own words, explain how a lock on a canal, or river, operates. If you have seen a lock operate, explain the operation to the class.
6. Explain which form of transportation discussed in this chapter was "best" for your county during the 19th century.

Working with maps...

1. Use the map of Ohio and compare the routes of the National Road, with US 40 and I-70.
2. Use the map of Ohio and pick out present highways that you could travel to explore Zane's Trace.
3. On the map of the United States, lay out two routes that settlers might have followed to move from New York City to Columbus, Ohio, in 1840.
4. On the map of your county, find the roads that (a) follow streams, (b) follow ridges, and (c) follow section lines.

Footnote
1. R. T. Howe

CHAPTER 8

How did people live during the 19th century?

Be ready to learn...

- why millions of people moved their homes to Ohio.

- what it was like to travel across the ocean.

- what it was like to live in a rural area.

- about devout religious people who came to Ohio.

In Chapters 4 and 5 you learned about the people who lived in our area before Ohio became a state. The chart on the next page shows how the population of Ohio grew during the 19th century. Now we will consider the questions: Why did 4 million people come to Ohio between 1800 and 1900, and how did they live?

Ohio Population Growth During the 19th Century

Census Year	Total Population	White Population	African- American Population	Number Born in America	Nunber Born Over Seas
1800	45,365	45,028	337	n.a.	n.a.
1810	230,760	228,861	1,899	n.a.	n.a.
1820	581,434	576,711	4,723	n.a.	n.a.
1830	937,903	928,329	9,574	n.a.	n.a.
1840	1,519,467	1,502,122	17,345	n.a.	n.a.
1850	1,980,329	1,955,060	25,279	n.a.	n.a.
1860	2,339,511	2,302,808	36,673	n.a.	n.a.
1870	2,665,260	2,601,946	63,213	n.a.	n.a.
1880	3,198,062	3,117,920	79,900	2,803,119	394,943
1890	3,672,316	3,584,805	87,113	3,213,036	459,280
1900	4,157,545	4,060,204	96,901	3,698,311	459,234

The Native Americans

As you have learned, Native Americans lived in the Ohio Country for thousands of years before Europeans knew there was such a place. You have also learned that after the War of 1812 the natives were assigned to reservations in the northwest corner of the state (see page 104).

Between 1829 and 1842, the United States government forced most of the Native Americans to move into *Indian Territories* west of the Mississippi River. By 1843 the only natives in our state were individual families who agreed to live as the government wanted them to live on small parcels of land in northwest Ohio.

Since the natives were not required to pay taxes to the state or federal governments, they were not permitted to vote. Neither were they counted in the ten-year **censuses** (counts of people) of the United States before 1960, but they have been counted since then.

In this chapter, you will learn how the success of the American Revolution and the establishment of a new form of government in the United States inspired Europeans to seek freedom for themselves. The map on the next page shows the countries we will be discussing.

Events in Europe

France

The French Government provided great help to the American Colonies during the Revolutionary War. When the people of France realized that it was possible to gain independence from a king, they united to overthrow the *House of Bourbon*, whose kings had ruled France for hundreds of years.

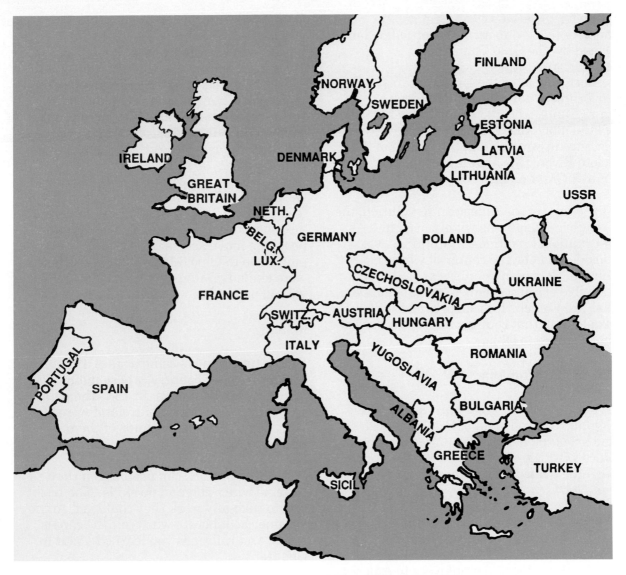

Map of Europe in 1939.

In 1790 a small group of French people planned to escape from the turmoil of revolution in their country. They paid money to buy land in Ohio, and came to America. Upon arrival in America, they learned that the salesman who had taken their money did not own the land he had "sold" them.

Some of these people were given permission to settle on land immediately west of the tract owned by The Ohio Company, which you can see by looking back to page 75. They crossed the mountains and settled on the north shore of the Ohio River in a place they called *Gallipolis*, which means "city of the Gauls." (Gaul was the ancient Roman name for the area we call France.) By mistake this group actually settled on land owned by The Ohio Company.

A short time later the United States Government gave the other French immigrants, who had been cheated, a tract of land along the Ohio River a short distance upstream from the mouth of the Scioto River. This area is labeled *The French Grant* on page 75.

At the time of the American Revolution, the French language was widely used in international relations, and France was considered to be the center of western culture. How many names can you find in the table of county names, in Appendix A, that are French? It is surprising that few people from that country migrated (moved their homes) to Ohio.

The United Kingdom

At the time of the American Revolution, England controlled all of Scotland, Wales, and six of the northern counties of Ireland. Since 1801 the official name of this area has been the *United Kingdom of Great Britain and Northern Ireland.*

During the 19th century, wealthy English families invested large sums of money in the development of the United States, and sent highly educated employees to America to manage their properties. At the same time life was very difficult for poor people in the United Kingdom. As a result, many Welsh, Scottish, Scotch-Irish, and English people migrated to the United States and Ohio.

Germany

For several hundred years, the nation we know as *Germany* was divided into small "princely states" that fought many battles with each other. In order to escape from this turmoil, thousands of German people came to the American Colonies before the Revolution .

During several years of the 19th century, German farmers could not produce enough food to feed all the people. These **famines** also caused tens of thousands of German people to move across the Atlantic Ocean and settle in Ohio. Many of these Germans were skilled craftsmen, and most were willing and eager workers.

Ireland

By the time Ohio became a state, Ireland was a very poor country, whose main farm crop was potatoes. In 1845 the potato crop failed. The people of Ireland were starving, so many thousands of them moved to America.

What kind of work can people do if they have no education and no skills? The Irish had to take any work they could get, so they became the laborers who built the canals, roads, and railroads you learned about in Chapter 7.

Italy

At the time of the American Revolution, the ordinary people of Italy had no freedom and lived in poverty. The country was divided into many small "states" that were constantly fighting. During the 1870s tens of thousands of these people moved to America, and many settled in Ohio, especially in the larger cities. By 1900 many

Street market

of the big cities in Ohio had areas called "Little Italy" that were filled with Italian immigrants. An artist sketched the scene above in the Italian neighborhood of a big city in 1895. Can you count how many people are trying to sell various items?

Scandinavia

The nations we call Denmark, Norway, and Sweden were once the homelands of the Vikings, the great sea people who, during the early Middle Ages, conquered much of Europe. By the year 1800, the Danes were skilled farmers, the Norwegians were skilled fishermen and lumbermen, and the Swedes were skilled at mining and working with metals. Unfortunately these three countries were often at war with one another, or with other nations. Many people of Scandinavia moved to America during the 19th century. Most of them migrated to states north and west of Ohio, but thousands of them brought their skills to our state.

133

Interior of a 19th century sailing ship

Russia

Throughout history the common people of Russia, and most of the vast land we now call the *Union of Soviet Socialist Republics* (USSR), were almost slaves to the very rich people who owned the land.

During the 15th and 16th centuries, when Christian people of Western Europe abused the Jewish people who lived within their nations, the rulers of Russia and the Russian Orthodox Church were more **tolerant** (they treated the Jews better). For these reasons, many Jewish people moved from Western Europe to Russia.

Near the end of the 19th century, the Russians began to **persecute** (abuse) these Jews, and the Jews began to flee to America. Between 1880 and 1920, more than 2,000,000 Jewish people left their homes in Eastern Europe to come to the United States. A very large number of Jewish people living in Ohio today have ancestors who were in this migration.

How the Immigrants Traveled

Travel by sailing ships was a slow and unpleasant experience. The picture on the previous page is an artist's idea of travel on such a ship. As you can see, even the wealthy people shown here traveled in crowded conditions, and everyone suffered equally when the sea was rough.

The poorest people traveled in **steerage**, that is, the lowest and least comfortable part of the ship. Their experiences were somewhat similar to those of slaves who were shipped from Africa to America, except that they were not chained in one place on board the ships as shown in the picture on page 137.

Men, women and children who had no money could come to the United States only as **indentured** servants. This means that they sold as many as the first five years of their lives in this country to a "sponsor" who agreed to provide food, clothing, and shelter, and sometimes small wages in exchange for the cost of travel. Immigrant women often tended children, cooked, and/or did housework for a family, or perhaps worked in a factory owned by a sponsor. Immigrant men contracted to work on farms, in mines, at lumbering, and other kinds of heavy labor. Immigrant boys contracted to work as apprentices to skilled craftsmen. By 1880, Ohio had 394,943 citizens who had been born in another country, as you can see in the table on page 130. By 1900 this number had grown to 458,734.

Excerpts from A Diary

What was it like to travel from Europe to Ohio 150 years ago? Here are excerpts from the diary of the leader of group that was **prosperous** (had money) enough to pay for their transportation. Almost all groups of immigrants had similar experiences.

Excerpts from The Diary of Matthias Durst (Page numbers refer to New Glarus 1845-1970)

On April 16, 1845, 196 people left their homes in Switzerland because economic conditions were very difficult. They traveled by boat to The Netherlands. On May 13 the party boarded a sailing ship, and the ship left Amsterdam for America. After fifteen days at sea, Matthias Durst wrote:

On the 28th we felt and saw the **consequences** of our fate. On this day we had to mourn two victims. The first ... after having suffered many deaths for several days gave up the spirit at 3 o'clock in the afternoon. She was bound in a coarse linen cloth with three buckets of sand placed at her feet to [make her] sink better. (p. 53)

After a bad storm he wrote:

In the morning of the 16th [of June] there was complete calm. We did not move from the spot, and so it went all day. We longed for wind but in vain. On the 17th we had better wind again, and on the 18th things went fine. ... We had that much more reason for longing to reach shore as soon as possible as on this day our main **staple** potatoes, have given out, ... There would have been potatoes for many more days if they were healthy. But in the beginning ...

Accidents destroyed many river boats.

we did not receive any, only to let them rot, because when one gets down to the **hold** of the ship one's nose is filled with such a **stench** that one is almost **repulsed** ... (p. 63)

On the 27th day of June he wrote:

The most joyful day of the whole sea voyage! ... At about 11 o'clock the *shout of joy* rang out: *Land!* (p.71)

Three days later the ship dropped anchor in the harbor of Baltimore, Maryland. A few days after that the people from Switzerland traveled by railroad and canal to Pittsburgh, Pennsylvania. On July 11th

they boarded a steamboat to travel down the Ohio River. Mr. Durst described the river trip as follows:

It went quite well until about 10 o'clock [P.M.], then we stopped and started again on the morning of the 12th. In the forenoon our ship ran into another steamboat so that we believed everything was in splinters. We learned later that it was done intentionally because of a **rivalry**; it is supposedly not rare that they greet one another in this manner so as to do damage to each other's ships. Luckily our ship remained the victor but it too was damaged some. It is inexcusable of the crew to undertake such a daring venture and to endanger the lives of the 250 people who were on our ship. It is said to be forbidden under penalty of 500 dollars but they do not care about that. (p.99)

The picture on page 136 shows how dangerous travel by steamboat could be.

The immigrants reached Cincinnati, Ohio, about 2 A.M. on July 18th, and Mr. Durst went sightseeing later that day. The population of the city at that time was about 72,000. The following note from the diary will show you what a stranger thought about the largest city in Ohio:

Today I looked around some of the town. It is one of the most beautiful and largest in the (United States). The streets are wide and paved, on both sides are walkways with cloths stretched over them and they all cross at right angles. The houses, all built of brick, in which an **extravagant** splendor is apparent. (p. 109)

Interior of a slave ship

Slavery

As you have learned, slavery created difficult problems for the founders of the United States. The representatives from

Maryland, Delaware, Virginia, the Carolinas, and Georgia demanded the "right" to own human beings as slaves, while representatives from the northern states opposed slavery. In 1808 Congress passed a law making it illegal to import slaves. In spite of this law, almost 250,000 more men, women, and children were brought to our country from Africa between 1808 and the outbreak of the Civil War in 1861.

The struggle over slavery increased as families from the East Coast moved across the Allegheny Mountains into "the West." Kentucky was settled by people from Virginia and the Carolinas, where all the large plantations had slaves. While Ohio had some settlers from Virginia and Kentucky, many more were from Europe and the non-slave states of the north.

The Underground Railroad

During the early years of the 19th century, some people in the Northern States began to work to **abolish** (end) slavery in the United States. By 1840 these *abolitionists*, as they were called, were operating *Underground Railroads* to help African-American slaves escape from the Southern States.

Have you ever seen a railroad that did not have tracks and locomotives? The Underground Railroad was a series of houses, called *stations*, scattered along several routes leading from the Ohio River to Canada. The owners of these houses helped escaping slaves gain freedom. The map on page 140 shows the "railroads" that operated in Ohio.

In this picture of a station on the Underground Railroad, Levi Coffin is the white man in the wagon, and Catherine Coffin is the white woman in the center of the picture.

The picture on this page is called *The Underground Railroad*. It was painted by Charles T. Webber, an Ohio artist, in 1891 for display at a great *World Fair* held in Chicago, Illinois to honor the 400th anniversary of Christopher Columbus "finding" America.

The Reverend John Rankin and his wife, Jane Lowry Rankin, lived in Brown County on the edge of a high hill above the town of Ripley on the Ohio River. The house could be seen from the hills of Kentucky, and the Rankins kept a lamp burning every night. Their home was the first stop on the Underground Railroad for about 2,000 escaping slaves, and you can visit it today.

How One Run-Away Slave Defended Himself

Ad White, a **fugitive** from Kentucky bearing the surname of his master, made his way to the place of rest for the **oppressed**, and thinking he was far enough away [from the South], had quietly settled down on the farm of Udney Hyde, near Mechanicsburg [in Champaign County]. His master had tracked him to the farm of Hyde and obtained a **warrant** for his arrest at the United States Court in Cincinnati. Ben Churchill, with eight others, undertook his capture. Ad was ... a powerful man ... and had expressed his determination never to return to slavery alive... Ad slept in the **loft** of Hyde's barn ... and one person only [could enter] at a time.

Here [Ad] had provided himself with such articles of defense as a rifle, a double-barrelled shotgun, revolver, knife and axe, and had the steady nerve and skill to use them ... Churchill and party arrived at Hyde's and found the game [Ad] in his retreat ....

Deputy-Marshall Elliott, of Cincinnati, [made] the first and only attempt to enter where White was, and as his body passed above the floor of the loft he held a shotgun before him, perhaps to protect himself, but particularly to scare White. But White was not to be scared away ... and, quick as thought, the sharp crack of a rifle rang out on the air, and Elliott dropped to the floor, not killed ...

[The slave owner sued Udney Hyde for protecting a fugitive slave. Mr. Hyde was found guilty of this crime, and he was required to pay the slave owner $1000 to "purchase" Ad.]

Quoted in Howe: vol. 1, pp. 384-6, from *Beer's History of Clark County*.

Levi Coffin and his wife, Catherine White Coffin, and their friends in Cincinnati, operated another important railroad. The Coffins were members of the *Religious Society of Friends* (people who are commonly called *Quakers*). Throughout the United States, the Friends took the lead in helping slaves escape from the South.

Not everyone in Ohio was in favor of helping runaway slaves. In fact some people, who were called **bounty hunters**, earned money by helping to recapture slaves. As you learned in Chapter 6, the Northwest Ordinance said that slave owners could enter any state that prohibited slavery — or send agents — to search for their "property." The anti-slavery people who worked with the "railroad" made many personal sacrifices as they violated the laws that favored slave owners.

Some slaves gained freedom in various ways before they moved into the Northern States. A few of these *freedmen* were highly skilled craftsmen, and some became educated in law, medicine, teaching, and preaching. The vast majority of free African-American people, or *Negroes* as they were then called, were very poor. Most of them settled in the cities of the North where they found work as laborers or as house

CANADA

MICHIGAN

LAKE ERIE

WILLIAMS · FULTON · LUCAS · OTTAWA · SANDUSKY · ERIE · LORAIN · CUYAHOGA · LAKE · GEAUGA · ASHTABULA

DEFIANCE · HENRY · WOOD · · · · HURON · MEDINA · SUMMIT · PORTAGE · TRUMBULL

PAULDING · · SENECA · · · · · · · MAHONING

PUTNAM · HANCOCK · WYANDOT · CRAWFORD · RICHLAND · ASHLAND · WAYNE · STARK · COLUMBIANA · PENNSYLVANIA

VAN WERT · ALLEN · HARDIN · MARION · MORROW · · HOLMES · TUSCARAWAS · CARROLL

MERCER · AUGLAIZE · · · KNOX · COSHOCTON · HARRISON · JEFFERSON

SHELBY · LOGAN · UNION · DELAWARE · · · GUERNSEY · BELMONT

DRAKE · CHAMPAIGN · · LICKING · MUSKINGUM · NOBLE · MONROE

MIAMI · CLARK · MADISON · FRANKLIN · · · MORGAN · OHIO RIVER

PREBLE · MONTGOMERY · GREENE · FAYETTE · PICKAWAY · FAIRFIELD · PERRY · WASHINGTON · WEST VIRGINIA

BUTLER · WARREN · CLINTON · ROSS · HOCKING · ATHENS

HAMILTON · CLERMONT · HIGHLAND · VINTON · MEIGS

BROWN · PIKE · JACKSON · GALLIA

ADAMS · SCIOTO · LAWRENCE

KENTUCKY

No one ever made an official map of the Underground Railroad.

servants. Because they were shunned by most white people, they often lived together in areas that later came to be called **ghettos**. The table on page 130 shows how the number of African-American citizens of Ohio increased from fewer than 400 in 1800 to almost 100,000 in 1900. About 40,000 of them moved into Ohio during the first 15 years after the Civil War.

Sojourner Truth made a very important speech in Akron.

Sojourner Truth

Throughout the 19th century, women were striving to gain equal rights with men. In 1851, in Akron, Ohio an African-American woman gave one of the best known speeches ever made for women's rights. Isabella was born as a slave in upstate New York about 1790. She was freed in 1827 and moved to New York City. She was a deeply religious person, and came to believe that God wanted her to work to abolish slavery.

In 1843 she changed her name to Sojourner Truth, and began to travel throughout the northern states arguing for freedom for the slaves, improved living conditions for freedmen, and more rights for women. Ms Truth is shown above.

A small group of women organized an American Women's Rights Convention in 1848. They held a meeting in Salem (Columbiana, County) in 1850, and a second meeting in Akron in 1851. Men were permitted to attend the Akron meeting and

Excerpt from "A'n't I a Woman? "
Delivered by Sojourner Truth
in Akron, 1851

"Wall, chilern, whar dar is so much racket dar must be somethin' out o' kilter. I tink dat 'twixt de niggers of de Souf and de womin of de Norf, all talkin' 'bout rights, de white men will be in a fix pretty soon. But what's all dis here talkin' 'bout?

"Dat man ober dar say dat womin needs to be helped into carriages, and lifted ober ditches, and to hab de best place everywhar. Nobody eber helps me into carriages, or ober mud- puddles, or gibs me any best place!" And raising herself to her full height, and her voice to a pitch like rolling thunder, she asked "And a'n't I a woman? Look at me! Look at my arm! (and she bared her right arm to the shoulder, showing her tremendous muscular power). I have ploughed, and planted, and gathered into barns, and no man could head me! And a'n't I a woman? I could work as much and eat as much as a man—when I could get it— and bear de lash as well! And a'n't I a woman? I have borne thirteen chilern, and seen 'em mos' all sold off to slavery,

and when I cried out with my mother's grief, none but Jesus heard me! And a'n't I a woman?

"Den dey talks 'bout dis ting in de head; what dis dey call it?" ("Intellect," whispered some one near) "Dat's it, honey. What's dat got to do wid womin's rights or nigger's rights? If my cup won't hold but a pint, and yourn holds a quart, wouldn't ye be mean not to let me have my litle half-measure full?" And she pointed her significant finger, and sent a keen glance at the minister who had made the argument. The cheering was long and loud...

And she ended by asserting: "If de fust woman God ever made was strong enough to turn de world upside down all alone, dese women togedder (and she glanced her eyes over the platform) ought to be able to turn it back, and get it right side up again! And now dey is asking to do it, de men better let 'em." Long-continued cheering greeted this. "Bleeged to ye for hearin' on me, and now old Sojourner han't got nothin' more to say."

From: Andrews & Zarefsky, *American Voices*, pp. 218-220

to speak. Several male leaders of the largest **denominations** (groups) of churches in America quoted the Bible to "prove" that women were not equal to men. Sojourner Truth, perhaps the person with the least schooling of anyone in the room, asked for the floor, and gave a speech. Frances D. Gage, the chairperson of the convention, wrote down the words to the best of her ability. Later Mrs. Gage said: "I have never seen anything like the magical influence that **subdued** (put down) the mobbish spirit of the day, and turned the sneers and jeers of an excited crowd into notes of respect and admiration."

Throughout the 19th century and into the 20th century farm families used few items they could not make themselves.

How People Lived in Rural Areas

As you can see from the census information in Appendix B, in 1800 everyone lived in rural areas. By 1900 only one-half of the people of Ohio lived in rural places, where "rural" included towns having fewer than 1,500 people. But even in 1900 there were more than twice as many citizens living in rural areas as in urban places in 53 of the 88 counties.

Have you visited a "historic village" to learn how people lived in rural areas during the 19th century? The *Ohio Village* in Columbus may have the best known collection of historic buildings in our state. The largest museums of 19th-century life in Ohio are: *Hale Farm* in northwest Summit County, *Auglaize Village* in Defiance County, *Century Village* in Geauga County, *Sharon Woods Village* in Hamilton County, *Roscoe Village* in Coshocton County, *Historic Lyme Village* at the corners of Seneca, Huron, Erie, and Sandusky Counties, Sauder Farm in Fulton County, and *Caesar's Creek Pioneer Village* in Warren County. Almost every county has one or more 19th-century houses that are open to visitors.

On Farms

The people who lived on farms had to do many things for themselves that we can pay someone else to do for us. In the earliest days of settlement, their houses were built from logs. They had only the simplest of furniture. They got water for themselves and their animals from a well, a spring, or a **cistern** (a large pit dug in the ground and lined with stones to store rain water which fell on the roof of the house or barn). Their toilets were outdoor "privies," that had to be located so that human wastes would not pollute the water supply.

The picture on page 143 is a typical rural scene btween 1850 and 1920. You can judge the depth of the well by the length of the pole used to lower or raise the water bucket.

The most important fuel in rural areas was wood. In the earliest days, a wood-burning fireplace provided heat for warmth and cooking, and light at night. Later, animal fat was cooked to make tallow candles for lighting. By 1870, if a farm was prosperous, the family could buy oil lamps for light and cast-iron stoves to heat the house. Families living in the southeastern counties of Ohio were among the first people to use coal.

In the earliest days, a farm family might raise some crops and animals for sale in the nearest market town, but every farm had a vegetable garden, fruit trees, chickens for eggs and meat, and cows or goats for milk for family use. Food was saved for winter use by smoking meat or packing it in salt, by canning vegetables and fruit, and by putting potatoes and other root crops and grain into rat-proof containers.

The only forms of transportation were walking or riding in a wagon, buggy, or sled, pulled by a horse or other animal. Going to church provided a chance to socialize with friends as well as an opportunity to worship God. Going to town was an important event because the farmers could sell their products and buy hardware, cloth, and "luxuries" they could not produce on their farms.

All kinds of jobs that involved hard work were also occasions for socializing. Neighbors often worked together to "raise" houses and barns. They went from farm to farm helping each other harvest and prepare food for the winter. The County Fair was a major social event each summer where the people "showed off" the vegetables, animals, and flowers they had raised, and the many things they had made for themselves. The picture on page 143 is a typical farm scene between the years 1850 and 1910.

By the end of the 19th century, the development of steam-powered farm machinery made it possible for some farm families to operate on large tracts of land. The railroads made it possible to sell farm products in the markets of the big cities of Ohio and the Eastern United States. But life on the small farms did not change much until the 1940s when electricity became available in rural areas.

In Small Towns

Living conditions in small towns were similar to those on the farms. One very noticeable difference was that farm families usually had more than fifty acres of land while town lots were seldom as large as one acre. The town lots were big enough that the owners could have a few fruit trees and raise vegetables — and often chickens — for their own use. If the family was rich enough

144

Johnny Appleseed and Ohio

One day early in the spring of 1801 as Isaac Stedden worked in the clearing near his cabin in Licking County, Ohio, he saw a strange-looking traveler approaching on horseback. Travelers were rare in those days, and, notwithstanding the odd appearance and manners of this man, Stedden offered him the scant **courtesies** of his cabin. He remained only a few days and had little to say of himself or his destination, but while he **tarried** as a guest he talked chiefly of planting apple trees so that settlers might have fruit in addition to the wild meat and fish found in the forests and streams. He took from his saddlebags a quantity of apple seeds and planted them about the cabin and then departed. This was one of the first recorded evidences of John Chapman's arrival in the Ohio Valley country. He was a young man in his early twenties at the time. Born in Leominster, Massachusetts, September 26, 1774, he spent his early years in western Massachusetts and had migrated to western Pennsylvania in his late teens or early twenties...

... For nearly fifty years he kept steadily at his work and, doubtless, there is no region in the United States where the early settlers planted more fruit trees than were grown in Johnny Appleseed's territory. There are still a few old apple trees alive which are claimed to have been taken from nurseries planted by "Johnny Appleseed." "The good men do lives after them."

From: *Johnny Appleseed: A Pioneer and A Legend*, A pamphlet prepared by International Apple Institute

Johnny Appleseed planted thousands of apple trees in Ohio

to own one or two horses, they kept the animals in a separate building called a "shed" or "stable." Wealthy citizens kept their animals in "carriage houses."

Many towns were located along creeks which could be dammed to provide water power to operate a mill. The town water supply might be the mill pond, a well in the market area, or cisterns in every yard. Some people earned their living by selling water, which they carried in barrels on "water wagons", from a pond to the houses of the town.

The people who lived in the town were usually craftsmen or merchants. The craftsmen included dressmakers, shoemakers, carpenters, blacksmiths, wagon makers, millers, tinsmiths, and furniture makers. The merchants bought the food produced by the farms of the surrounding area, and either sold it to the town people or transported it to a larger city. The merchants bought manufactured items in the city that could not be made in the town, and sold these things to the people living in and around the town.

Circuit Riders

Before Ohio became a state, people seldom enjoyed the services of doctors, lawyers, teachers, or religious leaders, and there were very few people trained in these professions. As the population of rural places grew during the 19th century, the families of a local area, such as a town or a township, worked together to build a school and employ a teacher for their children. You will learn in Chapter 11 how law courts of the state moved from place to place each year on a **circuit** (planned route). Since lawyers did most of their work in court, they "rode circuit" with these courts to carry justice to all rural areas.

Many of the people who settled in rural areas were deeply religious, and wanted **clergymen** (ministers, priests, rabbis) to lead them in worship, to perform marriage ceremonies, and to pray for them at time of death. Because few rural areas could support a full-time religious leader, clergymen also "rode circuit."

By far the best known of the circuit riders was John Chapman, who was born in 1775 and died in 1847. Mr. Chapman traveled through a large part of our state for many years, and planted apple seeds wherever he stopped. He planted so many of these trees in so many places that everyone called him Johnny Appleseed. An artist's idea of what

he looked like is shown on page 145. You can visit his grave in Ashland, the county seat of Ashland County. You can read a bit of this story on page 145.

Religious Communities

During the 19th century, there were three groups of people in Ohio who lived in some form of **communal** (shared) living. They believed strongly in the passage from the Bible known as Acts 4:32-35.

Mennonites

In 1524 a group of religious people in Switzerland organized themselves as the *Swiss Brethern*. In 1536 Menno Simons joined the Swiss Brethern, and by the time he died in 1561 almost everyone called the members of this group *Mennonites*.

By 1690, as new discoveries were made in science and new ways were developed for doing many things, some Mennonites decided to follow the teachings of Jacob Amman, who said that the old ways of doing things were best. The believers in the "old order" became known as the *Amish*, in honor of their leader.

When other Christians attacked the Mennonites in Europe, they fled to England, and later to William Penn's colony of Pennsylvania. The Mennonites settled a short distance to the northwest of Philadelphia, and named their community Germantown. (Today this is a neighborhood of Philadelphia.)

The basic teaching of the Mennonite faith was peace. Because of their love for peace, they would not fight in the War of the Revolution. Patriotic Americans condemned the Mennonites, so they moved westward in Pennsylvania, and later into Ohio.

*An Amish barn-raising project in
Holmes County.*

While riding along a rural road, have you ever seen a sign that says:
HORSE-DRAWN VEHICLES AHEAD ?
You can see many such signs in Geauga, Holmes, and Wayne Counties, in northeast Ohio, and in Williams and Fulton counties in the northwest Ohio, because many Amish and Mennonite people live in these areas. In fact, Holmes County has the largest number of Amish families of any county in the United States. Many Mennonites also live in Madison County. During the 1980s, a group of Amish families moved from northeast Ohio to Adams County.

The Mennonites and Amish people practice what can be called *communal responsibility*. Each family owns the land it lives on and the equipment it uses, but the people always help each other in times of need. But there are distinct differences between these two groups. For example, Mennonites use electricity in their homes, tractors on their farms, and own automobiles. The Amish use only oil for cooking food and lighting their homes, and horse-drawn equipment for farming and transportation. The picture on page 147 shows a dramatic picture of an Amish "barn raising" that took place in Holmes County in 1989.

Shakers

In 1774 Ann Lee and seven friends moved from a big city in England to New York City. Ann Lee had a vision that led her to believe ordinary people did not have to live in misery. They could solve their problems by establishing new communities that would practice the Bible story from Acts 4:32-35.

She also had a vision that led her to believe that the world would soon end. Her ideas

attracted a group of people, and together they formed the *Millenium Church of United Believers in the Second Coming of Christ*. Soon after the group was organized, the followers of Ann Lee were called Shakers because they were so moved by their religious experiences that their bodies shook violently.

A total of twenty-four Shaker communities were formed in the eastern United States between 1787 and 1896 — four of them in Ohio. The Whitewater community in the northwest corner of Hamilton County, was founded in 1824 and closed in 1907. The Watervliet community in Warren County was organized in 1806 and closed in 1910 . Union Village in Montgomery County was established in 1806 and closed in 1912. North Union Village was founded in Cuyahoga County in 1822 and closed in 1889. The buildings of North Union disappeared when *Shaker Heights* was built during the 1920s.

The Shakers lived simple lives of true communal style. No individual owned anything, and each was subject to the discipline of the group. They were hard-working people, and very **ingenious** (clever). They built all kinds of mechanical equipment to make their lives easier. They were the first people to harvest and package flower and vegetable seeds to sell in stores. They had one characteristic that helped to end their existence — they were so firmly convinced that the world was about to end that they did not marry and produce children.

Zoar

In 1817 a group of German people, who wanted to separate themselves from the established churches of that time, migrated to the Tuscarawas River in Ohio. They combined their resources and bought a large tract of land on the north boundary of Tuscarawas County, near an 18th-century trading post at Bolivar.

These German immigrants called themselves the *Society of Separates*, and named their community Zoar. They took the name Zoar from the Bible story in Genesis 19: 20-22. The members of the Society of Separates owned nothing as individuals, but worked together to build large brick buildings and create prosperous farms.

In 1898 the peace and harmony of the group ended, and the community broke apart. The people living at Zoar sold the land and buildings, and divided the money between them. For many years the property was under private ownership, but the Ohio Historical Society now operates a large part of it as a museum to show how a form of communal living once prospered in Ohio.

Stop and Think!

Ohio, the United States of America, and every country of the world, are what they are today because of the people who live in them. The earliest white settlers who came to Ohio were anxious to protect themselves from the natives of the area. By the beginning of the 19th century, whites outnumbered the Native Americans, and by 1842 all but a few families of natives had been driven from the state.

The settlers who moved to Ohio came for a variety of personal reasons, but all hoped to improve their positions in life. People came from most of the nations of Europe, and from slavery in the South, in search of freedom and opportunity. There were some wealthy people with good educations; there were many, many more who were penniless and uneducated.

During the first half of the 19th century, almost every rural family had to raise at least some of the food it needed. Some towns developed as central places where farmers could exchange their surplus crops for goods and services they needed. By the end of the century there were more than 4,000,000 people living in Ohio, with fewer than one-half of them living in rural areas.

Review the Chapter!

Building vocabulary...

abolish	loft
bounty hunter	migrate
census	neutral
circuit	oppression
cistern	persecute
clergyman	prosperous
communal	repulse
consequence	rivalry
courtesies	sojourn
denomination	staple
extravagant	steerage
famine	stench
fugitive	subdue
ghetto	tarried
hold (ship's)	tolerant
indentured	warrant (court order)
ingenious	

Meeting new people...

John and Jane Lowry Rankin
Sojourner Truth
Levi and Catherine White Coffin
John Chapman

Testing yourself...

Why is it true or false?

1. All of the immigrants to America during the 19th century were religious outcasts from Europe.
2. Runaway slaves were sure of freedom when they crossed the Ohio River.
3. By 1842 a majority of Native Americans had left Ohio to live on reservations in the west.
4. Gallipolis was settled by French immigrants.
5. Steerage was a form of travel.
6. Many Irish came to America because of a shortage of food in their homeland.
7. The vast majority of immigrants were skilled craftsmen.
8. Rankin House, in Ripley, Ohio, may be visited today.
9. Mennonites are often seen with their horses and buggies in Holmes County.
10. A good way to experience life in 19th century is to visit the Ohio Village.

What must be changed?
(You may change not more than three words to make each statement correct.)

1. Several county names in Ohio are related to Italian words.
2. In 1808 the General Assembly passed a law making it illegal to import slaves into this nation.
3. Switzerland provided great financial support to America during the Revolutionary War.
4. People who belong to the Society of Friends are called Amish.
5. A freedman was a craftsman who moved to Ohio.
6. Native Americans were assigned to live in cities.

7. Sojourner Truth made her speech in Toledo.
8. The Ohio canals had no trains or schedules.
9. Ohio Village is located in Fulton County.
10. The nations of Denmark, Norway, and Sweden are called Great Britain.

Thinking it through...

1. Why did people leave various countries in Europe to come to America during the 19th century?
2. Why did not the United States enforce the law of 1808 that prohibited bringing slaves to this country?
3. How were the following groups of religious people similar, how were they different, and why do some exist today while others do not? Mennonites, Amish, Shakers, Separatists.
4. Pretend that you are a reporter for your community newspaper, and Sojourner Truth has just delivered her speech in your school. Write a report of the speech for the newspaper.

Working with maps...

1. On your map of the world, locate the countries mentioned in this chapter.
2. On your map of the world, draw the route followed by the Swiss immigrants as they traveled from their former homes to Cincinnati. Measure the length of their route, and calculate their average speed per day. How long would it take you to make this trip today?
3. Using the mape on page 140 and your map of Ohio, locate the Underground Railroad lines that were closest to your home.
4. As a class project, find out where each member of your class lives today and where each was born. Locate each present home on a map of your county, and each birthplace on whichever map is best.

150

CHAPTER 9

How did the cities of Ohio develop?

Be ready to learn...

- the differences between settlements, towns, villages, and cities.

- why some settlements grew to become large cities.

- how people lived in cities during the 19th century.

- how transportation influenced cities.

In Chapter 8 you learned how the population of Ohio grew from just a few thousand people in 1800 to more than 4 million in 1900. You also learned that in 1900 only half of the people lived in rural areas, while the other half lived in cities. In this chapter we will explore the question: "How were the cities we know today created out of the dense forests that once covered most of Ohio?"

151

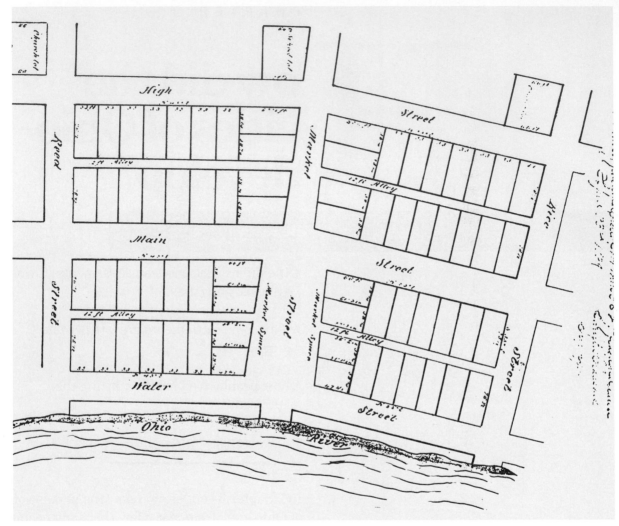

Plan for the town of Nassau established in 1829

Definitions

We have been using words like settlement, town, village, and city without being specific about meanings. Now we must be more exact in our choice of words.

Settlement

A **settlement** was made when a group of people left the place where they had been living and migrated to an undeveloped territory. Sooner or later they decided to "settle down" in what seemed to be a desirable place. They built shelters and tried to create a supply of food. Their main interest was in **survival** (existing), so they made few plans for the future of the

View of Akron, Ohio in 1846

settlement. Many of the early settlements in Ohio disappeared, many more continue to exist today as small groups of buildings near the intersections of roads, but others grew to become important cities.

Town

In some situations a land owner, or a group of owners, decided to create a planned town that would attract people to live there. Every planned town of the early 19th century had certain features. It had access to an existing route of transportation, such as a river, toll road, canal, or railroad. It had a planned pattern of streets and house **lots** (parcels). Certain areas were set aside for a market place, a school, a church, and a cemetery. The owners advertised the town

to people who had just come to the United States, and even to people in Europe.

The town plan shown on page 152 was created in 1829 and it appears to be a desirable place to live. There is a market place and lots set aside for a school and two churches. Three of the streets have direct access to the Ohio River, and Main Street was part of an important existing road. But no one living in Hamilton County would have bought one of these lots because the land slopes up steeply from the river to beyond High Street. In addition Water Street would have flooded at least once every year. Of course people in Europe, or on the East Coast of the United States, did not know about the terrain so they might buy the lots in hope of establishing new homes.

View of Akron, Ohio in 1890.

Incorporated Places

Do you know what a **corporation** is? The word *corporation* comes from the Latin word *corpus*, which means "a body." State laws permit groups of people to work together as single bodies to perform certain activities.

Ohio laws make it possible for people living near each other to form themselves into *municipal corporations* that have accurately described boundaries. This means that they can create units of government separate from the surrounding townships or counties. There are two kinds of incorporated places in Ohio, *villages* and *cities*.

Our word *village* comes from the Latin word *villa*, which means "country estate." In Ohio a village is an incorporated place that has fewer than 5,000 people.

Our word *city* comes from the Latin word *civitas*, which means "citizen." In Ohio a city is an incorporated place that has 5,000 or more people. The two views of Akron shown on page 153 and 154 show how quickly large cities can grow.

An *urban*, or *urbanized*, area has a large number of people living in a combination of incorporated and unincorporated places.

Why Some Towns Grew

If every urban area of Ohio began as a settlement, why did some grow to become large cities while others never grew? And why did the largest cities grow in the 50-mile (80-kilometers) wide diagonal band you learned about in Chapter 1? You could make a career — or life-time hobby — out of searching for answers to this question, but there are some general principles that are very important.

Location

A settlement can be made wherever there is a supply of water, good land, and material for shelter. The site must be free from natural hazards, such as flooding and land slides. If the site is so small that it can support only a few families, it is not likely to become a city.

Canal boat St. Helena II at Canal Fulton

Accessibility

As you learned in Chapter 7, an area of land is valuable only if people can get to it. The first settlements in Ohio were on the shores of the Ohio River and Lake Erie. Later, settlements sprang up along the streams that drain into the Ohio River and Lake Erie.

You learned in Chapter 2 that the southeastern half of Ohio is very hilly and has poor soil for agriculture, while the northwest half is level and has good soils. The original settlements along the rivers in the southeast half of the state did not grow into big cities because there were few locations suitable for growth. In the northwest half of the state, outside the diagonal band, only the settlement at Toledo became a large city.

As you learned in Chapter 7, new forms of transportation had great influence on the development of settlements. When the canals were built, new towns sprang up to serve as central places for farmers to ship their products to the markets of big cities. For example, a historical marker in Delphos, on the line between Allen and Van Wert Counties, tells how transportation affected that village.

Power Supply

When the earliest settlements were made, four sources of power were available for doing work — human effort, animal energy, wind, and water power. Water wheels were used to operate mills along streams that could be dammed to provide falling water. Since wind is not a reliable source of power in Ohio, animals were used to operate mills where water could not be used. By 1825 inventors had developed steam engines that were much more powerful than water wheels or animal-operated mills. Since steam engines could be operated anywhere, water power became less important in choosing a site for settlement.

When the Ohio and Erie Canal was built, a lock was needed at the northwest corner of Stark County. A new settlement was soon established at this lock to take advantage of the source of power and the improved transportation on the canal. Today people visit the village of Canal Fulton to ride the canal boat *St. Helena II*, shown on page 155, and to see the old canal directly behind the stores of the CBD.

Politics

Politics can be defined as the art of people living together in groups. Politics played a very important role in the development of every urban place in Ohio. For example, how was the decision made to locate the seat of government of your county? In some

---

Historical Marker at Delphos

Delphos began and **flourished** as a canal town. It was originally four separate settlements .... The town became a center of canal traffic **rivaled** in the west only by Fort Wayne, Indiana. The first canal boat ... passed through Delphos July 4, 1845. Farmers from miles around came to load their produce on the canal boats. However, the building of the Ohio and Indiana Railroad in 1854 from Crestline, Ohio, [in Crawford County] to Fort Wayne shifted the center of the trade and the rapid growth of Delphos **abated** ....

First Ohio captol and office buildings in Columbus

places, such as Marietta, Cincinnati, and Cleveland, the first settlement in the area immediately became the county seat. In later years, as existing counties were divided to create new ones, as you can see by turning back to page 93, the residents of several towns often competed to have their town named the county seat.

Chillicothe was made the first capital of Ohio for three reasons:
1. It was midway between the east and west boundaries of the state.
2. Most of the population was in the southern half of the state.
3. It was on a river for easy transportation.
As the population of northern Ohio grew, the people of that area wanted to be closer to the seat of government.

In 1808 the citizens of the small town of Putnam, on the west bank of the Muskingum River in Muskingum County, built a fine, large stone building that they offered to the General Assembly to be used as the state capitol. The people of Zanesville, a larger community on the east bank of the river, used greater political influence to have the capital moved to their town. Today Putnam is a suburb of Zanesville, and you can visit the *McHenry House* that the people of Putnam hoped would be the capitol.[1]

When the General Assembly met at Zanesville in 1810, it decided to create a new capital city closer to the center of the state. With an unlimited number of

157

How Columbus Became the Capital City of Ohio

In the winter of 1810 ... four citizens of Franklinton ... formed a company to establish the State capitol "on the high bank of the Scioto river opposite Franklinton." The villages of Dublin, Worthington and Delaware were **competitors**, but the geographical advantages of the Columbus site and the terms offered by them prevailed. Their proposal was to give the State two separate batches of land of ten acres each—one lot for the State House and one lot for the Penitentiary—the **foresighted** and **impartial** founders of the capital realizing that equal and immediate quarters should be provided alike for the law makers and the law breakers. In addition they agreed to build (at their expense) the capitol and **penitentiary** and "such other buildings as should be directed by the legislature to be built, not exceeding a total cost of $50,000."

Quoted from: Howe: vol. I, p. 619

choices, how did they make a decision? The story in the box above will answer this question.

The picture on page 157 shows the first capitol built in Columbus. Franklin County was established in 1803, and Franklinton served as the county seat until 1824, but it is now part of inner-city Columbus.

Entrepreneurs

Entrepreneurs are resourceful people who know how to achieve goals. They plan ahead and work hard to change their plans into reality. They also know that creative people like to associate with each other in centers of government and/or learning, such as college towns.

Some settlements in ideal locations did not grow because the people who lived there were happy with life as it was. They did not want to be disturbed by entrepreneurs and the changes that come with growth.

Boosters

Does your school have a *Boosters Club*? If it does, you know that the people who belong to the club work hard to raise money for school activities. Some settlements grew into major cities because they had **boosters**, that is, people who were so enthusiastic about the future of the town that they did everything they could to tell strangers about how wonderful it was. They wrote letters to friends and relatives in Europe and in the Eastern States. They had artists make drawings — there were no photographs before 1840 — and sent copies of these drawings to newspapers and magazines. They tried to show visitors how much better life was in their town than in other places. If there were two towns similar in all ways except that one had boosters and the other did not, the town with boosters grew faster!

The Role of Central Places

As you have learned, a *central place* is a site that provides goods or services needed by people living in the surrounding area. In the 19th century, mills for grinding grain and

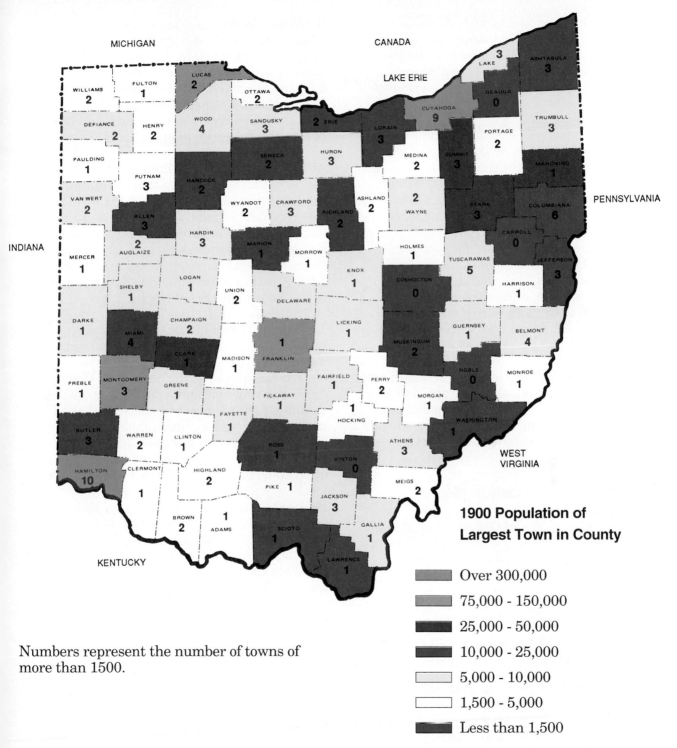

MICHIGAN

CANADA

LAKE ERIE

INDIANA

PENNSYLVANIA

WEST
VIRGINIA

KENTUCKY

County	Number
WILLIAMS	2
FULTON	1
LUCAS	2
OTTAWA	2
LAKE	3
ASHTABULA	3
DEFIANCE	2
HENRY	2
WOOD	4
SANDUSKY	3
ERIE	2
GEAUGA	0
CUYAHOGA	9
TRUMBULL	3
PAULDING	1
PUTNAM	3
HANCOCK	2
SENECA	2
HURON	3
LORAIN	3
MEDINA	2
SUMMIT	3
PORTAGE	2
MAHONING	1
VAN WERT	2
ALLEN	3
WYANDOT	2
CRAWFORD	3
RICHLAND	2
ASHLAND	2
WAYNE	2
STARK	3
COLUMBIANA	6
MERCER	1
HARDIN	3
MARION	1
MORROW	1
HOLMES	1
TUSCARAWAS	5
CARROLL	0
JEFFERSON	3
SHELBY	1
LOGAN	1
UNION	2
KNOX	1
COSHOCTON	0
HARRISON	1
DARKE	1
CHAMPAIGN	2
DELAWARE	1
LICKING	1
GUERNSEY	1
BELMONT	4
MIAMI	4
CLARK	1
MADISON	1
FRANKLIN	1
MUSKINGUM	2
NOBLE	0
MONROE	1
PREBLE	1
MONTGOMERY	3
GREENE	1
FAIRFIELD	1
PERRY	2
MORGAN	1
PICKAWAY	1
WASHINGTON	1
BUTLER	3
WARREN	2
CLINTON	1
FAYETTE	1
HOCKING	1
ROSS	1
ATHENS	3
HAMILTON	10
CLERMONT	1
HIGHLAND	2
VINTON	0
MEIGS	2
PIKE	1
BROWN	2
ADAMS	1
JACKSON	3
GALLIA	1
SCIOTO	1
LAWRENCE	1
AUGLAIZE	

**1900 Population of
Largest Town in County**

- Over 300,000
- 75,000 - 150,000
- 25,000 - 50,000
- 10,000 - 25,000
- 5,000 - 10,000
- 1,500 - 5,000
- Less than 1,500

Numbers represent the number of towns of
more than 1500.

Map of central places of Ohio in 1900

159

sawing lumber, blacksmith shops for making ironware, and stores for selling sugar, salt, and clothing were examples of small central places because almost everyone in the neighboring area needed these goods and services.

As the economy of a rural area improved, people were able to produce more goods than they needed for themselves. They also gained some free time for pleasure and recreation. Perhaps they wanted to buy books or rubber boots, or go to a theater. As soon as entrepreneurs in the region learned that there was a demand for such goods, some of them attempted to satisfy the needs. The town that had the first book store, boot shop, and/or theater then attracted customers from a wider area; therefore, it became a large central place.

As the economy continued to improve, some people wanted to buy better furniture, or perhaps a piano, or they wanted to hear an orchestra perform. Entrepreneurs in one of the growing towns set out to provide for these new wants, and their town grew even more.

Central Places of Ohio in 1900

The central places of Ohio developed in an interesting pattern. Certain towns grew as long as entrepreneurs filled the growing needs of the region — and "boosters" advertised the new attractions. But only a few towns can grow to become very large cities that offer the most highly specialized goods and services, because only a limited number of people need such items.

The map on the previous page shows populations of Ohio counties and the number of towns having more than 1,500 population in 1900. More than 381,000 people lived in Cleveland in that year, and

there were eight more towns of at least 1,500 people in Cuyahoga County. Almost 326,000 people lived in Cincinnati, and there were nine other towns of at least 1,500 people in Hamilton County. This means that Cuyahoga County and Hamilton County each had more than ten percent of the entire population of Ohio.

At first Cleveland grew because it had a harbor on Lake Erie, and the surrounding land was good for farming. Later Cleveland was the northern end of the Ohio and Erie Canal. At first Cincinnati grew because it had good land for farming and access by rivers to the north, south, east, and west. Later Cincinnati became the southern end of the Miami and Erie Canal.

The site of Toledo in Lucas County was as desirable as the site of Cleveland, but Toledo was in the area assigned to the Native Americans at the end of the War of 1812. For this reason, it could not be settled until long after Cleveland was established as the major central place of northern Ohio. By 1900 Toledo had grown to almost 132,000 people, but there was only one other town of 1,500 people in Lucas County.

By 1900 Columbus had more than 125,000 people because it was the center of state government. It was surrounded by excellent farm land and had a connection to the Ohio and Erie Canal, but there were no other towns in Franklin County.

How People Lived in Cities

In Chapter 8 you learned how people lived on farms and in small towns during the 19th century. Life in the big cities was quite different. While some cities may have started as unplanned settlements, within a few years town plans were created. Streets were laid out — but seldom paved — and

19th-century inner-city housing in Cincinnati

the land between the streets was divided into lots, as shown on page 152, so that individuals could buy land to erect houses, stores, workshops, places of worship, and other types of buildings.

Buildings

In most of the early towns of Ohio, the building lots were created about 25-feet by 100-feet in size. Almost all of the original buildings were two or three stories high, often with a store or workshop on the first floor and living space above. The buildings usually touched each other on both sides, and filled most of the depth of the lots. As the population of the town increased, buildings were made four or five stories high, but there were no elevators. The picture above shows a combination of fronts, sides, and backs of typical Cincinnati

houses of the mid-19th century when 100,000 people lived on two square miles (about 5.2 square kilometers) of land.

Public Health

It was not unusual for a family with six or more children to live in two or three rooms. After dark, people used candles or oil lamps to provide light. By the end of the 19th century, most houses had gas lights. The rooms were heated by burning wood or coal in a fireplace or cast iron stove. Some people earned their living by selling small amounts of firewood and coal from house to house. **Soot** (small bits of carbon from burned coal), fumes, and fire were common problems.

161

In the earliest days, unpurified water was available at public wells, pumps, or faucets along the streets, or from water wagons. Later a single water tap was installed for each house. By 1900, almost every living unit in a house had its own water tap.

Human and animal wastes were major problems. In the earliest days, each building lot had one or two outdoor toilets (privies), just as in rural areas. During the second half of the 19th century, many of the larger cities built **sewerage** systems by laying pipes underground to carry away the **sewage** (human wastes). The sewers were seldom flushed properly, and after a storm the sewage ran into creeks or rivers. **Epidemics** of typhoid fever, typhus, cholera, and dysentery — diseases that you seldom hear about today — killed large numbers of people. The story in the box on this page will give you some idea about the conditions in which the very poorest people lived.

Food

Because walking was the main form of transportation, people had to buy food close to where they lived. They had to buy some types of food almost every day because there was no refrigeration to prevent spoiling. Every neighborhood had stores that sold canned and dried foods, **produce** (fruits and vegetables), and meats, but very few stores sold all of these types of food. Small bakeries sold bread, rolls, and pastries baked in the building. Milk was sold from wagons like the one shown on the next page.

By the middle of the 19th century, entrepreneurs were selling blocks of ice for use in keeping meats, produce, and milk from spoiling. The canals and reservoirs of Ohio froze over during the winter months.

Excerpt from Cleveland Newspaper about Living Conditions

Starting in the New England block, under the guidance of the health officer, Dr. H. W. Kitchen, we entered the basement under the sidewalk. Here were a number of small rooms, fourteen feet below the street, having no **ventilation**, and all occupied by numerous families, who pay six dollars per month for two rooms. A narrow stairway leads us down into a cellar, below these rooms, occupied as a general **receptacle** for everything that seems unfit for any earthly use. There are old rotten boards, broken wheels, stove pipes, rags, pieces of carpets, old shoes and heaps of straw, all pitched together in a confusion natural to the locality. Emerging from this cellar the rear of the building is reached, and the most prominent feature of the disease-breeding nuisance here meets the eye. The rear is about three stories higher than the front, and the whole long block looks as if it were ready to slide down the hillside upon the smaller **hovels** fringing the [Ohio] canal.... Everything is thrown from the upper windows down this hill, and the whole neighborhood is pervaded by an unsupportable stench. The vaults, cesspools and water pipes are out of order, and the interior of the building is swarming with human beings.

Quoted in: Smith, Thomas H., Editor, *An Ohio Reader*, p. 94 from Cleveland Leader, July 10, 1873.

19th-century milk delivery wagon

The state sold rights to certain companies to cut ice from these water surfaces. After cutting the ice, the entrepreneurs had to haul it to the towns and provide heavily-insulated storage buildings so that the ice would not all melt before the next winter.

Problems of Poor Women

Poor women had particularly hard lives because they often had large families under very crowded and unsanitary conditions. They could not vote, they had few freedoms, and they were often subject to abuse by alcoholic husbands. Divorce was legal, but not socially acceptable, and single women with children led very difficult lives, as the story in the box on page 164 shows.

Wealthy People

Wealthy people faced all of the difficulties that ordinary people faced, but they could afford more pleasant ways to solve the problems. Those who chose to live in the cities often bought several small parcels of land so that they could build larger homes and have open space surrounding them. They built cisterns to catch rain water for private water supplies. They hired servants — who were often indentured, as you learned in Chapter 8 — to do most of the work around the house, including carrying the human wastes from "slop jars" in the houses to outdoor privies. They built their own storage places for food and for ice.

Most of all, wealthy people owned horses and carriages so that they could move to the outskirts of town "to get away from the noise and dirt of the city." When you visit a large city today, you can often find the 19th-century houses of the wealthy within one or two miles of the center of town. By 1950 most of these fine houses were in areas considered to be **slums** (run-down

Excerpts from A Widow's Story

In a small room of a **tenement** house on an alley we found a widow who was trying to support herself and a little boy by making vests. Everything about her spoke of better days, and when we stated our business she **flushed** and seemed unwilling to discuss the subject .... A pile of woolen vests lay on a table .. Although of inferior material, they were made as neatly ... as the finest broadcloth.

"If I work steadily all day, and quite late at night," she said, "I can make fourteen of these a week, but I hardly ever go to bed at all Friday night, as I must have them done by Saturday noon in order to get my pay.... When the time arrives [on Saturday afternoon to have the work examined] I tremble from head to foot with nervousness, for the fellow who [examines it] is invariably ... **insolent**. If he cannot find a flaw in the work, he will say, 'Can't you make more than a dozen vests a week?...' ... and it humiliates me so to take abuse from a person so utterly beneath me in every way."

"And what," we asked, "do you get for these vests?"

"Only fourteen cents each," was the answer.

"Then you make, with all this toil, $1.96 a week?"

"Yes, and sometimes even less, and the rent for this room is $2.00 a month."

"Then," we suggested, "you have only about $5.50 a month to live on?"

"Not even that, for my [sewing] machine is not yet paid for, and I ought to have $3.00 a month for payments on that. This I have been unable to do lately, for my child has been sick, and I had to buy dainties for him. I am ashamed," she continued, "to tell you how little we spend on food. I have all my life heretofore been accustomed to a **bountiful** table, and I would never then have believed that anyone could exist on what I have had to this winter."

Quoted in An Ohio Reader, pp. 153-4 from *"Women's Work"*, Third Annual Report of the Bureau of Labor Statistics, 1879, pp. 267-270

Birthplace of President William Howard Taft about 1870 showing Taft children in the yard.

housing). In recent years, some of these buildings have been remodeled into professional offices or residences for upper-income people who like to work near the center of the city.

Above you can see the house in which a President of the United States, William Howard Taft, was born in 1857. In fact one of the boys in the picture is "Billy" Taft. This house was built in 1840 on a hilltop about two miles from the heart of Cincinnati. In 1940 it was used as a tenement house for several low-income families. During the 1950s, people interested in preserving historic places

bought the house and turned it over to the National Park Service. You can visit the restored house today.

Urban Transportation

When a town reached a population of 3,000 to 4,000, it covered such a large area that some entrepreneurs began to offer transportation-for-hire. The earliest **omnibuses** (from the Latin *omnibus*, meaning "for everyone") were simple four-wheel wagons pulled by one or two horses. The owner put a few benches in a wagon and operated over a regular route. Anyone who wanted to ride could signal the operator to stop, pay the fare, climb aboard,

About Historic Preservation

By the year 1930, many of the oldest parts of the big cities of the United States were badly neglected. Even houses built by wealthy people during the first half of the 19th century were being used as apartments for low-income families. The fine store buildings of the 1850s were being used as warehouses. In 1934 as part of the *New Deal* sponsored by President Franklin D. Roosevelt, the Congress of the United States adopted a *slum clearance* program. Thousands of 19th-century buildings in Ohio were torn down and new housing was built for low-income families.

During the 1950s, Congress adopted more *slum clearance* projects, and established the National System of Interstate Highways that you will learn about in Chapter 13. These federal programs required the wrecking of tens of thousands of old buildings.

Some citizens of the older cities became alarmed that important parts of our **cultural heritage** (good things from the past) were being destroyed in the name of "Progress." These citizens urged Congress to stop using federal money to destroy history. As a result of their efforts, Congress passed the *National Historic Preservation Act of 1966*. Today no federal money can be used to destroy old houses, bridges, factories, or other structures until historians have studied the sites and decided that these things have no historic value. New structures cannot be built on unused ground until archeologists have studied the site. Most of the historic places you are learning about in this book, including the Taft home, are listed on the *National Register of Historic Places*.

and travel to the desired destination. Riding in an omnibus was a slow and rather painful experience because the streets were not paved, but it was often better than walking.

Street Railways

During the 1850s and 1860s, many cities of Ohio sold franchises to entrepreneurs who built *street railways* by laying tracks in city streets. Horse-drawn wagons could move along these tracks with greater speed and comfort because the wheels did not bog down in the mud. This improved form of transportation made it possible for the cities to grow because people could live farther from their places of work and shopping. On the next page you can see an early streetcar at Broad and High Streets in Columbus.

By 1870 there were several small towns within five miles of the centers of the largest cities. When the weather was bad, it might take five hours to travel five miles from one of these towns to the big city over unpaved roads. A similar trip over a paved turnpike might take two hours. When street

Horse-drawn street car in front of the state capitol in Columbus about 1880

railway tracks were laid in public roads — whether paved or unpaved — passengers could move five miles in one hour. This faster transportation encouraged land owners along the tracks to subdivide their property to create housing within easy walking distance of the street railway line.

By 1890 the largest cities were expanding by **annexing** (adding on) old settlements within five miles of their centers. This meant that the outlying areas became part of the central city, and the people became citizens of the city. By the end of the 19th century, construction of electric-powered street railway systems made it possible for some cities to became very large.

Ferry Boats

In Chapter 7 you learned that rivers were very important transportation routes. But how did rivers affect the growth of individual cities? The answer to this

167

question is that sometimes rivers were barriers to growth. Because there were no bridges, people had trouble getting across the water. Of course, whenever there is a need, entrepreneurs will try to meet it. In this case, they built ferry boats to move passengers and goods back and forth across the stream, but this was a slow and limited form of transportation. During the last half of the 19th century, entrepreneurs applied for franchises to build bridges across the streams, but ferry operators often objected to such interference with their business.

Influence of Railroads

Steam railroads had even more dramatic influence than the street railways on the development of the largest urban areas of Ohio. While the first steam railroad lines were built to join distant centers of activity, entrepreneurs quickly realized that they could attract city dwellers to live in new communities from five to fifteen miles from the center of the city. They advertised: "Live in the country, away from the noise and dirt of the city, and be only thirty minutes from your place of work."

In Hamilton County you can visit an outstanding example of a **suburban** (outside a city) railroad community. In 1852 the village of Glendale, shown below, was laid out about twelve miles north of Cincinnati as a model town for business leaders of that city. You can find similar communities around all the large cities of Ohio.

Patterns of Land Use

Everywhere you go, you see patterns of land use. On a farm you can find tracts of land used for wood lots, for pasture, for field

Artist's view of Glendale, Ohio, about 1870

View of Lancaster, Ohio in 1846

crops, for gardening, for the shelter of animals, and for human activities. During the 19th century, very few units of government tried to control patterns of land use. Today almost every large urban area has strong regulations, called **zoning** ordinances, that control how land can be used in various parts of the village, city, township, or county.

When walking was the only form of transportation, places where people lived, worked, banked, shopped, worshiped, and played were all within walking distance. Doctors, lawyers, and other professional people often had their offices on the upper floors of store buildings. Social organizations had their meeting halls on the upper floors. You can still see this pattern of land use in many small towns that developed before 1900.

As a town expanded to become a large city, a pattern of central places evolved within the city. A blacksmith shop might grow into a metal-working factory. A shoe repair shop might grow into a shoe factory. A

dress-making shop might grow into a clothing factory. The original street of small stores and workshops grew to become a Central Business District (CBD). For example, the pictures on this page and the next show how the CBD of Lancaster, the county seat of Fairfield County, changed from 1846 to 1886.

As new residential neighborhoods developed farther and farther from the center of town, entrepreneurs opened small stores and workshops in the new neighborhoods. These neighborhood stores sold **convenience goods**, such as food, work clothing, and simple household items needed on a daily basis. The stores in the CBD began to specialize in **shopping goods**, such as dress clothing, fine furniture, musical instruments, and other items which last for long periods of time. Theaters, concert halls, lodge halls, and professional offices remained in the CBD.

As the CBD became too crowded for manufacturing companies, the owners of these factories sometimes relocated them

Similar view of Lancaster, Ohio as on page 169 in 1886

outside the city limits. When factories were built beyond the lines of public transportation, the owners had to build housing near the new factories in order to attract workers. This action sometimes led to the formation of new towns, as you will learn in the next chapter.

Stop and Think!

Life was not easy in the cities of 19th-century Ohio, but we cannot say that the people of Ohio were less happy in 1900 than people are today. Most of the people who lived in cities felt that they were making progress toward better lives for themselves and their children. Certainly the situation in the United States was far more pleasant for ordinary people than it was in many other parts of the world. In addition, at the turn of the century the people of Ohio were enjoying advantages of scientific and engineering discoveries that people of 1850 could not have imagined! You will learn about some of these developments in Chapter 10.

Knowing what you do now, would you like to go back in time — if you could — and live in a city of Ohio in 1900? It would be like going to another world!

Building vocabulary...

abate
annex
booster
bountiful
competitor
convenience good
corporation
cultural
heritage
epidemic
flourish
flushed (face)
foresight
hovel
impartial
insolent
lot (land)
omnibus
penitentiary
politics
produce (noun)
receptacle
rival (verb)
sewage
sewerage
shopping goods
slum
soot
suburban
survival
tenement
ventilation
zoning

Finish the sentence ...

1. The main interest of people creating a settlement was ....
2. Metropolitan means ....
3. The people of .... built the McHenry House in the hope that it would become the state capitol.
4. The three villages along the Scioto River that wanted to be the capital city were .... , ..., and ....
5. A village that is now part of inner-city Columbus was once called ....
6. A "central place" provides ....
7. Some towns were established along rivers and streams because the moving water provided power for ....
8. Cleveland, Cincinnati, and Toledo all grew to become big cities because they were ....
9. A town plan always had a .... so that people could buy food.
10. A major cause of disease in 19th-century towns was the lack of ....

How are they related?

1. Cities and villages?
2. Townships and counties?
3. Sanitation and health?
4. Boosters and entrepreneurs?
5. Canals and ice?
6. Politics and colleges?
7. Omnibuses and streetcars?
8. Widows and work?
9. Central places and suburbs?
10. Delphos and Canal Fulton?

Thinking it through...

1. You now live in either a township, a village, a small city, or a large city. How would your life be different if you lived in the other three kinds of places?

2. What three ingredients were needed to make an early 19th- century settlement survive? If a group of people wanted to create a new settlement today within 100 miles (160 kilometer) of your home, what would they need to "survive"?

3. Why did the community in which you live (or your county seat) grow, or fail to grow?

4. What is the purpose of the National Historic Preservation Act of 1966? Find out how this act has been used in your county.

6. Find out how "boosters" help your school, organization, or town to prosper.

Working with maps...

1. If you live in an urban area, make a sketch map of the streets within about 500 feet (150 meters) of where you live. Sketch all the buildings, parks, playgrounds, and undeveloped parcels that may be in this area, and label each item. Can you see any evidence of town planning in your neighborhood? If you live in a rural area, do this activity in one of the towns near where you live.

2. Go to a town or business center near where you live that developed during the 19th century. Make a sketch map of one block of the business district. Look for dates on the buildings, and try to figure out the order in which the buildings were built. What has happened to this business district in the past twenty years?

3. Go to a public library near your home, and ask to see old maps of a town in the county. Compare the town on the old county map with the same town today.

4. On your county map, choose a highway that runs across the county in either the north-south, or east-west direction, and identify all of the settlements that may have existed along this road in 1900.

Footnote

1. Today Columbus is the *capital* city of Ohio. The building in which the General Assembly meets is the *capitol*.

CHAPTER 10

How did industry develop during the 19th century?

Be ready to learn...

- about the importance of energy and tools.

- about industries related to agriculture.

- about industries based on natural resources.

- how Ohio became one of the greatest centers of manufacturing.

What do you think of when you hear the word *industry*? Are you an *industrious person*? **Industry** can be defined as the making and selling of goods and services for profit. In 1800 the industry of Ohio was very simple. Water provided power to operate mills. Blacksmiths made simple objects out of iron. Merchants imported goods from the eastern states to sell on the frontier. By 1900 Ohio was one

173

The French settlers at Gallipolis were city people who knew little about survival in the forest.

of the leading industrial states of the world. In this chapter you will learn how this change took place.

Energy and Tools

You have learned that the principal energy resources available to workers in 1800 were human, animal, water, and fire. Another important resource is *knowledge*, because knowledge makes it possible for people to change the raw materials of nature into useful tools. For example the French settlers at Gallipolis, in Gallia County, had as good tools as any one else on the frontier, but they had little knowledge of how to use them. The picture on this page shows the dangerous methods they used in cutting down a large tree.

An old water-powered mill in Ohio

Water Wheels

Water wheels are ingenious devices for changing the energy of running water into useful mechanical action. The original wheels, built almost entirely of wood, were not very efficient. The picture above shows the water wheel of an old mill in Ohio. Many of the early mills were built to grind grain into flour, but others were used to saw wood, or prepare cotton and wool for spinning. Today the word *mill* is still used in certain industries, for example, steel mill, paper mill, carpet mill.

By the end of the 19th century, water wheels were made of iron or bronze, and designed to operate inside large pipes. Today such wheels — called **turbines** — are very efficient devices for using the energy of moving water.

Steam

As you know, steam is obtained by boiling water. About the year 1700, Thomas Newcomen of Scotland invented the first practical *steam engine* to use the energy of steam to operate machinery. Knowledge of how to control the energy of steam led to what we call the *Industrial Revolution*, but almost a hundred years passed before steam was used in America. In Chapter 7 we discussed how steam power improved transportation. Steam power was also used to operate machines, such as cotton gins, that turned natural resources into useful goods. Ohio played a leading role in the Industrial Revolution during the 19th century.

Efficiency

We discussed efficiency briefly in Chapter 7. The goal of almost all industries is to operate in the most efficient manner possible. If you could make use of every unit of energy put into a project, your efficiency would be 100 percent, but no operation can meet that goal.

For example, if a pioneer woman wanted to make a dress for herself, she had to go through a long process. First she had to either raise sheep, cut off the wool, and clean it, or raise **flax** plants and break them down into fibers. Next she had to spin the wool or linen fibers into thread. She may have used either of the devices shown on on this page to spin thread. She colored the thread by soaking it in dyes that she made from berries, leaves, or nuts. Next she wove the thread into cloth, using some kind of loom. She cut the material into pieces, using scissors made of iron, and sewed the pieces together to form a dress. Buttons were handmade from bone or shell. The dress might have been as lovely to look at, and as comfortable to wear, as any modern dress, but many hours of labor were required because the entire process depended on human energy and the use of simple tools. You can watch women do these tasks today at Hale Farm in Summit County.

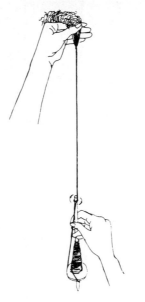

Two early ways to spin thread

176

Sizes of Ohio Farms
in 1900 and 1982

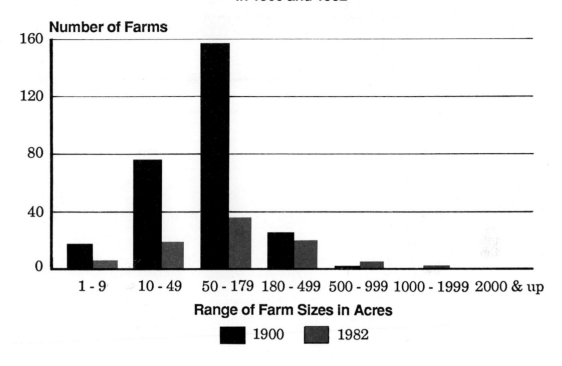

Number of Farms

Range of Farm Sizes in Acres

■ 1900   ■ 1982

When water-powered mills became available for spinning threads and weaving cloth, women usually found that it was less expensive, in terms of time and energy, to buy machine-made cloth to make a dress. Still later, after steam-powered factories were built to mass-produce dresses, most women found that they could not afford the time and effort required to make their own clothes.

Agriculture

In Chapter 5 you learned that almost everyone who came to the Ohio Country during the 18th and early 19th century expected to grow food for themselves. Even those who lived in small towns produced food in their yards. Cities began to grow only after the people living on farms could produce surplus food and transport it to the towns.

You also learned that the northwest corner of Ohio could not be settled until the natives were pushed out, and the land was subdivided on the Public Land Survey. The people who bought land in this region faced another major problem: the land was swampy! In fact a large area was called *The Black Swamp*. After the trees were cut, the farmers had to work together to build drainage ditches and install clay-tile drain pipes. When the area was finally drained, the soil was some of the most productive in the United States.

Ohio Agriculture in 1900

	No. of Farms	Improved Acreage	Value of Products	Value per Acre
State of Ohio (Totals)	276,719	19,244,472	$257,065,826	(average) $13.36
Main Products:				
Hay & Grain	80,809	6,651,265	$81,414,560	$12.24
Vegetables	7,171	184,999	$5,032,040	$27.20
Fruits	5,074	159,241	$3,515,880	$22.08
Live Stock	113,520	8,616,736	$110,669,116	$12.84
Dairy Produce	12,768	774,290	$14,782,140	$19.09
Tobacco	6,199	267,159	$5,580,440	$20.89
Sugar	60	2,216	$33,680	$15.20
Flowers & Plants	505	2,518	$1,402,940	$557.16
Nursery Products	147	9,867	$538,534	$54.58
Miscellaneous	50,466	2,576,181	$34,096,496	$13.24

By 1900, the average size of the 250,000 farms in Ohio was 88.5 acres. African-American families operated fewer than 2,000 of these farms. The graph on the previous page shows the distribution of sizes of Ohio farms in 1900: it also shows the distribution of farm sizes in 1982. The table on this page shows that corn, wheat, oats, and rye were the most important grains in 1900. Potatoes and sweet potatoes were the most widely raised vegetables, while apples, grapes, pears, and peaches were the most important fruits. Sugar was derived from sorghum grain. Almost one-half the farms sold **livestock** (cows, pigs, sheep, and goats). Many farms in the hilly, southern part of the state produced tobacco on small plots of land. As you can see, flowers, plants, and **nursery** products (shrubs, bushes, ornamental trees) were the most profitable items raised because people living in the cities wanted to buy these things to beautify their homes.

Agricultural Tools

In 1800 agricultural tools were very simple, like the plow shown on page 179. Only the cutting edges and a few other parts were made of iron. By 1900 almost every farm had horse-drawn tools like the plow shown on page 180. The largest farms had

An early 19th century plow

steel-powered equipment similar to that shown on page 181. A leather belt could be run from the **flywheel** (the large wheel behind the smoke stack on page 181) to operate threshing machines, shuckers, saws, pumps, and other equipment.

Industries Based on Agriculture

While grains could be stored for long periods of time, fruits and vegetables spoiled quickly unless they were preserved in some way. By 1900 there were large factories in Ohio that bought tons of fruits and vegetables from the farmers, cooked them, and packed them into sealed cans or glass jars.

Milk turned sour so quickly that much of it was immediately changed into cheese, either in the farm home, or in a nearby small factory. Today Amish people still change large quantities of milk into cheese at factories you can visit in Holmes County.

Meat Packing

Meat quickly became unusable if it was not properly prepared. When the canals made it possible for farmers to sell cows and pigs to

A late late 19th century John Deere plow

the **slaughter** houses (places where animals are changed into meat) of Cincinnati and Cleveland, meat processing became an important industry in those cities.

Farmers living near the big cities drove their animals to town on hoof. The toll roads described in Chapter 7 charged a small fee for each animal moving over the road. At certain times of the day, some of the streets of the city were filled with herds of animals. For example, by 1840

Cincinnati was known as "Porkopolis" because thousands of pigs were killed there each month. After the animals were cut up, the meat was packed into wood barrels with salt to prevent spoilage. These barrels were placed on steamboats for shipment to New Orleans and the big cities along the east coast of the United States.

By 1870 the farmers of northern Ohio could load animals onto railroad cars and ship them to slaughter houses in eastern cities. By that time, the farms of Illinois, Iowa,

Text within the image:

BLANDYS PORTABLE STEAM ENGINE AND SAW MILLS, ZANESVILLE & NEWARK OHIO

This is the Portable Engine and Saw Mill, that took the First Premium at the U.S Fair at Cincinnati over Six Competitors. Cutting 960 ft. inch lumber out of two logs in 8½ Minutes, Have taken the First Premium every where

Blandys' Machine Works are unequaled for completeness. They are capable of turning out ten Portable Engines & Saw Mills a Week.

BLANDYS' DOUBLE SAW MILL

BLANDYS' PORTABLE ENGINE & SAW MILL ARE OWNED AND OPERATED ALL OVER THE UNITED STATES FROM THE ATLANTIC TO THE PACIFIC MEXICO, CENTRAL AMERICA WEST INDIA IS SOUTH AMERICA EUROPE & EVEN FAR OFF AUS

Portable, general-purpose steam encgine of the 1850s.

and other midwestern states were also producing thousands of cows and pigs for the markets of eastern cities. The western farmers shipped their livestock on the rail lines across northern Ohio.

Byproducts of Animal Fat

During most of the 19th century, farm families cut the fat off animals they killed for family food. They used this fat to make **tallow** candles, or they mixed it with **lye** (the chemical potassium carbonate) obtained from the ashes of burned wood to make soap.

In 1837, as more and more animals were slaughtered in Cincinnati, William Procter and James Gamble, whose wives were sisters, formed a business to make soap and candles. This partnership was the beginning of the Procter & Gamble Company, which is now one of the largest corporations in the world.

A "forest" of leather belts in a typical machine shop of the 1860s.

Leather

Changing the hide of an animal into a piece of leather is a long, slow, smelly process called **tanning**. There were many tanneries in Ohio during the 19th century, but none are in operation now.

Today it is hard to imagine the number of uses that people of the 19th century had for leather. Had you asked someone in 1900 about the most important use of leather, the answer might have been "shoes," or "belts to drive machinery," or "saddles and

182

Ohio Extractive Industries
Changes in Value of Products

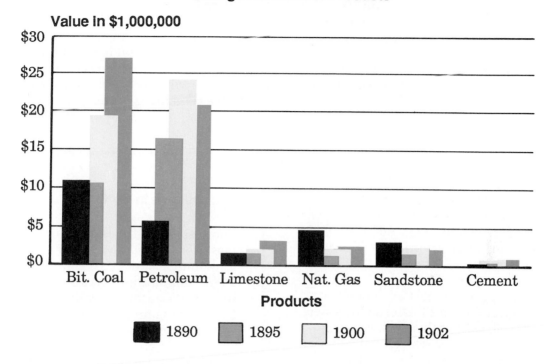

Value in $1,000,000

Legend: 1890, 1895, 1900, 1902

Products: Bit. Coal, Petroleum, Limestone, Nat. Gas, Sandstone, Cement

harnesses." The picture on page 182 shows a typical "forest of leather belts" that you could have seen in any large factory. For many years, Portsmouth in Scioto County was a very important center for making shoes, but the last of its shoe companies closed about 1960.

Extractive Industries

When you **extract** something, you take it away from its natural position and there is no way to replace it. Certain industries, such as quarrying, mining, and removing petroleum from the ground, are extractive industries because the material removed from the earth cannot be replaced. For over 200 years lumbering was an extractive industry in the United States, but since

1950 many companies plant as many new trees as they cut.

Quarrying and mining are very similar: both may be done underground or above ground. The removal of rocks is called *quarrying*, while the removal of metallic ores and coal is called *mining*. During the 19th century, miners had only hand tools and gun powder or dynamite to loosen the rock. The graph on this page shows how production of the extractive industries of Ohio changed from 1890 to 1902.

Stone

Stone has been an important building material throughout history because it does not decay. It can be removed from the ground and cut into useful shapes without the use of iron tools. Since wood rots quickly when it is in touch with the ground, many of the settlers in Ohio built their houses on stacks of flat stones that they set at each corner of the building. As the cities of Ohio grew during the 19th century, almost every house rested on stone foundation walls.

If you look back to page 12, you will see a sandstone quarry in northeastern Ohio. Many monumental buildings in Ohio, such as court houses and churches, were built of sandstone from this quarry. Sandstone was also used to make two types of *grindstones*. One type was used to sharpen all kinds of cutting tools, the other to grind grain. **Burr stones** (for grinding grain) from Ohio were used in many parts of the world.

There were several important limestone quarries in central and western Ohio. When the owners of some of these quarries stopped removing rock, the pits filled with water. In recent years several of these old quarries were changed into recreation centers for scuba diving.

Cement

From colonial times in America, **mortar** was used in all buildings built of brick or stone. The earliest mortar was made from a blend of lime, sand and water — a mix that forms a weak binding material when it dries.

During the 1870s, inventors in England found that by mixing limestone and shale in certain ways and heating it to a very high temperature they could make a cement that would hold bricks and stones together. Because this new cement looked like the rocks around Portland, England, the inventors called it **Portland cement**.

Concrete is a mixture of very small pieces of stone (sand), large pieces of stone (gravel), and a cementing material. When the cementing material is Portland cement, the mix is called "Portland cement concrete," or what is simply called *concrete*. When the cementing material is asphalt,

---

Youngstown in 1846

Youngstown is the largest and most flourishing town in Mahoning County.... It contains 1,200 inhabitants, has 12 **mercantile** stores, 3 warehouses for receiving and forwarding goods and produce on the canal....

Bituminous coal and iron abound in the immediate vicinity of the village ... adequate, it is believed, to the wants of a large manufacturing place. ... It has recently been determined that the coal in the valley of the Mahoning is well adapted in its raw state to the smelting of iron ore, and three furnaces ... each capable of producing from sixty to one hundred tons of pig metal per week have been erected ... near the village.... it is more than probable that the various railroads now projected in Ohio ... will be supplied with rails from this point.

From: Howe: vol. 2, p.178

The Brier Hill Iron Furnance in Mahoning County around 1890

the mix is called *asphaltic concrete*, or what is often called *blacktop*.

A few places in Ohio have the right combination of shale and limestone to make Portland cement. Today it is produced at Fairborn in Greene County and at Zanesville in Muskingum County.

Iron

Iron is an excellent example of the relationship between energy and tools. Although it takes large amounts of energy to obtain iron from its ore, the iron can be used to make very efficient tools. Two conditions are required to convert (**smelt**) ore to iron — a very hot furnace to melt the ore, and limestone to separate the iron from the ore. In the earliest days **charcoal** (made from trees) was used as the fuel. By the year 1900, only **coke** (made from coal) was used. The process of making charcoal and coke created great amounts of what we now call air pollution.

Hanging Rock Iron

In Chapter 2 we mentioned the *Hanging Rock Iron Region* of south-central Ohio, and you saw a picture of the Buckeye Furnace on page 27. This region covered parts of Perry, Hocking, Vinton, Jackson, and

Boys work in a coal mine.

Lawrence Counties in Ohio, and extended into eastern Kentucky and western West Virginia. It seems as though "Mother Nature" designed this area for the production of iron, because it contained high-grade ore, trees for charcoal, and limestone.

The first iron was produced in the Hanging Rock Region about the year 1845. When the Civil War began in 1861, there were eighty iron furnaces in this region of Ohio. The city of Ironton, in Lawrence County, developed as the shipping point for the iron.

The metal-working industry of Cincinnati grew rapidly by using this iron to produce machinery, steam boilers, and weapons. At Kennesaw Mountain, in northern Georgia,

the scene of a major battle during the Civil War, you can still see many cannons of the Union Army that were made in Cincinnati from Hanging Rock Iron.

Youngstown Area

Mahoning County lies to the northeast of the Hanging Rock Iron formation, but it covers a large deposit of excellent coal and it once had a large deposit of iron ore.

The picture page 185 ahows the Brier Hill Iron Furnace in Mahoning County as Henry Howe saw it in 1886.

By 1880 most of the iron ore of Ohio was used up. Fortunately for the United States, a tremendous supply of iron ore was discovered in northern Minnesota. The biggest problem was to get the ore from Minnesota to the furnaces of Ohio, because there were dangerous rapids at Sault Ste. Marie (the "Soo") between Lake Superior and Lake Huron (look back to page 54).

During the last half of the 19th century, the United States and Canada built a canal and locks at "the Soo" so that large boats could move safely through the strait. Cleveland had a good harbor to receive the ore and railroad and canal connections to the coal fields of eastern Ohio. By 1900 Cleveland had become one of the most important iron and steel manufacturing cities of the world.

Products from Iron

The material that comes from an iron furnace is called **pig iron**, which is a weak and brittle material that is used for only a few products such as window sash weights. But three essential materials are made from it: cast iron, wrought iron, and steel.

Cast iron can be molded into an unlimited number of shapes. In order to make such shapes, forms must be made from a special mixture of sand and clay. Pig iron is heated until it melts, and the liquid metal is poured into a mold. The metal is allowed to cool slowly. You may be surprised to discover that the fronts of many 19th-century store buildings in your county are made of cast iron.

Wrought iron is made by heating pig iron and then beating on it with a heavy hammer, or running it between heavy rollers. It is much stronger than cast iron, and blacksmiths used it to make such things as tools, hinges, and horse shoes.

Steel is a mixture of iron, carbon, and small amounts of other chemicals that improve the qualities of the iron. Again the pig iron is melted, the chemicals are added, and the molten steel is poured into large molds to cool slowly. After it has cooled to the proper temperature, the steel is rolled into a great variety of shapes.

Coal

In Chapter 2 you learned that southeast Ohio contains beds of coal. Early in the 19th century, all coal was mined by digging into a hillside where a layer of coal was visible. As coal became important for generating steam, land owners in southeastern Ohio began to drill holes into the earth in search of *black gold*, as coal was often called. Many of the layers of coal in Ohio are less than 12-inches thick, and none is more than 10-feet thick. In order to have space for miners to work, a coal layer had to be at least 30-inches thick. On the previous page you can see two boys working in a space about 30-inches high.

When a useful layer was found, the owner dug a shaft into the ground, built an elevator, and lowered workers down to the coal. The workers then loosened the coal, loaded it into small rail cars, and rolled the cars to the elevator. In Chapter 14 you will learn how coal is mined today.

As soon as the Pennsylvania and Ohio Branch Canal was built from Akron to Youngstown about 1840, (look back to map on page 120) mine owners in Mahoning

Tne Company Store

By Isaac Hanna, Engelwood,
Illinois, 1895

The lot of the miner
At best is quite hard,
We work for good money,
Get paid by the card;
We scarcely can live,
And not a cent more,
Since we're paid off in checks
On the company store.

Those great coal monopolies
Are growing apace,
They are making their millions
By grinding our face;
Unto their high prices
The people pay toll,
While they pay fifty cents
For mining their coal.

They keep cutting our wages
Time after time,
Where we once had a dollar,
We now have a dime;
While our souls are near famished,
And our bodies are sore
We are paid off in checks
On the company store.

Though hard we may labor
But little we have;
We are robbed of our rights,
Though we fought for the slave
Monop'ly keeps grasping
For more and still more;
They will soon own the earth
Through the company store.

From: Korson: *Coal Dust on the Fiddle*, p.78

County began to ship coal to Cleveland for use in operating the steamships on Lake Erie. In 1848 a young man named James Garfield worked on one of these boats: thirty-two years later, he was elected President of the United States.

In 1902 Ohio produced about 23,500,000 tons of coal, and ranked fourth among the states of the United States in production.

Life of a Miner

How would you like to work at least ten hours every day in a space half as high as you are tall, with your only light coming from oil lamps? Many boys began such work before they were sixteen, and continued until they died twenty, thirty or forty years later.

Who would work under such conditions? Most Ohio miners were immigrants who had worked in the mines of England, Wales, Germany, Sweden, Poland, Hungary, and other places in Europe. Many of the miners gladly came as indentured workers because they wanted to enjoy the freedom of the United States.

When a land owner decided to open a coal mine, he first had to build a town for the miners and their families. These towns were not planned like the towns described in Chapter 9. They were usually built in the cheapest possible way, with only one

The First Oil Well in Ohio

The first oil well in Ohio was drilled in 1814, near the town [of Caldwell, in Noble County] by [a man] drilling for salt brine; but striking oil, it was first covered up, oil not being what was wanted. About two years later, in 1816, a second well was drilled not far from the same spot, also for brine, when they struck oil mixed with the brine. This well was still running oil with the brine when we visited it [in 1846]. ...

The oil went by the name of Seneca oil. Peddlers were accustomed to gather the oil by soaking blankets in the spring, wringing them out of the oil and then travelling the country on horseback and selling it to farmer's wives for rheumatism, sprains, and bruises, for which in its crude state particularly it is especially [effective].

From: Howe: vol.2, p. 353

General Store that was operated by the mine owner. The song on page 188 tells about life in a **company town**.

Can you imagine digging out a ton of coal under the conditions described above? And there were NO *fringe benefits*, such as health, unemployment, or accident insurance!

Petroleum

You have learned about the different natural resources of northwest and southeast Ohio. These regions were similar in one way — both had large reservoirs of petroleum, in the forms of gas and oil, as you can see by looking back to page 24.

The Discovery of Gas in Morgan County

In 1830 Rufus P. Stone was boring near Malta (just east of McConnelsville) for salt water, which he struck at a depth of 400 feet, as well as a flow of natural gas. Mr. Stone, being interested in other **enterprises**, permitted this well to remain idle for some years ...

In 1878 [two men] while boring for oil some two miles south of Malta, struck gas at a depth of 400 feet. The gas was piped a distance of 800 yards, and used as motive power for engines in place of steam.... In addition to the amount used in the engines, a blaze some 30 to 40 feet in height illuminated the hills for miles around, so that fine print could be read at night half a mile distant. Gas was also used for cooking and heating.

From: Howe: vol. 2, p.309

The first oil well in the United States at Titusville, Pennsylvania as it looked in 1866.

190

Petroleum is a dark liquid material that nature created from decaying vegetable material that was buried millions of years ago by shifts of the Earth's crust.

The raw material called *petroleum* includes a great number of useful chemicals varying from gases called *natural gas* and *propane*, to thick fluids called *asphalt* and *paraffin*. Gasoline, kerosene, lubricating oils, and grease or also obtained from petroleum.

For thousands of years human beings have burned oil in lamps to create light. Before 1880 *whale oil* was such an important source of **illumination** (lighting) that thousands of these great sea mammals were killed each year. The **blubber** (fat) was cut off and cooked to make oil, and the rest of the carcass was thrown back into the ocean.

How Gas Was Discovered at Findlay

[People] called [Oesterlen] the "gas fool," and until 1884 he was regarded as a vain dreamer. But patience and **perseverance** at last prevailed and [in 1876] he succeeded in organizing a stock company to drill for gas. The well was a successful one, and when the gas gushed forth with a panting roar and shot a column of flame sixty feet into the air, people were alarmed for a time....

Findlay was a small and almost unknown town when gas was struck. It took a year for the news of the wonderful discoveries to spread, and it was not till 1886, when the great Karg well, with a capacity of 15,000,000 cubic feet daily, was struck, that the attention of the public was arrested by the developments and possibilities at Findlay.

From: Howe: vol. 1, p. 872

Southeast Ohio

You have learned how important salt was to the early settlers in Ohio. The early settlers in the southeastern part of our state knew that they could sometimes find salty water (**brine**) by drilling holes as much as 200 feet deep. The story in the box in the left xolumn on page 189 is about one search for salt. Geologists have learned that salt and petroleum are often found together.

The development of the petroleum industry began in 1859 at Titusville, in the northwest corner of Pennsylvania. By this time entrepreneurs knew that petroleum oil gave better light than whale oil. The picture on page 190 shows the oil well at Titusville in 1866.

Natural Gas

Natural gas is one of the lightest forms of petroleum, and it is often found with oil. However, it is not unusual to drill for petroleum and find gas but no oil. The box in the right column on page 189 is a story of finding of gas in Morgan County.

Northwest Ohio

Natural gas was discovered in northwest Ohio at about the same time it was found in the southeast, but it was ignored for a longer time in the northwest. For almost forty years, a man named Charles Oesterlen, of Hancock County, was convinced (believed deeply) that there was petroleum under the ground. The box on page 191 tells part of the story.

Within a short time gas and oil wells were being drilled throughout the northwest corner of Ohio.

During the first twenty years after petroleum was found in Ohio, two products were most important: kerosene to replace whale oil in lamps, and lubricating oil and grease to reduce **friction** (loss of energy due to rubbing) in machinery. Today few places sell kerosene, but two similar petroleum products, diesel fuel and heating oil, are used widely. All of our systems of transportation and manufacturing depend on lubricating oils and grease to maintain efficiency.

John D. Rockefeller

In 1839 a baby was born in upstate New York, and given the name John Davidson Rockefeller. By the time he died in 1937, he was one of the richest men in the world.

John's father earned his living by selling *Seneca oil*, that you read about earlier, and other *patent medicines*. The family moved to Strongsville, in Cuyahoga County, when John was fourteen years of age. Four years later John went into business with a friend, and they were very successful. A few years later, he became interested in refining petroleum, and by 1865 he and a partner were transporting, refining, and selling petroleum products in Cleveland. In 1870 John organized a new company and named it the *Standard Oil Company* as described in the box on this page.

U.S. Petroleum Production
During 19th Century

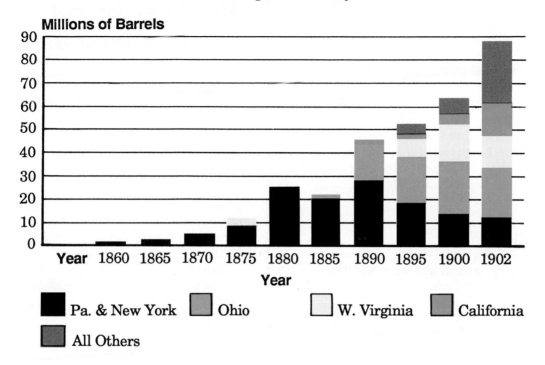

Millions of Barrels

Legend:
- Pa. & New York
- Ohio
- W. Virginia
- California
- All Others

Oil Pipelines

The discovery of large deposits of petroleum in northwest Ohio took place at about the same time the iron industry learned to make high-quality cast iron pipes. Since petroleum is a liquid, the easiest way to move it is through pipes. In 1887 there were 70 oil wells in the city of Lima in Allen County, and more than 300 wells in the Lima oil field, which reached into Auglaize and Mercer Counties. In fact the first underwater oil field in the world was developed in Auglaize and Mercer Counties in Grand Lake St. Marys. All of this oil moved to refineries through pipes.

The graph on this page shows petroleum production in the United States from 1860 through 1902. This clearly shows the importance of Ohio petroleum in the development of the United States. By 1902 a very small amount of gasoline was being made for automobiles.

Clay Products and Ceramics

Clay has little value as it is found in nature. If you mix certain kinds of clay with water, you can mold it into a wide variety of shapes. If you heat a molded shape in an oven, you can create a useful product, such as a brick or a piece of pottery. If you heat the molded clay to a very high temperature, in a **Kiln** (oven), you can produce a **ceramic** (from the Greek work meaning pottery) material. All furnaces that operate at high temperatures, including those used

193

to smelt iron, are lined with ceramic blocks called *fire bricks*. It was difficult to make such products before gas was available.

Farm Tile

You have learned that much of the land in northwest Ohio was swampy, and that the water had to be removed in order to create productive farms. Simple ditches were not effective until farmers learned how to use clay-tile pipes to carry the surface water to the ditches. By 1890 there were 500 factories in Ohio producing farm tile and other clay products.

East Liverpool

Good clay and natural gas were available in the vicinity of East Liverpool in Columbiana County. In 1840 the first factory was opened there for making ordinary dishes. During the Civil War the Congress of the United States levied a **tariff** (tax) on pottery and dishes brought into the United States from other countries. This tariff made the cost of clay products imported from England so expensive that few people could buy them.

Pottery owners in East Liverpool immediately expanded production of ordinary dishes and began to make higher-quality products. By 1890 East Liverpool had 18 potteries that employed almost 2,200 workers. On page 196 you can see the largest factory, which employed 613 workers. Today you can visit the Pottery Museum in East Liverpool to learn about this great industry, but very few clay products have been made there since World War II.

Manufacturing in Springfield

In 1838, James Leffel, whose name should be honored here and elsewhere as Springfield's greatest pioneer inventor and manufacturer, built the first foundry and machine-shop ever erected in this vicinity.... Here sickles, axes, and knives were manufactured, and various iron implements in use among the people were repaired. Mr. Leffel afterward invented the double turbine and waterwheel ... [that] is now manufactured by the firm of James Leffel & Co. in this city, and sent to all points of the globe. [Leffel turbines are still made and widely used today.] ...

In 1852 was born the great Champion industry, William N. Whiteley having in that year invented the Champion reaper and mower, which by 1887 has come to be much the largest and most important harvester industry in the world....

From: Howe, vol. 1, pages 399-400

Glass

In many places of the world, archaeologists have found glass objects made thousands of years ago. Glass is a ceramic material made from sand rather than clay. To make glass you need silica sand and a source of heat that can be controlled very accurately at high temperatures. Lucas County had deposits of the good sand, but no

Champion Factory in Springfield

satisfactory fuel. When natural gas was discovered to the south of Lucas County, several glass factories were built in northwest Ohio. Glass factories were also built in Muskingum and Guernsey counties. Most of the products made in Ohio were bottles and jars, plates and drinking glasses, and window glass for everyday use, but beautiful art glass was also created.

In 1902 Ohio ranked seventh among the states of the United States in the production of clay products and fourth in the production of glass. Today you can visit museums of glass products at Cambridge in Guernsey County and at the Toledo Museum of Art.

Manufacturing

The word *manufacture* comes from the Latin words, *manu* and *factus*, which mean "made by hand." For the past 200 years the word *manufactured* has been used to describe things made by machinery.

Springfield in Clark County was one of the first cities in Ohio to develop large-scale manufacturing. The box on page 194 tells a story related to the factory you can see above.

The city of Dayton had a great variety of manufacturing plants. The people living

195

The Knowles, Taylor & Knowles Pottery in East Liverpool, Ohio, was one of the largest in the world.

there today may be surprised to learn that in 1888 Dayton had more factories producing cigars than any other product: eleven companies employed a total of more than 1,200 people in that activity. In that same year the National Cash Register Company (NCR) employed only seventy-nine workers. You will learn more about NCR in Chapter 12.

Present citizens of Cincinnati may be even more surprised to learn that in 1888 more than 3,300 workers in that city made products from tobacco. In that year, over 14,000 workers in Cincinnati produced products made from iron, including

machine tools, that is, machines used to make other machines. In 1900 Cincinnati ranked ninth in total manufacturing production of all cities of the United States, and Cleveland ranked tenth.

If you want to see how the industry of Ohio, and the entire United States, evolved during the 19th century, you should visit *Greenfield Village* and the *Henry Ford Museum* at Dearborn, Michigan, just a few miles north of Toledo on I-75. Plan to spend a full day at each of these great museums of American history and industry.

Stop and Think!

When Ohio became a state in 1803, its citizens had three resources that the natives did not have: iron tools, knowledge of the basic principles of science, and the desire to have more comfortable lives.

Tools helped them to clear the forests for agriculture, and to use the natural resources of the earth. Knowledge of science helped them to use the power of steam and the products of petroleum. The economic system of the United States encouraged entrepreneurs to invest personal effort and money in trying new ideas. From these ideas came new ways of working that produced more goods from less human labor.

As Ohio became an industrial state, many people had to work at hard physical labor, but a majority of them were able to create better lives for themselves. A small number of people gained such great wealth and political power that they were able to exercise great influence over the state and federal governments, as you will learn in the next chapter.

Review the Chapter!

Building vocabulary...

blubber
brine
burr stone
cast iron
ceramic
charcoal
coke
company town
concrete
convince

distilling
enterprise
extract
flax
flywheel
illumination
industry
kiln
live stock
lye
machine tool
manufacture
mercantile
mortar
nursery (plants)
perseverance
pig iron
Portland cement
slaughter
smelt
steel
tallow
tanning
tariff
turbine
wrought iron

Meeting new people...

John D. Rockefeller   James A. Garfield

Testing yourself...

Fill in the Blanks...

1. Three forms of energy available to workers in 1800 were ...., ... and ....
2. Because milk sours quickly, farmers used it to make .... which lasts much longer.
3. Water wheels were used to power mills that .... or ....
4. The process of changing a hide into a piece of leather is called ....

197

5. Linen is made from .... plants.
6. .... and .... are extractive industries.
7. Many buildings in Ohio were built of Berea ....
8. An oven used to make pottery is called a ....
9. The city of .... was a center of pottery-making in the United States.
10. The main source of oil for lamps was once fat from ....
11. Petroleum was accidently discovered by a man drilling for ....
12. The heaviest products obtained from petroleum are known as .... or ....
13. Three important raw materials of Ohio were .... and ....
14. The process of making pig iron is called ....
15. In 1900, the two most important manufacturing cities in Ohio were .... and ....

Why is it true or false?

1. Pioneer women used nuts and berries to dye their yarns.
2. Many people worked at making tobacco products in Ohio.
3. The Hanging Rock Region was most important for its beautiful scenery.
4. Ceramic materials were used in iron furnaces.
5. Most of the iron ore used at Cleveland was carried there by railroad.
6. Pig iron is stronger than wrought iron.
7. When oil was first discovered in Ohio, the owner of the land was unhappy.
8. The first product made by Procter and Gamble was whale oil.
9. John D. Rockefeller founded the Standard Oil Company.
10. Northeastern Ohio was very swampy until the land was drained.

Thinking It through...

1. Explain the difference between cast iron, wrought iron, and steel. What is each used for?
2. How did the discovery of natural gas affect the development of industry in Ohio?
3. What does the song "The Company Store" reveal about working conditions of a coal miner?
4. How is stone better construction material than wood? Why is wood used more widely than stone?
5. What benefits did people of the 19th century receive from petroleum?

Working with maps...

1. Use the map on page 24 and your map of Ohio to identify counties where you would expect to find both coal and petroleum.
2. Use the map on page 4 as a guide to lay off the diagonal band 50 miles (80 km) wide on your map of Ohio. Which cities discussed in this chapter lie within the band?
3. On the map of the United States, lay out a route that boats followed to carry iron ore from Minnesota to Cleveland.
4. On the map of the world, locate the countries from which miners came to work in Ohio.

CHAPTER 11

How was Ohio governed during the 19th century?

Be ready to learn...

- how the first Constitution of Ohio guided development of our state.

- why a second constitution became necessary.

- about the development of education in Ohio.

- about the Presidents of the United States from Ohio.

- about the political and social problems of the 19th century.

In Chapter 6 you learned that the most important purposes of government are: (1) to protect citizens from turmoil within the boundaries of the unit of government and from enemies outside; (2) to keep records of all important events, and (3) to collect money, in the form of taxes, to pay for the necessary services. In this chapter you will learn how the earliest laws of Ohio tried to meet these purposes, and how developments during the 19th century forced changes in the laws. You can see how the population of each county grew by turning to Appendix B.

Types of Laws

Every year toy manufacturers develop many new games. If you receive a new game as a gift, what is the first thing you do after opening the box and examining it? You must read the rules! If there are too many rules, or if you cannot understand them, what do you do? Perhaps you never look at the game again. But if you do learn the rules, and are willing to play by them, you may have great pleasure from this gift. Life is pleasant in your community, your county, and your state only when everyone plays by the rules — which are called laws.

There are three basic types of laws in the United States: constitutional law, statutory law, and common law. A constitution is the legal framework for existence and operation of a government. All other laws must be written and enforced in ways that do not conflict with this constitution. The Supreme Court of the United States hears only cases that are related to the meaning of the Constitution of the United States. The Supreme Court of Ohio hears only cases related to the constitution of our state.

Units of government adopt *statutory* laws to guide the activities of citizens to achieve the goals of government. Have you ever heard someone say, "There ought to be a law against that!" If the problem the person is talking about has existed for a long time, there probably *is* a statutory law about it, although the law may not be enforced very well. On the other hand, if the problem

arises from a situation that no one has ever considered, it may be necessary to create a new *statutory* law.

Lawmaking bodies, from Congress to the General Assembly to a city council, can make laws only about conditions that exist or can be expected. As time passes and events change, *statutory* laws must be changed to meet the new conditions, but every statutory law must be in harmony with the constitution of the governmental unit.

How do you solve problems in daily living if there are no laws or *rules* to cover a situation? Do you try to use *common sense*? When such a situation arises in a legal argument, the court may have to follow the practices of *common law* in order to reach a fair decision. One example of common law that you may have heard is, "Your right to swing your fist ends one inch in front of my nose." Court decisions based on this principle cannot conflict with the constitution.

Constitution of the United States

The basic idea that guided the leaders who wrote the Constitution of the United States was "The less government there is, the better it is for the people." The first **article** (major division) of the Constitution of the United States defined the powers of the Congress and the relationship of the government of the United States to the governments of the individual states. For example, it said that no state could adopt a law that conflicted with a law of the United States.

The first ten amendments to the Constitution were adopted in 1791; they are known as the *Bill of Rights*. Three of these *rights* are very important to the operation of every state government.

You can still see 19th-century school houses along the rural roads of Ohio.

Many old schools like this one on Rt. 127 in Darke County are now used for a variety of purposes.

Amendment I. Congress shall make no law respecting an establishment of religion, or **prohibiting** the free exercise thereof; or **abridging** the freedom of speech, or of the press; or the right of the people peaceably to assemble, and to petition the government for **redress** of grievances.

Amendment II. A well-regulated militia, being necessary to the security of a free State, the right of the people to keep and **bear** arms, shall not be **infringed**.

Amendment X. The powers not delegated to the United States by the Constitution, nor prohibited by it to the States, are reserved to the States **respectively**, or to the people. You will learn more about these articles later in this chapter and in Chapter 15.

First Constitution of Ohio

In Chapter 6 you learned how leaders from the various counties of Ohio met at Chillicothe in 1802 to write a constitution for the state of Ohio. Although it was replaced by a new constitution in 1851, the first constitution still affects our lives because it guided the development of Ohio for almost fifty years.

The first three articles of the constitution of Ohio were directly related to the first three articles of the Constitution of the United States. The first articles of both defined the way laws would be made by representatives of the people in the Congress of the United States and the General Assembly of Ohio. The second articles defined how the chief executives — the President of the United States and the Governor of Ohio — would carry out the laws. The third articles defined how courts would be established to ensure justice in enforcing the laws.

Article VIII of the Ohio constitution was the State's *Bill of Rights*. It included some interesting "rights" not mentioned in the Constitution of the United States.

Section 1. "... all men ... have certain rights... [including] .. enjoying and defending life and liberty, acquiring, possessing, and protecting property, and pursuing and obtaining happiness and safety...."

Section 7. "[All courts shall be open to] every person, for injury done him in his lands, goods, person, or reputation ...."

Section 15. "[A person in debt] shall not be continued in prison after delivering up his estate for the benefit of his creditor ...."

Section 25. "... no law shall be passed to prevent the poor ... within this State from an equal participation in the schools ... [that receive money from] ... the United States ...."

Section 27. "... every association of persons, when regularly formed, ...

and having given themselves a name, may ... be entitled to receive letters of incorporation ...."

The remainder of the constitution was a plan for changing from the territorial form of government to the state form. We shall now look at how sections of this constitution related to the purposes of government listed in the introduction to this chapter.

To Protect Citizens from Turmoil

External Threats

Turmoil is always a threat to the life of a nation. If an enemy attacks a defenseless nation, it may be destroyed. During the 19th century, the United States was attacked once by a foreign nation — in the War of 1812. The Constitution of the United States gave Congress the power to create an army and navy to protect against external attacks.

Militia

When the American colonies decided to break away from Great Britain, they had no army or navy. Every community in the colonies had militiamen who met together to drill and practice shooting so that they could defend the community from outlaws or threatening natives. The "armies" that marched north out of Fort Washington under the leadership of Generals Harmar, St. Clair, and Wayne were made up largely of militiamen.

Because the militia was so important on the frontier, Article II, Section 10, of the original state constitution said, "[The Governor] shall be Commander-in-Chief of the army and navy of this State, and of the militia, except when they shall be called into service of the United States." Article V

Portrait of William Henry Harrison. This lithograph was made in 1846 from a daguerrretype.

William Henry Harrison's campaign for the presidency was the first to use advertising "gimmicks" like this.

said how the different levels of officers would be appointed.

When the second constitution was adopted in 1851, all items relating to the militia were combined in Article IX. Section 1 of this article said:

"All white male citizens, residents of this state, being eighteen years of age, and under the age of forty-five years, shall be

enrolled in the militia, and perform military duty ... as may be prescribed by law."

This requirement for service in the militia existed until the *National Guard* system was established throughout the United States shortly after World War I.

Right to Bear Arms

Section 20 of the Bill of Rights of the first constitution of Ohio said: "That the people have a right to bear arms for the defense of themselves and the State; and as standing armies in time of peace are dangerous to liberty, they shall not be kept .." Section 4 of Article I of the Second Ohio Constitution used almost the same words.

What do you know about "gun control" laws? If someone in your family has been killed or wounded by a bullet, your parents may be very active in a group that is trying to get your city, state, or national government to prohibit the sale of guns. If someone in your family is a member of the National Rifle Association, you have almost certainly heard that the Bill of Rights guarantees citizens the right to own guns. These differing opinions have created political turmoil for many years.

Internal Threats

A nation may also suffer from internal turmoil, such as that caused by uprisings of the Native Americans. Another form of internal trouble arises when citizens do not obey the laws of the land. If the government cannot control such turmoil, the nation may collapse or be overwhelmed by a foreign power.

Dishonest people who break fair laws create turmoil in the society. A person who drinks alcohol, then drives an automobile and injures or kills another person, is creating turmoil. On the other hand, some laws may be unfair to honest people, or a police officer may enforce a law unfairly. The Bills of Rights of the United States, and the first and second constitutions of Ohio protect the rights of all honest citizens, and even guarantee fair treatment for dishonest people.

Systems of Justice

Have you ever said, "All I want is a fair deal?" The basic idea of *justice* is that everyone concerned with a problem gets a "fair deal."

All three branches of government are important in our system of justice: the **legislative** branch creates laws; the **executive** branch, through a police system, enforces the laws; and the **judicial** branch decides on punishment for breaking the laws, or decides whether the laws are constitutional.

In the early days of statehood, it was very difficult for the judicial system to provide quick justice. There were only a small number of judges, the population was spread across a large area, and transportation was slow. Two sections of Article III of the first constitution dealt with this problem. Section 10 said that the Supreme Court of Ohio would meet in every county once each year. Section 11 said that the residents of each township would elect *Justices of the Peace* to serve as local judges.

Can you imagine how difficult it was for the Supreme Court to meet in each county every year? To solve this problem, the Constitution was amended in 1874 to create a system of twelve *Courts of Appeal*. The office of Justice of the Peace was abolished in 1957, but we still have courts operated by mayors of incorporated places.

Photograph of Ulysses S. Grant during his last year as President of the United States.

To Keep Records
of All Important Events

Do you keep a diary? Many people do keep diaries of the events of their lives — at least for a short time. Some of the most important sources of information about the early history of the United States are the diaries of people who wrote about their daily activities.

In order to have good government, it is **essential** (absolutely necessary) that every unit of government keep accurate written records of every action it takes. For this reason, the position of *Clerk* or *Secretary* is as important as the position of legislator, governor, or judge.

Many important records are kept in government offices; some in city offices, some in county offices, and some in state offices. If your parents lived in a city when you were born, your birth certificate should be in the records of that city. If they lived in an unincorporated area, your certificate should be in a county office. A record of your birth is very important in two situations: when you apply for *Social Security* benefits, and when you want a **passport** (proof of citizenship) to travel outside the United States.

For many people, the most important public records are those relating to the ownership of land. All land records for a given county must be on file in the office of the *County Recorder*. No one should buy a parcel of land until a lawyer who is skilled in searching land records is satisfied that all of the records for that parcel are in order!

To Collect Money
for Public Services

During the 19th century, the state of Ohio had very few sources of income, and provided very few services. The most important sources of income for the cities and counties were **real estate** taxes on land and buildings, and **personal property** taxes on private possessions, such as furniture, art work, jewelry, books.

As more and more people moved into Ohio, they wanted more and more services from the cities, counties, and the state. For this reason, the constitution had to be changed to create new ways to raise money.

Second Constitution

By 1850 the leaders of Ohio found that they could not operate efficiently under the existing constitution for three reasons. First, the population had reached almost two million people spread over such a large area that the court system could not provide prompt and fair justice. Second, the problems of the many villages and cities could not be handled by the General Assembly. And third, so many business corporations were being formed that the General Assembly could not consider each application. The people of Ohio, therefore, voted to call a Constitutional Convention. The convention began its work in May 1850 and finished in March 1851. The proposed new constitution was approved by the citizens of Ohio in June 1851. This Second Constitution had many new features. You have already read about a few of them and we can look at only a few more.

The first article of the new constitution was a *Bill of Rights*. This Bill of Rights was very similar to that of the First Constitution, but it included one new idea that is essential to the operation of government, namely, the principle of **eminent domain** (highest level of ownership).

Eminent domain

When people "buy" pieces of land, what they really buy is exclusive use of the described parcels. The real, or highest, "ownership" of the land continues to rest with the government. If the government needs a piece of land for public use — perhaps for a new highway or a new building — the government can buy the land whether or not the owner wants to sell it.

Public Debt

In Chapter 7 you learned that the people of Ohio were so eager to have better transportation that state and local units of government freely went into debt to build canals and railroads. By 1850 Ohio was so far in debt that the new constitution included a section that said: "The state may contract debts to ... meet expenses ... but the **aggregate** amount of such debts ... shall never exceed seven hundred and fifty thousand dollars...." One hundred years after this law was passed, it was changed, as you will learn in Chapter 15.

Corporations

All of the corporations formed before 1851 were established on an individual basis by the General Assembly. The new constitution said that the General Assembly would create general laws for forming new corporations, and would no longer make a new law for each new company.

Counties and Townships

Since the First Constitution made no provision for the incorporation of villages and cities, the General Assembly had to pass a law for each group of citizens that wanted to form a village or city. Article X of the new constitution instructed the General Assembly to adopt statutory laws to control the government of villages and cities, and appointed a person to supervise these laws. As long as the laws were followed, the incorporated places could make many decisions for themselves.

Article XV of Second Constitution —"Miscellaneous"

Article XV of the new constitution, headed MISCELLANEOUS, included three sections that are amusing today.

Section 5 said that no person who fought a duel, or helped someone else fight, could be elected to any public office.

Section 6 said, "Lotteries, and the sale of lottery tickets, for any purpose whatever, shall forever be prohibited in this state."

Section 9 said, "No license to [sell] intoxicating liquors shall ... be granted in this state; but the General Assembly may, by law, provide against the evils resulting [from such sale]."

President Grant was born in this house at Point Pleasant. The man shown is the physician who helped Mrs. Grant with the birth of Ulysses.

Proposed Constitution of 1874

By 1873 some people were unhappy with the constitution of 1851. Another Constitutional Convention has called, and another constitution was written. When the voters of Ohio were asked to decide whether to adopt the new document, they voted against it. The constitution we live under today is the one adopted in 1851 with amendments that have been adopted from time to time.

Education

As you learned in Chapter 5, the founders of the United States were well-educated people. They knew that the success of the new form of government they were creating depended on having well-educated citizens in the future. For this reason, they included the following ideas in the Public Land Act of 1785:

Currier and Ives lithograph made from a photograph of Rutherford B. Hayes made about 1877.

"There shall be reserved [section] No. 16, of every [public land survey] township for the maintenance of public schools within the said township; also one-third of all gold, silver, lead, and copper mines, to be sold, or otherwise disposed of, as Congress shall direct."

You can look back to page 71 to see where Section 16 is in every part of Ohio that has this pattern of subdivision. No gold, silver, lead, or copper was ever found in Ohio.

The land companies you learned about in Chapter 5 had to put Section 16 of every township they surveyed under control of a group of **trustees** (caretakers) who could rent the land. The rental income could be used only to pay for education. A different system was used for the Western Reserve and Virginia Military Reserve because there were no Sections. This proved to be an unsatisfactory system, and in 1826 the General Assembly sold all the school lands and put the money into a state fund to be used for financing public schools.

The second constitution made far more provisions for education than the first one. It gave the General Assembly power to raise taxes to support free public schools, but prohibited use of public money for private or church-related schools. As soon as the new constitution was approved by the voters, the General Assembly adopted a set of laws to guide the development of what they called "common schools" in Ohio. One part of this law said:

"The ... boards of education in this State ... are ... required to establish within their respective [school districts], one or more separate schools for colored children, when the whole number [of these children] by enumeration exceeds thirty ... ."

You must remember that this law was written in 1851 when there were very few African-Americans living in Ohio.

What Schools Were Like

Almost all of the earliest schools were one-room buildings built on small tracts of land donated by land owners. The buildings shown on page 201 are typical of 19th-century schools you can still see today. Many of these buildings have been unused for more than fifty years, but others are used for a variety of purposes.

Perhaps thirty children, ranging in age from six years to fourteen (few children went to school beyond age fourteen), learned from one teacher. The teacher usually had a high-school education, and received a small salary plus "room and board." This means that the teacher had a sleeping room and ate with a family that lived near the school. Classes were scheduled to permit the children to help on the farms when they were needed. You can visit one-room schoolhouses at Hale Farm in Summit County and at the Ohio Village in Columbus.

Before 1850, many city schools were private **academies** (private high schools) that charged tuition for the instruction. This means that children from poor families seldom went to school. As immigration began to swell the populations of the cities, many evening classes were offered to teach English and prepare newcomers for citizenship. By 1900 there were public schools in all the cities.

Some church groups, and especially the Roman Catholic Church, established schools for the children of their parishes. Because of laws relating to the "separation of church and state" in the constitutions of Ohio and

Ohio and the Three R's

Three young men from Ohio revolutionized the teaching of the "Three R's" of elementary education — "readin, 'ritin, and 'rithmetic" — during the 19th century.

William Holmes McGuffey was two years old in 1802 when his parents moved to what is now the city of Warren in Trumbull County. He received almost all of his education from his mother, Anna McKittrick McGuffey, until he was eighteen years of age. In 1818 he had a chance to go to an academy for two years. He did so well in this school that he enrolled in a college in western Pennsylvania.

When he finished college in 1826, he went directly to Miami University at Oxford, Ohio as an instructor in Greek, Latin, and Hebrew languages. He had great difficulty teaching these languages because his students spoke so many forms of English. To help his students, McGuffey wrote a "reading" book that proved to be so useful that he wrote five more. These books revolutionized the teaching of reading, and more than 130 million copies were used by generations of school children. Today you can buy reprints of *McGuffey Readers*.

Platt Roger Spencer was born in New York State in the same year as William McGuffey. At the age of nine, he became fascinated with writing, but he had no paper. He wrote on birch bark with a quill pen and ink made from berries, and in sand with a stick, but he wrote and wrote in a beautiful style. In 1810, his mother moved her family to Ashtabula County, and enrolled Platt in a school at Conneaut. Before long the teacher was letting Platt teach his classmates how to write clearly.

When he finished school, Platt Spencer had no trouble finding jobs in which clear hand writing was important. (Typewriters were invented about 1890!) When his fellow workers saw his beautiful writing, some of them paid him to teach them how to write. His system of *Spencerian handwriting* became the model for instruction in schools throughout the United States.

Joseph Ray was born in Cincinnati about ten years later than William McGuffey and Platt Spencer. By the time he was sixteen years old, he was teaching mathematics in Cincinnati. He then went to school at Ohio University at Athens, Ohio but did not have enough money to continue there. His father persuaded him to study medicine in Cincinnati. Even while practicing medicine, his first and only love was mathematics.

A few years after Woodward High School was organized in Cincinnati in 1831, Joseph Ray was hired to teach mathematics. The textbook assigned for the course was so difficult to understand that he wrote a new one. By the time his career ended, Joseph Ray had written fifteen books on mathematics that were used throughout the United States.

As you can see, three young men from Ohio had tremendous influence on education in the United States.

Based on Siedel, "Three R's", in *Out of the Midwest*

The Hayes family enjoying life in the White House.

the United States, no tax money could be given to these schools.

Earliest Colleges

When the Ohio Company and John Cleves Symmes purchased their large tracts of land from Congress, Congress required that they set aside land to support institutions of higher learning. The Ohio Company set

aside 46,080 acres (72 square miles or 185 square kilometers) in what is now Athens County. When the General Assembly met in 1804, the legislators established Ohio University on this land. Today Ohio University receives only about $4,500 income from this land each year.

When Congress sold him the land between the Miami Rivers, John Cleves Symmes

Photograph of James A. Garfield taken during the last year of his life.

214

An artist's idea of the assassination of President James Garfield.

agreed to set aside one township (36 square miles or 92 square kilometers) to support higher education. By the time the General Assembly was ready to establish a college in southwest Ohio, Symmes had sold all of his land between the Miami Rivers. The legislature, therefore, chose a tract of the same size in the territory between the Great Miami River and the Ohio-Indiana border, and established Miami University there. Miami opened as an academy in 1818, and became a college in 1824.

Morrill Act

In 1862 Congress passed what is known as the *Morrill Act* to provide financing, in the form of land, for each state to establish a school for "agricultural and mechanic arts." This act led to the founding of the Colleges of Engineering and Agriculture at The Ohio State University. The United States gave each state large areas of unsold public lands to finance these new schools, similar to the lands set aside for Ohio and Miami Universities. Since all of Ohio was subdivided by the time the Morrill Act became effective, the United States turned over to Ohio all parcels of land in the Virginia Military Reserve that had not yet been claimed. These tracts of land were sold, and the money was used for The Ohio State University.

The Role of Ohio in National Government

Political leaders from Ohio have played important roles in the history of the United States. You can turn back to Appendix C to see the names of the governors of our state,

215

and the more important national offices some of them held.

Many people in Ohio like to say that our state was the home of eight Presidents of the United States! It is true that eight men who served as President spent parts of their lives in Ohio, but other states in which some of them lived also take "credit" for them. While this chapter deals with government in the 19th century, we shall consider all of the Presidents with Ohio ties.

The system used today to solicit votes for the candidates for president is quite different than that used before the days of radio and television. But two features have not changed: it takes much hard work and a large amount of money to be elected.

William Henry Harrison

William Henry Harrison (1773-1841) was the ninth President of the United States, but he served for only a few weeks. On page 203 is a portrait of him. You learned several things about Mr. Harrison in Chapters 5 and 6. During the fifteen years following the end of the War of 1812, he served in a variety of state and national political offices.

In 1836 the leaders of the *Whig Party* of the United States were searching for a candidate for president who could defeat the popular Democrat Martin Van Buren. They nominated Mr. Harrison, but Van Buren won. In 1840, the leaders of the Whig Party again nominated Mr. Harrison to run against Van Buren. This time the Whig Party emphasized Harrison's role in the frontier wars, and created the slogan, "Tippecanoe and Tyler too!" to remind voters that General Harrison had won the Battle of Tippecanoe. James Tyler was the Whig candidate for Vice President.

The "buckeye" was adopted as a symbol of the campaign. On page 204 you can see a picture of a souvenir of the Harrison campaign.

We do not know what kind of President Mr. Harrison would have been because he became ill on the day of his **inauguration** (beginning of official duties) in March 1841, and died a few weeks later. Mr. Harrison was married to Anna Symmes, a daughter of John Cleves Symmes, but she did not even have an opportunity to move to Washington.

Ulysses Simpson Grant

Ulysses Simpson Grant (1822-1885) was the eighteenth President of the United States. He served two terms from 1869 to 1877. You can see his portrait on page 206. A boy named Hiram Ulysses Grant was born in 1822 at Point Pleasant, on the Ohio River in Clermont County, in the house shown on page 209. The man in the picture is the doctor who helped Mrs. Grant during the birth of Hiram. You can visit this house today.

In 1823 his parents moved to Georgetown, the county seat of Brown County. You can also visit Grant's boyhood home and school in Georgetown. In later years when asked about his earliest experiences in school, Mr. Grant said that his two men teachers gave more attention to beatings than to books. As a teenager "Lyss," as he was called, went to an academy at Ripley operated by the Rev. John Rankin. After Lyss finished this school, his father had enough political influence to get him an appointment to the U.S. Military Academy at West Point in 1839.

When Hiram Ulysses Grant presented himself for registration at West Point, there

216

An artist made this charcoal and chalk drawing of Benjamin Harrison about the time he became president.

An artist painted this portrait of William McKinley shortly after he became president.

was no record of him because the appointment had been made in the name of Ulysses Simpson Grant (Simpson was his mother's family name). Grant immediately changed his name in order to enter the academy. Never again did he live in Ohio.

During the Civil War, General Grant led armies of the North to great victories at Vicksburg, Mississippi, and Chattanooga, Tennessee. In April 1865, his troops defeated the Confederate Army under General Robert E. Lee, and ended the Civil War with the treaty signed at Appomattox, Virginia.

At this point the **political bosses** (people who control political decisions) of both the Democratic and Republican Parties encouraged this famous man to run for president with their party. (The Republican Party grew out of the former Whig Party.) No one knew what Mr. Grant thought about any public issue when he finally agreed to run as a Republican in 1868. The United States faced many great problems in trying to restore the economic and political health of the South. Mr. Grant had some good ideas about solving these problems, but he was surrounded by assistants who were determined to punish the South and members of Congress who were trying to gain wealth and power for themselves.

Ulysses S. Grant completed his second term as president in 1877. Later, he received a contract from a publishing company to write his autobiography. This well-written book, *Personal Memoirs*, was completed while he was very ill, and he died in New York in July, 1885 just four days after finishing the writing.

Rutherford Birchard Hayes

Rutherford B. Hayes (1822-1893) was the nineteenth President of the United States, serving from 1877 to 1881. Mr. Hayes, whose portrait is on page 210, was born in Delaware, Ohio, in 1822, about two months after his father had died. He attended Kenyon College, in Knox County, and then studied law at Harvard University. He practiced law in Fremont, Sandusky County. In a few years, he moved to Cincinnati and became a prosperous lawyer. He then married Lucy Ware Webb, who proved to be a great help in his career.

In 1864 he was elected as a Republican to the U.S. House of Representatives. He served as Governor of Ohio from 1868 to 1872. When he finished the second term as governor, Hayes moved his family back to Fremont, and had his home there for the rest of his life. When the Republican Party asked him run for Governor again in 1875, he was re-elected. In the following year, Republican Party leaders nominated him to be President of the United States. The voting was so close, that Congress had to decide in March, 1877 that Mr. Hayes had won.

The United States faced many difficulties while Mr. Hayes was president, including **reconstruction** (rebuilding) of the South, and growing conflicts between big businesses and workers. Many members of Congress were controlled by wealthy businessmen, so Mr. Hayes had little influence over the laws that were passed.

When he was elected, Hayes said that he would serve only one term, so in 1881 he returned to his home in Fremont. Mr. Hayes was a devout family man, and pictures of his family in the White House, like that shown on page 213, made people feel confident about the president. Today you can visit the Hayes home and the Hayes Presidential Center in Fremont.

James Abram Garfield

James A. Garfield (1831-1881) was elected the twentieth President of the United States in 1880, but he served for only a few months before dying from a gunshot wound. You learned a bit about his youth in Chapter 10. His portrait is on page 214.

James Garfield was born in Tuscarawas County while his father was in charge of building a section of the Ohio and Erie Canal. The family soon moved to Cuyahoga County, where the father died when James was two years old. His mother, Eliza Ballou Garfield, worked very hard at low-paying jobs so that her son could go to school.

James Garfield was one of the first students to enroll in Hiram College in Portage County, and earned part of his expenses by helping to build the college. At the age of twenty-seven, he was appointed President of Hiram College.

Mr. Garfield was elected to the Ohio Senate in 1859. While serving as an officer in the Civil War, he was elected to the United States House of Representatives as a Republican, and served well for almost twenty years. In 1880 he attended the Republican National Convention to support another Ohio citizen — John Sherman — in his bid for nomination as President. Mr. Sherman was born in Fairfield County, but lived as an adult in Richland County. The leaders of various **factions** (sides) of the Republican Party could not agree on a candidate. When someone suddenly

suggested Mr. Garfield for the position, he received the nomination.

The various factions did work together to elect Garfield in November, 1880, and he was sworn in as President in March, 1881. He appointed strong people to assist him, and made a good start at being President. On July 2, 1881, Mr. Garfield was shot by a mentally ill man to whom he refused to give a government job. Garfield died two months later and was buried in Lakeview Cemetery in Cleveland. The picture on page 215 shows a reporter's idea of the shooting.

Benjamin Harrison

Benjamin Harrison (1833-1901) was the twenty-third President of the United States, serving from 1889 to 1893. A portrait of him is on page 217.

Mr. Harrison was born in 1833 at North Bend in Hamilton County at the home of his grandfather, William Henry Harrison. After graduating from Miami University in Butler County in 1852, he studied law. In 1853 he married Caroline Lavinia Scott, and they moved to Indianapolis, Indiana, where they lived the remainder of their lives.

Mr. Harrison became deeply involved in politics and church work and always put moral considerations before political advantage. He served one term in the United States Senate from 1881 to 1887, and attracted the attention of the powerful leaders of the Republican Party.

Benjamin Harrison was elected President in 1888. In his inaugural speech to the nation, he promised reforms in the employment policies of the government, pensions for veterans of the Civil War, and the right for

The people of Ohio honored William McKinley by building this memorial to him in Canton. The picture was taken on the day of dedication.

African-Americans to vote. He could not fulfill these promises because he was overpowered by the people who controlled the Republican Party. In 1893 Benjamin Harrison returned to his home in Indianapolis, and died there in 1901. You can visit that home in Indianapolis today.

William McKinley

William McKinley (1843-1901) was the twenty-fifth President of the United States,

serving from 1897 until he was assassinated in 1901, at the beginning of his second term in office. The picture on page 218 is a portrait of him as president.

Mr. McKinley was born in 1843 at Niles in Trumbull County. He attended a college in western Pennsylvania for a short time, and then enlisted in the army during the Civil

An artist made this etching of President Wiliam Howard Taft in 1911.

War. Later he studied law in New York State. In 1867 he established a law office in Canton in Stark County, and became active in political affairs. He married Ida Saxton in 1871.

Mr. McKinley served in the United States House of Representatives from 1877 to 1883, and from 1885 to 1891. He was then elected Governor of Ohio for two terms. Marcus A. Hanna, a wealthy owner of steel mills and coal companies in Cleveland, persuaded the political leaders of the Republican Party to nominate McKinley for the Presidency in 1896. At the urging of Hanna, Mr. McKinley conducted his entire campaign from his home in Canton, and won the election.

McKinley was a hard-working and capable president at a time when the United States was having problems with Spain. In 1898 these problems led to the Spanish-American War. When the war ended a few months later, Cuba became an independent nation, and the United States gained control of Puerto Rico, Guam, and the Philippine Islands.

William McKinley was re-elected president in 1900 by a large majority. On September 6, 1901 in Buffalo, New York, he was shot by an **anarchist** (person who does not accept the rule of law), and died eight days later. Vice President Theodore Roosevelt was immediately sworn in as president.

A very large number of people attended the dedication of a beautiful memorial building built to honor Mr. McKinley in Canton, as you can see on page 221. You can also visit a nearby museum of his life and work. From the time of his first campaign for political office, Mr. McKinley wore a "lucky" scarlet carnation is his coat lapel. Shortly after he died, the General Assembly adopted this carnation as our state flower.

William Howard Taft

William Howard Taft (1857-1930) was the twenty-seventh President of the United States, serving from 1909 to 1913. You learned something about his birthplace in Chapter 9. You can see a portrait of him as president on page 222. As you can see, he was a very large man, weighing more than 300 pounds.

Mr. Taft graduated from Yale University, and from the Cincinnati Law School in 1880. He married Helen Herron, and they had two sons and a daughter who made great contributions to Ohio political life. Members of the Taft family are still active in Ohio politics.

As soon as he graduated from law school, Mr. Taft began to hold positions in the judicial branch of government. At the close of the Spanish-American War, he was named the first civil governor of the Philippines.

Mr. Taft was a loyal supporter of President Theodore Roosevelt, and when Mr. Roosevelt decided not to run for re-election in 1908, he helped Mr. Taft win the nomination of the Republican Party. Taft worked hard to be a good president, but never felt comfortable in the position. In the process of passing several laws to limit the powers of big business, Mr. Taft created turmoil within the Republican Party. He ran for re-election in 1912, but was badly defeated.

Portrait of Warren Harding in his last year as President of the United States (Inset: Harding's home.)

224

After he left office Mr. Taft became a Professor of Law at Yale University and carried out several special assignments for the United States during World War I. In 1921 he was named Chief Justice of the United States Supreme Court, and served in that position until he died in 1930. You can look back to page 165 to see him as a boy at his home in Cincinnati.

Warren Gamaliel Harding

Warren G. Harding (1865-1923) was the twenty-ninth President of the United States, serving from 1921 to 1923. He was born in 1865 near Blooming Grove, a small town where Crawford, Marion, and Richland Counties meet. He graduated from Ohio Central College and entered the newspaper business in Marion. You can see a portrait of him as president on page 224.

In 1891 Warren Harding married Florence Kling De Wolfe, a very capable woman who helped him make a success of the newspaper. Harding was very handsome and friendly. When he became interested in politics, he was easily elected to the General Assembly, and later served as lieutenant governor of Ohio. He was defeated when he ran for governor in 1910. Five years later, Warren Harding was elected to the United States Senate.

Ohio attracted nationwide attention in the presidential campaign of 1920 because both candidates were from our state. James M. Cox, a newspaper publisher in Dayton, was Governor of Ohio when the Democratic Party nominated him to be its candidate for President. Warren G. Harding, a newspaper publisher in Marion, was nominated as the Republican candidate for President. Mr. Harding was elected.

Because of trouble created by President Harding's advisors, his brief term of office was filled with some of the greatest scandals in the history of the United States. In the summer of 1923, President and Mrs. Harding and a group of friends took a trip to the western states and Alaska. Shortly after they reached San Francisco on the way back to Washington, D.C., the President died of an unknown cause.

The people of Marion were certain that their friend Warren was not responsible for the scandals, and in 1931 they erected the beautiful memorial you can see on page 227 to mark the graves of President and Mrs. Harding. You can also visit the Harding home in Marion.

Problems at the End of the 19th Century

In chapters 7 through 10, you read about the great changes that took place during the 19th century. Almost everyone had a better life in 1900 than their ancestors had in 1800, but there were several severe social problems in Ohio and the nation that we must consider.

Laissez-faire

Laissez-faire is a French term that means "let the people do as they please." During the last half of the 19th century, some entrepreneurs were able to make huge fortunes "doing as they pleased" by **exploiting** people and natural resources. The basic meaning of *exploit* is "to use," but under the motto of *laissez-faire*, many entrepreneurs had as their goal making money without regard for their workers, the general public, or nature.

Some very rich people essentially "bought" and "sold" political leaders, including mayors, governors, representatives, and even presidents. As you learned, President Taft lost his bid for re-election when he introduced laws to control the activities of such people.

The Labor Movement

In Chapter 10 you learned how some mine and factory owners treated their employees. The political cartoon on page 228 shows how workers felt about their situations, and information in the box below tells how some government officials viewed the situation.

In 1873 representatives of workers throughout Ohio met in Cleveland to organize the National Industrial Congress. In that same year, representatives of coal miners in Ohio met in Youngstown and organized the Miner's National Association of the United States. One of the goals of the miners' group was to encourage immigrants to become citizens so that they could vote for political candidates who would represent the interests of the workers.

In 1886 labor representatives from all over the United States met in Columbus, Ohio, to organize the American Federation of Labor. In 1890, miners from all parts of the nation met in Columbus to organize the

Factory Work
in the Late 19th Century

My attention has been frequently called to the alarming growth of women and child labor ... Good girls to do kitchen work are hard to find in the cities at three and four dollars a week and board, but girls can be found in the factories, and in the planing mills running planers, and in the potteries doing men's work, receiving from 50 to 75 cents a day, while men working beside them get from $1.50 to $2.00 for the same kind and quantity of work.

Children are crowded into workshops at twelve years, and at fifteen they are able to do a man's work, but their wages are fixed at thirty, forty and fifty cents a day. They are given work at **meager** wages until they reach the years of manhood, when they are thrown out of employment to make room for some other boys ... I have found boys ... struggling for a **livelihood** in a room heated 120 degrees, Fahrenheit.

From: Fassett, "Labor's Competitors" in *An Ohio Reader*, p. 158

The people of Marion, Ohio, built a beautiful memorial to honor their neighbors Warren and Florence DeWolfe Harding.

United Mine Workers. Later you will learn about the activities of these labor unions in the 20th century.

Women's Suffrage

An equally serious problem was the unequal treatment of men and women. In Chapter 6 you learned how Abigail Adams worked to have the Constitution of the United States grant rights to women. In Chapter 8 you read what Sojourner Truth said about women's rights. By 1900 women were still struggling to gain the right to vote. The word **suffrage** comes from a Latin word meaning "vote" or "political support"; people interested in women's *suffrage* were seeking the right for women to vote in public elections.

African-American Citizens

African-Americans continued to live under difficult conditions. In 1800 almost all of them were slaves. In 1863 President Lincoln declared that all slaves would be

During the last years of the 19th century working people often felt that they were slaves to the owners of big businesses.

free at the end of the Civil War. Between 1865 and 1868, the Constitution of the United States was amended three times to guarantee African-Americans all of the rights of citizenship.

In 1900 almost 100,000 African-Americans lived in Ohio under conditions not much better than their parents and grandparents had known as slaves. Almost one-half

lived in seven counties that had large manufacturing companies, while many others lived in the counties of southeast Ohio where lumbering and mining were important. Because the African-Americans were widely scattered and small in number, white political leaders did little to help them.

The Women's Temperance Crusade met outside a saloon in New Vienna, Ohio, to protest the owner selling alcohol to their husbands.

Oberlin College

One school in Ohio became known throughout the United States for its leadership in dealing with social problems. Oberlin College was founded in Lorain County in 1833 by leaders of the Congregational Churches of New England. It was the first four-year college in the United States to encourage women and African-Americans to become students. It was also an important "station" on the Underground Railroad.

In 1843 a young woman named Lucy Stone left her home in Massachusetts to be a student at Oberlin. After graduating in 1847, she returned to Massachusetts to become a leader in the Women's Suffrage Movement. When she married in 1855, she was one of the first women to keep her given family name after marriage.

John Mercer was born in Virginia in 1825. While John was in his "teens", a white man named Langston recognized his abilities and encouraged John to enroll in Oberlin College in 1841. Later John Mercer honored his friend by changing his name to John Mercer Langston.

While a student at Oberlin, he began to work hard for the rights of African-Americans. He was the first of his race to receive a degree in **theology** (preparation for Christian ministry) from Oberlin. He returned to Virginia and became the first African-American licensed

229

to practice law, to be elected to public office, and to recruit African-American troops for the Civil War. Later he was named the first dean of the law school at Howard University, and served as the only African-American representative of Virginia in Congress.

Alcoholism

The last problem we can consider is alcoholism. The production of alcoholic beverages was a very important industry in Cleveland and Cincinnati at the end of the 19th century. With the crowded living conditions that existed in the cities, saloons were important places for people to socialize. Sausage, cheese, and bread were often free to those who bought alcoholic drinks in these saloons.

The *Women's Temperance Crusade* was organized in several counties of south-central Ohio to reduce the evils of alcohol. On December 23, 1873 a speaker from New York met with the women of Hillsborough (now Hillsboro), the county seat of Highland County, to tell them about a program under way in his home town to stop alcoholism. Fifty women of Hillsborough agreed to work together to close the places selling alcohol in their town.

As a first step, they wrote letters to the owners of the saloons and drug stores asking them to stop selling alcoholic drinks. If the owners did not agree, the women held prayer meetings in front of the places of business. A picture of one of these gatherings at New Vienna, near Hillsboro, is on page 229. Soon women in the surrounding counties were using this approach to reduce the use of alcohol. The *Women's Christian Temperance Union* continued to work for many years to reduce the use of this drug, but used less dramatic methods.

Stop and Think!

The *Rule of Law* is essential for large numbers of free people to live together harmoniously in a small area, but free people want as few laws as possible. In 1803, when there were slightly more than 400,000 people scattered over the 40,000 square miles of Ohio, the citizens adopted a simple constitution to guide their lives. Each year thereafter the General Assembly adopted new laws to deal with problems that had not existed, or had been ignored, a few years earlier.

By 1851, when there were almost two million people living in Ohio, many of the old laws were no longer appropriate, so the state adopted a new constitution. While the Constitution of 1851 is still the basic law of Ohio, many amendments have been made over the years.

In a period of less than sixty years, from 1868 to 1924, eight citizens of Ohio were elected President of the United States. While most of them were capable political leaders, they had little influence over the government of our nation. Two of them died of natural causes while in office, and two others were assassinated.

Ohio was the first place in which the United States made provision for financing education. During the 19th century, citizens of our state made many important contributions to improve the education of children and adults, and to promote social reforms. Unfortunately some of the problems of the 19th century — dishonesty in government, alcoholism, and lack of equal opportunities for women and African-Americans — remain unsolved.

Building vocabulary...

abridge
academy
aggregate (total)
anarchist
article (law)
bear (verb)
common law
constitutional law
eminent domain
essential
executive
exploit
faction
inauguration
infringe
judicial
legislative
livelihood
meager
passport
personal property
political boss
prohibit
real estate
reconstruction
redress
respectively
statutory law
suffrage
temperance
theology
trustee

Meeting new people...

William H. McGuffey
Platt R. Spencer
Joseph Ray
Ulysses S. Grant
Rutherford B. Hayes
James A. Garfield
Benjamin Harrison
William McKinley
Warren G. Harding
Lucy Stone
John Mercer Langston

Why is it true or false?

1. Income taxes support schools operated by churches.
2. State laws may overrule federal laws.
3. Ohio has had two state constitutions.
4. The first constitution of Ohio included plans to change from a territorial government to a state government.
5. Many political leaders of Ohio have achieved national importance.
6. William Henry Harrison's term as president was the shortest ever served.
7. Benjamin Harrison was William Henry Harrison's grandfather.
8. Ulysses S. Grant was a general during the Revolutionary War.
9. President Garfield once worked on the Ohio and Erie Canal.
10. William Howard Taft is the only person to be Chief Justice of the Supreme Court and President of the United States.

Find the years and tell which came first.

1. President McKinley or President Harding?
2. The Spanish-American War or the Civil War?
3. President Hayes or President Garfield?

231

4. The National Federation of Labor or the Women's Temperance Crusade?
5. Miami University or The Ohio State University?

Make each statement correct by filling in the blanks.

1. .... University is located in Athens County.
2. The introduction to the Constitution of the United States is called the ....
3. The chief executive of the United States is called .... and the chief executive of Ohio is called ....
4. Civilians who served temporarily as soldiers were ....
5. The Supreme Court and all other courts are the .... branch of government.
6. The legislative branch of Ohio government is called ....
7. William Henry Harrison was President for only .... days.
8. .... promised that he would serve only one term when he was elected president.
9. .... was the last Ohioan to be elected president.
10. The right of women to vote is called Women's ....

Thinking it through...

1. Why was it important for Ohio to have a militia when the first state constitution was written? What has taken the place of the militia?
2. Divide the presidents from Ohio among the members of the class, and have each group prepare a report on its assigned president.
3. Explain the principle of eminent domain. How could this affect the property that your family, relatives, or friends may own?

4. Stage a debate about labor unions, their good points and bad. Compare labor unions today with those of 1900.
5. Take a vote in your class to find out who favors and who opposes gun control laws. Choose sides and have a debate on this issue. Please do not break up any friendships because of this debate.
6. Alcoholism has been a problem for many years. Hold a round-table discussion about what you might be able to do to reduce alcoholism and drug abuse.

Working with maps...

1. On the map of the world, locate all the places mentioned where William Howard Taft served our nation. Assume that a ship could move at 15 miles per hour, for 24 hours per day. How long did it take Mr. Taft to travel from San Francisco, California to Manila, Philippine Islands?
2. On the map of the United States, plot the route that Lucy Stone might have followed to go from Boston, Massachusetts, to Oberlin College in 1843. Use information in Chapter 7, and estimate the time it might have taken for this trip.
3. Using information in Chapter 7, how would the delegate from your county have traveled to Columbus to help write the Second Constitution in 1851? Using the map of Ohio, how would you make the same trip?
4. With help from a historical atlas of the United States, plot on your map of the United States the states that existed in the year when each president from Ohio was elected.

Ohio in the 20th Century

A person who was born in the United States at the beginning of the 20th century, and who died near the end of it, lived through more changes than anyone had experienced in any earlier century. As the population of Ohio increased from about 4 million in 1900 to almost 11 million in 1990, the variety of people increased greatly. Farms increased in size and decreased in number. The largest cities grew rapidly until 1950, and then all except Columbus began to decline as urbanized areas mushroomed around them. The use of energy increased tremendously as people discovered more ways to use it.

In 1899 the Superintendent of the United States Patent Office resigned from the position because he believed so many wonderful things had been invented that his job was no longer needed. At the end of that year, about 800,000 patents had been issued. By the year 2000, more than 5 million will be in effect. During the 20th century, some of the social problems of the previous century were eased, though few were completely solved. Progress was made on some of the old political problems, but almost as many new ones arose.

While studying this period of history, you should talk to your grandparents or other older folks as often as possible to learn how their lives changed during the 20th century.

For example, the picture on page 234 will help them recall various ways they traveled in earlier years.

This remarkable picture was taken in Montgomery County about 1910. It may have been specially arranged. On the far left you can see the Great Miami River, which was an important artery of transportation until 1833. To the right of the river, you can see an electric interurban car, which was an important way to travel between 1895 and 1930. On the highway, which may have been one of the first paved roads in the county, you can see an automobile. To the right of the highway, you see a canal boat on the Miami and Erie Canal, which was little used after 1900. On the right side of the picture you can see a steam-powered railroad train. Railroads put the canals out of business during the 19th century, while highways and motor vehicles greatly reduced the importance of railroads during the 20th century.

The Ohio you enjoy today is the result of millions of people working to improve their own lives during the 20th century.

Bringing History to Life

In Part III we will look at life in the 20th century through the eyes of three well-known men of Ohio: Charles Franklin

Five forms of transportation circa 1910.

Kettering (1876-1958), who believed that all problems could be solved by scientific methods; Louis Bromfield (1896-1956), who lived on a farm in close touch with nature; and Carl Burton Stokes (1927-), who has lived in the center of political action.

Kettering

Charles F. Kettering was born on a farm in Ashland County, about three miles north of Loudonville. As a boy he helped on the farm and loved to experiment with mechanical devices. He won a scholarship to Loudonville High School, and walked back and forth between home and school each day. On the basis of his high school record, Charles was offered a job as teacher in an elementary school at Bunker Hill, three miles east of Loudonville. The following year he taught in Mifflin High School, seven miles north of his home.

By 1898 he had saved enough money to enroll in The Ohio State University to study engineering. When eye problems forced him to drop out of college after the first year, he took a job installing some of the first telephones in Ashland County. He

continued to study, read scientific literature, and experiment. He also met Olive Williams of Ashland, Ohio, whom he later married.

Kettering returned to The Ohio State University in 1901, and earned a degree in electrical engineering in 1904, at the age of twenty-seven. Because of his outstanding record at Ohio State, he was offered a position in the research department of the National Cash Register Company (NCR) in Dayton, Ohio.

During his five years at NCR, Kettering invented devices that made NCR machines the most popular cash registers in the world. He then began to invent devices for automobiles, including the first electric starting system. By 1918 he was Vice President for Research of the General Motors Corporation, and remained in that position until 1956.

The Ketterings built a large house in Montgomery County and named it *Ridgeleigh Terrace*. They lived there until Olive died in 1946 and Charles in 1958. They were both buried in Montgomery

County. Their son, Eugene, built Kettering Memorial Hospital for the people of Kettering, Ohio, and gave Ridgeleigh Terrace to the hospital.

Bromfield

Louis Bromfield was born in Mansfield, Ohio, the county seat of Richland County in 1896. His father operated a small business in Mansfield, and his mother's parents owned a farm about ten miles from where Charles Kettering was born. Bromfield loved to visit his grandparents' farm. After graduating from high school in 1914, he went to Cornell University to study agriculture. During his freshman year, his grandfather died and Louis was asked to help at home. Within a year, his mother decided to sell the family farm.

Because Louis enjoyed writing, he enrolled at Columbia University to study **journalism** (professional writing). Before the end of his first year at Columbia, he enlisted in the United States Ambulance Corps to work in France during World War I. He returned to the United States in 1919, married, and at the age of twenty-seven published a long novel based on life in Mansfield, Ohio. This book made Bromfield famous and wealthy.

In 1925 he moved his family to France, where they lived until 1939. During this time he traveled throughout the world, wrote many novels and several scripts for motion pictures, and became world-famous. Shortly before the outbreak of World War II, he moved the family back to Richland County, Ohio and bought several neighboring farms near his grandfather's old place. In the following years he wrote stories about farming.

Bromfield loved farm life, and he set out to create a successful farm based on the idea of working in harmony with nature. He named this farm *Malabar* after the beautiful west-coast area of southern India. In 1956 Louis Bromfield died after a long illness that had cost most of his fortune. During the 1960s, the State of Ohio bought Malabar Farm, and maintains it as a tribute to a man who loved the soil, and as a museum of successful farming by natural methods.

Stokes

Carl B. Stokes was born in Cleveland, Ohio in 1927, two years after his brother Louis. His father died two years later, and his mother, Louise, struggled to support her children by working at the poor-paying jobs available to uneducated, African-American women.

In 1945 Carl dropped out of high school and enlisted in the United States Army. He served in Germany during the post-World War II period, and said of this experience:

"My attitudes had been changed. The contact with educated black men in the Army had made me see a new value in going to school. More important, I now had money I had saved, and I had the G.I. Bill ...." (The "G.I. Bill" was a federal program to help members of the armed services return to civilian life.)[1]

Stokes graduated from Western Reserve University in Cleveland in 1950, and a few years later earned a degree in law. He then took a job in the enforcement division of the Ohio Department of Liquor Control, with work assignments in Canton, Toledo, and Cincinnati. Through his work in law enforcement, he became interested in politics. In November, 1962 he became the first African-American member of the Democratic Party to be elected to the Ohio General Assembly. As he was finishing his third term in the General Assembly, he was elected to the position of Mayor of Cleveland. He served two 2-year terms as mayor, during which time he helped to elect his brother Louis as the first African-American representative from Ohio to Congress.

Political pressures made Carl Stokes decide not to run for re-election as mayor in 1971. In 1990 he was serving as a judge in the Municipal Court of Cleveland, while his brother Louis continued to serve in Congress.

Footnotes

1. Stokes, *Promises of Power*, p. 29.

How did the quality of life change?

- why people came from many parts of the world to live in Ohio.

- how working conditions changed during the 20th century.

- how the Great Depression affected our state.

- about cultural activities in Ohio.

- about opportunities for recreation in Ohio.

It is fairly easy to measure the *quantity* of life — how long people live, how many "things" they have, how far they travel, and so on. It is much more difficult to measure the *quality* of life, because quality is related to how individuals *feel* about their lives. Today there are people living in Ohio who have all of the "advantages" of modern life, such as reliable electric service, radios and television, clothes that are easy to clean, and comfortable transportation; but they

World conflict that affected Ohio during the 20th century.

Start	End	USA Involved	Name of Conflict	Location
1894	1895	No	Sino-Japanese War	China and Korea
1898	1898	Yes	Spanish-American War	Cuba
1899	1902	Yes	Phillippine Rebellion	Phillippine Islands
1904	1905	No	Russo-Japanese War	East coast of Russia
1903	1906	No	Russians persecute Jews	Russia
1905	1906	No	Revolution in Russia	Russia
1905	1949	No	Turmoil in China	China
1910	1917	Yes	Turmoil in Mexico	Mexico
1912	1912	No	Revolt of SE Europe from Turkey	Southeast Europe
1914	1918	Yes	World War I (U.S. entered in 1917)	Europe and Near East
1915	1925	No	Turmoil in Middle East	Turkey, Greece, Armenia, Palestine
1916	1925	No	Irish Rebellion	Ireland
1917	1920	No	Russian Revolution (Start of USSR)	Russia
1919	1948	No	Nonviolent campaign for independence	India
1921	1922	No	Economic collapse in Russia and Ukraine	USSR
1925	1953	No	Stalin creates turmoil in USSR	USSR
1934	1941	No	Hitler creates turmoil in Europe	Europe
1936	1939	No	Spanish Civil War	Spain
1939	1945	Yes	World War II	Most of the World
1945	1989	No	Communists control East Europe (Cold War)	East Europe
1947	1947	No	Separation of India and Pakistan	India and Pakistan
1948	1991	No	Communists control China	China
1948	1991	Yes	Conflicts between Jews and Arabs	Israel
1949	1991	No	Refugees from China seize Taiwan	Taiwan
1950	1953	Yes	Korean War	Korea
1950	1954	No	Communists drive French out of SE Asia	Vietnam
1955	1991	No	Independence and turmoil in Africa	Africa
1956	1973	Yes	Vietnam War	Vietnam
1959	1991	Yes	Communists control Cuba	Cuba
1967	1991	Yes	Turmoil in the Near East	Near East

are unhappy. On the other hand, there are people who have few material possessions but live happy, useful lives.

In this chapter we will look at how events such as conflict, working conditions, health care, education, recreation, and cultural activities, have affected the people of Ohio during the last hundred years.

How Conflicts Affected the Population of Ohio

During the first half of the 19th century, most immigrants to Ohio came from western Europe. During the last half of that century, thousands of peasants and laborers from eastern and southern Europe came to work in the large industries you learned about in Chapter 10. In addition, almost 100,000 freed African-Americans moved to Ohio from the southern states in the hope of finding better lives. At the beginning of the 20th century, the population of Ohio was about 4 million: today it approaches 11 million. Much of this growth was related to conflicts in other parts of the world. The table on page 238 is a time line of these events.

Wars in Russia

Between 1890 and 1920, the area we know today as the Union of Soviet Socialist Republics (USSR) was in turmoil. The rulers of Russia, which is now the largest part of the USSR, conquered the lands of the Ukraine and Armenia. The Communist Party stamped out all opposition and discouraged Jews and Christians from practicing their religions. As a result, millions of Jews, Ukranians, and Armenians fled to the United States — many of them to Ohio. Between 1920 and 1987, the Communist Party refused to let people leave the USSR. When that nation adopted new policies of "openness" during the late 1980s, people of the Jewish faith were permitted to emigrate, and many more of them came to Ohio.

World War I

Life was very difficult in the nations of Eastern Europe during the early years of the 20th century. Millions of people emigrated to the United States before World War I began in 1914. During those same years, economic conditions in the southern part of the United States were very poor, but Ohio industry was prospering. This combination of conditions encouraged unemployed people of Europe and the South to move to Ohio. The stories in the boxes on page 240 tell how Akron was affected.

Why Poor People Moved
to Akron During World War I

By 1915 [Akron] was a boom town, and with a **vengeance**. The word spread over the country, 'There's work in Akron,' and men swarmed in by the thousands. Thirty thousand workers converged on the city in 1916; in one decade, 1910-20, the population jumped from 69,000 to 209,000.

Over the Ohio border from West Virginia and Kentucky the **recruits** came pouring.... Manpower scarcity was sending the wages up and now the most effective advertising of all—word of mouth— was working for the [rubber] kings. In the Slav lands of Europe the mispronounced name of Akron was [discussed]. Through the black belt of America ran the rumor of [high wages] to be picked up ... working for Massa Seiberling and Massa Firestone. In the hills of Scotland the Akron wage news was told, the hills of Albania, the hills of Tennessee.

From: *The Ohio Guide,*
WPA Writers' Program, p. 171

How African-American Workers
Were Recruited

Meantime, northern industry's war production had created a demand for labor. Northern industrialists gave added impetus to the migration by sending labor agents into the South to recruit Negro workers. These factors and the increasing racial discrimination and segregation in the South were conducive to a greater Negro migration to the North.

Ohio industrialists stimulated the migration into the state by actively recruiting Negro workmen in the South.... "'Some Cleveland industrialists paid their labor agents one dollar for every Negro workman recruited.... The agents of some Cleveland firms carried pictures of the homes of wealthy Negroes which were shown to southern **sharecroppers** as examples of 'the sort of places you'd live in up in Cleveland."

From: W.W. Giffin, *The Negro in Ohio,*
1914—1939, pp. 19-21

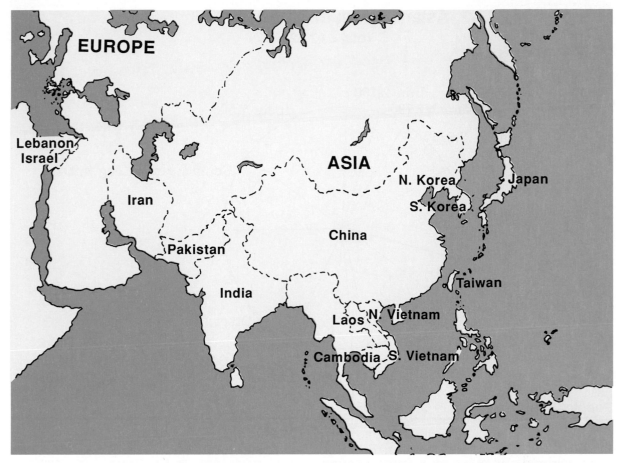

Nations of Asia mentioned in this Chapter .

At the close of the war, thousands of young people who participated in the war effort married and had children. These new families also helped to increase the population of Ohio.

World War II

It seems safe to say that the ten years between 1940 and 1950 brought more changes to the lives of people living in Ohio and the United States than any other single decade. At the peak of the war effort, there were almost 14 million men and women serving in the armed forces of the United States in all parts of the world. Many of the

children born after World War I married before they began military service in World War II. Still more young people married after they were released from military duty. Beginning in 1946, the number of babies born each year jumped dramatically. Your parents, or grandparents, may have been part of the "baby boomers", as the post-World War II generation was called.

Conflicts in Asia

You will want to look at the map of Asia on this page as you study this section. Asia is the largest continent and home to more

241

Asians Living in Ohio in 1980
Total = 47,322

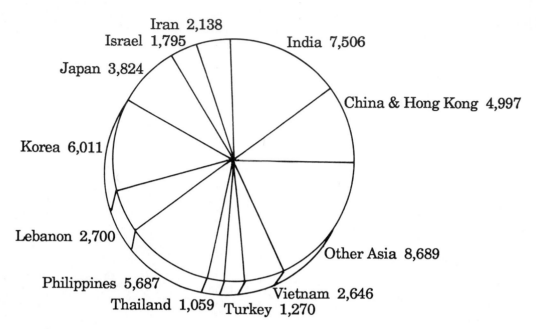

Iran 2,138
Israel 1,795
Japan 3,824
India 7,506
China & Hong Kong 4,997
Korea 6,011
Lebanon 2,700
Other Asia 8,689
Philippines 5,687
Vietnam 2,646
Thailand 1,059
Turkey 1,270

People from Asia Living in Ohio in 1980

| | Totals | Year Arrived | | | | | |
		1975-1980	1970-1974	1965-1969	1960-1964	1950-1959	Pre 1950
China	3,269	971	732	456	302	313	495
Hong Kong	728	259	263	107	57	32	10
India	7,506	3,251	2,257	1,308	403	213	74
Iran	2,138	1,564	189	165	123	79	18
Israel	1,795	647	326	262	145	304	111
Japan	3,824	925	616	552	417	1,141	173
Korea	6,011	2,290	2,203	896	371	241	10
Lebanon	2,700	1,118	332	226	118	211	695
Philippines	5,687	1,857	1,695	1,241	385	352	157
Thailand	1,059	484	474	93	6	2	0
Turkey	1,270	218	159	163	68	168	494
Vietnam	2,646	2,340	240	49	12	5	0
Other Asia	8,689	5,138	1,515	792	466	449	329
Total Asia	47,322	21,062	11,001	6,310	2,873	3,510	2,566

than 2 billion people. Only the countries mentioned below are identified on the map.

When the nation of Israel was established in the Near East in 1948, conflicts developed throughout the region that have not yet been resolved. These conflicts caused thousands of people, especially from Lebanon and Iran, to migrate to the United States, and many settled in Ohio.

In the five years following the close of World War II, many changes took place in India and China. The people of India gained freedom from Great Britain, and the people of Pakistan broke away from India. Communists seized control of China, and a small group of Chinese fled to the island of Taiwan to establish the Republic of China.

In 1950 the United States took the lead in the United Nations to prevent Communist China from seizing Korea. This action involved thousands of United States military personnel in fighting for almost four years. Some of our armed forces were still in Korea in 1990.

During the 1950s, students from India, Pakistan, Korea, and the Republic of China (Taiwan) began to attend colleges in the United States, and hundreds of them came to Ohio. Some of these students returned to their homelands after graduation, but many more remained here and brought their families to live with them.

In 1955 the United States began to help the people of South Vietnam protect themselves against the Communist rulers of North Vietnam. After the United States decided to withdraw from Vietnam in 1973, hundreds of thousands of refugees from South Vietnam, and the neighboring countries of Cambodia and Laos, came to the United States, and many of them moved to Ohio.

By 1970 the people of the United States were buying so many products made in Japan that Japanese companies began to build factories in this country. As a result, hundreds of Japanese executives and their families have moved to Ohio in recent years. You will learn more about this in Chapter 14. The diagram on page 242 shows when people from various parts of Asia came to live in Ohio. Appendix B shows the migrants from Asia living in each county of Ohio in 1990.

Working Conditions

At the beginning of the 20th century, wages and prices were very low by our standards, and few people could save as much as one dollar per week. A very small number of people, such as John D. Rockefeller, became very wealthy as they controlled the natural resources and industry of the nation. A growing number of small merchants and craftsmen formed what we now call the "middle class." Here is how Helen Santmyer described working conditions in Waynesboro, the imaginary town in her book ... *and Ladies of the Club*....

Working Conditions at Rausch Cordage Company in 1904

[Mary, a granddaughter of Captain Bodien who managed the Rausch Cordage Company in Waynesboro, is home from college. She and a friend, Franz, have become interested in the lives of poor people, and they go to the rope factory to talk to Ludwig Rausch, the president. Mary begins the conversation:]

"I want to talk to you about labor conditions in this mill."

"What's wrong with them? A **ropewalk** isn't a very clean place to work, but they are used to the tar— and even to [the fiber used to make rope], smell though it does. They're satisfied, far's I know."

"What do you pay them?"

"Mary, that isn't any of your damn' business. An' most of 'em would say so, if you ask them. But ... I might as well tell you. The [rope twisting] girls, six dollars a week. Unskilled labor ... seven. Skilled labor ... it depends: eight to ten dollars a week. Anything wrong with that? A dollar a day is a good wage, even for skilled labor."

"It's **abominable**. How many hours do they work?"

"Fifty-four, since we've been shutting down Saturday afternoons. Unless there are orders we have to finish."

"And they don't realize they are being **exploited**?"

"If they don't like their wage and pay, they can always quit."

From: Santmyer, ...and Ladies of the Club... pp 894-5

In this story, Ludwig Rausch took great interest in each of his employees, giving them personal help when they had special needs. This practice was called **paternalism** (the employer acted as "father"). During the early years of the 20th century, many companies, including the National Cash Register Company of Dayton, Ohio treated employees in this way.

National Cash Register Company

In 1879 the Ritty brothers of Dayton invented a machine popularly called a "thief catcher." Five years later, John Henry Patterson, a descendent of Robert Patterson, one of the founders of Dayton, bought the Rittys' idea and created the National Cash Register Company (NCR). In Chapter 10 you read that this company employed 79 people in 1888.

Patterson was very successful at selling cash registers, and did everything he could to make his workers happy. As one author described the situation:

"... he paternally plied his employees with fringe benefits that were pioneer efforts at industrial welfare: showers, lockers, swimming pools, hot lunches, medical care, and inspirational lectures. Women employees were taught how to manage their homes, and children of employees were taught how to save their money, how to chew their food, and how to avoid scattering germs when they sneezed. In return, he demanded absolute obedience and high productivity."[1]

The entire future of the company changed in June, 1904 when Charles Kettering was hired as an "electrical expert." Within two years Kettering invented devices that made it possible to operate cash registers by electricity. By 1910 NCR was making 90 percent of the cash registers used in the United States.

In 1972 NCR employed 20,000 people in Dayton, but it had not improved its products to compete with the new electronic devices made by competitors. That year a new president began to lead the company back to its earlier position as world-wide leader in business machines. He changed the company name to NCR Corporation, reduced employment in Dayton to about 5,000, and built new factories in places where pay scales were lower. In 1990 NCR employed almost 56,000 people throughout the world and was the leading manufacturer of automatic bank-teller machines, a product unheard of just a few years ago. It still practices good labor relations, but not the paternalism of earlier years. In April, 1991 the American Telephone & Telegraph Company gained control of NCR.

Labor Unions

In Chapter 11 you learned that some workers organized trade unions before 1900 to protect themselves from unfair treatment. As companies expanded during the first twenty years of the 20th century, more and more workers found that they had to join labor unions to protect their interests.

You also learned that several unions had joined together in 1886 to organize the American Federation of Labor (AFL). These unions represented skilled and semi-skilled craftsmen (there were almost no women) who worked independently, or in small groups. For example, carpenters, painters, and electricians formed their own unions, but cooperated with each other through the AFL.

Because workers in mass-production industries, such as steel, automobiles, and clothing, faced other kinds of problems, they organized themselves differently. The International Ladies Garment Workers Union, for example, was organized to deal with the problems created by *piece work* you read about in Chapter 9. In 1935 Congress passed the National Labor Relations Act [often called the *Wagner Act*] to make it easier for these mass-production workers to form unions. Several of these unions quickly joined together to create the *Congress for Industrial Organization (CIO)*.

During the last half of the 1930s, four of the largest CIO unions had thousands of members in Ohio: the United Automobile Workers (now called International Union of United Automobile, Aerospace and

During the late 1930s CIO members staged several "sit down" strikes in automobile factories.

Agricultural Implement Workers of America); the United Mine Workers of America; the United Rubber Workers (now called United Rubber, Cork, Linoleum and Plastic Workers of America); and the United Steelworkers of America. Each of these unions staged *sit-down* strikes for better wages and working conditions. This means the workers went to work one morning, and then refused either to work or to leave the factories or mines. The picture above shows a sit-down strike in an automobile factory. When the United States entered World War II, Congress passed a law prohibiting strikes in industries making war **materiel** (all goods needed for the war effort).

In 1947, over the **veto** of President Harry S. Truman, Congress passed what is commonly called the *Taft-Hartley Act.* (Robert A. Taft was a Senator from Ohio and a son of former President William H. Taft.) This law put some limitations on the ability of unions to strike in cases of national interest, such as against electric-power, telephone, water, and other essential services that are called *public utilities.*

During the Great Depression people did many things to try to earn money.

The various unions making up the AFL and CIO sometimes quarreled over the right to represent particular industries, but in 1955 the two organizations joined to form what is usually called the *AFL-CIO*. A few strong unions, including the United Mine Workers of America and the International Brotherhood of Teamsters, Chauffeurs, Warehousemen, and Helpers of America, refused to join the AFL-CIO, and they continue to operate as independent groups. The total membership of the AFL-CIO peaked at 14,070,000 in 1975, but dropped to 12,702,000 by 1987.

The Great Depression

Throughout the history of the United States, there have been alternating periods of economic **prosperity** (times when jobs

During the Great Depression many farmers lost their land because they could not repay loans.

are plentiful) and **depression** (times when many people are out of work). People who depend on wages are often hurt more by a depression than people who have other sources of income. Between the end of World War II and 1991, there were a few **recessions** (mild economic depressions) but no serious economic troubles.

During the first nine months of 1929, a large percentage of the people of Ohio were optimistic and prosperous. Many low-income people still lived in tenement houses (the type of housing you can see on

page 161), but most had electric lights and indoor toilets. The number of middle-income families had increased greatly, and many owned homes and automobiles.

In October, 1929 the financial market of the United States collapsed, and within two years the economies of most nations fell into the deepest and longest depression in history. Thousands of businesses closed, and millions of people lost their jobs. Those who were able to continue working accepted drastic cuts in pay. Hundreds of banks collapsed, and people lost money they had saved "for a rainy day." The pictures on pages 247 & 248 show scenes that were very common during the 1930s.

In 1932 Franklin D. Roosevelt was elected President of the United States on the promise that he would solve the economic problems of our nation. During 1933 Congress established dozens of programs to deal with the emergency. We will look at four programs that had lasting influence on Ohio.

Works Progress Administration (WPA)

The goal of WPA was to provide work for tremendous numbers of both skilled and unskilled people while producing long-lasting benefits. Most WPA workers were paid forty cents an hour. Many unskilled workers built or remodeled city streets using hand tools such as picks, shovels, and wheelbarrows. On the other hand, professional historians wrote histories of Ohio and its larger cities, including *The Ohio Guide* quoted on page 240. In some areas the most reliable history book available today was written as a WPA project.

Public Works Administration (PWA)

Unlike the WPA program, with which it is often confused, the PWA program provided Federal money to states and local units of government to build public buildings. One or more school buildings in your county were probably built under this program. Perhaps a post office or a municipal building in your county was also financed by the PWA. Every building financed by PWA has a **plaque** (plate) near the entrance stating this fact. Contractors who built these buildings were required to pay union wages.

Civilian Conservation Corps (CCC)

The purpose of the CCC program was to put young, unmarried men to work repairing damaged soils and forests. For example, a large part of the drainage basin of the Muskingum River (look back to the map on page 22) was unusable because of poor farming practices and destruction of the forests. The Muskingum Conservancy District was established, and men from several CCC camps worked to stabilize the soil and plant new trees. Louis Bromfield's Malabar Farm was in this region.

Some CCC projects were the beginnings of state parks such as Lake Hope State Park in Vinton County, and Shawnee State Park, in Scioto County. The workers were given room and board, and paid about twenty-five cents an hour.

Federal Housing Programs

The Federal housing programs created during the 1930s had such tremendous effect on the cities of Ohio, and of the entire United States, that we will consider most of them in the next chapter.

For the moment, we will look at the program that had great effect on poor people in large cities. Migrants from Appalachia and the South, who came to Ohio in search of jobs during World War I, could afford housing only in the old tenement houses of the big cities. The owners of these tenements lived in outlying areas, and did no more to maintain the buildings than the law required; therefore, many of the neighborhoods became slums.

In 1933 President Roosevelt said, in a speech relating to housing, "one third of our nation is ill-fed, ill-housed, and ill-clothed." Shortly after this speech, Congress passed a law to create *Metropolitan Housing Authorities* (MHA) to help cities provide good housing for the poor. Large numbers of poorly-kept houses were bought and **razed** (torn down), and groups of modern apartment houses were built. The picture on page 251 shows a typical building created by this program. You can see buildings similar to this in many cities. Here is the story of how this program helped two men who became political leaders in Ohio.

The MHA program is still in operation in all large cities. It continued to build groups of large apartment buildings through the 1960s, but today cities prefer to build one or two-family buildings scattered throughout the area.

Health Care

Today almost every one of us knows more about health, physical fitness, and foods than medical doctors did in 1900. Today the

---

How Public Housing Helped the Stokes Family

"... My mother, Louis and I [Carl B. Stokes] lived ... in a rickety old two-family house. We covered the rat holes with the tops of tin cans. The front steps always needed fixing, one of them always seemed to be missing. The coal stove kept the living room warm; we used heated bricks and an old flatiron wrapped in flannel to keep warm in the bedroom. The three of us shared one bed.

"Poor people are herded into such neighborhoods, where survival too often means that they are forced to prey on each other. When my mother washed the clothes on Saturday night, she hung them in the kitchen to dry. Hanging them outside meant you didn't want them anymore. When Louis and I would take our wagon down to get the surplus dried peas, flour, rice and dried milk that was dispensed to welfare clients, we took along a baseball bat to get the food home past the other kids and sometimes even adults."....

"We were delivered from the most oppressive physical presence of our poverty in 1938, when I was eleven. Cleveland was the first city in the country to construct housing for the poor with federal funds. For some time after the plans for the housing were known and Mother had made an application for an apartment, we lived in day-to-day anticipation of getting out of our rickety old house. She would tell Louis and me about steam heat, painted walls, beds of our own, but I'm sure these things meant little to us at the time. We had no experience to give these words meaning.

"The day we moved was pure wonder. A sink with hot and cold running water, a place where you could wash clothes with a washing machine, and an actual refrigerator. And we learned what it was to live in dependable warmth. For the first time, we had two bedrooms and two beds. My mother for the first time had a room and a bed of her own."

From: Stokes, *Promises of Power*, pp. 22 - 25

During the late 1930s metropolitan housing authorities built many housing projects for low-income people.

healing professions include doctors of medicine, nurses, dentists, **pharmacists**, **chiropractors**, and **paramedics**, and there are few details about the human body that are not known. Today Ohio has outstanding schools of medicine, dentistry, nursing, and pharmacy. The larger hospitals of our state are equipped with the newest instruments to help patients with almost any kind of health problem.

We also know many more things about preventing illness. For example, ever since 1960 almost every person in the United States — and in many other parts of the world — has taken the polio serum developed by Dr. Albert B. Sabin and his helpers at the Children's Hospital Research Center in Cincinnati. The picture on page 252 shows people lined up in front of the Children's Hospital in 1960 to take the new "wonder drug."

Before 1960 thousands of children and adults were crippled by infantile paralysis ("polio").

Dr. Albert B. Sabin

Albert Bruce Sabin was born in Russia in 1906, and came to the United States with his parents during the great migration of Jews you learned about earlier in this chapter. He joined the faculty of the College of Medicine of the University of Cincinnati in 1939, and worked for many years to develop a medicine to prevent *infantile paralysis*, which is also known as *poliomyelitis*, or **polio** for short. Dr. Sabin retired from the University of Cincinnati in 1971 to do research and teach in many other places.

Education

What kind of work would you like to do someday? No matter what your answer may be to this question, you can almost certainly find a place in Ohio to learn that skill.

In Chapter 8 you learned about rural schools in the 19th century. These schools did not change much until the 1930s. One of the many new Federal programs adopted during the Great Depression encouraged local boards of education to build **consolidated** (several similar things put together) schools. Paved roads made it possible for buses to travel through farm areas and small towns. The buses took children to centralized schools that provided many more educational facilities than the old one-room buildings. By 1950 there were no one-room schools in operation in Ohio.

Status of Public Schools

For about 100 years, from 1860 to 1960, publicly-owned, tax-supported schools were the most important cultural features in the big cities of Ohio. Public schools made it possible for immigrants to learn the English language and become citizens of the United States. They made it possible for children in each neighborhood to grow up together, and for parents to become acquainted through activities of Parent Teacher Associations (PTAs). Because not all children were equally anxious to learn, those who did not want to learn were separated from those who did.

Beginning about 1950, cities began to change, as you will learn in Chapter 13, and by 1970 the public schools of large cities had also changed drastically. Thousands of parents, who could afford to do so, enrolled their children in private schools, including new schools created by various religious organizations. The boxes on pages 254 & 256 contain two stories about public schools — one from a rural area and the other from a big city.

Leonard Slye at School in Duck Run

Leonard Slye was born in Cincinnati in 1910. His family lived on Second Street, which is now called *Pete Rose Way*. His father, Andy, worked for the United States Shoe Company, which you will learn more about in Chapter 14. In 1919 the family moved to a farm on Duck Run Road in Scioto County, about ten miles north and five miles west of Portsmouth. The farm could not support the family, which had grown to include four children, so Andy took a job in a shoe factory in Portsmouth. Leonard, as the oldest child, had to help his mother, Mattie, operate the farm. Here is how a writer described Leonard's school days at Duck Run:

"Leonard grew up skinny but well-**coordinated**. He had a good arm and a good eye. He was a poor student though, feuding with the underpaid and undertrained teachers who were exiled to the one-room Duck Run schoolhouse. Then in 1926 Guy Baumgartner relaxed the school's harsh discipline and improved the learning environment…. He took a special interest in the shy yet rebellious Leonard Slye…. All his life, Leonard said it was Guy Baumgartner who **coaxed** him out of his shell by getting him to try difficult things like appearing in a school play as Santa Claus, his first stab at acting.

"Baumgartner also had some formal training in voice and … taught Leonard to sing …. Later in high school, Leonard took up the clarinet. He was already a regular in the local barn dance circuit, both as a guitar player and a dance caller."

During the Great Depression of the 1930s, the Slyes were **migrant workers** on the farms of California, and suffered all of the problems of poverty. Leonard entertained the other workers by playing his guitar, singing, and calling square dances. He teamed up with two other young men, and they began to earn money singing and "strumming" in nearby cities. In 1934 Leonard adopted the name "Dick Weston," and organized a group called "Sons of The Pioneers": this group played in a few movies made by Republic Pictures.

By 1950 Leonard Slye accomplished many things, including adopting the name *Roy Rogers, King of the Cowboys*; marrying Frances Octavia Smith who adopted the name *Dale Evans*; and teaching two horses—both named *Trigger*—to perform tricks few other horses could do.

Today you can see reruns of Roy Rogers movies, visit a Roy Rogers Museum in Portsmouth; travel on Roy Rogers Road in Duck Run, and eat in a Roy Rogers Restaurant near your home.

From: Fleischman, "Lonesome Trail from Duck Run," in *Ohio*, Oct. 1989, p 118

During World War I women did jobs that had always been considered to be men's work.

Carl Stokes Writes
About School in Cleveland

"Adolescence hits a boy like a fist, and if he is at all close to more than one world of activity, he is likely to find himself shoved toward the seamier. Until I reached the ninth grade I had been the pride of the classroom, getting excellent grades, singing in the glee club, and that sort of thing. But about that time I began to develop other talents—[pitching] pennies, shooting craps, playing poker, forging my mother's name on a paper excusing me from school. I was caught, of course, and my mother was severely disappointed in me. I felt her disappointment, but didn't change my ways. Whether I would have changed in a different high school, I don't know, but I went to East Technical High School, which offered the best vocational training in the city. It was located in my all-black neighborhood, but it was attended by white kids who commuted from all over. The student body, in fact, was about ninety percent white. (I wonder how those white kids, now [1973] middle-aged, feel about busing today.)

"East Tech had produced a number of internationally famous black track stars in the 1930s and 1940s—Jesse Owens, Harrison Dillard, Dave Albritton. One of the reasons the black kids were so good in that sport is that they were actively discouraged from going out for the team sports, football, basketball, and baseball."

From: Stokes, *Promises of Power* pp. 25-26

Women

As you learned in Chapter 11, by 1900 some women were working hard to gain the same legal rights that men enjoyed. Before World War I very few students went to school beyond the eighth grade. Most girls and boys of upper-income families went to a public high school or a private academy. While some girls went to college, many others went to **Normal Schools**. Every state had one or more Normal Schools to train school teachers. After World War II most of these schools were changed into junior colleges or four-year colleges, and the term "normal" disappeared.

During World War I, as several million young men entered the army or navy, women moved into a variety of jobs that they were previously thought to be "unfit" to do. The picture on page 255, for example, shows a woman operating a machine in a war plant. As more and more women demonstrated that they could work as effectively as men, the men finally approved

Women helped to win World War II in a great many ways.

two amendments to the Constitution of the United States that women had worked to achieve for at least forty years. In 1919 the Eighteenth Amendment prohibited the manufacture and sale of alcoholic beverages. In 1920 the Nineteenth Amendment gave women the right to vote.

Throughout the 1920s and 30s, far more young women went to high school and college, but most found employment as school teachers, nurses, librarians, or office workers. During the Great Depression, women had difficulty finding jobs because many people thought that they were "taking jobs away from men who needed them." When the United States entered World War II, women again filled many jobs that had been closed to them. The picture on page 257 shows how women were recruited for work during the war. "Rosie the Riveter" became a national symbol of patriotism. Women even became members of the Armed Forces of the United States in noncombatant positions.

Between 1945 and 1965, many more career opportunities opened for women, but very few were admitted to professions — other than nursing, library work, and teaching — or to executive positions in business. Between 1978, when it was established, and 1990, the Ohio Women's Hall of Fame honored only two women as leaders of manufacturing companies: Jayne Baker Spain, of Hamilton County, who retired about 1980, and Joan E. Lamson of Cuyahoga County.

Joan E. Lamson

Ms. Lamson was born in Denver, Colorado, in 1937. As a youth she helped her parents operate a small drug store. She married at age eighteen, had three children, and divorced at age twenty-nine. She found employment as a receptionist with a company that moved her and the children to Cleveland, Ohio. When the Federal *Equal Employment Opportunity Program* (that you will learn about later in this chapter) was announced, Ms. Lamson decided to improve her skills. In 1975 she enrolled in a special program for Women in Management, and earned a Master of Business Administration degree without a previous college degree. In 1980 she and a partner formed a small company in Cleveland — *Castite Systems, Inc.* It is quite possible that your family automobile includes one, or more, parts that have been treated by this company. The giant machine you can see on page 307 may also have parts treated by Castite. You can see Ms. Lamson above. The box gives a brief statement about her life.

The Great Society

During the 1960s, under the leadership of President Lyndon B. Johnson, Congress adopted a program that was called *The Great Society*. A major part of this program was written to promote equal opportunities in education and employment for all citizens, especially women, African-Americans, Spanish-speaking people (often called *Hispanics*), and other *minority* groups. Out of this came the *Affirmative Action Program* and the *Equal Employment Opportunity Program*. Today every organization that wants to do business with the United States government must demonstrate that it takes positive steps to employ minority persons and to use the services of businesses owned by minority persons.

Religion

There are two questions that almost every person asks at one or more times in life: "What is the meaning of life?", and "What is the meaning of death?" The great majority of people look for answers to these questions in some form of religion. During the 20th century, as people came to Ohio from all over the world, they brought with them ideas about religion that they learned as children. Today in almost every large city of Ohio, you can attend religious services of many kinds. There are a variety of Christian churches, Jewish synagogues and temples, Moslem mosques, and centers of Buddhist and Hindu worship. As you can see on pages 260, some of the most beautiful buildings in Ohio are centers of worship.

On the other hand, many people reject the teachings of organized religions but believe in a *Supreme Being*. The Native Americans lived very close to nature and worshipped the *Great Spirit*. The ideas expressed in the box on page 261indicate that Louis Bromfield accepted the beliefs of the natives.

St. Peter in Chains cathedral was built during the 1850s.

Isaac M. Wise Temple is the home of reformed Judaism in the United States.

The Moslem center of worship in Perrysburg is the largest mosque in Ohio.

Recreation

Have you ever thought of recreation as *re-creation*? Human beings need variety in their activities, including both work and play. People find recreation in many forms varying from doing hand work at home to traveling to distance lands. For example, every county has an annual fair that may be the biggest social event in the county. The Ohio State Fair, held in Columbus in August, advertises that it is the greatest fair in the United States.

In every county you can find recreation areas operated by a city, the county, or the State of Ohio where you can enjoy very active — or very quiet — recreation. Several county and state parks have been created in connection with flood control projects of the United States Army Corps of Engineers. The Ohio Historical Society owns at least sixty historic sites, and publishes a calendar of events held at them.

Of course, Ohio also has many recreation facilities that cost money. You can take boat rides on Lake Erie or the Ohio River. You can go to athletic events varying in skill from the *Little Leagues* to the highest-paid professional teams. You can go to world-class amusement parks at Cedar Point in Erie County or Kings Island in Warren County. You can visit zoos in several cities, and even go to a *Sea World* in Portage County — hundreds of miles from the sea.

During summer months, you can visit outdoor dramas that re-enact important events in the early history of our state. "Trumpet in The Land" is presented in Tuscarawas County near the site of the massacre at Gnadenhutten. "Tecumseh" is presented in Ross County where that Shawnee leader lived as a boy. "Blue Jacket" is presented in Greene County on the site of the village where he lived.

Ohio has been the home of so many popular sports and entertainment figures that only a few can be mentioned. During the 1960s and 70s, Oscar Robertson and Jerry Lucas were among the all-time great college and professional basketball players. Robertson graduated from the University of

Cincinnati; he now lives in Hamilton County and operates several businesses. Lucas attended The Ohio State University; he now lives in his native Butler County and develops new forms of educational materials. Jack Nicklaus, a graduate of The Ohio State University and a resident of Dublin, Ohio, is one of the best-known professional golfers in the world. Pete Rose, a native of Cincinnati and longtime star of the Cincinnati Reds baseball team, holds more baseball records than any player in history. At age fourteen, Tina Marie Bischoff of Columbus won the national long-distance swimming championship. Four years later, in 1976, she cut thirty minutes off the world record time for swimming across the English Channel.

Creative and Performing Arts

Throughout history wealthy people have given financial support to individuals who are especially talented in singing, acting, painting, sculpting, writing, dancing, playing musical instruments, or other activities we call the *creative and performing arts*. Some have given money to build concert halls and art museums; others have given collections of books and art to libraries and museums. Still others have given money so that musicians and actors can study or perform for the public.

Art

In 1932 Edna Maria Clark published a comprehensive study titled: *Ohio Art and Artists*. This book was such an important source of information that it was republished in 1975. In it, Ms. Clark made the statement:

"Every one concedes the **preeminence** of Cincinnati over other western cities, during the middle and late nineteenth century, in

the fields of art, literature, and public spirit. There are many valid reasons for this supremacy. Cincinnati was older than the other cities; for instance, Chicago was a mere fort and trading post when Cincinnati was a city of twenty-five thousand people with a definite social culture."[2]

Artists were attracted to Cincinnati because wealthy people of the city encouraged them by buying their works and helping them improve their skills. Nicholas Longworth, one of the wealthiest men in Ohio in the first half of the 19th century, helped many artists including Robert Duncanson, the first African-American to achieve fame as a painter. You can see some of Duncanson's works on the walls of the former Longworth home — which is now the Taft Museum in Cincinnati.

You can find paintings by Frank Duveneck in many art museums of the United States. Mr. Duveneck was born in Covington, Kentucky directly across the Ohio River from Cincinnati, but spent most of his professional career, from 1874 to 1919, in Cincinnati. His painting *Whistling Boy*, shown on the next page, has been shown in art museums throughout the United States.

Several of the other illustrations in this book are reproductions of works of prominent Ohio artists, and these have been identified where they are shown. Between 1982 and 1990, more than 19 million people viewed the Vietnam Veterans Memorial in Washington D.C., a creation of Maya Lin of Athens County.

Have you ever attended or shown your own handiwork in a *craft fair*? If so, you know that *folk art* is very popular today and takes many forms, including ceramics, quilting, and whittling. At Dover, in Tuscarawas County, you can visit the folk art museums

The Whistling Boy is a very popular painting by an Ohio artist, Frank Duveneck.

The home of Paul Laurence Dunbar in Dayton is now owned by the Ohio Historical Society.

of Ernest and Frieda Warther. Ernest has carved a large number of railroad trains from blocks of wood and ivory. Frieda has collected over 73,000 buttons and arranged them into a variety of "pictures."

Literature

Ohio has been the birthplace and/or workplace of many widely-known writers, but we can mention only a few. Harriet Beecher Stowe grew up in a family that was deeply involved in the 19th-century movement to abolish slavery. When her book, *Uncle Tom's Cabin*, was published it became a "best seller", and a strong influence in the movement to free the slaves in the southern states.

One of the best known American poets of the early 20th century was Paul Laurence Dunbar of Dayton. His former home in Dayton is maintained as a museum of his life and writings. The picture above shows him at home. The parents of Paul Dunbar were both born into slavery, but escaped to Dayton by way of the *Underground Railroad*. Paul was born there in 1872. Paul's mother worked and sacrificed to make it possible for him to attend high school, where he was the only African-American student. One of his classmates, neighbors, and friends was Orville Wright, whom you will learn more about in Chapter 14.

In high school Paul became editor of the school magazine and wrote the graduation song for the class of 1891. The only job he could get before or after graduation was operating an elevator in downtown Dayton at $4 per week for eleven hours a day.

Paul spent all of his free time reading and writing. When he was nineteen, he decided to publish a newspaper for the 5,000 African-American citizens of Dayton. This was possible only because his friends Wilbur and Orville Wright — who had opened a printing shop near his home — were willing to help Paul. The Wrights also helped him publish a small book of poetry.

During the late 19th and early 20th centuries, William Dean Howells, a native of Belmont County, Ohio, was one of the most respected writers in America. He was also editor of the literary magazine *Harper's Weekly*, which is still published. When Howells was given a copy of Paul Dunbar's book, he was so impressed that he published a feature article about Paul in the same edition of *Harper's Weekly* that honored William McKinley on his re-election as President of the United States. With this introduction to the world of literature, Paul's poetry became famous throughout the English-speaking world.

One critic wrote: "Dunbar's writing, either prose or verse, in ordinary English shows little more than the average

talent possessed by thousands of **literary-minded** young writers, whereas his **dialect** songs and stories have seldom been exceeded for simplicity, tenderness, and **lyric** sweetness."[3]

"Harriet Beecher Stowe

She told the story, and the whole
    world wept
At wrongs and cruelties it had not known
But for this fearless woman's voice alone.
She spoke to consciences that long
    had slept:

Her message, Freedom's clear reveille,
    swept
From heedless hovel to complacent throne.
Command and prophecy were in the tone
And from its sheath the sword of
    justice leapt.

Around two peoples swelled a fiery wave,
But both came forth transfigured from
    the flame.

Blest be the hand that dared be strong
    to save,
And blest be she who in our weakness
    came —
Prophet and priestess! At one stroke
    she gave
A race to freedom and herself to fame."[4]

By thirty years of age he suffered from two problems, alcoholism, and **tuberculosis** (a fatal disease of the lungs that was once very common). He died in 1906, and was buried in Dayton.

Stop and Think!

In 1900 Ohio had only 4 million people spread over the 88 counties. There were only two very large cities — Cleveland with

264

almost 382,000 people and Cincinnati with almost 326,000 — and two others of over 100,000 — Toledo and Columbus. For most people, each day was a struggle to gain the necessities of life. Very little was known about science or health. A few people had electricity in their homes and all depended on public transportation. Nevertheless, a great majority of people felt that their lives were better than in earlier years.

During the 20th century, conflicts in many parts of the world caused millions of people to migrate to the United States — many of them to Ohio. As improvements were made in public health, more people lived to be much older. As a result of these events, almost 11 million of us now live in Ohio — the great majority in urban areas. Today even the poorest of people can enjoy things that were not available to the richest people of 1900, but who can say whether our lives are really "better" than those of a century ago?

Review the Chapter

Building vocabulary...

abominable
chiropractor
coax
consolidate
coordinate
cordage
depression
dialect
literary minded
lyric
materiel
migrant worker
normal school
paramedic
paternalism
pharmacist

philosophy
plaque
polio
preeminence
prosperity
raze
recession
recruit
ropewalk
scenario
self-sustained
sharecropper
tuberculosis
vengeance
veto

Meeting new people...

Charles F. Kettering
Louis Bromfield
Carl B. Stokes
Louis Stokes
Robert A. Taft
Maya Lin
John Henry Patterson
Leonard Slye
Paul Laurence Dunbar
Franklin D. Roosevelt
Albert B. Sabin
Joan E. Lamson
Lyndon B. Johnson
Oscar Robertson
Jack Nicklaus
Pete Rose
Tina Marie Bischoff

Match them up ....

1. World War I	a. depresion
2. World War II	b. Muskigum River
3. Vietnam	c. Roy Rogers
4. India	d. serum
5. NCR	e. baby boomers
6. AFL	f. folk art
7. 1932	g. mosque
8. WPA	h. refugees

265

9. CCC   i. Ohio Guide
10. FHA   j. Malabar
11. poliomyelitis   k. CIO
12. Duck Run   l. growth of industry
13. Lamson   m. women in industry
14. Moslem   n. housing
15. Warthers   o. Dayton

Complete the thought...

1. During World War I, workers moved to Akron from ...., ..., and ....
2. Children born during the ten years after the end of World War II were called ....
3. The National Cash Register Company hired Charles Kettering as ....
4. .... believed that successful farming depended on working with nature.
5. Workers organized .... to help them gain better working conditions.
6. When almost everyone has a job, our nation is enjoying ....
7. When many people are out of work, our nation is suffering from a ....
8. The full names of two federal programs that provided work during the 1930s were ....and ....
9. .... schools were created by joining several small local schools.
10. Two large unions that did not join the AFL-CIO were .... and ....

Thinking it through...

1. Use information in Appendix B to calculate the percentages of 1990 residents of your county who were African-American and Asian people.
2. Ask your parents about how your ancestors came to live in Ohio, and share this information with your classmates.
3. Pick a company, school, or social program that you would like to learn more about, and make a list of places where you might get information about this subject.
4. Choose an important person who now lives in your community, city, or county, and prepare a report on how this person helped your community.
5. Write a report on what you think of the "quality of life" in your community, and what your and your classmates might do to improve the situation.

Working with maps...

1. On the map of your county, locate five centers of recreation that are closest to your home.
2. On the map of Ohio locate five state parks, forests and/or historical sites that you could visit on one-day trips from your home. Make plans to visit these sites while traveling from place to place on a bicycle.
3. On the map of the United States, locate the places from which people moved during World War I to get jobs in Akron.
4. On the map of the world, locate ten of the nations of Asia and three parts of the USSR mentioned in this chapter.
5. On the map of the world find the English Channel, which separates England from the rest of Europe. If Tina Marie Bischoff swam across the narrowest part of the channel in nine hours and three minutes, what was her average speed?

Footnotes

1. Moskowitz, et.al.: *Everybody's Business*, p.443
2. Clark, *Ohio Art and Artists*, p. 73
3. Kunitz and Haycraft, Editors, *American Authors 1600—1900*, pp. 232-233
4. Dunbar: *Lyrics by the Hearthside*, p.97

CHAPTER 13

How did patterns of living change?

- about new forms of energy and transportation.

- how life in rural and urban areas changed.

- how federal housing programs affected urban areas.

- how laws affected urban areas.

- how metropolitan areas developed.

In 1900 about half the residents of Ohio lived in incorporated places and the other half lived in rural areas. In general, the boundary of each incorporated place could be clearly seen: if you stood on the boundary and looked in one direction, you saw the town; if you looked in the opposite direction, you saw farmland. People living in rural areas had the advantages of clean air and freedom from congestion but had to provide their own water, dispose of their wastes, and accept isolation from medical help and cultural activities. People living in urban areas had

267

the advantages of public water supply and waste disposal, and easy access to medical help and cultural activities, but they had disadvantages of crowded housing and air filled with smoke and **soot** (small bits of carbon) of burning coal.

By 1950 a large majority of the citizens of Ohio lived in incorporated places, but it was not always easy to identify the boundary between areas that were urban and rural. As energy resources and personal transportation improved after 1950, more and more people chose to live in **suburban** areas (areas surrounding the cities). At the same time, shopping centers and places of employment moved outward. As a result, the large cities of Ohio lost hundreds of thousands of residents and millions of dollars of taxes. In this chapter you will learn about the patterns of living in Ohio today. It will help if you will review the various population figures for each county shown in Appendix B and the 1900 pattern of central places of Ohio shown on page 159.

Changes in Energy Resources

In Chapter 10 you learned about the importance of coal to the development of railroads and industries during the 19th century. By 1900 electricity, petroleum, and natural gas were available, and these new sources of energy greatly changed the pattern of living.

Energy in Homes

In 1900 most urban and rural families burned coal or wood — in a small fireplace or cast-iron stove — to heat each room. By 1940 most city houses had central heating systems that burned coal in furnaces to provide cleaner and more uniform heat. But coal furnaces were inconvenient, inefficient, and dirty by modern standards. During the

1950s, electrically-controlled furnaces became available to heat urban buildings by burning natural gas and rural buildings by burning fuel oil. After 1965 many houses in both urban and rural areas were built with electric heating systems.

In 1900 many homes had cook stoves heated by burning coal or wood, but natural gas, or **manufactured gas** (made from coal) was available in the larger cities. By 1950 all homes in cities were using gas or electricity for cooking, and many farm homes were using **bottled gas,** that is, liquified butane or propane.

By 1900 some houses in large cities also used natural or manufactured gas for illumination. In that year the houses built for wealthy people often had both gas and electric lighting systems: electricity was more effective, but gas was more reliable.

Energy in Factories

Before World War II, almost every factory in Ohio burned coal to create steam. The steam was used to heat the buildings and to operate steam engines that turned shafts to move the "forest of leather belts" you saw on page 182. Some factories generated their own electricity. The picture on page 269 shows a typical factory power plant that you could see in any factory, but you can only see such equipment in a museum today. Since World War II, almost all factories have used gas or oil for heating and electricity for operating machinery.

Electricity

The diagrams on page 270 show the sources of energy used in Ohio and the U. S. in 1982. As you can see, coal was the most important fuel in Ohio while petroleum was second and natural gas third. You can also

Factory steam boiler and engine at Greenfield Village, Dearborn, Michigan.

see that in the entire United States petroleum was the most important fuel while natural gas was second and coal third.

If homes and factories no longer use coal, why is it the most important fuel in Ohio today? The chart on page 271 gives the answer to this question. As you can see, the vast majority of electric energy generated in Ohio is from coal-fired power plants like the one you can see on page 272. A small amount of electricity is generated by diesel-powered units, but these are used only in times of maximum demand for power. There are two nuclear-powered electric plants in Ohio and some nuclear power is imported from western Pennsylvania. You will learn about problems of nuclear energy in Chapter 16. All of the hydroelectric power shown in the diagram is generated in northwest Pennsylvania. Almost all of the coal-fired power plants are along the Ohio River and Lake Erie, because they need large quantities of water and low-cost transportation for the coal.

Have you ever stopped to think about what your life would be like if there were no electricity? Perhaps you have thought about this when a storm or an accident

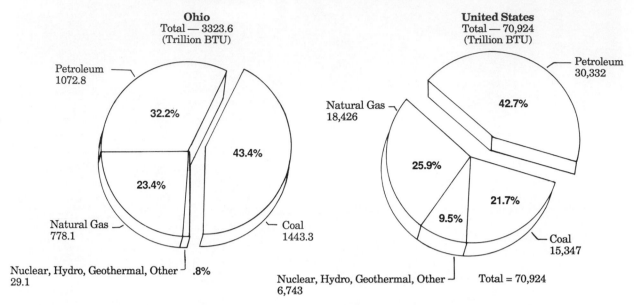

Gross Energy Consumption by Fuel, 1982, Ohio and U.S.

Ohio
Total — 3323.6
(Trillion BTU)

Petroleum
1072.8

32.2%

43.4%

23.4%

Natural Gas
778.1

Coal
1443.3

Nuclear, Hydro, Geothermal, Other .8%
29.1

United States
Total — 70,924
(Trillion BTU)

Petroleum
30,332

Natural Gas
18,426

42.7%

25.9%

21.7%

9.5%

Coal
15,347

Nuclear, Hydro, Geothermal, Other
6,743

Total = 70,924

The sources of energy used in Ohio are the same as those used in the entire United States, but the proportions are different.

interrupted the power service to your home. In the late 19th century, two natives of Ohio — Thomas Edison and Charles Brush — were leaders in making electricity useful.

Thomas Alva Edison

Thomas Edison was born in Milan in Erie County in 1847. The Edison family moved to Michigan when Tom was seven years old, and he never again lived in Ohio. Electricity was something that scientists experimented with in laboratories before Thomas Edison began to work with it. Edison invented a way to generate electricity, and to distribute it to potential users. He is best known for the many electrical devices he invented, including light bulbs, motion picture projectors, and sound recording devices. On page 273 you can see his birthplace as it

looks today. If you visit Greenfield Village in Dearborn, Michigan, you can see the laboratories in which he created many devices we use daily.

Charles Francis Brush

Charles Brush invented the first practical **dynamo** to generate direct-current electricity — the form of electricity used to power all electric streetcar systems, interurban lines, and arc lamps. He also invented electric arc lights, which were the only source of very bright lighting until about 1970. Mr. Brush was one of the founders of the Cleveland Electric Illuminating Company.

Another Ohioan — Charles Kettering — was one of the first inventors to make it possible for people in rural areas to have

Electric Power Generation
by Ohio Companies

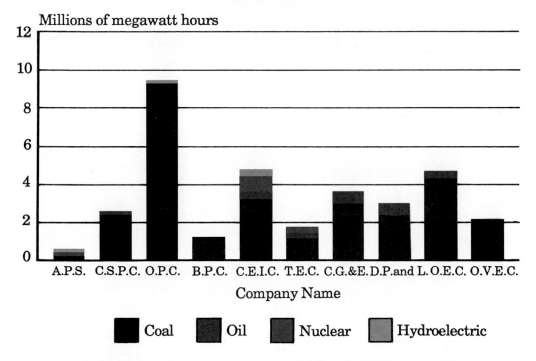

Millions of megawatt hours

Coal **Oil** **Nuclear** **Hydroelectric**

A.P.S. — Allegheny Power System
C.S.P.C. — Columbus Southern Power Company
O.P.C. — Ohio Power Company
B.P.C. — Buckeye Power Company
C.E.I.C. — Cleveland Electric Illumination Company

T.E.C. — Toledo Edison Company
C.G.&E.E. — Cincinnati Gas & Electric Company
D.P.andL.C. — Dayton Power and Light Company
O.E.C. — Ohio Edison Company
O.V.E.C. — Ohio Valley Electric Corporation

The electric energy you use comes from one of these companies.

electricity. In 1913 he built a small electric generating system, and he experimented with the system at his parents' farm in Ashland County. In 1916 he established the Domestic Engineering Company in Dayton to produce such systems for public sale. Some Ohio farms may still have the original wiring from their first Kettering system.

By 1920 almost every incorporated place in Ohio had an electric power plant, but only Kettering systems were used in rural areas.

During the Great Depression of the 1930s, Congress created the Rural Electrification Administration (REA) to encourage farmers to form independent companies to gain access to electric power. By 1940 almost half the farms of our state had electricity, and by 1950 all farms were electrified.

The Acme power plant in Jefferson County is an example of modern sources of electricity.

Changes in Transportation

In 1900 almost all railroads and boats were powered by steam engines. Although travelers became dirty from the smoke and soot, few people complained because steam power provided faster and more comfortable travel than walking or animal power. Prior to 1950 almost one-third of all steam **locomotives** (railroad engines) in the United States were made at Lima, in Allen County. By 1960 there were only a few steam engines still in use, and today you must go to the Railroad Museum in Worthington, to Lincoln Park in Lima, or to

the Henry Ford Museum at Dearborn to see "Iron Horses," as they were once called. During summer months, you can ride the steam-powered train shown on page 274 in the Cuyahoga Valley National Recreation Area south of Cleveland. Today all railroads in the United States use diesel or electric locomotives.

In Chapter 9 you learned about the development of suburban railroad communities. Railroads had two other important effects on urban development. First, since all factories depended on coal for energy, they had to be built next to a

Thomas Edison was born in this house in Milan. It is two-stories high in the rear.

transportation route. A few factories were built along the Ohio River and Lake Erie so that coal could be delivered by boats, but most were built near railroads. Second, as automobiles provided greater **mobility** (ease of movement) after 1920, many families moved "away from the noise and dirt" of railroads and factories. You will learn more about this movement later in the chapter.

The Good Roads Movement

By the end of the 19th century, many of the streets of the big cities were paved so that vehicles could move over them in all weather conditions. These improved streets encouraged use of a new form of transportation that was inexpensive, clean, and faster than walking — *bicycles*! On page 275 you can see a cartoon about people going to school to learn how to ride these marvelous inventions.

You can ride on this train in the Cuyahoga Valley National Recreation Area.

During the 1880s and 90s, thousands of bicycle owners joined the *League of American Wheelmen*. By 1900 this League was conducting a *Good Roads Movement* to encourage county and state governments to pave rural highways so bicycle riders could take trips into the countryside on Sundays and holidays. Unfortunately, these units of government had no money to improve the roads.

By 1916 travel in rural areas had become so difficult that Congress passed the *Federal Aid Road Act of 1916*. This act established a *Bureau of Public Roads*, and authorized the bureau to spend $75,000,000 over a period of five years. This was the first time, since the federal government built the National Road across Ohio and Indiana during the first half of the 19th century, that Congress approved the spending of money for highways.

Can you imagine learning to ride a bicycle under conditions like this?

In 1925 the Bureau of Public Roads established the system of numbered highways that we have today. The most dramatic change in highway transportation came in 1956 when Congress created the *National System of Interstate and Defense Highways* that you know as the *Interstate System*. These new high-speed highways also encouraged people to move away from the big cities.

As rural highways were paved during the 1920s, entrepreneurs began to offer travelers a new form of transportation — intercity bus service that could operate on city streets or rural roads to provide more flexible service than the interurban rail lines.

Public Transportation

Between 1890 and 1930, the cities of Ohio were changed greatly because land development and electric streetcar service were closely related. A company formed

In 1900 electric streetcars were the most important form of transportation in cities.

to provide streetcar service often became involved in land development. It bought tracts of land outside the city limits, annexed the land to the city, and developed residential subdivisions. Other entrepreneurs created residential subdivisions and negotiated with the owners of the streetcar system to have service extended to their land. In some cases, streetcar companies developed large amusement parks so that people would use the streetcars to go to these places for recreation.

The picture above shows how popular streetcars once were in cities of Ohio. As time passed, the cars used in the largest cities were made much larger and more comfortable. By 1940 bus service had replaced streetcar systems in small towns, and buses were used to create new transit routes in larger cities. Streetcars disappeared from Ohio during the 1950s,

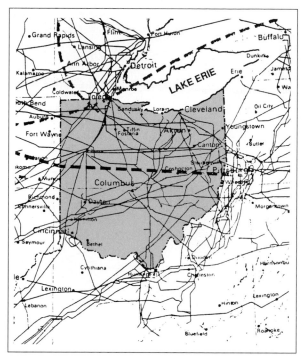

Several thousand miles of pipe lines carry petroleum products below the surface of Ohio

For military purposes during World War II, the United States built thousands of miles of pipelines to move petroleum from the fields of Louisiana, Oklahoma, and Texas to New England, and other places on the East Coast. At the end of the war, in 1945, some of these pipe lines were **converted** (changed) to transport natural gas. During the 1950s and 1960s, many thousands of additional miles of gas lines were built. The map on this page shows the pipelines that carry petroleum and gas to and through our state.

Motor Vehicles

Ohio has played a leading role in the development of motor vehicles, as you will learn in Chapter 14. The term *Motor Vehicle* includes all automobiles, trucks, and buses. If you had to decide whether electricity or a motor vehicle was more important to your life, how would you answer? It is almost impossible to think of life today without both of these conveniences.

The graph on page 278 shows how the population of Ohio, the number of motor vehicles, and the number of horses and mules, changed during the 20th century. (In this chart you must subtract the total number of automobiles from the total number of motor vehicles to get the combined number of trucks and buses.) You can see that the number of motor vehicles has been increasing more rapidly than the population. There are many households today that have as many vehicles as people, and a few that have more vehicles than people!

except for one high-speed line in Cleveland that is still heavily used. The only large streetcar systems in the United States today are in Pittsburgh, Philadelphia, Boston, Chicago, and San Francisco. You can see a few electric streetcars in the Railroad Museum at Worthington, and several in the Henry Ford Museum at Dearborn, Michigan.

Role of Petroleum in Transportation

Crude petroleum, and many of the products obtained from it, are used to power modern transportation systems. During the first half of the 20th century, crude oil (which was often called "bunker oil") was frequently used instead of coal to power steam ships.

Ohio Transportation Statistic
Horses, Autos, Total Vehicles & Population

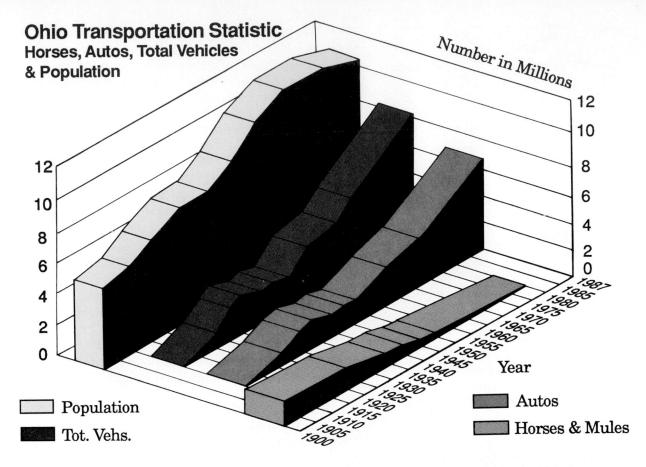

Number in Millions

Legend:
- Population
- Tot. Vehs.
- Autos
- Horses & Mules

Year axis: 1900, 1905, 1910, 1915, 1920, 1925, 1930, 1935, 1940, 1945, 1950, 1955, 1960, 1965, 1970, 1975, 1980, 1985, 1987

The number of motor vehicles in Ohio has increased faster than the number of people while horses and mules have almost disappeared.

Trucking

Do you have any idea how much your life depends on trucks? While not every single thing you use today has traveled on a truck, it is hard to think of things that have never been on a truck, either as raw materials or as finished products. Today the Norfolk Southern Corporation has semitrailer trucks that operate over highways on rubber-tired wheels to a railroad yard. At the yard, the semitrailers are fitted with steel wheels to operate on tracks as shown on page 279. These railcars are moved to a city hundreds of miles away where the rail wheels are removed. The semitrailers again travel over highways to their destinations. This is one example of how railroads are trying to compete with trucking companies.

Changes in Rural Life

Agriculture has always been an important industry in Ohio, but life on farms changed dramatically during the 20th century. If you look back to page 177, you can see how Ohio farms changed between 1900 and 1982. You can see that the number of farms was reduced while the sizes of farms increased.

As the number of farms declined, more than 9 million acres (3,321,000 hectares) were removed from the production of crops. What happened to all the land that was farmed in 1900 but not in 1982? Almost 400,000 acres (162,000 hectares) were converted to park and forest lands, including 177,000 acres (72,000 hectares) in Wayne National Forest, and more than 45,000 acres (18,000 hectares) in the Muskingum Conservancy District. In addition, large tracts of land in southeast Ohio are now owned by coal companies, and companies that grow trees on previously stripped land. During the last half of the 20th century, large areas of rural land were "urbanized," as you will learn later in this chapter.

Today people living in rural areas have the same standard of living as people in urban areas because electricity is available everywhere. Many rural families must provide their own water, but electric pumps simplify this problem. Few people in rural areas have sewer service, but modern, self-contained sewage treatment systems work effectively.

Modern farm machinery, like that shown on page 280 and 281, makes it possible for a family to operate a farm of several hundred acres (hectares). **Herbicides** (chemicals that kill weeds) eliminate the once difficult task of removing weeds during the early weeks of the growing season. **Pesticides** (chemicals that kill insects) prevent insects from damaging the crops. Fertilizers increase the productivity of the soil. But all these "labor saving" advantages cost money,

The Norfolk Southern railroad now uses vehicles that can operate as highway trucks and as rail cars.

Modern farm machines make it possible for one family to farm hundreds of acres of land.

and many farm families find it desirable — or necessary — to earn additional income. Unfortunately, these chemicals are creating environmental health problems you will learn about in Chapter 16.

Patterns of Land Use

Every part of every urban area reflects the most important form of transportation available when that area was developed. In Chapter 9 you learned how walking and horse-drawn omnibuses influenced the growth of cities. You can still see these effects in the oldest parts of Ohio towns. When electric streetcar lines were built, each route influenced development of the area it served. In 1920 automobiles began to affect the development of land, and today motor vehicles are the most important influence in every part of our state.

Modern farm machines like this are used to pick tomatoes.

Housing

You can look back to page 161 to see typical housing of average-income people in a big city of 1870. As electric streetcar lines extended outward, people could live further from places of employment and shopping, and housing conditions changed. By 1900 parcels of land in the suburban areas were larger than in the walking city, and houses did not cover all of the land area. As you can see on page 282, typical houses of this era had a front porch and one "blind" side, that is, no windows. The porches were used as

outdoor living rooms on summer evenings, and the omission of windows on one side provided privacy.

As automobiles became popular during the 1920s, land developers began to subdivide areas within the city that were not served by streetcar lines. In addition, farmers sold large lots to people who wanted to live away from the "noise and dirt of the city." Every new house had a garage because automobiles of that time could not be left out in the cold. When the owners of older houses purchased autos, they often added garages to their property.

New subdivision houses of the period around 1900.

Beginning in 1940, urban development changed drastically because of federal programs designed to encourage construction of new housing, and because of new laws related to housing and the growth of cities. You will learn about these things later in this chapter.

Shopping

As transportation changed during the 20th century, so did shopping. For example, the Kroger Company is now one of the largest retail food companies in America. It was founded in the 1880s by Barney Kroger as the neighborhood store you can see on page 283. By 1920 The Kroger Grocery & Baking Company had small stores along streetcar routes in almost every neighborhood of

Cincinnati. By 1980 there were Kroger *superstores* in many parts of the United States and every one had a parking lot to accommodate hundreds of automobiles.

Before World War II, the central business district (CBD) of every city was the most important area for shopping, business, and entertainment. Almost all streetcar lines entered the CBD. When people began driving automobiles to the CBD, parking became a serious problem. Businessmen tried to solve this problem in two ways: some built multistory garages, while others simply razed old buildings and created parking lots.

Barney Kroger's first grocery store in the 1880s.

As the streetcar lines were extended outward, entrepreneurs built shopping areas to serve the new suburbs. Places where streetcar lines crossed or branched were especially important locations, and you can still see these shopping areas along **arterial** (main) streets. Small food stores were often established at streetcar stops along the busiest streets. The most important suburban business districts of big cities were as large as the CBDs of small towns. As these suburban centers were built, investors built large apartment houses nearby with no provisions for automobiles.

By 1960 many of the streetcar-era shopping centers had lost importance. During the 1970s and 80s, local business people remodeled some of these business districts and built parking areas with the help of federal funds for urban renewal, but few of them are as prosperous today as they were in 1950.

One interesting change in shopping prior to World War II was the creation of places to sell and to service automobiles. The sales rooms had to be located where customers could get to them by streetcar. Auto service stations were established at the intersections of major streets. Below is a story about the first gasoline station in the United States.

As more people moved to outlying areas, and as interstate highways were constructed between 1957 and 1970, entrepreneurs began to build large shopping centers in outlying areas. The largest centers were built near interchanges of the new interstate highway system.

These centers are now called *malls* from the old English term *pall-mall* (pronounced *pell-mell*) meaning alley.

Businesses in the central business district reacted to this shift in population in one, or more, of three ways. First, they tried to have the city government build parking facilities in the CBD to attract auto drivers to the downtown. Second, the largest stores opened branches in the new shopping

The First Gasoline Station in America

Pataskala is a small town in the southwest corner of Licking County. About the time The Standard Oil Company started to make *coal oil* (now called kerosene) to light the lamps of the world, Harvey Wickliffe began to sell it to his neighbors in Pataskala. He carried the kerosene in a big tank on his horse-drawn wagon.

When a young man in town bought an automobile, Harvey decided to expand his business to include gasoline, so he bought a second tank and marked it *Gasoline — Danger, Inflammable*. He immediately lost business because old customers would not let him approach their homes with this dangerous liquid.

One of Harvey's customers, George Hunsaker, operated a *General Store*, and he put a gasoline tank and pump outside the store to sell fuel to passing motorists. Harvey noticed that people who wanted to buy gasoline had to wait until George took care of customers inside the store. Harvey said to the

store owner, "You know what I think George? I think the grocery business and the gasoline business don't mix. Maybe there ought to be a regular gasoline store with a man waitin' to fill up their tanks the minute they drive up to the pumps."

"Be all right for the automobile guys - but a fella'd starve to death in such a business."

"I'm not so sure," Harvey said thoughtfully. "You mad enough to sell me your gas pump?"

"I'm mad enough if you're crazy enough to buy it."

"All right," Harvey said, "I'll be after it as soon as I find a place to put it."

Harvey found an old building at the corner of Oak and Young Streets in Columbus, and created the service station you see on page 285.

From: Siedel, *Out of The Midwest*, pp. 99-104

The first gasoline station in the United States opened in Columbus in 1912.

malls. Third, small businesses moved to outlying malls.

Places of Employment

When walking was the main form of transportation, people lived close to their work. When electric streetcars became available, factories were built along the transit lines so that employees could get to work. Some of these factories are still used today, but many have been converted to other uses or razed.

In 1940, the United States began to supply war materiel to England, France, and the USSR to help them fight against Nazi Germany. The government built new factories in outlying areas that were one-story in height, and entirely oriented toward motor vehicle transportation. Special bus service was provided to transport workers who did not have

The Federal Housing Administration helped thousands of Ohioans to buy houses during the 1950s.

automobiles. After the war a few of these factories continued in operation under government supervision, but many others were taken over by private corporations.

Wartime factories established the pattern of industrial development you see today. The spread of gas and electric service after the war and the growth of the trucking industry made it possible for companies to build factories and warehouses anywhere that zoning laws and terrain permitted.

Institutions

All hospitals, schools, museums, and places of public entertainment are also located in relation to available forms of transportation. For example, during the 19th century, every college was built within walking distance of the center of a town. Later campuses in urban areas were located along streetcar lines, and local students often said that they went to a "streetcar college." Since 1950 *parking* has been an important problem for every school, hospital, and museum.

Before World War II, many people who moved to the suburbs continued to use streetcars to attend churches in the center of the city. Others went to new churches built within walking distance of the new housing subdivisions. Today some churches operate buses to transport their members, and every large church has some arrangement for parking.

From 1890 to 1950, motion picture theaters were important places of entertainment, and the largest and fanciest movie houses were in the central business district. Many small movie theaters were built in suburban business districts so that people could walk to them. When television became available during the 1950s, most of the downtown and neighborhood theaters closed. Some of these buildings were changed to other uses, but many were razed. Today most theaters are adjacent to shopping centers that have large parking areas.

Before 1900 professional people, such as physicians, dentists, and engineers, had their offices in the CBD. By 1910 some doctors and dentists established their offices in suburban areas along the streetcar lines. In 1940 many physicians made *house calls*, because they had automobiles but their patients did not. Today very few physicians make house calls, but growing numbers of them have two or more offices in different locations so that patients do not have to drive so far for medical help.

Federal Housing Programs

In Chapter 12 you learned about the Federal Housing Administration (FHA) program to provide better housing for low-income families. Several other programs had much greater effect on the cities of Ohio during the last half of the 20th century.

FHA Mortgage Guarantee

During the 1930s, a family could build a very comfortable house for less than

$10,000, but few people could afford the down payment of 20 percent ($2,000) required by banks or savings and loan companies. The FHA helped by guaranteeing these lending agencies that they would not lose money if a purchaser could not meet the monthly **mortgage** (loan to purchase house) payments. In exchange for this guarantee, the lending agency accepted a down payment of only ten percent.

During the late 1930s, this program encouraged construction of new houses on vacant land within existing cities. It also encouraged builders to create new subdivisions — sometimes called *plats* — outside city limits.

Very few houses were built during World War II. In 1945, the Congress created a program that permitted veterans of the armed services to buy homes with a down payment of only five percent of the cost of the house. When the war ended, this program led to a tremendous demand for new housing, and new subdivisions were **platted** (planned) wherever builders could find suitable land. You can see a typical house built under the FHA program on page 286.

Housing Act of 1968

By 1968 Congress became concerned that low-income families could not afford to rent or buy adequate housing. A new program, called *Section 8* housing, was created to help such people. The first part of the new law encouraged builders to create new houses — or remodel old ones — that low-income families could buy for a down payment of one percent, with monthly payments to be made over a period of forty

The three largest counties of Ohio changed in many ways during the 20th century.

	Cuyahoga	Franklin	Hamilton
1900 Total Population	439,120	164,460	409,479
Population of Largest City	381,768	125,560	325,902
Number of Other Towns over 1500	8	0	9
Population of Other Towns	24,187	0	23,671
Rural Population	33,165	38,900	59,906
1990 Total Population	1,412,140	961,437	866,228
Population of Largest City	505,616	632,910	364,040
Number of Other Villages & Cities	50	20	34
Total Population of Other Places	891,862	103,250	228,486
Total Population in Unincorporated areas	14,662	225,277	273,702

years. This program has not been too successful, and today you can find advertisements like the following in your local newspaper. These ads are paid for by the United States Department of Housing and Urban Development.

The second part of the 1968 housing act encouraged developers to build apartments for low-income families in suburban areas. The owner of the apartments could set the rent price high enough to pay for the cost of construction, maintenance, and operation of the building, and provide for a fair profit. In exchange for this guarantee of profit, the owner agreed to rent some of the apartments to low-income families, and to charge each family not more than 25 percent of the family's income. The federal government then paid the owner the balance of the rent.

Many of these projects were built in Ohio, but the need for housing for low-income families is almost as critical today as it was fifty years ago. In April, 1989 the Ohio Housing Finance Agency published the following facts:
1. For every two people in Ohio who needed low-cost housing, only one unit was available.
2. As many as 200,000 Ohians were unable to find rents that fit comfortably within their budgets.
3. There were almost 40,000 families waiting to move into public housing projects.[1]

Laws Relating to Urban Growth

Since adoption of the Second Ohio Constitution of 1851, a variety of laws relating to annexation and incorporation have influenced the development of urban areas. We will look at four types of laws.

Annexation

Annexation (from the Latin *annectere*, meaning "to connect") is the process by which cities grow in area. The simplest form of annexation has always been for the owner of land outside a city to offer it for

annexation before subdividing it. Between 1875 and 1925, as the cities of Ohio installed new public utilities, such as water lines, sewers, transit lines, or electric systems, people living outside the city wanted access to these services so they asked to be annexed to the city. Later in this chapter you will learn how Columbus has continued to use this system since 1940.

Incorporation of Towns

Requirements for incorporation of a village or city in Ohio have changed from time to time. Since World War II many towns have incorporated to avoid being annexed by an older village or city. To form a municipal corporation, the people living in an area must meet together to define the boundaries of the new village, or city, and adopt a form of government. This process may require several years of effort. When these steps have been completed, every citizen living within the proposed boundaries must have an opportunity to vote for, or against, the plan for incorporation. The table on page 288 shows how the processes of annexation and incorporation affected the three largest counties of Ohio between 1900 and 1990.

Zoning Regulations

Ohio laws permit incorporated places to adopt *Zoning Regulations* to eliminate many conflicts about the use of land. These regulations usually define areas for residences, offices, retail sales, manufacturing, and open-space uses. Counties and townships may also adopt zoning regulations, but they are usually weaker than those of incorporated places. Any group of citizens living under a zoning ordinance may **petition** formally ask the local unit of government to have changes made in the zoning of their neighborhood.

In 1950 Ohio had more cities of 100,000 population than any other state, but many changes took place in the last half of the 20th century.

	1950	1990
Cuyahoga	1,389,532	1,412,140
Franklin	503,410	961,437
Hamilton	723,952	866,228
Lucas	395,551	462,361
Mahoning	257,629	264,806
Montgomery	398,441	573,809
Stark	283,194	367,585
Summit	410,032	514,990
Cleveland	912,840	505,616
Columbus	362,205	632,910
Cincinnati	502,010	364,040
Toledo	303,725	332,943
Youngstown	168,065	95,732
Dayton	243,050	178,920
Canton	116,785	84,161
Akron	273,710	223,019

Subdivision (Plat) Regulations

Every incorporated place and every county in Ohio may adopt regulations to guarantee a certain minimum quality of subdivision development. Since the goal of land developers is to maximize profits, few subdividers build better projects than local laws demand. If a builder has a choice of creating a new subdivision inside an incorporated place that has strong standards, or in an unincorporated that has weak standards, the subdivision will usually be made in the unincorporated area.

Recent Changes in the Largest Cities

In 1950 Ohio was the only state with as many as eight cities with more than 100,000 people. By 1990 Ohio had only six cities of more than 100,000. The table above shows the relationships between the cities of Akron, Canton, Cincinnati, Cleveland, Columbus, Dayton, Toledo, and Youngstown and their counties in 1950 and 1990.

The graph on page 291 shows the 1950 and 1990 populations of each of the eight counties. You can see that the population of each county grew during the 40-year period, but only Franklin and Montgomery

Population Changes
of Largest Counties 1950 to 1990

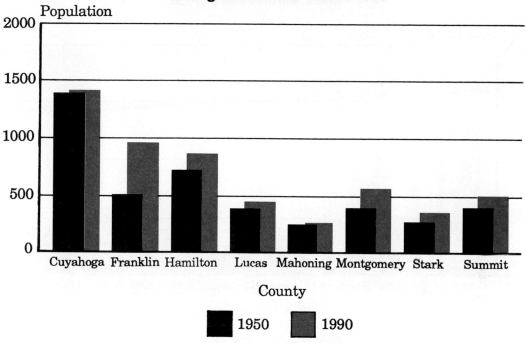

Between 1950 and 1990 Franklin County grew more than any other county in Ohio.

Counties had large percentage growths. The graph on page 292 shows the 1950 populations of the eight counties and their major cities. You can see that each major city, except Canton in Stark County, had at least half of the county population in that year. The graph on page 293 shows similar information for the 1990 populations. In that year only the cities of Columbus and Toledo had more than half the populations of their counties.

Metropolitan Areas

By 1940 some of the largest urban areas of the United States were very complicated, with mixes of incorporated and unincorporated areas. For this reason, the United States Bureau of Census created the idea of *Standard Metropolitan Area* (SMA). **Metropolitan** is from the Greek word *metropolis*, meaning "mother city." Each of the eight largest cities and counties of Ohio was part of an SMA. In 1960 this name was changed to *Standard Metropolitan Statistical Area* (SMSA). **Statistics** are numbers relating to a subject. The Bureau of Census map on page 294 shows the SMSAs of Ohio. If you look back to page 4, you can see how the diagonal lines fit the pattern of SMSAs. The SMSAs along the Ohio River that include Ohio counties exist because of cities in Kentucky and West Virginia.

Population of Counties
and Central Cities in 1950

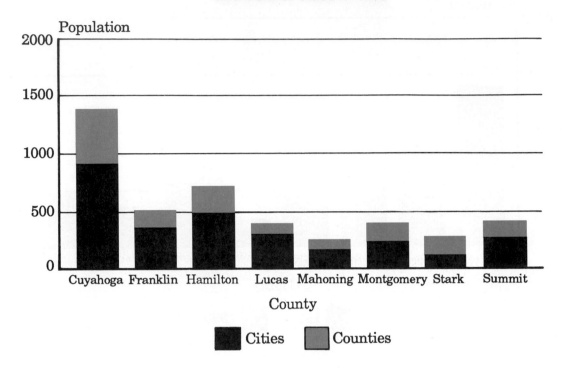

In 1950 each of the eight largest cities of Ohio had at least half the entire population of its county.

The SMSAs of Ohio

The basic principles of transportation and development you learned about in Chapter 7 can be used to explain why each of the SMSAs of Ohio developed as it did. But another very important principle has also been at work — *politics* — what we defined in Chapter 6 and 11 as the art of people living together in groups. Following are some examples.

Throughout history people have wanted to live in the best places they could afford (remember the Theory of Optimization).

When walking was the main form of transportation, wealthy people lived on the outskirts of town because they owned horses to move them longer distances. When steam railroads were built, those who could afford to ride the trains often moved to suburban communities. When automobiles became widely available, people who could afford to do so often moved to outlying areas and created new towns that had large building lots.

As automobiles grew in popularity, and housing, shopping, and industrial developments moved outward during the 1950s and 60s, settlements that had existed

Population of Counties
and Central Cities in 1990

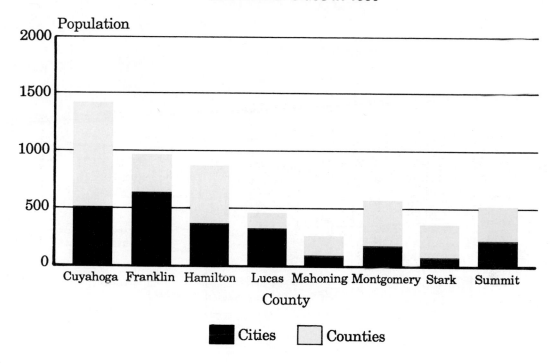

In 1990 only Columbus had more than half the population of its county.

for many years — perhaps as stagecoach stops in the early 19th century — were incorporated to include as much of the new development as possible. Towns incorporated during the 19th or early 20th century annexed as much surrounding land as they could manage. Each incorporated place adopted zoning laws that would, in so far as possible, attract only the "best" people to the community. The result of these actions was that low-income people became concentrated in the old central cities while upper-income people moved outward.

Beginning in 1968, federal housing laws were designed to help low-income people

find new housing. Since that time suburban developments related to federal housing programs have attracted low-income families to outlying areas. But many incorporated places have used a variety of political maneuvers to prevent such housing from being built in their areas. Looking at these two pages, can you guess which large city of Ohio avoided these problems? Yes, it was Columbus! The box gives Carl Stokes' explanation of the situation in that city in 1973. Conditions have not changed since then.

James A. Rhodes moved from the office of mayor of Columbus to Auditor of the State

293

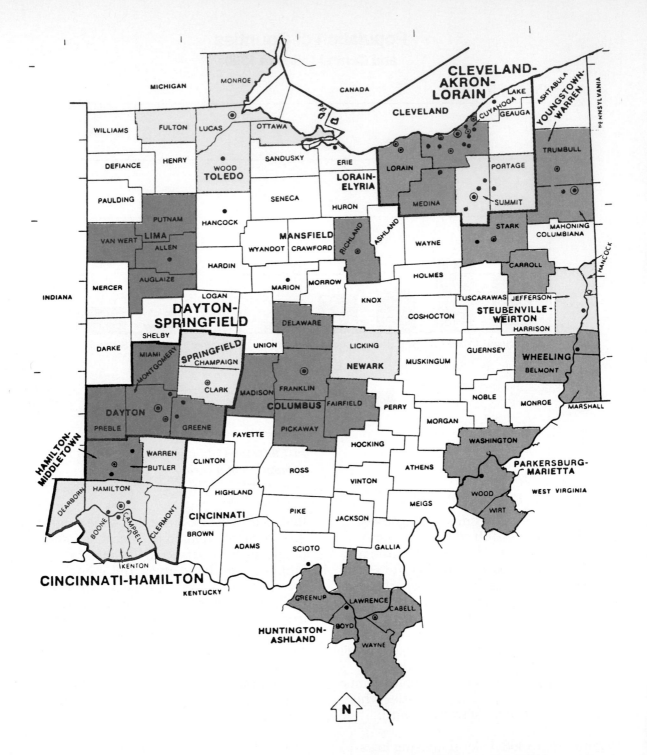

MICHIGAN

CANADA

CLEVELAND-
AKRON-
LORAIN

CLEVELAND

MONROE

WILLIAMS FULTON LUCAS OTTAWA

Lake

Cuyahoga GEAUGA

ASHTABULA

YOUNGSTOWN-
WARREN

PENNSYLVANIA

DEFIANCE HENRY

WOOD
TOLEDO

SANDUSKY

ERIE

SENECA

TRUMBULL

PAULDING

LORAIN-
ELYRIA

LORAIN

PORTAGE

PUTNAM

HANCOCK

HURON

MEDINA

SUMMIT

VAN WERT

LIMA
ALLEN

WYANDOT CRAWFORD

MANSFIELD

RICHLAND

ASHLAND

WAYNE

STARK

MAHONING
COLUMBIANA

HANCOCK

INDIANA

MERCER

AUGLAIZE

HARDIN

LOGAN

MARION MORROW

KNOX

HOLMES

COSHOCTON

CARROLL

TUSCARAWAS JEFFERSON

STEUBENVILLE-
WEIRTON

DAYTON-
SPRINGFIELD

DELAWARE

DARKE

SHELBY

MIAMI

MONTGOMERY

SPRINGFIELD
CHAMPAIGN

CLARK

UNION

LICKING

NEWARK

MUSKINGUM

GUERNSEY

HARRISON

WHEELING
BELMONT

MONROE

MADISON

FRANKLIN

COLUMBUS

FAIRFIELD

PERRY

NOBLE

DAYTON

GREENE

FAYETTE

PICKAWAY

MORGAN

MARSHALL

PREBLE

WARREN

BUTLER

CLINTON

ROSS

HOCKING

ATHENS

WASHINGTON

PARKERSBURG-
MARIETTA

HAMILTON-
MIDDLETOWN

DEARBORN

HAMILTON

BOONE

CAMPBELL

CLERMONT

HIGHLAND

CINCINNATI

BROWN

PIKE

VINTON

JACKSON

MEIGS

WOOD

WEST VIRGINIA

WIRT

KENTON

ADAMS

SCIOTO

GALLIA

CINCINNATI-HAMILTON

KENTUCKY

GREENUP

LAWRENCE

CABELL

HUNTINGTON-
ASHLAND

BOYD

WAYNE

N

*A great majority of the people of Ohio now live in
standard metropolitan statistical areas.*

Above: View of Cincinnati from Carew
Tower in 1957

Below: View of Cincinnati from Carew
Tower in 1991

of Ohio. From this office, he was elected governor of Ohio in 1962, 1966, 1970, and 1974. He ran again in 1978, but was defeated.

The cities of Ohio you know today are the results of events described in this chapter. You will learn more about the government of Ohio in Chapter 15.

Why Columbus Grew After World War II

[James A.] Rhodes never went beyond high school, but nobody ever questioned his [political] expertise. And he understood power. He was mayor of Columbus at the crucial time of suburban expansion for that city, the 1940s. Unlike the mayors of Cleveland, who couldn't see beyond their reelections, Rhodes saw that the suburbs had to be forced to incorporate as part of Columbus if the central city was to survive. Whenever a newly developed area decided it wanted water lines, Rhodes laid down his hard line. The suburb either submitted to annexation or it got no water. As a result, Columbus today has the largest land area of any city in the state. Had the same policy been followed in Cleveland [Mr. Stokes hometown], our city would not have been strangled economically by the surrounding suburbs who paid low sewer and water rates for Cleveland water, and used the availability of cheap water to attract industry and business from Cleveland.

From: Stokes, *Promises of Power*, p. 66

Stop and Think!

In Chapter 12 you learned that the decade of the 1940s brought great changes in the individual lives of most of the people of the world. In this chapter you have learned that urban areas also changed dramatically during the same period. Today people in rural areas of our state have the same energy resources and ease of transportation as those living in cities.

On the other hand, most of the large cities of our state are not as strong as they were in 1940. In 1900 almost everyone living in a rural area looked forward to trips to the big cities for shopping and recreation. Today many citizens of the big cities do their shopping and seek recreation outside the city limits. But the picture on page 297 — shows how exciting life can be in a big city! In Chapter 14 you will learn how industry affected these changes, and in Chapter 15 you will learn about the problems of government that have arisen because of the changing patterns of living.

Cincinnati celebrates a variety of festivals with fireworks.

Review The Chapter!

Building vocabulary...

arterial
bottled gas
convert
dynamo
herbicide
manufactured gas
metropolitan
mobility
mortgage
pesticide
petition (verb)
platted
statistic

Meeting new people...

Thomas Alva Edison
Charles Francis Brush
James A. Rhodes
Barney Kroger

Give an example of where you can...

1. See an oil lamp?
2. See a steam engine?
3. See an electric power plant?
4. Visit Thomas Edison's laboratory?
5. See a steam locomotive?
6. Travel on a U.S. numbered highway?
7. Ride on an electric streetcar?
8. See a greenhouse?
9. See a building built before 1900?
10. See a store that does not have a

parking lot?
11. See a school that does not have a parking lot?
12. See a church that does not have a parking lot?
13. See a factory that does not have a parking lot?
14. Read an ad about a house for sale?
15. Find a medical doctor who has more than one office?

What doesn't fit?... and why doesn't it?

1. (coal) (dirt) (natural gas) (soot)
2. (Brush) (Edison) (Kettering) (Rhodes)
3. (automobiles) (locomotives) (pipelines) (trucks)
4. (airplanes) (automobiles) (buses) (streetcars)
5. (fertilizers) (greenhouses) (herbicides) (pesticides)
6. (farms) (lots) (subdivisions) (towns)
7. (CBDs) (factories) (malls) (stores)
8. (annexation) (incorporation) (wealth) (zoning)
9. (Akron) (Cleveland) (Columbus) (Toledo)
10. (counts) (numbers) (people) (statistics)

Thinking it through...

1. Go to a community in your county that was established before 1900, and prepare a report on what has been done by the merchants along both sides of one block of one street to provide parking for their customers. You may have to look at a larger area to find a common parking lot or garage.
2. Which electric power company serves your home? Find out where the power plants of this company are located, and show them on the map of Ohio. How far does electricity travel from the nearest plant to your home?
3. Walk around your neighborhood and make a sketch map of the subdivision you live in. As a guide, all of the houses that are similar in appearance were probably built at the same time. On the map show any buildings that seem to be older than most of the houses.
4. Discuss with your parents what your family would do if your electric service was cut off for a period of three days. Make plans to "survive" such an emergency.
5. Discuss with your parents what your family would do if it had no automobile transportation for a week.

Working with maps...

1. Choose an old town in your county and visit it. On your county map, sketch the part of the town that was built before 1900, the part that was built between 1900 and 1940, and the part that was built after 1950. Prepare a report on how automobiles have affected each of these three areas.
2. Use the map of Ohio to prepare directions to guide your parents to drive to the state capital in Columbus. Estimate the time it will take to make this trip. (If you live in Columbus, plan a trip to one of the former capitals at Chillicothe or Zanesville.)
3. Use the maps of Ohio and the United States to prepare directions to guide your parents to visit Washington, D.C. Estimate the time it will take to make this trip.

Footnote

1. *Cincinnati Post*, April 18, 1989, pp. 1B-2B

298

CHAPTER 14

How did the economy of Ohio change?

Be ready to learn...

- about the problems of owning a business.

- how agriculture changed in the 20th century.

- how some of the largest companies changed.

- about the role of Ohio in the "space age."

You have learned how the population of Ohio increased from 4 million to almost 11 million during the 20th century and how ways of living changed during that time. Now we must consider how the **economy** of our state grew during the past hundred years. Whenever you make a purchase, you are affecting the economy of your family and the company that owns the store. When you sell Girl Scout cookies or school candy, or operate a "lemonade stand," you are performing an economic activity.

Status of Ohio Industries in 1986

	Number of employees in various industries	Total year's payroll in various industries	Number of companies in various indurtries
Agriculture, Forestry, Fishing	14,940	$234,620,000	2,719
Mining	26,947	$797,479,000	1,286
Contract Construction	149,492	$3,738,816,000	18,577
Manufacturing	1,123,722	$30,727,383,000	16,952
Transportation & Public Utilities	183,872	$4,864,575,000	7,729
Wholesale Trade	258,004	$5,895,827,000	17,452
Retail Trade	794,336	$8,242,421,000	60,480
Finance, Insurance & Real Estate	238,289	$4,776,448,000	19,539
Services	982,211	$15,036,830,000	75,149
Unclassified	26,320	$451,297,000	15,000
Totals	**3,798,133**	**$74,765,696,000**	**234,883**

The economy of Ohio is very complex because it includes many kinds of activities, which have changed rapidly since World War II, and especially since 1980. The table above shows the types of industries included in the census of Ohio industries in 1986, the number of jobs in each industry, the number of companies in each industry, and the total payroll of each industry. We will look back at this table several times, but we must learn something about how the ownership of business has changed over the years.

Ownership of Business

Just as every city in Ohio began as a small settlement, so every business began with only one person or a small group of people.

The great majority of all businesses remain small, but some grow to employ thousands of workers.

It has always been easy to start a new business in Ohio, but it is very difficult to make it successful. Each of the following steps is important to success:
1. You must have an idea for a product or service that people need or want.
2. You must be aware of the laws relating to what you want to do, and the related fees and taxes.
3. You must have enough money, time, and energy to develop your idea.
4. You must make the public aware of your product or service.

5. You must find people to help you create the product or service.

Because needs and desires change over the years, businesses must seize new opportunities if they are to survive, as these two examples will show:
1. In 1900 several companies in Ohio made very good leather harnesses for horses. Some owners of these companies decided that automobiles would never be popular and continued to make harnesses. Others decided that they would have a brighter future if they made leather seats for the *horseless carriages*. Which companies do you think were still in existence in 1925?
2. In 1903 the Wright Brothers patented their method of making a "flying machine," but they did not create a company to manufacture a large number of airplanes. Other entrepreneurs like William Boeing used the ideas of the Wrights to build planes. Boeing also organized United Airlines as the first company to fly passengers on a regularly scheduled flights. Who contributed most to modern life?

In the United States **free enterprise** (private ownership of business) is the basic principle of our economy. This means that entrepreneurs have the right to succeed — or fail — depending on their efforts, ability, and resources. If a company — or person — cannot produce goods or services at a profit, it must close or sell out to another company. If a company borrows money that it cannot repay, it can go to court and ask to be declared **bankrupt**, which involves three steps:
1. the company will close or be taken over by another company,
2. the owner(s) will give up all interest in the company, and
3. in return the company debts will not have to be paid.

On the other hand, some companies are very successful. In Chapter 10, for example, you learned that John D. Rockefeller recognized the possibilities of selling petroleum and had the ability to organize a company to do so. Rockefeller created such a large petroleum company that it **monopolized** (completely controlled) the production, refining, and sale of petroleum products throughout the United States. The brands you know as Amoco, Chevron, Mobil, Texaco, Exxon, and once knew as SOHIO (now BP), all came from the Standard Oil Company that he organized.

Conglomerates

Shortly after World War II, some entrepreneurs began to buy a variety of operating companies and combined them into **conglomerates**. In recent years this word has been used to describe "a business corporation made up of a number of different companies that operate in widely different fields." Since 1970 conglomerates have changed the ownership of Ohio industries so rapidly that no one can know all of them. Perhaps someone in your county had a good idea for a new business, carried out all of the steps mentioned above, and created a business that was the pride of your community. What happened when that person died, or wanted to retire? Perhaps a family member took over management. Perhaps the stockholders hired someone new to manage the company. Perhaps the employees joined together to buy the company and continue operations. Perhaps a conglomerate bought it and continued to operate it. Or perhaps the new owners closed the business or moved it to another location.

You will learn about some particular conglomerates later in this chapter. We will now look at the industries of Ohio in the order they are shown on page 300.

Agriculture, Forestry, Fishing

Agriculture has always been an important industry in Ohio. Cows are raised for both milk and meat, pigs for meat, and sheep for wool. For many years every farm raised a few chickens for eggs and meat; today thousands of chickens are raised under controlled conditions to create the maximum number of eggs and quantities of meat. Today the most important field crops are corn, soy beans, hay, and wheat. Ohio also produces large quantities of tomatoes, celery, sugar beets, grapes, and other fruits and vegetables.

The smallest modern farms shown on page 177 are special places. Some of them have *greenhouses* in which vegetables and/or flowers are grown throughout the year, even within a city. In addition, some farm families own a small area, but raise crops on several hundred acres (hectares) of rented land. The very largest farms are owned by corporations that operate them like manufacturing businesses.

The food-processing industry of our state uses the fruits, vegetables, and grains to make food products that are sold in many places. For example, the La Choy Food Products Company at Archbold, on the boundary between Williams and Putnam Counties, is one of the largest producers of canned and frozen Chinese foods in the world.

Condition of the Land

In Part II you learned how fertile the land was when the first settlers arrived in the Ohio Country. Unfortunately, very little was done during the 19th century to protect the soil. By 1930 large areas of land, especially in the southeast, were in poor condition because most of the trees had been cut for lumber and the topsoil had washed away.

As you learned in Chapter 12, the Civilian Conservation Corps program (CCC) put hundreds of young men to work to improve conditions in the drainage area of the Muskingum River. In 1939 Louis Bromfield bought four farms covering almost 1000 acres (405 hectares) in the southeast corner of Richland County. This land was just upstream from the Clear Fork Reservoir, which was built as part of the conservation program. Bromfield's goal was to restore the land to its original fertility. The box on page 304 tells how he described his experience shortly before he died in 1956.

Migrant Workers

Some crops require large numbers of workers during periods of planting and/or harvesting. Do you know what a migrant worker is? For many years, the federal government permitted thousands of families from Mexico to migrate northward through the United States to pick crops from Texas into Michigan. Every member of a family, except the smallest children, put in long hours in the fields. Today farmers in northwest Ohio provide simple housing like that shown on page 303. The information in the box on page 305 is from an official report about migrant workers in 1958.

Migrant farm workers live in small houses like those shown in this picture.

Far fewer migrant workers are used today than were used in 1958 for two reasons:

1. Many field crops have been standardized through the process of **genetic engineering** so that plants grow to a uniform size and mature at the same time.

2. Machines have been developed to speed the harvesting of crops. For example, genetic scientists developed new types of tomatoes that can be picked by machines like that shown on page 281.

Summary of Louis Bromfield's Work at Malabar

When the snow was gone [in 1940], I discovered that the valley of my childhood was no longer there. Something had happened to it. It had been ravaged by time and by the cruel and careless treatment of the land. As a small boy I had never noticed that these once small, lovely, rich valleys throughout our countryside had already begun to change, growing more gullied and bare with each year, or that the pastures grew thinner and more weedy and the ears of corn a little smaller each season.... Some of the farms [nearby] no longer raised crops at all. They had been rented out to [people] who took everything off them until they would no longer grow anything. The houses were occupied by industrial workers who spent their days in the [Mansfield] factories...

Today, fifteen years later, we at Malabar have ... found .. a tangible world of great and insistent reality, made up of such things as houses, and ponds, fertile soils, a beautiful and rich landscape and the friendship and perhaps respect of my fellow men and fellow farmers. The people who come to the Big House are ... plain people and farmers and cattlemen from all parts of the world.

Perhaps it will turn out that I have left behind some contributions not only to the science of agriculture, which is the only profession in the world which encompasses all sciences and all laws of the universe, but the realm of human philosophy as well.

From: Little, *Louis Bromfield at Malabar,* pp. 220-222

Forestry

Forestry has always been an important industry in southeast Ohio. Today large areas in this part of our state are protected as state or national forests. Saw mills are given the right to cut trees of certain size to make lumber or pulp for paper. In many cases, areas of perhaps fifty acres are "clear cut," and later reseeded to grow new trees. In this process, trees of all sizes are cut, and the wood is used in the most economical way.

Fishing

Fishing is not an important industry for the economy of Ohio. There are a few *fish farms* where the owners raise fish under controlled conditions for sale to wholesale distributors. For several years prior to 1970, commercial fishing on Lake Erie was not economical because of the polluted condition of the water. Regulations enforced by the United States and Ohio Evironmental Protection Agencies (EPA) led to cleaning

**Excerpts from Report
of Governor's Committee
on Migrant Labor in 1958**

"The migrant worker has been playing an increasingly important role in Ohio's agricultural economy as many growers are almost totally dependent on this mobile labor force to help plant and harvest the crops. Their services are needed during the critical periods when the success or failure of handling a crop [depends] upon having an adequate labor supply. ... "

The committee report included the following statements from two church groups:

1. "Generally the attitude of the farmers is good in Wood county. The farmers realize the workers are necessary and they treat them as people. Part of this is due to the fact that there are small camps on many farms. The farmers enthusiastically welcome the Migrant Ministry for their workers.

"This fall some of the children from the Wood County Canning Company ... enrolled in school." {From "United Church Women Report on Wood County"}

2. "Of the 10,000 migrants who work in Ohio field crops each summer, the majority are Texas Mexicans. Of these, 95% are Catholic. ...

"Men and women of the parish are organized to teach in the camps. They supervise the distribution of clothing and food to those who are in need. They work with the parish priest to perform many services; for example, furnishing transportation to the Health Clinics, recruiting nurses, providing playground facilities for children, 'selling' the community on the importance of accepting the migrant as a fellow citizen."

{From "Report of the Work of the Catholic Church"}

Quoted from: Smith (ed.) *An Ohio Reader*, pp. 399-405

the lake water so that fish could live. Since 1988 this industry has faced new problems in the form of **zebra mussels** carried to the Great Lakes by ships that passed through the St. Lawrence Seaway. These small, useless shell creatures reproduce rapidly eating the food needed by small fish. By the end of 1990, scientists had found a way to kill these pests, but they had already spread to some of the smaller lakes.

Mining and Quarrying

The table on page 300 show that in 1986 almost 27,000 Ohio workers were employed in mining — which includes quarrying. You learned about 19th-century quarrying in chapter 10, and the industry has scarcely changed except for the machinery used. The most important products of Ohio mines are salt, **gypsum** — a very soft rock used to make plaster — and coal. Almost one-third of the salt used in the United States comes from Wayne and Cuyahoga Counties, but

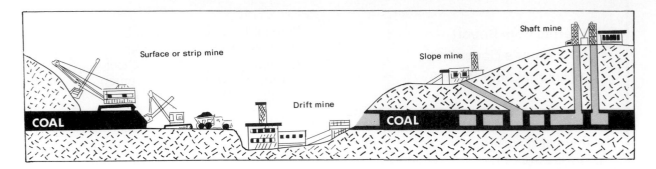

Coal is mined in a variety of ways, but most of it is removed by surface or strip mining.

the total number of workers required for this production is small. The gypsum mined in Ottawa County is the source of plaster that is used in the construction of almost every house in Ohio.

Coal Mining

In Chapter 10 you learned about coal mining in the 19th century. The diagram above shows all possible ways to remove coal from the earth. As larger and larger pieces of earth-moving equipment were developed, **strip mining** methods were adopted. Today huge machines, like the one shown on page 307, remove thousands of cubic yards (meters) of earth and rock to uncover seams of coal in southeastern Ohio. They can move a volume of material equal to the size of an average classroom at one time. Machines similar to the one shown are made by Dresser Industries, Inc. in Marion County, and used all over the world.

For many years, the coal companies merely tore up the landscape, as shown on page 308, took the coal, and moved to another location. Since 1980 no company can open a strip mine until it has submitted plans for how it is going to restore the landscape to a usable condition.

As coal mining changed from underground to stripping methods, the number of workers dropped greatly. In January 1990 the United Mine Workers (UMW) met in Columbus, Ohio to observe the 100th anniversary of the founding of the organization in that same city. A news release from the meeting said that the active membership nationwide was 600,000 in 1940, but there were only 190,000 active members in 1990 while 127,000 retired miners were receiving union pensions. For example, more than 3,000 coal mining jobs disappeared from Harrison County between 1970 and 1990. You can look back to page 24 to see where coal was mined in Ohio in 1987.

Contract Construction

All large structures are built by the *contract construction* industry, which operates in the following way:
1. An individual, a company, or a unit of government needs a new structure, such as a house, store, church, factory, or an airport, harbor, railroad, highway, pipe line, sewer, electric power line, dam, or power plant.
2. When this need is advertised, **contractors,** who can do the work study

The American Electric Power Service Corporation put this machine in operation near Zanesville in 1989. Machines like this are made by Dresser Industries, Inc. in Marion County.

the plans and decide how much it would cost to build the structure.

3. Various contractors submit written proposals (**bids**) to build the structure for a certain amount of money.

4. The individual or organization that needs the structure looks at all the proposals, and signs a written **contract** with the contractor offering the "lowest and best bid."

5. The winning contractor then organizes all the workers and materials needed to build the structure and manages the construction.

6. When the project is finished on time for the agreed amount of money, everyone has benefited.

Unfortunately, the forces of weathering and erosion you learned about in Chapter 2 affect the structures in the same way they affect mountains. Structures also weaken under the stresses of daily use; therefore, some construction companies specialize in repairing existing structures.

Infrastructure

Do you know about the **infrastructure** of your community? During the 1980s, many speeches were made and many articles written about problems with the infrastructure of local communities. The word "infrastructure" was created to represent all of the fixed facilities that are important to your daily life — schools, highways, power lines, water lines, sewers, and other public works. You have learned how the public utility systems of Ohio grew over the years. Today there are many sewers and water pipes that have been in use for seventy-five to a hundred years. Many of these old pipes must be replaced because they are broken or overloaded. During the last fifty years, government officials have been so busy planning for new growth of urban areas that they have paid little attention to existing facilities. Today political leaders are faced with the combined problems of demand for new facilities in new outlying areas, and repair of the infrastructure in the old cities. This means that there is a large amount of work available in contract construction IF cities, counties, and the state can raise money to pay for these needs.

Before laws were adopted to control strip mining, companies took coal and left the landscape looking like this scene in Southeastern Ohio.

Manufacturing

For many years Ohio, Indiana, Illinois, Michigan, and Wisconsin — the states created out of the old Northwest Territory — were called *The Industrial Heartland of America* because so many products were manufactured in these states. Beginning about 1970

manufacturing declined in this region to such an extent that by 1980 some writers were referring to the area as *The Rust Belt*.

How has this situation affected Ohio? Between 1966 and 1988, the population of Ohio increased slightly, from 10,726,007 to 10,784,200, but the number of manufacturing jobs dropped from 1,409,766

Between 1966 and 1988 many factories moved from the eight largest counties of Ohio into surrounding rural counties.

Metropolitan Areas	1988 Manufacturing Jobs	1966 Manufacturing Jobs	Change
Cuyahoga	207,997	274,740	-66,743
Mahoning	16,404	37,036	-20,632
Stark	52,788	65,362	-12,574
Summit	67,501	90,508	-23,007
Astabula	10,576	11,815	-1,239
Columbiana	9,845	11,175	-1,330
Geauga	9,897	4,874	5,023
Lake	27,863	20,155	7,708
Lorain	32,246	30,035	2,211
Medina	9,866	5,458	4,408
Portage	12,475	8,989	3,486
Trumbull	49,055	39,283	9,772
Tuscarawas	9,041	10,092	-1,051
Wayne	15,306	11,716	3,590
Net Change			-90,378
Franklin	73,432	81,526	-8,094
Delaware	5,608	3,522	2,086
Fairfield	7,884	10,319	-2,435
Licking	11,154	12,625	-1,471
Pickawy	5,153	3,535	1,618
Madison	1,822	551	1,271
Union	9,670	2,355	7,315
Net Change			290
Hamilton	140,825	152,368	-11,543
Butler	28,031	22,106	5,925
Clermont	7,676	1,134	6,542
Warren	7,407	1,971	5,436
Net Change	1/2 Warren		3,642
Lucas	62,533	61,871	662
Fulton	7,297	4,615	2,682
Ottawa	3,750	3,538	212
Sandusky	11,500	8,607	2,893
Wood	12,799	7,817	4,982
Net Change			11,431
Montgomery	87,386	111,410	-24,024
Greene	7,095	3,281	3,814
Miami	17,944	14,344	3,600
Preble	2,957	1,334	1,623
Warren	7,407	1,971	5,436
Net Change	1/2 Warren		-12,269

SOHIO logos were changed to BP.

to 1,328,426. The table on page 309 shows what happened to manufacturing jobs in the eight largest counties and their metropolitan areas. The map on page 311 shows the same information in graphical form. You can see that all the largest counties, except Lucas, lost manufacturing jobs while many of the surrounding counties gained such jobs. This movement of jobs is directly related to the decline of the largest cities and growth of the metropolitan areas you learned about in Chapter 13. We will now look at a few examples of manufacturing companies that have played important roles in the economic history of our state.

Petroleum

In 1911 the United States government forced John D. Rockefeller to break up his Standard Oil Company into several smaller companies. One of the new units was The Standard Oil Company (Ohio). The offices

and refinery of this company were in Cleveland, and the symbol *SOHIO* became well-known throughout the state. During the 1960s, the company ran into problems and received help from The British Petroleum Company (plc), a world-wide petroleum company. By the end of 1987, British Petroleum owned all of The Standard Oil Company (Ohio), and announced that the name was being changed to *BP America*. During 1991 the long- familiar SOHIO signs were replaced by the new *BP* signs as shown on page 312.

In 1887 fourteen small oil-producing companies in northwest Ohio united to form the *Ohio Oil Company*, with headquarters in Findlay, Ohio. By 1946 Ohio Oil was using the brand name *Marathon*, and in 1962 the company name was changed to *Marathon Oil Company*. In 1982 the United States Steel Corporation bought the Marathon company, and in 1988 United States Steel became *USX Corp.*

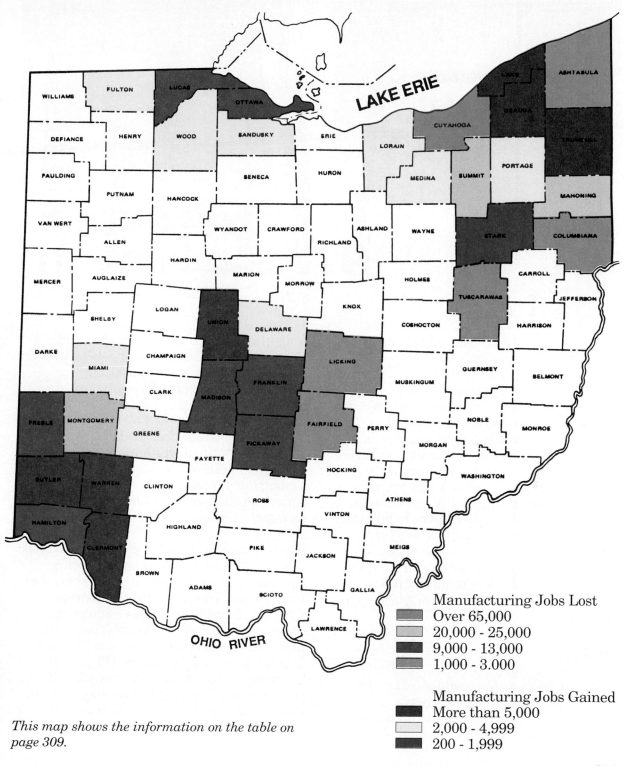

LAKE ERIE

OHIO RIVER

Manufacturing Jobs Lost
Over 65,000
20,000 - 25,000
9,000 - 13,000
1,000 - 3,000

Manufacturing Jobs Gained
More than 5,000
2,000 - 4,999
200 - 1,999

This map shows the information on the table on page 309.

311

SOHIO signs were replaced by BP signs in 1991.

Headquarters of Marathon Oil Company are still in Findlay.

Do you know what *leaded* gasoline is? If not ask your parents or grandparents about it. Up to 1930 automobile engines were inefficient and made strange noises while running. Charles Kettering assigned some research people to solve these problems. They discovered a chemical they named **tetraethyl lead**, which — when added to gasoline — caused auto engines to operate smoothly. Unfortunately, lead is a poisonous material, and automobiles were discharging it into the air. For this reason, Congress passed a law requiring use of *unleaded* gasoline in all automobiles made after 1975.

Steel

In 1920 Ohio was the home of five of the largest steel companies in America: United States Steel Company in Lorain, Republic Steel Corp. in Cleveland, Jones & Laughlin Steel Corp. in Cleveland and Youngstown, Youngstown Sheet & Tube Company in Youngstown, and The American Rolling Mill Company, Inc. in Butler County. By 1985 three of these corporations were owned by LTV Corp., a large conglomerate that owned LTV Steel. By 1989 LTV Steel was bankrupt, and the large steel mills of Cleveland and Youngstown were closed or razed. The American Rolling Mill Company, Inc. changed its name to ARMCO, Inc.

Nevertheless, in 1990 Ohio was the second largest steel-producing state, with only Indiana producing more. By that year, the three largest companies had Japanese partners. In addition to these companies, there were several small mills that made new steel out of scrap metal — a long-used form of "recycling." On page 313 you can see a picture of steel making at the ARMCO steel mill in Middletown. You may want to compare this picture to the picture of the Buckeye Furnace on page 27.

The liquid steel you see here in the ARMCO Steel Company at Middletown may be part of a refrigerator or automobile your family owns.

Glass

Throughout the world for thousands of years, each piece of glass was made by hand. About 1900, Michael J. Owens invented a machine to mass-produce glass bottles, and then organized the Owens Bottle Machine Company in Toledo, Ohio in 1907. For most of the 20th century, Toledo was known as an important center of the glass-making industry in the United States. By 1965 the company name had been changed to Owens-Illinois, Inc. In 1990 the world headquarters of Owens-Illinois were still in Toledo, and the company operated several factories in Ohio, but none of them made glass products. In 1987 the company was taken over by a **corporate raider** (a financial company that buys a big corporation and then sells off pieces of it).

In 1938 Owens-Illinois joined with the Corning Glass Company of Corning, New York to form the Owens-Corning Fiberglas Corporation. This new company produced an excellent insulation material called **Fiberglas**. In 1990 Owens-Corning had its home office in Toledo and a factory and large research center in Licking County. The company also had factories in several other states and foreign countries.

A third company, Libbey-Owens-Ford Company was founded in Ohio in 1916, and established its headquarters in Maumee (Lucas County). It had large factories in Lucas and Wood Counties to manufacture flat glass used for windows and mirrors, and safety glass for automobiles. Over the years it moved into other types of manufacturing, including sheet and film plastics, and stopped making glass in the late 1980s.

Paper and Printing

In 1986 more than 30,000 people were employed in making paper in Ohio. Almost 70,000 were employed in printing and publishing — the industry that uses a large percentage of the paper manufactured. Several of the paper factories that were built along the Miami and Erie Canal during the 19th century are still in operation. One of these, the Fox Paper Company in Hamilton County, closed in 1988 after operating for more than a hundred years.

In 1846 Daniel Mead bought part interest in a paper mill in Dayton, Ohio. By 1882 he owned the entire company and changed the name to Mead Paper. In 1890 Mead bought a paper mill in Chillicothe, Ohio, and one hundred years later this factory, which you can see on page 315, was the largest center of employment in Ross County. In 1988 Mead was the largest manufacturer of school supplies in the world.

Have you ever heard of *McCall's Magazine*? Your grandmothers, and perhaps your mother, knew it very well! The McCall Corporation was established in 1897 to produce patterns for women who made their own clothing. The company began to publish magazines, and built its printing plant in Dayton. In 1968, 8,500,000 copies of *McCall's Magazine* were printed in Dayton every month, plus 4,400,000 copies of *Redbook* magazine. First one conglomerate, then another bought the company, and each new owner changed it. While *McCall's Magazine* and *Redbook* are still published, they are not nearly so popular as they once were.

314

Large modern factories, like this Mead paper mill at Chillicothe, cover several acres of land. Parking for employees may require more land than the factory. A large part of the "smoke" from the tall stack is water vapor.

Rubber and Plastics

During the 19th century, rubber was used for a wide variety of products, but it became even more important during the 1880s for bicycle and carriage tires. In 1870 Benjamin Franklin Goodrich organized The B.F. Goodrich Company to make such tires in Akron, Ohio. In 1898 F. A. Seiberling also decided to make rubber tires in Akron. He

organized a company and named it Goodyear Tire & Rubber Company to honor Charles Goodyear, who had discovered how to make natural rubber more useful. In 1900 Harvey S. Firestone organized The Firestone Tire & Rubber Company in West Virginia to sell rubber carriage tires. In 1902 he too began to manufacture tires in Akron. General Tire and Rubber Company was established in Akron in 1915. By 1920

40 percent of all the rubber products in the world were made in Akron, and the city was called *The Rubber Capital of the World*.

What is the situation today? During the 1980s corporate raiders tried to buy Goodyear Tire & Rubber Company. This action caused great turmoil in the company. In 1988 Goodyear was the 31st largest company in the United States. The main offices were still in Akron, but no tires were made there. In 1988 The B.F. Goodrich Co. was the 115th largest company, with headquarters in Akron, but it made no rubber products there. By 1980 it had transferred its tire manufacturing to Uniroyal-Goodrich, and in 1990 this company became part of the Michelin Tire Company of France. Michelin established its United States office in Akron, but makes no tires there. During the late 1980s, the Bridgestone Corp. of Japan bought the Firestone company, and in 1989 *Bridgestone* replaced the brand name *Firestone*. The tire factory was closed several years ago and the Bridgestone offices moved from Akron to Tennessee in 1991.

The General Tire and Rubber Company began to buy other businesses, including radio and television stations, and in 1984 changed the corporate name to GENCORP Inc. GENCORP sold its tire factories to a German company that now has offices in Summit County, but does not make tires there. The Cooper Tire and Rubber Company continues to make tires and rubber products in Hancock County.

In Chapter 10 you learned about the importance of leather during the 19th century. Many of the items that were once made of leather or rubber are now made of **plastic** (from a Greek word *plastikos*, meaning "to mold"). In 1920 only three forms of plastics were used: celluloid,

Bakelite, and Formica which is an Ohio product. *Celluloid* was used for motion picture film, but the most popular use was to make detachable collars and cuffs for men's shirts. The shirts were worn for several days and the celluloid parts washed each night. *Bakelite* was widely used as an insulating material for electrical equipment. *Formica* was created in Cincinnati to be used in place of mica as insulating material for electrical equipment, but for many years it has been used to make long-wearing and easy-to-clean surfaces for table tops and other flat surfaces. Today Formica and a great variety of other "plastic" raw materials and finished products are created in Ohio.

Machinery

Thomas White, who loved to build mechanical gadgets, began to manufacture sewing machines in Cleveland in 1866. Almost a hundred years later, a new group of people took over control of The White Sewing Machine Company, and closed all the factories in the United States. You can still buy White sewing machines, but they are made in foreign countries. In 1957 the new owners began to buy other manufacturing companies.

In 1950 you could buy major household appliances, such as refrigerators, radios, washing machines, and clothes dryers with the brand names Bendix, Crosley, Gibson, Kelvinator, and Philco. By 1971 The White Sewing Machine Company owned all of these and had changed its corporate name to White Consolidated Industries, Inc. (WCI). During the 1950s, the Westinghouse company built a very large factory in Franklin County to make clothes washers and dryers. In 1976 WCI bought this plant and changed the name to White-Westinghouse.

Winton automobiles, made in Cleveland, were the first cars to travel across the United States in both directions. This one made the trip from east to west.

All electric-powered cooling systems operate by compressing and expanding a gas that is called the **coolant**. The early coolants were very dangerous gases that were both poisonous and **flammable** (burn easily). When he became concerned about this problem, Charles Kettering assigned a research team to find a safer coolant. In 1930 a new gas coolant was patented by General Motors that actually put out fires. You know it today as *freon*. Kettering was the first person to use it in the refrigeration system in his home at Ridgeleigh Terrace in Montgomery County. Today freon is considered to be a *dangerous* gas because of its effect on the atmosphere.

Do you call the appliance that keeps food cold a *fridge*? In the early 1920s, General Motors Corp. made the first "mechanical ice box" in Dayton, and called it *Frigidaire*. For many years the popular name for all electric *refrigerators* was *Frigidaire*, but now many people say "fridge." In 1979 General Motors decided to stop making Frigidaires, and within a short time WCI had bought the brand name and the factory. If your school, or church owns a *Ditto* machine to make copies of "handout sheets" or programs, WCI also owns that company. By the end of 1990, WCI had been purchased by the Electrolux Corporation of Sweden.

During most of the 20th century, Cleveland and Cincinnati were centers for the manufacture of machine tools, which are used to make all kinds of machinery, including parts for automobiles. Prior to 1970, Cincinnati boasted of being "The Machine Tool Capital of The World": you could find machine tools in large and small factories around the world with "Cincinnati" on them. By 1990 many of the small machine-tool companies of Ohio were no longer in business, while several of those that remained had Japanese partners.

Motor Vehicles

Since 1950 almost one-seventh of all jobs in the United States have been related to **motor vehicles**. If you consider all the hotels, motels, and restaurants that get their business from people traveling in automobiles, the importance of motor vehicles to our economy is even greater.

By 1890 several inventors were experimenting with small steam engines that burned petroleum products, and some of these engines were used to create "horseless carriages." By 1900 some inventors were calling their self-propelled vehicles "automobiles" (from the Greek word *autos*, meaning self, and the Latin word *mobilis*, meaning to move).

In addition to making sewing machines, during the 1890s, Thomas White also made roller skates and bicycles. When his son Rollin graduated from a college of engineering, Thomas supported his experiments with steam-powered automobiles. By 1900 Rollin had built and operated four such vehicles, and his father set up a factory to build 193 steam cars in 1901. In 1906 the family established The White Company to manufacture steam-powered automobiles. They built a large factory in Cleveland, and made about 1,500 "steamers" (as they were called) each year until 1910. At that time Rollin began to make trucks powered by gasoline engines. White trucks are still made today in Virginia by Volvo, a large Swedish manufacturer of automobiles and trucks.

Like Thomas White, Alexander Winton manufactured bicycles in Cleveland during the 1890s. Like Rollin White, Winton began to experiment with building horseless carriages, but Winton used **internal combustion** (burn fuel in engine) engines rather than steam. In 1898 he made and sold 25 machines for $1,000 each. The next year, he sold 1000 machines for $2,000 each. In 1903 a physician from Vermont and his **chauffeur** (driver) made the first cross-country automobile trip in a Winton automobile, from San Francisco to New York City in 64 days! A short time later, the Winton automobile you see on page 317 was used to travel from New York City to San Francisco. You must remember that there were almost no paved highways in 1903 except for the turnpikes in eastern states. The last Winton automobile was made in 1924.

318

The manufacturing of automobiles is an important industry in Ohio.

City	1987 Auto Assemblies		1987 Truck Assemblies	
	Number	% of US	Number	% of US
Chillicothe			4,758	0.1
Dayton			906	
Lorain	232,661	3.1	236,622	6.2
Lordstown	234,494	3.2	123,314	3.2
Marysville	317,718	4.3		
Moraine			219,835	5.7
Norwood	138,837	1.9		
Springfield			75,972	2.0
Toledo			222,889	5.8
Ohio Total	923,710	12.5	884,296	23.1

In 1899 a young engineer named Ward Packard bought a Winton automobile in Cleveland and drove it to his home in Warren, the county seat of Trumbull County. He did not quite reach home before the auto broke down, and he had to hire a farmer with two horses to pull his new auto the rest of the way. After making several changes on the auto, Packard drove it back to Cleveland to tell Alec Winton how his product could be improved. Winton told Packard that if he knew how to build better cars, he should do so. Ward Packard returned to Warren and began to make high-quality Packard automobiles, and his company continued to make them until World War II. The company slogan was "When better cars are built, Packard will build them."

In 1908 while Charles Kettering was working for NCR, he began to experiment with making an electric starting device for automobiles. In 1909 Edward A. Deeds joined with Kettering to establish the Dayton Engineering Laboratories Company (DELCO) to manufacture self-starters for Cadillac automobiles. When the General Motors Corporation was organized in 1918-19, DELCO became part of the new company, and Kettering was named vice president in charge of research. He held this position until 1956, and remained a member of the board of directors of General Motors until he died in 1958.

The table above shows the production of **motor vehicles** (all automobiles, trucks, and buses) in Ohio during the "model year" beginning August 1, 1986, and ending July 31, 1987. In that year Ohio produced more than 12 percent of all autos made in the U.S. — second only to Michigan in the number produced. In addition Ohio produced more than 23 percent of all trucks made in the United States — more than any other state.

Toledo has been a center for manufacturing automobiles for many years, but today you must go to a museum to see most of the cars that were once made there. The most widely known vehicle built in Toledo is the *Jeep*. If you talk to anyone who served in the armed forces of the United States at any time since 1940, he/she can almost certainly tell you of an experience with a Jeep. Many of the vehicles used to deliver mail are "civilian" forms of the original military Jeeps.

In the table on page 319, the numbers of "trucks" assembled in Lorain by the Ford Motor Co., in Lordstown by General Motors, and in Toledo by Chrysler Corp., seem to overshadow the number produced in Springfield. However, the "trucks" produced by the "Big Three" auto makers in Ohio are all pick-ups and vans that many people use as passenger cars. The Navistar International Transportation Company factory at Springfield produces more heavy-duty trucks than any other factory in the world.

For several years, Ohio was also an important source of public transit buses. Does your city, or county seat, have transit buses built by The Flxible Company. Flxible — there is no "e" in the name — was established in Loudonville, Ashland County, in 1915 to make *sidecars* for motorcycles. Hugo Young, of Ashland County, got a patent on his idea for a sidecar, but needed money to build the vehicles. Charles Kettering heard of Young's idea and agreed to help him create the Flxible Side-Car Company in Loudonville. In contrast to the thinking of Louis Bromfield, Kettering believed that the only hope of survival for small towns was to have small factories!

Flxible built thousands of sidecars for the U.S. Army during World War I. In the 1920's, with guidance from Kettering, the company began to build motorcycles, funeral cars, ambulances, and intercity buses.

During the 1960s and 70s, Flxible and General Motors were the largest makers of urban transit buses in the United States. During the 1970s and 80s, Flxible was owned by two different aerospace companies, but the employees bought it during the late 1980s.

Entrepreneurs from the Far East have also moved into the auto industry of Ohio. Marysville, the county seat of Union County, had a population of fewer than 7,000 in 1980. In 1979 the Honda Corporation of Japan decided to build a factory near Marysville to assemble motorcycles from parts made in Japan. In 1982 Honda built another factory nearby to assemble automobiles. During 1989 Honda of Ohio exported some of the autos made at Marysville to sell in Japan! In the Spring of 1990, Honda began building automobiles in a second factory near East Liberty, in Logan County. In 1989 the Panda Company of the Peoples Republic of China purchased the former General Motors auto factory in Butler County.

If you look at auto production figures for 1989 and later, you will no longer find General Motors listed in Norwood, in Hamilton County. GMC demolished this factory in 1989.

Trade

Trade is one of the most important economic activities among people in all parts of the world. If you add together the figures on page 300 for the numbers of people working and the numbers of companies engaged in wholesale and retail trade, you see how important this activity is to the economy of our state.

Katharine Wright played an important role in the success of her brothers Wilbur and Orville.

Wholesale Trade

People engaged in wholesale trade buy large quantities of goods, and sell them in smaller quantities. For example, the La Choy Food Products Company in Archbold, Ohio, creates thousands of cans of Chinese food, and then sells hundreds of boxes filled with its products to each of several dozen wholesale grocery companies throughout the United States. Each wholesale grocery company stores the boxes in a **warehouse**, and then sells a few boxes at a time to many individual restaurants and grocery stores.

Retail Trade

Every time you make a purchase you are engaging in *retail trade*. Merchants buy goods in large quantities from wholesale distributors, and sell single units to individual customers. In 1988 four of the largest retail trade companies in the United States had their corporate offices in Ohio. The fourth largest of these was The Kroger Company, that sells groceries and related items throughout the eastern United States. In 1988 The Kroger Company was completely reorganized to resist purchase by a corporate raider.

The eighth largest retailer in the United States was Federated Department Stores, Inc. which owned several of the best known department-store chains, including the Lazarus stores in Ohio. In the winter-spring of 1988, Federated was bought out by Robert Campeau, a Canadian entrepreneur. By the winter of 1990, the company was bankrupt.

The thirty-eighth largest retailer was Revco Discount Drug Centers of Twinsburg, in the northeast corner of Summit County. Revco began in the 1950s as a single drug store in Detroit, Michigan. In 1988 there were 1,200 Revco drug stores throughout the United States. By 1989 Revco was in great financial trouble.

The forty-first largest retailer was The United States Shoe Company, Inc. of Cincinnati. U.S. Shoe manufactures shoes in several small towns of Ohio, and sells a

Wilbur (left) and Orville (right) Wright dressed in this way in their shop and when they flew. Here they are prepared to fly a bolt of silk cloth from Dayton to Columbus.

variety of well-known brands of clothing and shoes throughout the United States. In the winter of 1989, the management of U.S. Shoe suddenly announced that the company was for sale, but no one has bought it.

As you can see, the ownership and management of all types of companies have been in turmoil since 1980.

During World War I 3,000 airplanes like this were manufactured in Dayton.

Finance, Insurance, and Real Estate

In 1950 there were fewer than 90,000 people working in banks, savings and loan associations, insurance companies, real estate, and similar companies in Ohio. As you can see from page 300, in 1986 there were almost three times as many people employed in these activities. Perhaps you have been wondering why the City of

Columbus and Franklin County have grown so rapidly in recent years when they were losing manufacturing jobs: the explanation lies partly in the growth of finance and insurance activities. The Nationwide Insurance Company in Columbus, for example, processes all federal **Medicare** (health insurance program for senior citizens) claims for a large part of the eastern United States. State government activities and wholesale trade have also expanded greatly in Franklin County.

323

Ask your parents about the bank they use. Does it have the same name it had ten years ago? Before 1980 there were many restrictions on banks, including the size of the geographic area each could serve. Today there are few limitations, so that large Ohio banks are buying smaller Ohio banks, and/or joining larger banks of other states.

Service Industry

Have you ever asked someone to do something for you that you did not want to do yourself? Have they answered, "Do you think I'm your servant — or slave?" We often say that the pioneers who settled Ohio were *self-reliant* and *rugged individuals*. Of course anyone who traveled through the wilderness alone during the 18th century was such a person, but the early settlers depended heavily on each other for help. Groups of people got together to "raise" houses, or barns. They helped each other harvest and/or thresh grain, and in general, they *served* each others' needs. Today our society is so complex that we cannot be "self-reliant." In addition, family and friends are so busy that we cannot always count on them, so we turn to the service industry for help. In 1950 there were fewer than a half million jobs in service industries of Ohio. As you can see on page 300, there were almost one million *service* jobs in Ohio in 1986. Physicians, dentists, and nurses provide health-care services. Barbers and beauticians provide personal-care services. Auto mechanics, appliance repair people, and telephone operators provide specialized technical services. Professional athletes and television stars offer entertainment services. Ministers, priests, rabbis, and church secretaries are classified as service workers. Hotels, motels, and amusement parks are service industries.

Education and Research

Is education an industry? Are you a product? Educational institutions are included under Services in the table on page 300. The educational system of Ohio is of great concern to the leaders of industry in this state. In the 1890s industries needed many employees for heavy physical work; in the 1990s they need employees for complicated mental work. If the schools do not "produce" enough young people who have the ability to operate increasingly complex systems, the industries will have to either bring better-educated employees from other states or move their businesses out of Ohio.

Today the simplest of products are produced by very complicated machines, and the day is fast approaching when machines will build machines. But human beings will still have to design and build the machines that build machines. Electronic computers can now do things that stagger the imagination, but human imagination strives to make these "brains" ever more life-like. Fortunately, we do not have to understand why everything works as it does, but we must be smart enough to understand what the machine can — and cannot — do. And human beings must still repair the machines when they break down.

New products and new ways of performing jobs are developed through **research**. Every company that hopes to stay in business for a long time has some employees, or managers, thinking about ways to improve the existing activities of the company. The most profitable companies have large groups of people exploring new fields of knowledge in the hope of discovering new products and services they can sell in the future.

General Electric Aircraft Engines made in Hamilton County provide power for almost half the large airplanes of the world.

The search for new knowledge is an essential part of the overall economy of Ohio. The Ohio State University in Columbus, Case Western Reserve University in Cleveland, and the University of Cincinnati have contributed many new ideas to advance the industries of this state.

During the 1980s, the State of Ohio established several Institutes for Advanced Manufacturing Systems in connection with the larger Colleges of Engineering in the state. These research centers will continue to make many contributions to help the industries of Ohio.

All of the large companies of Ohio do research relating to their own businesses, but the Battelle Memorial Institute in Columbus is the largest private research organization in the world. Battelle has carried out important research projects in the physical and biological sciences for many years. It has laboratories in six cities of the United States, and in three cities of Europe.

Air Transportation

Air transportation is not listed in the table on page 300, but it is essential to the economy of the United States today. Ohio has played important roles in the development of this industry. By the time of the Civil War in the United States, there was some "travel" by air. Hot-air balloons were used to lift soldiers above the ground to spy on the enemy, and specially-trained pigeons were used to carry what might be called "airmail" messages. But it was the Wright brothers of Ohio who discovered the secret of controlled flight.

The Wright Brothers and Their Sister

Wilbur was the youngest of the three sons of Milton and Susan Wright while the family lived in Indiana. In 1869 the Wright family moved to Dayton, Ohio, because Milton had been elected an officer in the Church of The United Brethren in Christ, in that city. In 1871 the family moved into a new house at 7 Hawthorn Street, very close to the home of the Dunbar family you learned about in Chapter 12. Within four years of this move, another son, Orville, and a daughter, Katharine, were born.

When the United Brethren in Christ assigned Milton to travel throughout the states west of the Mississippi River, the family moved to Iowa. In 1884 they returned to 7 Hawthorn Street in Dayton. When their mother died in 1888, Katharine was only fifteen years old, but father Milton assigned her to take care of the family as Susan had.

After graduation from high school, Wilbur and Orville did not know what they wanted to do, but Orville liked to build mechanical devices. One day Orville created a simple printing press, so the brothers decided to go into the printing business. As you learned in Chapter 12, they printed Paul Dunbar's newspaper and a small book of poems he wrote.

In 1892 the Wright brothers rented a store around the corner from their home and opened a second business selling and repairing bicycles. In 1896 they began making bicycles using machines that Orville created. During these years, Katharine studied at Oberlin College in Lorain County, while father Milton traveled widely for his church.

In 1896 Wilbur and Orville read an article in a newspaper that said the invention of a heavier-than-air flying machine would probably be the work of a bicycle builder. At that point the Wright Brothers became **aeronautical** (the science of flight) engineers in addition to printers and bicycle repairmen. They began to spend all their free time studying and experimenting with **gliders** (heavier-than-air machines that have no motor) and with internal combustion engines. After Katharine graduated from Oberlin, she found a position teaching Latin in the Dayton public

John H. Glenn, Jr. of Mushingum County was the first person to circle the earth three times in outer space.

schools, but she continued to manage the home at 7 Hawthorn Street. As one recent writer described the situation:

"Wilbur and Orville enjoyed the benefits of life within a warm and stable family, while escaping the responsibilities that consumed the time and energy of married men. Katharine, far more than others, paid a considerable physical and psychological price. It was her most important and least recognized contribution to the work of the Wright brothers."[1]

The picture on page 321 shows Katharine at about this time.

By the autumn of 1900, the Wrights were ready to test a glider they had built. They learned from the United States Weather Service that the best weather conditions for their purposes could be found on the sand dunes at Kitty Hawk, North Carolina. They returned to Kitty Hawk in the autumns of 1901, 1902, and 1903 — each time with a more complicated flying machine. In 1903 they stayed on, experimenting constantly until they achieved success. On December 13, 1903, they flew above the ground a distance of 120 feet in 12 seconds, and later the same day they flew 852 feet in 59 seconds.

Within a few days, Wilbur and Orville Wright were known throughout the world, but their problems were just beginning! Other people had also been experimenting with flight: some of them said that the Wrights had stolen their ideas while others tried to steal the Wrights' ideas. Every newspaper and magazine wanted to print stories about them, and several nations wanted to honor them. The brothers, however, wanted to continue to improve their airplane. Katharine Wright gave up her teaching career and became the manager of her brothers' affairs. On page 322 you can see the Wright Brothers prepared to fly *freight* — a bolt of silk cloth — from Dayton to Columbus, Ohio on November 7, 1910.

Wilbur died of typhoid fever in May 1912, just a few days after the family had purchased land in Oakwood, to the south of Dayton, to build a new home. Less than a year later, before they could move to Oakwood, the family home on Hawthorn Street was surrounded by flood water. You will learn about the flood of 1913 in Chapter 15. As their father grew older, Katharine became more and more responsible for the family affairs.

In 1910 Katherine was named to the Board of Trustees of Oberlin College, and after the death of Wilbur, Orville attended board meetings with her. At these meetings she met a widowed classmate, and — against the wishes of Orville — married him in 1926 at the age of 52 years. Three years later Katherine died, but Orville lived until 1948.

Today you can visit the scene of the Wright Brothers' flight in North Carolina; you can see their first airplane in the Smithsonian Institution in Washington, D.C.; and you can visit both their home — in Greenfield Village at Dearborn, Michigan — and their bicycle shop on Williams Avenue in Dayton. You can see their second airplane and a reproduction of their shop in the Carillon Historical Museum at Dayton. You can actually fly in a reproduction of their 1911 model "B" plane at the Dayton General Airport on S.R. 741.

Neil A. Armstrong of Auglaize County was the first person to walk on the moon.

Lighter-than-Air Craft

How many times have you played with a balloon filled with helium? As you know, sooner or later, one of three things happens to such a balloon: it floats away from you; it breaks; or the gas leaks out. Today you can pay to take rides in hot-air balloons at county fairs and small airports.

By the end of the 19th century, inventors in Germany and the United States were experimenting with very large balloons filled with hydrogen, the lightest of all gases, but one that is very flammable. During World War I, the British army named one type of observation balloon "Balloon, Type B, limp," and this was quickly shortened to **blimp**.

Have you ever seen a blimp? There are still a few of them used for advertising purposes. If you attend any event that attracts tens of thousands of people, you may see a Goodyear blimp circling overhead and carrying advertising signs that light up at night!

About 1910 German engineers began to build huge lighter-than-air craft that had "cabins" hanging from the gas bags. The cabin contained a gasoline engine and a steering system. Such vehicles were called **dirigibles** (from the Latin word *dirigere*, meaning "to steer"). Later Count von Zeppelin designed metal frames to maintain the shape of the vehicles, and these dirigibles were called *zeppelins*.

In 1922 Goodyear Tire and Rubber Company formed a new organization called Goodyear-Zeppelin Corporation. This new company helped to build a very large zeppelin that was filled with non-burning helium gas: it was named Shenandoah. The frame of the *Shenandoah* was the first aircraft of any kind to be made of aluminum.

In 1929 Goodyear built a "garage" for airships in Akron that was the largest single building ever constructed. The present owner of this building, Loral Systems Group, is looking for suggestions about what to do with it.

Airplanes

In 1916 Charles Kettering and Edward Deeds joined with Orville Wright to organize The Dayton Wright Airplane Company in Moraine in Montgomery County. Shortly after the United States entered World War I on April 3, 1917, this new company received a contract to build 400 training planes by the end of that year. There were not more than 100 airplanes in the entire United States at that time. Airplanes were much more difficult to build than automobiles, but the Dayton factory produced 1,000 planes by July, 1918, and a total of almost 3,000 before it went out of business. On page 323 you can see a picture of one of these planes that is on display at the Air Force Museum in Greene County.

In 1920 the United States Army Air Force began doing research on flying at Wright Field in Greene County. Today this is known as *Wright Patterson Airbase*, the largest center for aircraft research in the United States. You can visit the U.S. Air Force Museum, on the grounds of Wright-Patterson Airbase, and see the largest collection of military airplanes in the United States.

Judith Resnik of Summit County was on her first trip in space when this picture was taken. She died when the Challenger *exploded in 1986.*

During World War II, hundreds of military planes were made in Columbus, and engines were built at the Curtiss-Wright plant in Hamilton County. The first civilian jet plane service in the world began in May, 1952, and this event opened a new era of transportation. Today GE Aircraft Engines has its headquarters and one of its main factories where the Curtiss-Wright factory once stood. GE is a world leader in the production of jet engines for civilian and military aircraft. You can see one of the large jet engines made by GE Aircraft Engines on page 325.

In 1943 the Federal Government established a laboratory to study aircraft engines at the Cleveland Airport. In 1958 the National Aeronautics and Space Administration (NASA) was formed, and named this laboratory the *Lewis Research Center*. Today it specializes in developing engines for space travel.

Space Exploration

In April 1957, the USSR surprised the world by announcing that it had shot a capsule, called **Sputnik**, into space, that it had circled the Earth in less than two hours, and had landed safely. Almost five years later, in February 1962, John H. Glenn, Jr., a native of New Concord, in Muskingum County, became the first U.S. citizen to circle the Earth three times in a space capsule. A picture of him is on page 327. In July 1969, Neil A. Armstrong, a native of Wapakoneta, the county seat of Auglaize County, became the first human being to walk on the moon. Today you can visit the Neil Armstrong Air and Space Museum at Wapakoneta and learn many things about space exploration. There is a picture of him on page 329.

After retiring from the space program John Glenn became a businessman and made his home in Grandview Heights, in Franklin County. In 1981 the citizens of Ohio elected him to the United States Senate, and re-elected him in 1987. After leaving the space program Neil Armstrong moved to a farm in Warren County, Ohio. He served on the faculty of the University of Cincinnati for ten years, and continues to serve our state in ways that do not attract attention.

Judith Resnik of Akron, whom you can see on page 331, was the second woman astronaut in outer space. While working toward a doctoral degree, she applied to be an astronaut. In 1977 she was accepted for training in the first group that included women. In 1984, just six seconds before her second space flight was to "blast off," something happened to the engines so that the flight was cancelled. In January, 1986 just a few seconds after her third spacecraft, the *Challenger*, was launched, it exploded and killed Judith and her six associates.

Stop and Think!

By the year 1900 Ohio was a leading manufacturing state in the United States. Manufacturing is still very important, and products made in this state are used throughout the world. During the last quarter of the 20th century, Ohio lost many of its early 20th-century factories that employed thousands of workers, but it gained many new factories that make products of the "plastics age", "electronics age", and "spage age." In addition, as the number of jobs in manufacturing declined, opportunities in the fields of finance and service expanded.

By 1900 about 800,000 patents had been issued. By 1990 more than 4,600,000 had been issued. It is unlikely that the head of the U.S. Patent Office during the 1990s will resign for the same reason as the superintendent did in the 1890s.

Review the Chapter!

Building vocabulary...

aeronautical
bankrupt
bid
blimp
chauffeur
conglomerate
contractor
coolant
corporate raider
dirigible
economy
Fiberglas
flammable
free enterprise
genetic engineering
gypsum
infrastructure
internal combustion
Medicare
monopoly
motor vehicles
plastic
research
Sputnik
strip mine
tetraethyl lead
warehouse
zebra mussel

Meeting new people...

Edward Deeds   Ward Packard
Harvey S. Firestone   F.A. Seiberling
B.F. Goodrich   Alexander Winton

Daniel Mead   Katharine, Orville
Michael J. Owens   and Wilbur Wright
John H. Glenn, Jr.   Neil Armstrong
Judith Resnik   Thomas White

Why is it true or false?

1. The United Mine Workers have lost many members.
2. SOHIO will always be a familiar brand name of gasoline.
3. Large amounts of glass are now made in Toledo.
4. A majority of the tires made in world are made in Akron.
5. The first automobile to travel across the United States was made in Ohio.
6. The Mead Corp. makes paper in Chillicothe.
7. Battelle Institute is one of Ohio's leading universities.
8. The Kroger Company was purchased by a Canadian company.
9. Migrant workers have never been important to Ohio.
10. The industries of Ohio have changed greatly since 1950.

Fill in the blanks...

1. Three natural resources that are still mined in Ohio are ...., ..., and ....
2. These three things help farmers operate larger farms today: ...., ..., and ....
3. Three parts of the infrastructure of a city are ...., ..., and ....
4. The earliest names of plastics were................, ..., and..............
5. Formica is used for ....
6. A company in .... Ohio makes most of the large trucks used in the United States.

7. .... automobiles were invented in World War II.
8. Akron was once known as
   ....
9. Mead Corp. is the largest maker of .... in the world.
10. The .... established by Ohio do research on manufacturing.

Match them up and tell where you found each answer.

1. Mead Corp.	a. Toledo
2. Katharine Wright	b. White Consolidated Industries
3. BP	c. Cincinnati
4. Akron	d. Battelle
5. buses	e. airplanes
6. machine tools	f. paper
7. U.S. Steel	g. SOHIO
8. Frigidaire	h. tires
9. Jeeps	i. Loudonville
10. research	j. Marathon Oil

Thinking it through...

1. Go to the library and get information about agriculture in your county. What are the most important agricultural products in the county? What type of food processing is done in the county?
2. Go to the library and ask for *Thomas's Register of Manufacturers*, and/or *Harris' Industrial Guide of Ohio*, and find what you can about the largest and the most unusual manufacturers in your county.
3. Talk to a member of a labor union, and get her/his opinion of the importance of unions today. Share the information with the class. Compare information with other students.
4. Look at ten items in your home made of cloth. Write down the country in which each item was made. Outline the steps of trading that might have been followed to get that item to your home.
5. Make a list of all the things in your house that are made of plastics. Alongside each item, list alternate materials [such as glass, steel, wood] that the item might have been made from. How difficult would it be to use something other than plastic for each item?

Working with maps...

1. Using a telephone directory and the map of your county, pick out one type of business (for example, drug stores, auto repair garages, lawyers) of interest to you. Plot the locations of these businesses on the county map. How far would you have to travel to go from your home to the nearest shop? If you live in a big urban area, do only the places within a mile of your home.
2. Take the information you gathered in Project #4 of *Thinking it through...* and plot the location where each item was made on the map of the world, or of the United States.
3. Go to the shopping area that your parents usually use, and make a sketch map of all the stores, noting what each store sells. Try to figure out why some stores are busier than others. Ask your parents why they use particular stores.
4. With the help of a grandparent, or older neighbor, plan a trip to travel by automobile from San Francisco to Washington, D.C., with a stop at your home. You cannot use any sections of Interstate Highways. You cannot travel for more than 12 hours each day and must stay in a town each night. How long will the trip take?

Footnote

1. Crouch, *The Bishop's Boys*, p. 125

CHAPTER 15

How is Ohio governed today?

Be ready to learn...

- how the role of government has changed.

- how Ohio is governed.

- how the principle of "One person, one vote" is achieved.

- how elections are held.

- how laws are created.

- how local governments are organized.

- how government is financed.

In Chapter 11 you learned about the government of Ohio during the 19th century. You also learned that Ohio adopted a new constitution in 1851. In this chapter you will learn how the government of Ohio changed during the 20th century.

Our Capitol was built between 1831 and 1869. The tall Rhodes State Office Building on the right was built during the 1980s.

As you know, Columbus is the center of government for Ohio. The State Capitol, shown above, was built over a period of twenty-two years from 1839 to 1861. Since 1970, the open space you see around the capitol covers a large parking garage. The newest State Office Building, on the north side of Broad Street across from the capitol, was completed in 1989. It appears on the right side of the picture above. The State Office Building shown on page 339 was completed in 1933. State offices are also located in several other places in Columbus, and in most of the larger cities of Ohio.

Changing Role of Government

In Chapter 11 you learned that the three most important roles of government were to protect citizens from turmoil, keep records of all important events, and collect money to pay for these services. During the 20th century, the citizens of Ohio decided that government should provide many more services relating to the **general welfare** of the state — that is, the health, happiness, and prosperity of the people. They also agreed that they would be willing to pay higher taxes to have these services. The diagram on page 340 shows all elected officials and a list of twenty-three "department heads appointed by governor." The table on page 342 shows how each elected official and department is related to the basic purposes of government.

The people who wrote the constitutions of the United States and Ohio could not predict the exact changes that have occurred, but they did include instructions about how these documents could be amended to meet new conditions. The Constitution of the United States has been amended only twenty-six times in more than 200 years. The Constitution of Ohio has been changed more than a hundred times since 1851, with thirty-three changes in 1912 alone. Almost all the amendments have related to additional services for improving the "general welfare" of the people and providing money to pay for these new services.

Elected Officials of Ohio

The government of Ohio, like the government of the United States, is organized so that all power is divided between three groups of people elected by the voters: the legislative branch, which creates laws; the executive branch, which enforces laws; and the judicial branch, which insures that all laws are in agreement with the constitution and enforced fairly.

General Assembly

In Ohio the legislative branch is called the General Assembly. This body corresponds to the Congress of the United States, and like

the Congress, it has two *houses*: the House of Representatives and the Senate (from the Latin word *senatus* meaning "old man"). All representatives are elected every two years for two-year terms. One-half the senators are elected every two years for four-year terms to insure that there will be some experienced people in the Senate at all times.

Representatives to Congress are elected in the same way as representatives to the General Assembly, but only one-third of all United States Senators are elected every two years for six-year terms. Later you will learn how Ohio lawmakers are elected.

Article II of the Ohio Constitution guides all aspects of work of the General Assembly. For many years the General Assembly **adjourned** (ended) its sessions in March or April, but now it meets throughout the year except for **recess** periods when the **legislature** (another name for the General Assembly and/or Congress) does not meet. Later you will learn how laws are created and changed.

Executive Branch

Article III of the 1851 Constitution described the executive branch of our government as follows:

"Section 1: The Executive Department shall consist of a governor, lieutenant governor, secretary of state, auditor, treasurer, and an attorney-general, who shall be chosen by the electors of the state ...."

This section was amended in 1976 so that candidates for governor and lieutenant-governor are elected as a team for four-year terms. The people holding the other offices are also elected for four-year terms but have no direct political relationship with each other. This means that the governor and lieutenant governor may be members of one political party, and the four other officers members of the other parties. We will look at these offices in the order they are listed.

Governor

The governor participates in creating laws by either approving — called *signing* — or disapproving — called *vetoing* — acts of the General Assembly. In addition, the governor is responsible for enforcing all laws of the state, with the help of the other elected executive officials. The lieutenant-governor serves as chief executive officer in case of an emergency that prevents the governor from taking action. The governor may serve for a total of eight years, but may be re-elected again after being out of office for four years. The president and vice president of the United States serve similar terms, but the elections are not in the same even-numbered years.

In Appendix C you will find a list of all of the governors of Ohio, and the other high political offices some of them have held.

The **secretary of state** is responsible for keeping accurate records of all the laws of Ohio, and for enforcing laws relating to elections.

The **auditor** makes certain that money is available to pay for all projects approved by the General Assembly. The Auditor examines the records of every county, township, incorporated place, and all other legal bodies in the state to make certain that all laws and regulations are obeyed. The auditor is also responsible for all records relating to state-owned lands, including the public land surveys and canals you learned about earlier.

The **treasurer** receives all taxes paid to the state, and pays all bills for all departments of the state. Everyone who works for the state receives pay checks signed by the treasurer. The treasurer is also responsible for the investment of all state funds, including the large sums that finance the various state retirement systems.

The **attorney general** is the lawyer for all departments of the executive branch of the state government. Whenever anyone has a question about the meaning of a state law, the attorney general can issue an *opinion* on the meaning. If the questioner does not like the opinion, the court can be asked to decide the question.

Supreme Court

The Supreme Court of Ohio, like the Supreme Court of the United States, has two purposes: to decide whether or not particular laws are in harmony with the intent of the constitution, and to decide whether laws are enforced as required by the constitution. There are three differences between the Supreme Courts of Ohio and of the United States:
1. State **justices** are elected for six-year terms while federal justices are appointed to serve for life, or until they choose to retire.
2. State justices are elected with the support of political parties, while federal justices are appointed by the President.
3. There are seven judges on the Ohio Supreme Court and nine on the United States Supreme Court.

Organization of State Government

The diagram on page 340 shows how the branches of state government fit together. We will now look at the details of this diagram.

The State Office Building on South Front Street was built during the 1930s.

Department Heads

The heads of the twenty-three departments, listed under the governor's office on this diagram, are appointed by the governor. The role they play corresponds to that of the cabinet of the President of the United States. Some of these departments are mentioned regularly in our local newspapers, but others perform important "housekeeping" duties we seldom hear about.

State Board of Education

The State Board of Education is made up of people elected from various parts of Ohio. The board is responsible for making the General Assembly aware of the needs of the schools of Ohio, and for enforcing laws relating to education. The members meet monthly in Columbus, and do most of their work through the superintendent of public instruction, who is an employee of the board.

339

Organization Chart of Ohio State Government

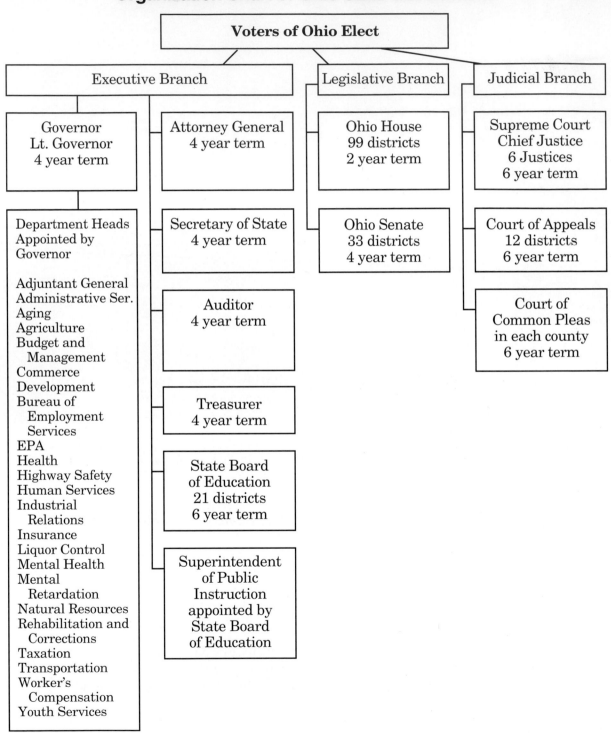

Voters of Ohio Elect

Executive Branch

Legislative Branch

Judicial Branch

Governor
Lt. Governor
4 year term

Attorney General
4 year term

Ohio House
99 districts
2 year term

Supreme Court
Chief Justice
6 Justices
6 year term

Department Heads
Appointed by
Governor

Adjuntant General
Administrative Ser.
Aging
Agriculture
Budget and
   Management
Commerce
Development
Bureau of
   Employment
   Services
EPA
Health
Highway Safety
Human Services
Industrial
   Relations
Insurance
Liquor Control
Mental Health
Mental
   Retardation
Natural Resources
Rehabilitation and
   Corrections
Taxation
Transportation
Worker's
   Compensation
Youth Services

Secretary of State
4 year term

Ohio Senate
33 districts
4 year term

Court of Appeals
12 districts
6 year term

Auditor
4 year term

Court of
Common Pleas
in each county
6 year term

Treasurer
4 year term

State Board
of Education
21 districts
6 year term

Superintendent
of Public
Instruction
appointed by
State Board
of Education

State Courts

As you can see in the organization diagram, there are two levels of courts below the state supreme court: *Courts of Common Pleas* and *Courts of Appeal*. Complaints about decisions of the Courts of Common Pleas are decided by one of the nine district *Courts of Appeal*. The Supreme Court of Ohio hears only complaints about decisions of the Courts of Appeal.

The Court of Common Pleas of each county has at least one judge, but the larger the population of a county, the more judges it has. These judges are elected by the people of each county. In the largest counties, the Court of Common Pleas includes two special courts for probate and juvenile affairs. Probate courts deal with various records relating to the lives of citizens — birth, adoption, marriage, divorce, death, and estates of people who die. Juvenile courts deal with the problems of children and young people under eighteen years of age.

Municipal Courts

Every village and city may have its own court system. In small towns this is called the *Mayor's Court*. State law permits incorporated places within a metropolitan area to combine their courts into *Municipal Courts* with the judges elected from the entire county.

Apportionment

In a free society the largest possible number of people are given the right to vote, and all votes have equal value. It is easy to decide who may vote, as you will learn in the next section. It is much more difficult to insure that all votes have equal weight.

For example, since the members of the executive and judicial branches of Ohio government serve the entire state, these officials are elected **at large**, that is, all voters throughout the state have equal influence.

On the other hand, members of the General Assembly are elected to represent the *districts* in which they live. The Constitution of 1851 called for one hundred representatives and thirty-five senators. In 1967 these numbers were changed so that there now are ninety-nine members of the House of Representatives, and thirty-three members of the Senate. As the population of Ohio has increased, and as people have moved about within the state, it has been necessary to change district boundaries to preserve the principle commonly stated as "One person, one vote!"

The principle of *apportionment* is used to solve this problem. After each U.S. Census of Population, district lines are adjusted so that areas that lost population will not have more representation than areas that gained population. For example, in one district a legislator might represent 90,000 people, and in another, a legislator might represent 110,000 people, and this is not "equal" representation.

The map on page 343 shows districts used to elect the ninety-nine members of the House of Representatives between 1982 and 1992. The districts in the six most populated counties cover such small areas they cannot be shown individually. The map on page 344 shows the thirty-three districts used to elect senators. If you try to fit these two maps together, you will find that each senate district is made up of three **adjacent** (touching) house districts.

Role of Government in the Late 20th Century

Prevent Turmoil

Governor and Lieutenant-Governor
Judicial Branch
Attorney General (elected official)
Adjutant General
Highway Safety
Liquor Control
Rehabilitation and Corrections

Keep Records

Auditor (elected official)
Secretary of State (elected official)
Budget and Management

Raise Money

Treasurer (elected official)
Taxation

General Welfare

State Board of Education
Aging
Agriculture
Commerce
Development
Employment Services
Environmental Protection
Health
Human Services
Industrial Relations
Insurance
Mental Health
Mental Retardation
Natural Resources
Transportation
Workers' Compensation
Youth Services

How can district boundaries be so complicated? The answer to this question is the old adage: "To the victor belongs the spoils." The district lines are created by a five-member *Apportionment Board*, which includes the Governor, Auditor, Secretary of State, and one representative each of the Republican and Democratic parties. The political party that has the majority of members on the committee draws the district lines so that candidates from that party are most likely to be elected.

The map on page 346 shows the Congressional Districts of Ohio from 1982 to 1992. These district lines are also drawn by the Apportionment Board, but have no direct relationship to the districts of the General Assembly. Between 1982 and 1992, Ohio sent twenty-one representatives to Congress. Since several states grew more rapidly than Ohio during that period, Ohio will have only twenty representatives after 1992. This means that all of the districts on this map may be changed.

Elections

The original Constitution of the United States limited the right to vote to white males citizens aged twenty-one, or older. The Fifteenth Amendment, adopted in 1870, extended the right to vote to African-American male citizens. The Nineteenth Amendment, adopted in 1919, extended the right to vote to female citizens aged twenty-one or older. In 1971, the Twenty-sixth Amendment to the Constitution of the United States lowered the voting age to eighteen years for all citizens. Throughout the years, the Constitution of Ohio was changed each time the Constitution of the United states was amended; therefore, in 1977 the Ohio Constitution was amended to permit eighteen-year-olds to vote in state elections.

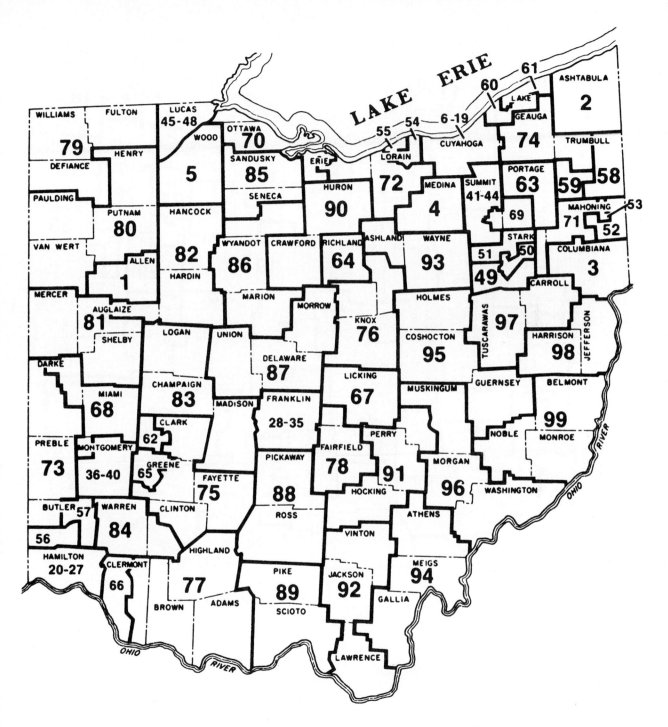

Voting districts of the Ohio House of
Representatives from 1982 to 1992

343

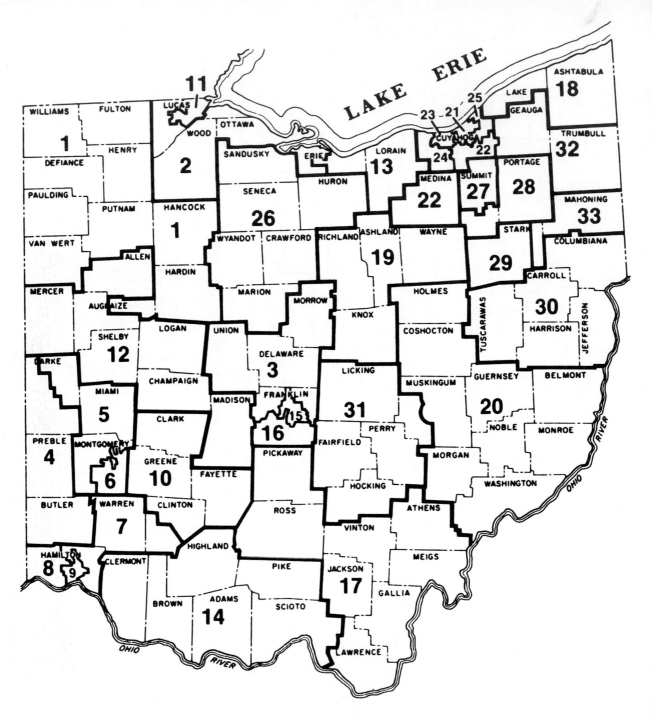

Voting districts of the Ohio Senate from 1982 to 1992

344

Registering to Vote

Article V of the Ohio Constitution says that people who want to vote must **register** (sign up) with the Board of Elections of the county in which they live. The Board of Elections may require proof that the person is at least eighteen years of age, and lives at the address given within the county. The Board of Elections then informs the new voter about the **polling** (voting) place where she/he must report to vote. If a person who is registered to vote does not actually vote in any election over a period of four years, the Board of Elections will erase the name so the person cannot vote until he/she registers again. This system is designed to keep elections honest.

When you enter your assigned polling place, you must tell the *election judges* who you are and where you live. If they find your name on the list of registered voters, you must sign your name on the list before they will give you a **ballot** (form on which choices are marked). If the judges cannot find your name on the registration list, they will not let you vote.

Primary Elections

Primary elections are held in Ohio on the first Tuesday after the first Monday in May of each year. (This means that *election day* cannot come on May 1.) Primary elections are held to select representatives of the major political parties who will run for office in the general election the following November. Many types of issues, varying from local tax questions to constitutional amendments, may also be voted on at a primary election.

General Elections

General elections are held in Ohio on the first Tuesday after the first Monday in November. All state, county, and township officials are elected in even-numbered years. Incorporated places may elect their leaders in either odd or even-numbered years as they choose. In addition to voting for candidates running for various offices, you may be asked to vote on a variety of other issues.

Special Elections

A special election may be called at any time by any unit of government to meet an emergency, so long as the appropriate legal requirements are met. Has your school district ever called a special election for a school tax levy? More special elections are called in Ohio for school issues than for any other purpose.

How Laws Are Created

As you learned in earlier chapters, laws are created to solve particular problems relating to public safety and public welfare, and to raise money to pay for these services. You also learned that laws can become **obsolete** (no longer useful).

In 1945 the General Assembly created a Bureau of Code Revision to make sense out of the many outdated and conflicting laws of Ohio. In 1951, on the basis of recommendations from this bureau, the General Assembly **repealed** (cancelled) 2,361 obsolete laws, and reorganized all the remaining laws into what is now called the *Ohio Revised Code*. But many more laws have been passed since 1951 that are no longer important in the 1990s.

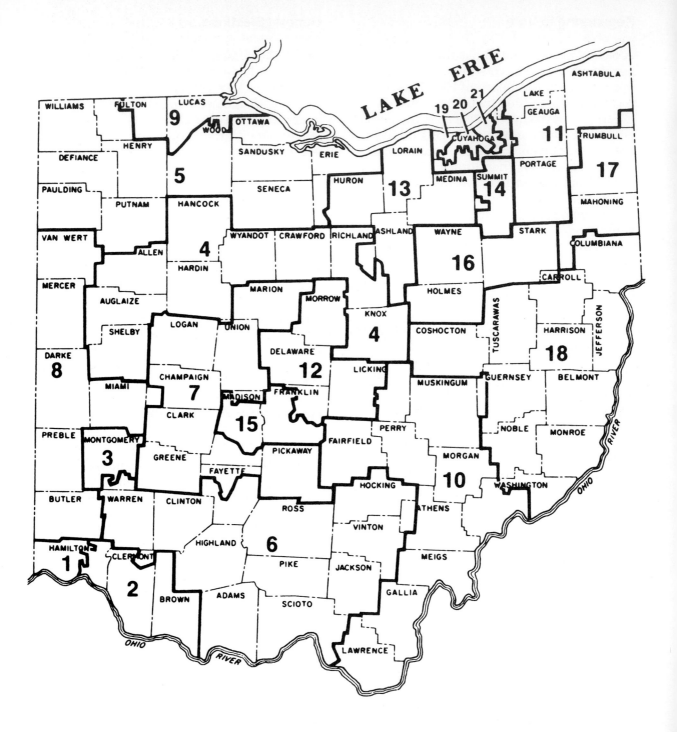

Voting districts of Ohio representatives to Congress from 1982 to 1992.

346

On page 348 you will find a diagram to help you understand the steps that must be taken to create a new law after a **bill** (proposed law) has been offered to the General Assembly. New laws may be proposed in several ways:

1. The governor may recommend a new law.
2. The Supreme Court may rule that an existing law is unconstitutional and the General Assembly may decide to change the wording to make it acceptable.
3. A special-interest group may use the process called **lobbying**.
4. Individual citizens may use the processes called **initiative** and **referendum**. We will look at only the processes of lobbying, initiative, and referendum.

Lobbying

Have you ever been in a *lobby*? Almost every hotel, motel, and movie theater has a lobby where people can assemble (and buy snacks at the movies). Have you ever been part of a *special-interest group*? If you beg your parents for permission to do something that they are reluctant to permit, you are acting as a special-interest group for your cause. What do lobbies have to do with special-interest groups?

In free societies, when one person comes to believe that a change should be made in the way the government acts, that person will try to interest other people in the idea. The more people who favor a change, the more likely it is to occur. Many special-interest groups, including professional organizations, business groups, farm organizations, and social groups, hire agents, called *lobbyists*, to make certain that legislators know about laws these groups want them to pass or defeat. The agents talk to the legislators about these matters in the lobbies of the Capitol and of nearby hotels. At election time, they **contribute** (give) money to the campaign committees of legislators who help them.

Initiative and Referendum

Do you ever surprise your parents or teachers by doing something nice without their asking you to do it? If so, you are showing *initiative*. Have your parents or teachers ever told you and your brothers, sisters, or classmates, to do something you didn't want to do, and you said: "Wait a minute! Let's take a vote on that!"? If so, then you have called for a *referendum*. The *initiative* and the *referendum* are two of the most powerful tools the citizens of a free nation have, but they did not come to the people of Ohio until the constitution was amended in 1912.

The initiative and referendum processes require large amounts of work by concerned citizens, and the actions are usually taken only after the process of lobbying has not produced desired results. If a group of citizens believes strongly that a new law should be passed, or an existing law should be changed, they ask registered voters to sign an *initiative* petition requesting the secretary of state to put the question on the ballot at the next general election so that the voters of the state can decide whether the change should be made. If enough people have signed the petition correctly, the secretary must put the issue on the ballot .

On the other hand, if a group of citizens is opposed to a law that the General Assembly has passed, they can ask registered voters to sign a *referendum* petition that requires the secretary of state to allow voters to decide whether or not to keep the law.

Simplified Diagram of How a Bill Becomes a Law in Ohio

House of Representatives

	Senate

House of Representatives

Senate

A proposal is presented by a representative, and is given a 1st reading.

A proposal is presented by a senator, and is given a 1st reading.

Proposal is given 2nd reading and sent to a committee.

Proposal is given 2nd reading and sent to a committee.

The committee holds public hearings on the proposal, and makes changes as necessary.

The committee holds public hearings on the proposal, and makes changes as necessary.

The proposal, as changed by the committee, is given a 3rd reading and voted on by the house.

The proposal, as changed by the committee, is given 3rd reading and voted on by the senate.

If defeated, proposal dies.

If approved, proposal goes to other house, and process is repeated.

If defeated, proposal dies.

If second houses makes changes in wording, a committee is formed of members of both houses to work out compromise. Compormise goes back to both houses for new vote.

If both houses agree on same wording, proposal goes to the governor for review.

If governor vetos, proposal goes back to both houses for new both houses vote for the proposal ...

If governor does nothing with proposal for 10 days...

If governor signs approval ...

... proposal becomes a law.

Example of Initiative and Referendum

Can you find West Chester on a map of Ohio? It is located in the southwest corner of Butler County, on what is now called Cincinnati-Dayton Road. Before I-75 was opened for traffic between Cincinnati and Dayton in 1960, West Chester was a small settlement along US Route 25. The picture on page 350 shows a building that was once a general store in the settlement along the main road between Cincinnati and Dayton.

As the processes of urban growth that you learned about in Chapter 13 took place in the northeastern part of Hamilton County, land developers built new housing projects in the southern parts of Butler and Warren Counties. The City of Fairfield was incorporated in Butler County. The old village of Mason in Warren County expanded to become a city. In addition, thousands of people moved into subdivisions built on what was once farmland between these two places, and said they lived in *West Chester*.

About 1985 some of the residents of *West Chester* decided that the area should incorporate as a new city. They followed all the legal steps of the *initiative* process to bring the question of incorporation to a vote. When everyone in the area had a chance to vote on the issue, a majority voted against incorporation.

Political Parties

Every citizen of the United States has her/his own ideas about government, but there can be no rule of law unless individuals are willing to cooperate. One important way in which they work together is through *political parties*.

Have you ever heard someone say, "There are two sides to every question!"? While there may be more than two ideas about a particular problem, they almost always break down into **liberal** and **conservative** points of view. *Liberals* are usually in favor of change, while *conservatives* tend to oppose change. One of the most important reasons for the strength of government in the United States has been the fact that one political party has represented the *liberals* and a second party the *conservatives*. Over the years the names of the parties have changed, but during the 20th century, the members of the two largest parties throughout the United States have been called *Democrats and Republicans.* As a general rule, whenever members of either party control the government of the city, county, state, or nation for too long a time, the quality of government declines. From another point of view, the party in power will say that voters should stay with their "proven" program, while the party out of power will say "It's time for a change!"

Charter Committee of Greater Cincinnati

During the last twenty years of the 19th century and the first twenty of the 20th century, the Republican Party controlled the City of Cincinnati. The Democratic Party elected the mayor and a majority to city council only twice, in 1911 and 1913. By 1920 Cincinnati was said to be "The worst governed city in America."

In 1920 a small group of concerned citizens began to discuss what they might do to change the situation. In 1924 the group organized the *Charter Committee*, made up of Democrats, dissatisfied Republicans, and people unhappy with both parties. This committee circulated petitions to have the form of city government changed from the

This building was once a general store in the Butler County settlement of West Chester.

federal system to the *council-manager system* — you will learn about these later. The Republican Party did all that it could to discourage the movement for change, but the citizens gave it strong support. By 1930 Cincinnati had adopted a new system of public records, a new system of employment, a master plan for future development, and was called "The best governed city in America." The political cartoon on page 353 shows what one artist thought of the situation.

From 1925 to 1959, the Democratic Party cooperated with the Charter Committee in city government. In 1959 the Republican Party convinced the voters that they should change the method of electing members to City Council. From 1959 to 1970, the Republican Party controlled City Council because the Democrats and the Charter Committee did not cooperate. In 1971 the Democrats and Charterites reunited and controlled City Council until the Democrats broke away again in 1981. Since 1981 none of the three local parties has had a majority on council and the government has been weak.

In 1991 the Charter Committee of Greater Cincinnati was the oldest continuously operating political reform party in the United States.

County Government

There are two points of view about laws:
1. You can do only those things that the law says you can, or must, do.
2. You can do anything so long as the law does not prohibit it. In general, state laws require that county and township governments follow the first point of view, while municipal governments can choose to follow the second.

The form of county government in Ohio was satisfactory before World War II, but it leads to many problems today, especially in the metropolitan areas. For example, each of the county officials shown in the diagram on page 354 is elected independently for a four-year term. This means that the county will have many problems if the elected officials do not cooperate with each other. We will look at these offices in the order in which they are shown in the diagram. All of the officials shown are elected in even-numbered years to four-year terms, and may be re-elected any number of times.

Board of County Commissioners

In all Ohio counties except Summit, three people are elected as *county commissioners* — two at one election and the third at the next — to conduct all business of the county not assigned by law to other elected officials. They may adopt **resolutions** that are intended to resolve particular problems, but they cannot create laws. Their greatest power lies in their control over the budgets of the other elected officials.

All citizens of a county take part in electing the county commissioners, but the commissioners have no control over activities within incorporated places in the county. In heavily populated counties, the commissioners must deal with complex urban problems such as water supply, waste disposal, and public transportation.

Auditor

The county auditor has some of the same duties, at the county level, that the state auditor has at the state level. People who move to Ohio from another state have trouble understanding that the county auditor is responsible for assessing real estate taxes. Many other states have a position called *tax assessor*. The Auditor determines the "fair market value" of each parcel of land in the county, and of any "improvements" (houses, etc.) on each parcel. The Auditor then calculates the real estate tax for each parcel.

Engineer

The county engineer is responsible for construction, maintenance, and operation of county roads in unincorporated areas, and for all bridges in the county. The engineer is not responsible for township roads or state highways. Most of the money used in this department comes from the highway user taxes collected by the state. The engineer must be registered as a professional engineer and surveyor in Ohio. Since few such qualified people live in rural areas, some counties with small populations share an engineer to save expenses.

Recorder

The county recorder must keep copies of all legal documents relating to land in the county. You should be able to go to your county recorder's office and learn who owned every square foot of land in your county in every year since the county was formed. Unfortunately, some records have been destroyed by fire in past years, and some records are so poorly indexed that it takes a long time for even an experienced person to find anything.

Treasurer

The duties of the county treasurer are very similar to those of the state treasurer. All local taxes, except municipal earnings taxes, are paid to the treasurer.

Coroner

Candidates for the office of coroner must be licensed to practice medicine in Ohio. The coroner must determine the cause of death in any situation where there is a question about why a person died. For example, the coroner may be asked to examine the body of a pedestrian killed in an accident involving an automobile: if alcohol is found in the blood, the pedestrian may have caused the accident. The coroner acts for the entire county including the municipalities.

Prosecuting Attorney

The prosecuting attorney represents the public interest in all court actions involving violations of state laws. The prosecutor also serves as the attorney for all other elected officials, and for all departments of the county. Candidates for this office must be licensed to practice law in Ohio.

Sheriff

The sheriff acts as the chief of police in unincorporated parts of the county and cannot make arrests in incorporated places. This elected official appoints as many **deputies** (assistants) as may be needed — or that the funds granted by the county

commissioners permit. The sheriff also operates the county jail. In a large county, some incorporated places may have their own jails, or all may send their prisoners to the county jail.

Clerk of Courts

The clerk of courts is responsible for keeping all records created by the court system of the county. All of these records must be indexed so that any citizen can find information about any case.

Alternate Form of County Government

In Chapter 13 you learned about the problems of annexation and incorporation. In 1933 the Constitution of Ohio was amended so that counties could adopt better forms of government than what you have just learned about. In 1957 the constitution was amended again to give the people of each county some choice in their form of government. As of 1990, only one county has had a group of citizens willing to follow the process of *initiative* you learned about earlier in order to change the form of their county government. During the late 1980s, the people of Summit County adopted a county council form of government with seven members of the council, all of whom were men in 1990. In that year the other 87 counties were supervised by 230 men — one of whom was African-American — and 31 women. Montgomery and Portage Counties were the only ones with two women commissioners.

Townships

As you have learned, townships were created as units of local government in an era when it was difficult to move about. The residents of the various unincorporated areas of each county elect three township

During the 1920s the Charter Committee changed Cincinnati from the worst-governed city to the best-governed city.

Organization of County Governments

Three County Commissioners

- Approve the budget for each of the other divisions of the county.
- May operate one, or more, of the following: Sewer District, Water District, Park District, Regional Planning, Building Inspection, Transit District, Animal Shelter, Cemetery, Land-Use Zoning, Hospital, and Help for the Poor.

County Auditor

- Keeps track of how every department of county spends it money.
- Sets value of every parcel of land in county, and assesses real estate taxes.

County Engineer

- Builds and repairs all roads owned by the county. Supervises all bridges in county.
- Makes — and keeps up-to-date — maps of all parcels of land for Auditor.
- Must be a registered professional engineer and land surveyor.

County Recorder

- Keeps a copy of every legal paper relating to the ownership of every parcel of land in the county.
- Keeps a copy of every other legal paper that anyone wants to put on public record.

County Treasurer

- Collects all taxes paid to the county.
- Pays all employees of the county, and all bills of all branches of county.

Coroner

- Determines the cause of death in any case that is doubtful or suspicious.
- Must be a licensed physician.

Prosecuting Attorney

- Serves as lawyer for every branch of county government.
- Represents the public in all cases where a state law has been broken.
- Must be a licensed lawyer.

Sheriff

- Enforces state laws in unincorporated parts of county.
- Operates the county jail.

Clerk of Courts

- Keeps all records and documents relating to county court activities.

Common Pleas Court

- Every county has at least one judge. The larger the county, the more judges it has.
- Hears all cases involving possible violation of state laws.
- May have a special court to handle juvenile cases.
- May have a special court that handles probate cases.
- Judges must be licensed lawyers.

trustees and a township clerk for four-year terms. Township trustees are responsible for all roads not on the state or county highway systems, and may operate a cemetery within the township.

Townships receive small amounts of money from the county commissioners. The citizens of some townships vote to pay special township taxes to hire police officers and/or to provide fire-fighting equipment for a volunteer fire department. Perhaps the most important role the trustees play is to represent the interests of their citizens in the broader problems of the county.

The existing form of township government may still be satisfactory in rural areas, but it is completely obsolete in the largest metropolitan areas. If you look back to page 288 for example, you can see that in 1990 more than 220,000 citizens of Franklin County and 270,000 citizens of Hamilton County lived in highly urbanized areas under the township form of government. In that same year, the General Assembly passed a law to make it possible for urban townships to have a stronger form of government. Governor Richard Celeste vetoed the act because lobbyists had encouraged the General Assembly to add undesirable features to it. In June 1991 the General Assembly passed another bill and Governor George Voinovich signed it into law so that people living in a township will be able to adopt a better form of government if they want it.

Special Districts

All of the boundary lines you see on maps in this book, including state, county, township, and municipal boundaries, were created by human beings to solve particular political problems. But these boundaries are meaningless in relation to the forces of nature: for example, the drainage systems and natural resources of our state are not related to such lines.

Special-purpose *districts* are often formed to solve problems that cross political boundaries. Each district is operated by a **board**, **authority**, or **commission**, that is, a special group of people appointed or elected to perform certain executive duties. Every *district* has the power to raise money to finance the activity for which it was created.

Some of the earliest special districts in our state were formed to drain the Black Swamp that once covered a large part of northwest Ohio. Everyone knew what had to be done, but the counties had neither money nor legal authority to take action. The land owners finally worked together to persuade the General Assembly to pass a "ditch law" that permitted them to organize drainage districts that crossed county lines.

You learned about the Muskingum River Conservancy District in connection with federal work programs of the Great Depression in Chapter 12. Now we will look at three types of *districts* that are very important today — the Miami Conservancy District, school districts, and sewer districts.

Miami Conservancy District

In 1913 the people living in the drainage area of the Great Miami River suffered from a tremendous flood. The people of Dayton, Ohio, suffered greatly, as you can see on page 357, and read in the box on page 356.

Effects of 1913 Flood on Dayton

The Dayton Flood nearly destroyed [Charles Kettering's] promising young [DELCO] company. On March 25, 1913, after several weeks of heavy rains and spring thaws, the dams and levees holding the four rivers flowing through Dayton to the Ohio [River] gave way. At dawn a torrent of water twelve feet high crashed down on the unprepared city, choking the downtown with mud, and leaving the city without gas, water, or electricity.

In the confusion, witnesses could only guess the extent of the damage. One early news dispatch claimed that "Dayton is tonight nothing less than a seething river three miles wide, a mile and a half on each side of Main Street, its principal thoroughfare. It is estimated that 2,000 to 5,000 people have perished." Actually, the damage was much less, and when the waters receded two days later, about 350 people were found dead and $120 million in property destroyed. ...

George Smith ... president of the Dayton Chamber of Commerce ... sent a telegram to Ohio Governor James Cox asking for food, medical supplies, and the state militia.

Years later, at a reunion of flood survivors, Smith asked if anyone knew how the telegram was delivered. From the back of the room, Kettering spoke up:

"Well, maybe I can help you out, George. I guess I was the guy. I took one of the copies of the telegram when you called for volunteers. I had a buck-board automobile out at the curb, with no top, no dash, no fenders, and no body except a slat bottom and a seat for two. [A colleague from] the Delco factory was with me. It was raining and sleeting, but we had on our rubber coats, hats, and boots. We had an idea that if we went far enough north, we would find a bridge across the [Great Miami] river. We rode for hours, it seemed. I have no idea how long. We came to a railroad bridge and drove across it. At the other end we got water in the **carburetor** and the car stopped on the **submerged** track. I climbed out and lifted the hood and wiped the water out of the carburetor with my handkerchief and got the car going. Then we started northward again. We drove some distance and finally saw a light ahead. It appeared to be a tower. When we reached it we found it to be a railroad train dispatcher's tower, and he had a telegraph key open, and a limited line of communication available ... It was still raining and sleeting. We reached home about daylight. That is how it happened."

From: Leslie, *Boss Kettering*, pp. 53-4

Dayton, Ohio, suffered severe damage in the great flood of 1913.

John Patterson, whom you learned about in Chapter 12, took the lead in organizing relief work for flood sufferers. The National Cash Register Company provided shelter and food for hundreds of people. A short time after the flood, Mr. Patterson also led the campaign to encourage the General Assembly to pass a law that made it possible for citizens living in a drainage area to form a **conservancy district** in order to pay for construction of flood control structures. In 1914 the people living in the drainage area of the Great Miami River voted to create the *Miami Conservancy District*. This project is still recognized throughout the United States as an outstanding example of people working together to solve problems that cross political boundaries.

School Districts

Every school in Ohio, whether public, private, or church-related, is in a *school district*. What are the boundaries of the district in which your school is located? If you are in a local district (part of a county system) does your district include any

General Revenue Fund Sources
(Excluding Federal Aid)
Fiscal Year 1989
Total $8,983.6 Million

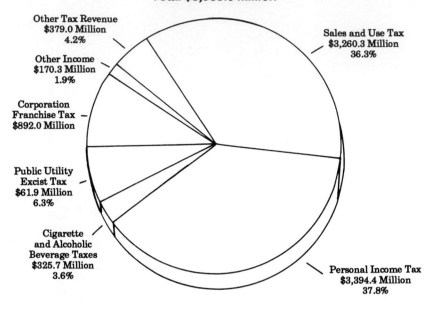

Other Tax Revenue
$379.0 Million
4.2%

Other Income
$170.3 Million
1.9%

Corporation
Franchise Tax —
$892.0 Million

Public Utility
Excist Tax
$61.9 Million
6.3%

Cigarette
and Alcoholic
Beverage Taxes
$325.7 Million
3.6%

Sales and Use Tax
$3,260.3 Million
36.3%

Personal Income Tax
$3,394.4 Million
37.8%

Revenue Sources		Fiscal Year 1989
		(million of dollars)
Personal Income Tax		$3,394.4
Sales and Use Tax		3,260.3
Corporation Franchise Tax		892.0
Public Utility Excise Tax		561.9
Cigarette Excise Tax		210.4
Alcoholic Beverages Taxes		
Alcoholic Beverage Excise Tax	$43.0	
Liquor Gallonage Tax	22.3	
Liquor Profits	50.0	
Total Alcohol Taxes		$115.3
Other Taxes		
Domestic Insurance Tax	$38.8	
Foreign Insurance Tax	207.1	
Intangible Personal Property Tax	5.1	
Horse Racing Tax	3.0	
Estate Tax	57.0	
Miscellaneous	68.0	
Total Other Taxes		$379.0
Other Income		
Earnings on Investments	$68.4	
Miscellaneous	101.9	
Total		$170.3
Grand Total		**$8,983.6**

towns? If you are in a city system, does the school district include any areas outside the city limits? In Cuyahoga County some adjacent incorporated places share a single school district; for example, the one with the longest name is Cleveland Heights-University Heights City Schools. In Hamilton County, the Princeton School District includes the following six villages and cities: Evendale, Glendale, Lincoln Heights, Sharonville, Springdale, and Woodlawn.

Members of your local board of education are elected to four-year terms and have complete responsibility for the public schools of your district. For example, the board hires all administrators, teachers, and other employees of the system, adopts all textbooks, makes all purchases. It also supervises state-financed programs for private and parochial (church-related) schools within the district. Perhaps the most difficult problem for every board of education is to raise the money needed to operate the schools. And the members of your board of education receive no pay for their work!

Sewer Districts

Sewer systems must be built so that waste waters flow freely to treatment plants. Many of the people who moved from cities to rural areas during the 1930s and 40s used septic tanks to dispose of sewage. When FHA loans were granted to buy houses in outlying subdivisions, the subdivisions were required to have local sewage treatment facilities. During the 1970s, the Environmental Protection Administration required that all existing and new buildings be connected to sanitary sewer systems, and that all wastes be thoroughly treated. The only way these requirements could be met was by forming special sewer districts.

Municipal Corporations

You have learned many things about the villages and cities of Ohio, but very little about the forms of government used in *municipal corporations*, as they are called in the Ohio Revised Code. If the citizens of an unincorporated area decide to form a village or city, they must choose one of three forms of government: the commission plan, the council-manager plan, or the federal plan.

Every municipality must have officials who serve as treasurer, auditor, clerk, and **solicitor**. The *solicitor* is an attorney who has duties similar to those of the attorney general and county prosecutor. In a municipality, these officials are usually appointed by the elected council or the manager.

Under the commission plan, five people — *commissioners* — are elected by all the voters in the municipality, and the commissioners appoint all other officials. The commissioners elect a chairperson to conduct their meetings, but all five have equal authority and responsibility. Dayton is the largest city in Ohio that has the commission form of government, but it was also the first large city in the United States to hire a city manager.

Under the council-manager plan, a city council is elected by the voters. The council elects one of its members to conduct the meetings of council, and to represent the municipality in ceremonies. This person may have the title of *mayor*. The council appoints a *city manager* to be in charge of the day-to-day operations of the government. The manager then appoints

General Revenue Fund Expenditures
(Excluding Federal Reimbursements)
Fiscal Year 1989
Total $8,686.5 Million

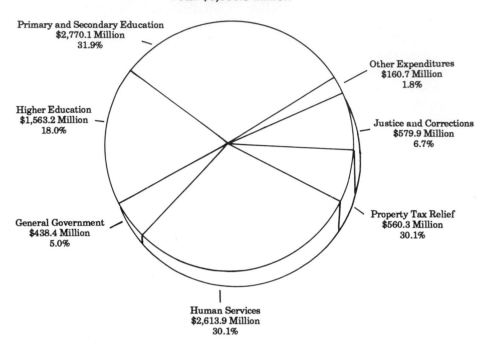

Primary and Secondary Education
$2,770.1 Million
31.9%

Other Expenditures
$160.7 Million
1.8%

Higher Education
$1,563.2 Million
18.0%

Justice and Corrections
$579.9 Million
6.7%

General Government
$438.4 Million
5.0%

Property Tax Relief
$560.3 Million
30.1%

Human Services
$2,613.9 Million
30.1%

Expenditure Category	Fiscal Year 1989 Expenditures	
	(million of dollars)	
Primary and Secondary Education		$2,770.1
Higher Education		1,563.2
Human Services:		
Public Assistance	$1,896.7	
Mental Health & Retardation	598.0	
Miscellaneous	119.2	
Total		$2,613.9
General Government:		
Transportation	$40.7	
Environment & Natural Resources	91.3	
Economic Development	79.9	
Miscellaneous	226.5	
Total		$438.4
Property Tax Relief		560.3
Justice & Corrections		579.9
Other Expenditures		
Capital Improvements	$36.0	
Debt Service	71.1	
Miscellaneous	53.6	
Total		$160.7
Grand Total		**$8,686.5**

assistants who serve at the pleasure of the manager. The council may replace the manager at any time. Earlier in this chapter you learned how Cincinnati adopted this plan. For many years, it was the largest city in the United States to have the county-manager form of government.

The federal plan is similar to the form of state government in Ohio. The voters elect a mayor as the chief executive officer, and a council as a legislative body. The mayor appoints assistants, and they serve at the pleasure of the mayor. The council may have as few as five members, but not more than fifteen, depending on the population of

Carl Stokes' Thoughts on Forms of City Government

... In Cleveland the mayor-elect is inaugurated the Monday after he is elected. That gives him only six days to try to put together a group of people to take over and to try to understand the workings of the machine he is supposed to control. This in the nation's eighth largest city, with over 825,000 people.

The other reason is built into the political process. Politics is a difficult, demanding, exhausting, sometimes exhilarating arena in which **gladiators** win and lose. But a city is a business—a non-profit service corporation. In Cleveland, when I took over, it did an annual business of $76 million a year, and three years later it had grown to more than $100 million a year. As a politician, a man learns what the social issues are and what services he thinks government

ought to provide, and he makes of his understanding political issues, campaign issues. But that understanding is an understanding of his society, not of management practices. I had never employed more than three people in my life, and now I found myself in charge of ten thousand. It was no longer a matter of standing in a public lot and saying, "Elect me and houses will spring up here." Now I have this foreman standing in front of me saying that seven of his trucks are broken down, and should he double up on the work crews or send the men home.

The trouble with the strong-mayor form of government in a big city is that the mayor is administrator, chief political officer and chief ceremonial officer for the entire city; everything flows to him directly. If he tries to directly handle all these duties, he becomes immobilized. This is a good argument for the city manager form of government.

From: Stokes, *Promises of Power* pp. 108-9

the municipality. The council may be elected at large, or by **wards** (districts). If elections are by wards, the boundaries of the wards must be adjusted by the principles of apportionment. Cleveland and Columbus are the largest cities in Ohio that use this form of government.

Some people think that the federal plan is the most democratic form of local government. Carl Stokes once felt that way, but he changed his mind after he was elected as the strong mayor of Cleveland in 1967, as you can read on page 361.

Each of the forms of government is used by some cities and villages in Ohio. Each type is "good" if all of the elected officials work together harmoniously to promote the general welfare of the municipality. Unfortunately, this goal is seldom reached over a long period of time, except perhaps in small communities where outstanding people serve without expectation of personal benefit, and the citizens do not seek personal profit at public expense.

Taxes

One of the most popular slogans of candidates running for public office is, "No new taxes!" But sometimes you can save money by paying more taxes! For example, in Chapters 7 and 13 you learned how improved highways reduce the cost of transportation. Since 1920 most of the cost of building and repairing highways has been financed by taxes on motor vehicles and petroleum products.

We have used the words *wealth* and *wealthy* several times in this book without defining them, but almost all taxes are related to *wealth* on the basis that the more *wealthy* a person is, the higher the taxes he/she should pay. **Wealth** involves the ownership

of *property*, and when a person dies the property goes into her/his *estate*. There are three basic forms of property — **real property**, **personal property**, and **intangibles**. *Real property* relates to the ownership of land and the buildings that may be on individual parcels of land. *Personal property* includes all the objects you own, such as clothing, toys, books, bicycles, and jewelry. *Intangibles* include money, stocks, bonds, patents, copyrights, and other legal papers that represent wealth.

Taxes relating to real property and personal property are the oldest forms of taxation in the United States. We can only look at a few taxes that are paid by people in Ohio. The most important ones for individual citizens are related to real property, purchases, income, and highway use.

Real Estate Taxes

Real property is usually referred to as *real estate*. Everyone who owns real estate in Ohio pays taxes twice each year to the county treasurer. A very small part of this payment goes to the State of Ohio, a very large part goes to the school district in which the property is located, and the remainder goes to the county, township, special districts, and/or municipality in which the property is located. Real estate tax rates can be increased only by the people living in an area voting for such an increase.

Personal Property Tax

Ohio no longer has a personal property tax for individuals. When a person dies, an estate tax must be paid on all forms of wealth owned at the time of death. Small estates must pay 2 percent of the estimated value, and very large estates must pay up to 7 percent of the value.

Sales Tax

Ohio adopted a sales tax in 1934 because income from other sources dropped greatly — due to the depression. At the same time more people needed financial aid from the state. For many years, the state sales tax has been at the rate of 5 percent of the cost of all goods except carryout foods and prescription drugs. In recent years, the sales tax has been levied on a variety of services.

Counties are permitted to collect up to an additional 1-1/2 percent sales tax for local purposes if the commissioners so desire. Local public transit authorities may also collect up to 1-1/2 percent sales tax if the voters of the transit district approve.

Income Tax

Ohio adopted an income tax in 1971. The state was desperately in need of new money to pay interest and principal on bond issues that were approved between 1963 and 1970. Between 1975 and 1982, the state borrowed still more money through bond issues. In 1983 the General Assembly increased the income tax to help pay for these bonds.

Everyone who works in Ohio has state and federal income taxes deducted from her/his pay check. This makes the tax very easy to collect, and relatively "painless" because you never actually have the money. The tax is considered to be "fair" because people with high incomes pay higher percentages of income in taxes than people with low incomes. In fact, people with very low incomes pay nothing.

Many cities in Ohio have a form of income tax that is really an earnings tax because it applies only to income from wages and salaries. If the voters in a municipality approve of an earnings tax, it must be paid by every employed person who lives or works in the municipality.

Excise Taxes

An **excise tax** is a form of sales tax levied on a specific item. Excise taxes on tobacco products and alcoholic beverages are sometimes called *sin taxes* because these products are harmful to the person using them. Excise taxes on fur coats, boats, and expensive automobiles are sometimes called *luxury taxes* because these items are used by wealthy people.

Highway User Taxes

The State of Ohio collects several forms of taxes related to motor vehicles. These are called *highway user taxes* because the income from them is used only for building, repairing, and operating the highway systems of Ohio.

The most visible form of highway user tax is the *registration fee*. When the owner of an automobile, motorcycle, truck, or bus pays this fee, she/he is given a pair of license plates (or a new sticker for the present plates) that must be put on the front and rear of the vehicle. The fee for a private automobile is quite low, but the fee for a large truck is very high.

Two other forms of highway-user taxes are less "visible." First, every person buying a gallon of gasoline or diesel fuel must pay state and federal fuel taxes. Second, every company operating a heavy truck in Ohio must pay an *axle-mile* tax. In 1989 highway users paid a total $1,262 million in these state taxes. The federal government also collects highway user taxes, and returns most of the money to the states for use in building and repairing highways.

Other Sources of Income

In a box in Chapter 11, you read part of Article XV of the Second Constitution of Ohio concerning liquor and lotteries. Over the years, this article was amended several times, and today lotteries and the sale of liquor are big businesses for our state. In addition Ohio receives several hundred millions of dollars each year from the United States for a variety of purposes.

Sale of Liquor

In Chapter 12 you learned that the Eighteenth Amendment to the Constitution of the United States banned the use of alcoholic beverages. During the 1920s, this law led to so much turmoil that it was repealed by the Twenty-first Amendment in 1933. As soon as it became legal to drink alcoholic beverages, Ohio amended its constitution so that the state would be the only seller of beverages containing high percentages of alcohol. In the **fiscal year** 1989 (July 1, 1988 to June 30, 1989) our state had a net income of about $50 million from this business.

Lottery

During the 1970s, the voters of Ohio approved another change in Article XV of the Second Constitution, so that it now reads as follows:

"Lotteries, and the sale of lottery tickets, for any purpose whatever, shall forever be prohibited in this State, except that the

General Assembly may authorize an agency of the state to conduct lotteries, to sell rights to participate therein, and to award prizes by chance to participants, provided the entire net proceeds of such lottery are paid into the general revenue fund of the state and the General Assembly may authorize and regulate the operation of bingo to be conducted by charitable organizations for charitable purposes.

In 1987 this section was amended again so that the net income from the lottery is now used for education.

In 1985 Ohio had a net income of over $400 million from the lottery. As you may have noticed, the state lottery is advertised widely as a "game", but it was created for two reasons: first, other taxes would not have to be raised; and second the lottery would eliminate the *Numbers Game* operated by criminal gangs. Thousands of people all over Ohio — and almost all other states — once made small bets of money on numbers that were drawn each day by an organized crime group.

Federal Grants

In 1985 one-fifth of our total state income was from federal grants, but such grants are not "free." The only source of federal income is taxes collected from the people of Ohio and the other states. Every dollar of *federal aid*, as it is often called, encourages Ohio to do certain things that may really not be necessary or desirable, and requires our state to put up some of its own money to match the federal funds.

Fiscal Year 1989

The graph on page 358 shows the taxes collected by the State of Ohio between July 1, 1988, and June 30, 1989, that is, during the fiscal year 1989. The graph represents what is called the General Fund of the state. Highway-user taxes are not included because they can be used only for highway purposes. Income from the lottery is not shown because it can be used only for education. From this graph you can see that more than one-third of the total income was from the sales tax and a similar amount was from the state income tax.

The graph on page 360 shows how the General Fund was used in 1989. Five percent of the income from state taxes was used to operate the government, including salaries of all elected officials and employees, all supplies and equipment, and transportation expenses for employees. Almost 50 percent was used for education, and 30 percent for human services, including health and welfare. Less than 7 percent was used for operation of the criminal justice system.

Stop and Think

One of the most important features of a free society is that citizens understand the form of their government, and participate by voting. The surest way for citizens to lose their freedom is to say that government is of no concern to them. When a few people live in an area, the form of government can be very simple, but the greater the number of people, and the greater the area, the more complicated government becomes.

The government of Ohio is similar in general form to that of the United States and the government of every other state. The operations of Ohio counties are similar to each other even though the counties differ greatly in population. As the populations of metropolitan areas grow and spread over larger areas, new levels of

government must be created, in the form of special districts, to deal with problems that do not recognize political boundaries.

Review the Chapter!

Building vocabulary...

adjacent	justice (judge)
adjourn	legislature
apportionment	liberal
attorney general	lobbying
at large	obsolete
auditor	parochial
authority	personal property
ballot	polling place
bill (law)	real property
board	recess
carburetor	referendum
commission	register (vote)
conservancy district	repeal
conservative	resolution
contribute	revenue
deputy	secretary of state
district (voting)	solicitor
excise tax	submerged
expenditure	torrent
fiscal	treasurer
general welfare	ward (voting)
initiative	warded off
intangible property	wealth

Why is it true or false?

1. The state auditor receives all tax monies.
2. A village solicitor performs the same duties as the attorney general, but at a lower level.
3. The sheriff is the head of the police force of a county.
4. Every county has four commissioners.
5. The governor may veto a proposed law.
6. The Ohio Constitution has been changed over 100 times.

7. The constitution is changed by the process of annexation.
8. Candidates are elected to office at the primary election.
9. School board members are paid for their services.
10. The secretary of state is in charge of elections in Ohio.

Match these ...

1. constitution	a. flood
2. state senators	b. cause of death
3. law enforcement	c. highways and bridges
4. birth and death	d. keeps records
5. county engineer	e. a privilege
6. conservancy districts	f. amendment
7. coroner	g. 33
8. voting	h. executive branch
9. attorney general	i. probate court
10. clerk of courts	j. lawyer

Fill in the blanks

1. The .... makes the laws of Ohio.
2. A ruling on cause of death is made by the ....
3. A city may have the following kinds of government: .... , ..., or ....
4. The .... branch of government is responsible for enforcing laws in Ohio.
5. A .... court deals with problems of children.
6. Profits from the lottery are used for ....
7. The legal age to vote in Ohio is ....
8. There are .... representatives in the General Assembly.
9. Ohio has .... senators in Congress.
10. .... and .... are called municipalities.

Thinking it through...

1. Make a chart to show how the government of Ohio is similar to that of the United States.
2. Find out who represents your county in both houses of the General Assembly.
3. Find out who represents your county in the Congress.
4. Have you ever been involved in a political campaign? If so, share your experiences with the class.
5. Write a report on all of the units of government that affect the place where you live. Include municipal, township, county, and all special districts.

Try this ...

Stage an election for class president. Let two or more students volunteer to run, or assign two or more to do so. Then divide the class into groups to support each candidate. Choose one or more issues that "liberals" would like to change but "conservatives" would like to leave unchanged. Have the candidates make speeches about what they will do if elected. Set up a system to register voters. Have an election by secret ballots. When the election is over, have a discussion about what various students learned from this experience.

Working with maps ...

1. On the map of Ohio, draw the boundaries from the maps on pages 343, 344, and 346 that enclose your home.
2. On the map of your county, draw the boundaries of all school districts.
3. If there are any special districts in your county, locate the boundaries on the county or state map.

CHAPTER 16

What are the challenges of the 21st century?

We must learn to......

- preserve the balance of nature.

- preserve natural resources.

- reduce the volume of waste.

- regain financial stability.

Two things are certain about the future:
1. There will be changes.
2. No one can predict exactly what the changes will be.
Nevertheless, a major objective in studying history is to try to understand why events took place in the past. If we can determine how people acted in past years, we may be able to predict how they will act in the future. In this chapter we shall look at some of the major problems that Ohio and the United States face as the 21st century approaches. The political cartoon on page 368 shows one of the most important problems.

Jim Borgman, the prize-winning political cartoonist for The Cincinnati Enquirer, *created this cartoon in 1990.*

Conservation of Resources

When white people came into the Ohio Country, they found a treasure house of resources. In this section we will review what has happened to these natural resources in the past, and consider what must be done to protect them in the future.

Trees

The first settlers found the forests to be both a source of lumber for building homes and furniture, and an obstacle to agriculture. They cut and burned trees as quickly as possible with the simple tools they had. As the population of Ohio and the

United States increased during the 19th century, most of the trees of Ohio were cut to create farms and/or to provide lumber to build the rapidly-growing cities.

By 1930 many of the areas that had been cleared of forests were badly eroded, and the streams were filled with soil. You have learned that the Muskingum Conservancy District was created to deal with this problem. Wayne National Forest and several state forests were created in southeast Ohio to hold soil on the hillsides and to reduce flooding. Farmers throughout the state were encouraged to create "wood lots" and to plow their fields in ways that reduced erosion. Since 1950, however, thousands of acres of woodlands have been destroyed as urban areas expanded into the countryside.

In the grand scheme of life, green plants play an essential role because of the process of **photosynthesis**. Humans and animals need oxygen to live, and they give off carbon dioxide as a waste product. Green plants need carbon dioxide from the air, and water and minerals from soil. They give off oxygen as a waste product. Trees are especially important in this process because they have so much leaf area. Throughout history, nature has maintained a balance between the oxygen, nitrogen, and carbon dioxide in the atmosphere. In the last half of the 20th century, human beings have been creating more and more carbon dioxide as a waste product from burning coal and petroleum. At the same time, they have been destroying trees throughout the world. As a result, the natural balance between oxygen and carbon dioxide in the atmosphere has been disturbed.

Raw Materials

You learned that Ohio was a leading producer of iron ore during the 19th century, but the supply was exhausted by the end of that century. You also learned that Ohio became a great center of steel-making during the 20th century because iron ore could be obtained easily from northern Minnesota. By 1977, so much steel was being imported from Europe and Asia that the General Assembly of Ohio passed a law requiring that all steel used in construction of state and local government projects must be made in the United States. (Section 153.011 ORC.) Today all the major steel companies in Ohio are partly owned by Japanese companies, and the state law is ignored.

You learned that in 1900 Ohio was one of the most important sources of petroleum and natural gas in the world. In 1990 Ohio was the eighth largest producer of these raw materials in the United States, but we use far more petroleum than we produce. In fact, almost half of the petroleum used in the United States now comes from other nations. When the Organization of Petroleum Exporting Countries (OPEC) threatened to cut off oil shipments in 1973 and greatly increased the price of crude oil, the United States started an emergency program to develop alternate sources of liquid fuel. Three important experiments were conducted, two of which were of great interest to Ohio. The first was to develop liquid fuel from coal, and the second was to find cheap ways to make alcohol fuels from grain. The third project was to obtain petroleum from vast deposits of oil-bearing shale in certain western states. Hundreds of millions of dollars were invested in these projects. Each of the three experiments produced liquid fuels, but the costs were several times the present cost of petroleum. Nothing more will be done with these alternate sources until there is another emergency in the petroleum industry.

Recycling of Resources

Does your community practice recycling of resources? Does your school or social organization collect newspapers, aluminum cans, and/or glass bottles? If so, you are part of the recycling process. The early settlers in Ohio practiced recycling of everything made of iron because iron was so useful and so scarce. In fact, when they found it necessary to build a new house, they often burned the old one to recover the nails.

During the Great Depression, some people eked out a living by going through neighborhoods collecting old newspapers and magazines, rags, and scrap iron. During World War II, so many resources were needed for the war effort that a national slogan was, "Use it up! Wear it out! Do without!" Everyone was required to save tin cans, glass bottles, and grease from cooking and these materials were collected each week.

At the end of the war, everyone was tired of being careful with resources, and recycling almost disappeared, except for newspapers. In the following years, as labor costs increased more rapidly than costs of materials, emphasis was placed on saving labor with little regard for saving materials. When "supermarkets" and "fast food" restaurants developed, more and more materials went into packaging to reduce the labor needed to complete a sale. Today it is not unusual for the packaging material you throw away to be larger than the product you purchase. In addition, many of the plastics used in packaging cannot be recycled.

Today the Ohio Department of Natural Resources (ODNR) sponsors an annual *Recycle Month* to encourage every

individual to conserve and recycle natural resources. The box tells you about this program.

Alternate Sources of Energy

You have learned many things about production, consumption, waste, and conservation of energy in Ohio. Now we must look at challenges for the future.

Energy from Waste

Prior to 1930 most cities of Ohio disposed of their solid wastes by throwing them into **dumps**, which were located in places where few people lived. As the cities began to expand during the 1940s, land developers created new subdivisions near these dumps. People bought the new homes without studying the neighborhood and later complained about the smells and rodents associated with the wastes. Cities then built **incinerators** (large furnaces) to burn the trash. In 1970 the newly-organized United States Environmental Protection Administration (USEPA) began to enforce regulations about air pollution from these

---

Why Should I Recycle?

Ohioans generate an enormous amount of waste—more than 12 million tons a year. Each of us contributes about six pounds a day. Over a lifetime that adds up to at least 900 times our adult weight in waste!

At the same time Ohio is producing massive amounts of solid waste, it is facing a landfill crisis. In 1989, the

Ohio Environmental Protection Agency estimates that 63 of Ohio's 88 counties have insufficient solid waste capacity.

We cannot continue to just throw waste away because there is no "away." Each of us can reduce waste by reusing and recycling. In addition to extending the life of our landfills, recycling reduces disposal costs and saves energy and natural resources.

From: Brochure, *Recycling at Home*, ODNR, rev. 7/89.

incinerators. Many cities decided that they could not afford the cost of cleaning the exhaust gases from burning trash, so they began to use *sanitary land fills* — which were really *dumps* in which the trash was covered with earth each day.

As urban areas continued to expand, some people fought against the construction of new incinerators, while others opposed development of new land fills. During the 1980s, a new slogan developed out of these protests — *NIMBY*, which means "Not in my back yard!" By 1990 most urban areas were considering going back to incineration of trash under a new process called **cogeneration**. When you travel on I-71 just south of Columbus, you can see the building shown on page 372. This is the Columbus Municipal Electric Plant that burns solid wastes to generate electric power. It was built by the City of Columbus in the early 1980s on the site of a sanitary land fill that occupied an abandoned sand and gravel quarry. Modern cogeneration plants differ from the old incinerators in two ways: The exhaust gases meet the requirements of the USEPA, and the heat is used to generate electricity.

If you have been reading your community newspaper while studying Ohio, you must have found several articles about *hazardous wastes*. Almost all of the wonderful products that we use to make our lives more pleasant involve chemicals that are dangerous to our health. For many years, manufacturers of these products gave little thought to getting rid of their wastes, but today there are strict regulations about such disposal. High-temperature burning is one of the most effective forms of disposal. Industries that need very high temperatures, such as manufacturers of Portland cement, have found that they can reduce their fuel costs by burning waste

products of other industries. Unfortunately, when people living nearby learn that hazardous wastes are being burned, they cry "NIMBY!"

Nuclear Power

At the close of World War II, when the world knew about the overwhelming power of an atomic bomb, nuclear scientists talked about the potential advantages of nuclear energy for generating electricity. The greatest advantage they claimed was that nuclear energy is "clean," meaning that it does not create air pollution.

Nuclear energy, for both generating electric power and making bombs, is obtained from a form of the chemical element *uranium*. In the early 1950s, the United States Atomic Energy Commission (AEC) built two large factories in Ohio to separate uranium from its ore. One factory was near the center of rural Pike County, and the other was near Fernald, a settlement in the rural western part of Hamilton County. Since the process of refining uranium requires large amounts of electrical energy, two new coal-fired power plants had to be built along the Ohio River to supply this energy. In 1988 people living near the processing plant at Fernald began to complain that the air and ground water of the area were polluted with radioactive materials. In 1989 these citizens won a preliminary case against the operators of the AEC plant for more than $100 million in damages.

In the early 1970s, three Ohio power companies decided to cooperate in building a nuclear power plant along the Ohio River in Clermont County. Almost fifteen years passed before the plant was completed because local citizens contested the safety of the project. In 1979 a nuclear power unit at Three Mile Island near Harrisburg,

During the 1980s Columbus, Ohio began to convert its solid waste into electrical energy at this plant built on the old city dump.

Pennsylvania, had a serious accident. No one was injured, but people throughout the United States were frightened by the potential danger. In 1986 a nuclear power plant at Chernobyl in the USSR exploded, shooting radioactive gases into the atmosphere of the entire world. Many Soviet citizens died as a result of this accident. The nuclear power plant in Clermont County was ready for initial test operations when the Chernobyl accident occurred. As citizens of the area raised even more cries of *NIMBY*, the three power companies decided to raze the nuclear plant, and build a coal-fired plant on the site.

The Toledo Edison Company built a nuclear power plant during the 1970s. The cost of construction and maintenance proved to be so high that the company was forced to merge with the Cleveland Electric Illuminating Company to form the Centerior Energy Corporation. By 1986 there were ninety-two nuclear power plants in operation in the United States and twenty-eight more under construction, but some of those under construction, including the Clermont County project, were abandoned.

The biggest problem with nuclear power is the fact that during the years of operation the equipment becomes so radioactive that it is a hazard to all plant and animal life. The only solution that nuclear scientists have been able to devise is to bury the used equipment deep in the earth, but the cry of *NIMBY* is heard from people living in the region. Is nuclear energy a good source of electric power?

Transportation

You have learned how motor vehicles influenced the development of Ohio during the 20th century. These same vehicles are the cause of some of our most difficult environmental problems.

Shortly after the oil crisis of 1973, the federal government announced goals for reduced fuel consumption by requiring that all cars produced by each manufacturer should travel an average of twenty five miles per gallon of gasoline. Bigger "gas guzzlers" could be made if enough smaller fuel-efficient vehicles were sold to achieve the overall company average.

The auto manufacturers immediately began to "down-size" their vehicles, and the public responded by buying smaller cars to reduce their transportation costs. When gasoline prices dropped from over $1.50 per gallon to about $1.00 per gallon, many buyers wanted larger automobiles. The manufacturers immediately asked the federal government for permission to build less efficient vehicles. When the federal government announced in 1990 a goal of forty miles per gallon of gasoline for every automobile, the auto manufacturers said all automobiles would have to be small. Are big automobiles important to the future of our nation?

Motor Vehicle Emissions

In addition to producing large amounts of carbon dioxide, automobiles create other **emissions** (exhaust gases) that are poisonous. When exposed to sunlight, these gases produce smog, a word that was created from "smoke" and "fog."

In 1986 the USEPA said that the air in both northeast and southwest Ohio was so unhealthful that the State of Ohio would have to reduce exhaust gases created by motor vehicles in these areas. After months of political debate, the Ohio EPA decided to require a simple inspection of the exhaust-gas control devices on all automobiles built since 1980. Early in 1989, the USEPA said that the inspection system used during 1988 had not reduced pollution in the region of Cuyahoga County. What can Ohio do to reduce auto emissions?

Scrap Vehicles

In addition to creating atmospheric pollution, motor vehicles are a major source of solid wastes. The motor vehicle industry is proud of the fact that it manufactured more than eleven million automobiles and trucks in 1987. If you look ahead to 1997, they also produced eleven million units of junk! Auto scrap dealers buy old cars, cut them apart, and separate the metal items from the plastics and rubber items. The scrap metal can be recycled, but what can be done with the plastic and tires? Several experiments have been tried using tire rubber in highway pavements or as fuel for generating electric power, but millions of old tires are accumulating.

A few cities have built automobile scrap yards where large machines, cut old autos into small pieces. The iron and steel scrap

This automobile junk yard was replaced by an interstate highway.

can be removed by magnets. The plastic cloth scrap can be blown aside. The remaining metal scraps can be sorted by other methods.

Financial Resources

Money is a form of stored energy. If you save money during your working years, you can draw upon it in later life when you can no longer work. The Federal Social Security Program is based on this principle.

Ideas about the value of money changed drastically during the last half of the 20th century. For example, in 1950 a salary of $10,000 per year was in the upper five percent of all incomes, but in 1990 it was below the poverty level for a two-person family.

Buying a Home

As you have learned, thousands of people moved to Ohio with the dream of getting land to farm, but by 1900 half the residents of the state lived in cities and villages. The dream of the city people was to own their own homes. Hundreds of *Building and Loan Societies* were organized in Ohio. Friends and neighbors would meet together and pledge to deposit a small amount of money each week with the group. When enough money was accumulated to make a down payment on the purchase of a house, members of the group would "draw straws," or have a lottery, to determine which member would get the money for a house. As a result of this cooperation, over a period of several years, many families could own their homes. During the 1970s and 80s, many of these organizations changed their names from *Savings and Loan Associations* to *Savings Banks*. Have you heard about the "savings and loan crisis" in the United States? This crisis began in Ohio in 1985 when the *Home State Savings & Loan Bank* suddenly went bankrupt.

Personal Finance

By 1900 stores that sold durable goods, such as clothing, housewares, hardware, and other items that last a long time, learned that they could increase sales by offering *layaway plans*. The customer picked out a desired item and made a payment on it. The merchant put the item into storage with the customer's name on it. The customer continued to make payments and received the merchandise when the full price had been paid.

During the 1930s, merchants discovered that they could increase sales greatly by changing from the layaway plan to a *credit plan* — what came to be called "buy now and pay later." All major department stores developed credit systems and issued *credit cards* so that reliable customers could purchase goods throughout the month and pay for them at one time without an **interest** charge. (*Interest* is the price of using someone else's money for a period of time.)

During the 1950s *personal finance* companies came into existence. These companies loaned money at high rates of interest to people who could not qualify for the credit plans of the larger stores, and to people who wanted to buy from small stores that did not have credit plans. During the early 1970s, some of the personal finance companies were advertising: "Get completely out of debt! Borrow from us and pay all your bills!"

About 1970 a few banks began to issue general credit cards of the type you know as *Visa and Mastercard*. Thousands of small merchants quickly recognized the value of these cards to their businesses, because they could let a customer pay with a credit card and know that they would be paid by the bank issuing the card. The banks were then responsible for collecting from the card holder, and the banks could charge interest on unpaid amounts. By the early 1980s, some banks were making nationwide mailings of offers of credit cards, and some people had ten or more credit accounts.

During the 1930s, banks would lend good customers as much as $1,000 to purchase a new automobile, with the loan to be repaid in one year with interest. During the 1980s, many banks would lend $10,000 or more to almost anyone to purchase a new car, with the loan to be repaid over five years. As a result of all this "easy" credit, people see little reason to save money for future purchases.

Ohio Financing

In Chapter 11 you learned that the Constitution of Ohio said that the General Assembly could not go into debt without approval by the voters. In 1951 the citizens of Ohio voted for a $500 million bond issue to improve highways, and for special taxes to pay for the bonds. During the 1960s, the citizens approved several more bond issues,

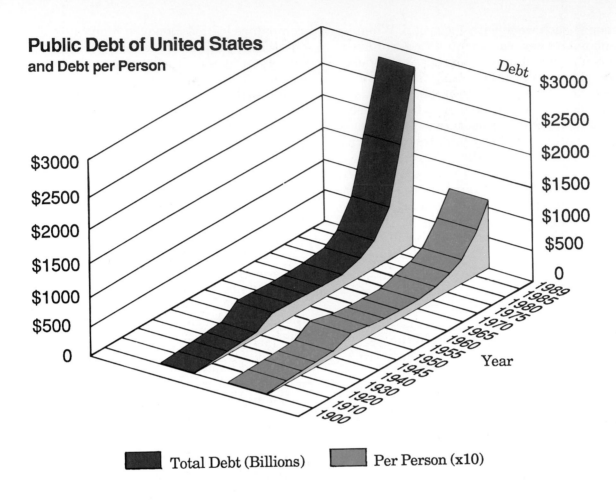

Public Debt of United States
and Debt per Person

Debt

Year

Total Debt (Billions)   Per Person (x10)

totaling at least one billion dollars, with no new taxes to pay for them. By 1989 the General Assembly was trying to find ways to pay the interest and principle on this debt while continuing the many services needed in our state.

Federal Financing

As you learned in Chapter 11, the Constitution of the United States gives Congress the power to levy and collect certain taxes, and to borrow money on the credit of the United States. The graph above shows how the federal

borrowing has grown over the years, and the portion of the debt owed by every person.

In 1981, during his first year in office, President Ronald Reagan persuaded Congress to reduce federal income taxes in order to stimulate the economy. This lowering of income taxes also contributed to the increase in debt, and the public debt went over $3 trillion in the early 1990s.

With personal and public debts increasing so rapidly, can you predict what the financial condition of our nation will be five years from now?

Social Problems

Almost everyone who lives in Ohio today has a more comfortable life than any citizen of our state enjoyed in 1900. Unfortunately many social problems of 1900 are still unsolved.

Social Security

The average worker today is much better off than a worker of 1900. Today every worker contributes money to the federal *Social Security Program*, that provides retirement payments to all workers and income for disabled persons. The State of Ohio operates a *Workmen's Compensation Program*, paid for by employers, that provides income for workers who lose their jobs or are injured while at work. The National Labor Relations Board protects workers against illegal actions by employers.

Health care insurance became available during the 1930s through the *Blue Cross — Blue Shield* programs. By 1960 many employers provided health insurance programs as fringe benefits. By 1989 these programs were costing more than $3,000 per year per employee.

Women's Rights

After many years of struggle, in 1919 women gained the right to vote. Their next challenge was to gain the right to be elected to public office. During the 1950s, a few women were elected to serve on municipal councils in Ohio. Several women have served as mayors in the municipalities of Ohio, and a few have been elected to executive offices of the state. Of the twenty-one Ohio citizens elected to the U.S. House of Representatives for the 1987-88 term, two were women. Two other women candidates were defeated for this office.

Beginning with the Great Society program of the 1960s, women have entered many more careers than ever before, but relatively few of them have been promoted to upper levels of management.

Substance Abuse

How many times have you been asked in a "secret survey" whether you use alcohol or drugs? The use and/or abuse of tobacco, alcohol, and a wide variety of drugs creates personal health problems and major social problems in our state and nation. Many people who use harmful substances like to say that it is their "right" to use their bodies as they please, but all too often substance abuse hurts innocent people even more. For example, at least 50 percent of all deaths from automobile accidents are caused by alcohol or drugs. A large majority of crimes are committed by people under the influence of alcohol or drugs.

Native Americans

As you have learned, very few Native Americans lived in Ohio after 1840. Today they are back in the news in Ohio! Before 1970 all information about the population of the United States was gathered by *census takers*, who went from house to house asking questions of the residents. In 1970 the Bureau of the Census decided to mail a census questionnaire to every household, and to have census workers collect and check the completed forms. This system worked so well that it was used again in 1980 and 1990.

You can see this statue of Chief Seattle near the City Hall of Seattle, Washington.

On the 1980 census form, under the heading of Race, people were asked to identify themselves as one of the following: White; Black; American Indian, Eskimo, and Aleut (natives of the Aleutian Islands to the southwest of Alaska); or Asian and Pacific Islander. In response to this question, 12,239 residents of Ohio indicated that they were American Indians. Appendix B shows the number of people in each county who chose to say that they were Native Americans in the 1990 census.

During the 1960s, Native Americans began to file law suits against the United States for violations of treaties of earlier years. In December, 1988 an international news magazine carried an article about the Native Americans, that said, in part:

... Thus 16 Indian leaders found themselves at the White House [with President Reagan] on December 12 [1988] for an exchange of views.

Indian affairs have always been a nuisance to American presidents. Federal policy has swung back and forth between **assimilating** Indians into the American mainstream and the current policy of maintaining tribal traditions, religions, and government. It is a confusing policy — one that has even confused the president. On May 31st [1987] Mr. Reagan told students at Moscow University [in the USSR] that American Indians

"from the beginning announced that they wanted to maintain their way of life.... Maybe we made a mistake. Maybe we should not have **humored** them into wanting to stay in that kind of primitive lifestyle. Maybe we should have said, "No, come join us: be citizens along with the rest of us." ...

Even so, the Indian leaders at the White House were encouraged. ... A special committee appointed by the Senate ... to investigate problems on Indian reservations is due to report early [in 1989].[1]

In June 1989 a news item from Washington, DC, reported on the work of this special committee:

After investigating for 17 months, collecting a million pages of documents and holding 20 days of public hearings, a Senate **panel** is preparing a report detailing the [United States] government's failed responsibility to Indians. ...

"I cannot think of any area where the federal government has so completely **abdicated** its responsibility as it has in Indian affairs," ... Dennis DeConcini ... chairman of the special committee said ... "Why weren't these problems discovered and dealt with earlier?"[2]

Shawnees Reclaim Land, Home in Ohio.

Separated by war, government **intervention**, broken treaties and time, they became one of the nation's most splintered groups, but now the Shawnees have an Ohio home.

The Shawnee Nation United Remnant Band recently purchased 20 acres south of Urbana, a west-central Ohio city, in Champaign County.

It's not much of a home for a people who once called much of western and southern Ohio home, but still a home.

"This is ours," said Hawk Pope, 48, of Dayton, chief of the Shawnee tribal band. "It was (a) rather hurtful thing to drive by miles and miles of land that used to belong to your people.... This puts an end to that." ...

Although the land purchased by the band has no historic significance, it does lie between a former Shawnee village and one of the last known campsites of Tecumseh, a Shawnee chief and famed Indian freedom fighter, Pope said.

Quoted in: *The Cincinnati Enquirer*: May 18, 1989, p. D-7

Letter from Chief Seattle to President Pierce

We know that the white man does not understand our ways. One portion of the land is the same to him as the next, for he is a stranger who comes in the night and takes from the land whatever he needs. The earth is not his brother, but his enemy, and when he has conquered it, he moves on. He leaves his fathers' graves, and his children's birthright is forgotten. The sight of your cities pains the eyes of the red man. But perhaps it is because the red man is a savage and does not understand.

There is no quiet place in the white man's cities. No place to hear the leaves of spring or the rustle on insect's wings. But perhaps because I am a savage and do not understand, the clatter only seems to insult the ears. The Indian prefers the soft sound of the wind darting over the face of the pond, the smell of the wind itself cleaned by a mid-day rain, or scented with a pinon pine. The air is precious to the red man. For all things share the same breath—the beasts, the trees, the man. Like a man dying for many days, he is numb to the stench.

What is man without the beasts? If all the beasts were gone, men would die from great loneliness of spirit, for whatever happens to the beasts also happens to man. All things are connected. Whatever befalls the earth befalls the sons of the earth.

It matters little where we spend the rest of our days, they are not many. A few more hours, a few more winters, and none of the children of the great tribes that once lived on this earth, or that roamed in small bands in the woods, will be left to mourn the graves of the people once so powerful and hopeful as yours.

The whites, too, shall pass—perhaps sooner than other tribes. Continue to contaminate your bed, and you will one night suffocate in your own waste. When the buffalo are all slaughtered, the wild horses all tamed, the secret corners of the forest heavy with the scent of many men, and the view of the ripe hills blotted out by talking wires, where is the thicket? Gone. Where is the eagle? Gone. And what is it to say good-bye to the swift and the hunt, the end of living and the beginning of survival? We might understand if we knew what it was that the white man dreams, what he describes to his children on the long winter nights, what visions he burns into their minds, so they will wish for tomorrow. But we are savages. The white man's dreams are hidden from us.

Quoted from: *Native American Testimony*, pp. 107-9, "All Things Are Connected"

In May of 1989, the Cox News Service, of Dayton, released the story in the box on page 379 about Native Americans in Ohio.

Perhaps someday you will be able to visit the land of the Shawnee Nation United Remnant Band and learn what Native Americans think about Ohio history.

Stop and Think About The Book!

After several months of study, you should have some understanding of the State of Ohio. What do you think Ohio will be like when your children study its history? Of course no one can give an exact answer to this question, but *YOU* can play an important role in the unfolding drama of our state. Even now you can be a good citizen by keeping yourself informed about what is happening in your community, county, and state, and by discussing these events with your parents, relatives, and friends. The most effective way of learning about local and state affairs is by reading newspapers and news magazines. The best television and radio news programs can only make you aware of general ideas, while the printed word can give you many details. At election time, you can study the candidates for office and the issues to be decided so that you can become an intelligent voter. You can volunteer your services to work for or against an issue or candidate.

And every day in a variety of simple ways you can do things to help preserve our natural heritage. Leaders in this movement like to quote from a letter written in 1855 to the President of the United States, Franklin Pierce seen in the box on page 380. Chief Seattle was the leader of two tribes that lived in the vicinity of the present city of Seattle, Washington. About 1990, the people of Seattle erected the statue shown on page 378 to honor the man for whom their city is named.

Native Americans lived in the Ohio Country for thousands of years in harmony with nature. In the past 200 years, white "settlers" have made so many changes the natives would never recognize it if they could return. Unfortunately, not all the changes have been for the better.

The more you learn about your community, state, and nation, the more challenges you will discover. The American system is not perfect, but is the best political system that human beings have ever lived under. What role will you play in keeping it that way?

Review the Chapter!

Building vocabulary...

abdicate
assimilate
cogeneration
dump (waste)
emissions
humor (verb)
NIMBY
interest (money)
intervention
incinerator
panel (group)
photosynthesis

What doesn't fit ... and why doesn't it?

1. nuclear, electricity, petroleum, natural gas
2. clothing, ice cream, hardware, housewares
3. savings, credit card, debt, charge account
4. exhaust, pollution, autos, gases

381

5. VISA, MASTERCARD, BLUE CROSS, CREDIT
6. Pike County, Lucas County, Champaign County, Hamilton County
7. trees, carbon dioxide, oxygen, acid rain
8. scrap vehicles, solid waste, emissions, tires
9. recycling, reusing, throwing away, making do
10. Chief Seattle, Ronald Reagan, Franklin Pierce, George Bush

Fill in the blanks ...

1. Durable goods include such things as ...., ..., and ....
2. In 1900 people put money into a Building and Loan Association in order to be able to ....
3. The .... plan was used by people who could not afford to pay the full price of durable goods.
4. During the 1970s scientists experimented with making motor fuel from ...., ..., and ....
5. Nuclear power was believed to be a good source of energy because it does not .... the air.
6. The chemical element used to produce nuclear power is ....
7. In 1987, residents of .... began to complain about radioactive pollution.
8. Automobile manufacturers prefer to built big cars because ....
9. The future will involve .... but no one can predict ....
10. Photosynthesis is important because ....

Thinking it through ...

1. What are the dangers of using credit cards too much?
2. Do some research on atomic energy and conduct a debate on the topic, "More nuclear power plants should be built in Ohio."
3. Study the transportation activities of your family for a week, and suggest ways that you all might reduce the energy used in transportation.
4. Investigate the opportunities to recycle newspapers, aluminum, and glass in your community. If there is a program, how are the materials reused? If there is no program, try to develop a plan that your school could use.
5. Think about your life for the next five years, and write out a plan that you can follow to become a better citizen than you now are. Try to follow the plan, and five years from now grade yourself on what you have accomplished.

Working with maps...

1. Go to the place where your community disposes of its solid wastes. Make a sketch map of the area. Use you county map to scale off the distance that solid waste travels from your home to the disposal area.
2. On the map of the United States, locate Seattle, Washington.
3. On the map of Ohio, locate all the places mentioned in this chapter.

Footnotes

1. *The Economist*, December 17, 1988, pp. 31-32

2. *The Cincinnati Post*, June 10, 1989, p. 3A

Information About Ohio Counties

County	County Seat	Year	Area	Source of Name
Adams	West Union	1797	586	President John Adams
Allen	Lima	1820	405	Uncertain origin
Ashland	Ashland	1846	424	Henry Clay's home in Kentucky
Ashtabula	Jefferson	1808	703	Indian for "Fish River"
Athens	Athens	1805	508	Athens, Greece, center of learning
Auglaize	Wapakoneta	1848	398	Indian for "fallen timbers"
Belmont	St. Clairsville	1801	537	Fr. "belle monte" (beautiful mountain)
Brown	Georgetown	1818	493	General Jacob Brown of War of 1812
Butler	Hamilton	1803	470	General Richard Butler of Indian wars
Carroll	Carrollton	1833	393	Charles Carroll of Declartion of Indep.
Champaign	Urbana	1805	429	French for "plain"
Clark	Springfield	1818	398	Genl. George Rogers Clark of Revolution
Clermont	Batavia	1800	456	French for "clear mountain"
Clinton	Wilmington	1810	410	Vice Pres. George Clinton
Columbiana	Lisbon	1803	534	From "Columbus" and "Anna"
Coshocton	Coshocton	1810	566	Indian for "Black Bear Town"
Crawford	Bucyrus	1820	403	Col. William Crawford of Indian wars
Cuyahoga	Cleveland	1810	459	Indian for "winding stream"
Darke	Greenville	1809	600	General William Darke of Revolution
Defiance	Defiance	1845	414	Location of Fort Defiance
Delaware	Delaware	1808	443	Indian tribal name
Erie	Sandusky	1838	264	Indian tribal name meaning "cats"
Fairfield	Lancaster	1800	506	Beauty of "fair fields" of area
Fayette	Washington CH	1810	405	General LaFayette of Revolution
Franklin	Columbus	1803	543	Benjamin Franklin, U.S. Statesman
Fulton	Wauseon	1850	407	Robert Fulton, inventor of steam boat
Gallia	Gallipolis	1803	471	"Gaul", ancient name of France
Geauga	Chardon	1805	408	Indian for "raccoon"
Greene	Xenia	1803	416	General Nathanael Greene of Revolution
Guernsey	Cambridge	1810	522	Isle of Guernsey, home of settlers
Hamilton	Cincinnati	1790	412	Alexander Hamilton, Sec. of Treasury
Hancock	Findlay	1820	532	John Hancock, of Declaration of Indep.
Hardin	Kenton	1820	471	General John Hardin of Indian wars
Harrison	Cadiz	1813	400	General William Henry Harrison
Henry	Napoleon	1820	415	U.S. Statesman Patrick Henry
Highland	Hillsboro	1805	553	High land of the area
Hocking	Logan	1818	423	"hock-hocking"Indian for "bottle river"
Holmes	Millersburg	1824	424	Major Holmes of War of 1812
Huron	Norwalk	1809	494	Indian tribal name
Jackson	Jackson	1816	420	General Andrew Jackson of War of 1812
Jefferson	Steubenville	1797	410	Vice President Thomas Jefferson
Knox	Mt. Vernon	1808	529	General Henry Knox of Revolution
Lake	Painesville	1840	231	Located on Lake Erie
Lawrence	Ironton	1815	457	Naval Capt. James Lawrence, War of 1812
Licking	Newark	1808	686	Licking River flows through area
Logan	Bellefontaine	1818	495	Benjamin Logan, a local hero
Lorain	Elyria	1829	495	French province of Lorraine
Lucas	Toledo	1835	341	General Robert Lucas of Ohio border war
Madison	London	1810	467	President James Madison
Mahoning	Youngstown	1846	417	"mahoni", Indian word for "at the lick"
Marion	Marion	1820	403	General Francis Marion of Revolution
Medina	Medina	1812	422	Arabian city of Medina
Meigs	Pomeroy	1819	432	Return J. Meigs, Governor of Ohio
Mercer	Celina	1820	457	General Hugh Mercer of Revolution

Miami	Troy	1807	410	Indian for "mother"
Monroe	Woodsfield	1813	457	President James Monroe
Montgomery	Dayton	1803	458	Genl. Richard Montgomery of Revolution
Morgan	McConnelsville	1817	420	General Daniel Morgan of Revolution
Morrow	Mt. Gilead	1848	406	Jeremiah Morrow, Governor of Ohio
Muskingum	Zanesville	1804	654	Indian for "town at the river's side"
Noble	Caldwell	1851	399	James Noble, an early settler in area
Ottawa	Port Clinton	1840	253	Indian tribal name
Paulding	Paulding	1820	419	John Paulding, captor of spy John Andre
Perry	New Lexington	1818	412	Commodore Perry of War of 1812
Pickaway	Circleville	1810	503	Indian for "a man formed out of ashes"
Pike	Waverly	1915	443	Genl. Z.M. Pike discovered Pike's Peak
Portage	Ravenna	1807	493	Indian "Portage Path" across area
Preble	Eaton	1808	426	Naval Capt. Edward Preble of Revolution
Putnam	Ottawa	1820	484	General Isiah Putnam of Revolution
Richland	Mansfield	1808	497	Rich soil of the area
Ross	Chillicothe	1798	692	James Ross of Pennsylvania
Sandusky	Fremont	1820	409	Indian for "cold water"
Scioto	Portsmouth	1803	613	"scionto", Indian word for "deer"
Seneca	Tiffin	1820	553	Indian tribal name
Shelby	Sidney	1819	409	Isaac Shelby, 1st Gov. of Kentucky
Stark	Canton	1808	409	General John Stark of Revolution
Summit	Akron	1840	412	Highest land on Ohio Canal
Trumbull	Warren	1800	612	Jonathan Trumbull, Gov. of Connecticut
Tuscarawas	New Philadelphia	1803	570	Indian for "open mouth"
Union	Marysville	1820	437	Union of parts of 4 counties
Van Wert	Van Wert	1820	410	Isaac VanWert, captor of spy John Andre
Vinton	McArthur	1850	414	Samuel F. Vinton, Ohio Statesman
Warren	Lebanon	1803	403	General Joseph Warren of Revolution
Washington	Marietta	1788	640	President George Washington
Wayne	Wooster	1808	557	General "Mad Anthony" Wayne
Williams	Bryan	1820	422	David Williams captor of spy John Andre
Wood	Bowling Green	1820	619	Col. Wood built Ft. Meigs, War of 1812
Wyandot	Upper Sandusky	1845	406	Indian tribal name

Appendix B

Population Data For Ohio Counties

	1990 Total Pop.	1980 Urban Pop.	1990 Afr.-Amer.	1990 Native Amer	1990 Asian	1950 Total Pop.	1950 Urban Pop.	1900 Total Pop.	1900 Urban Pop.	1850 Total Pop.
Adams	25,371	2,791	47	67	30	20,499	0	26,328	2,003	18,883
Allen	109,755	75,482	12,313	202	572	88,183	53,664	47,976	25,886	12,109
Ashland	47,507	23,204	460	49	271	33,040	16,810	21,184	5,668	23,813
Ashtabula	99,821	313,829	3,138	196	350	78,695	42,076	51,448	22,424	28,767
Athens	59,549	167,810	1,678	167	1,374	45,839	16,505	38,730	10,642	18,215
Auglaize	44,585	21,216	66	50	177	30,637	12,005	31,192	9,274	11,338
Belmont	71,074	39,539	1,308	81	129	87,740	45,786	60,875	25,356	34,600
Brown	34,966	3,467	406	28	30	22,221	0	28,237	3,777	27,332
Butler	291,479	207,366	13,134	379	2,659	147,203	103,909	56,870	35,139	30,789
Carroll	26,521	5,210	135	65	29	19,039	4,244	16,811	0	17,685
Champaign	36,019	10,762	992	68	113	26,793	9,335	26,642	8,425	19,782
Clark	147,548	103,898	13,031	294	653	111,661	82,284	58,939	38,253	22,178
Clermont	150,187	52,835	1,291	218	453	42,182	0	31,610	1,916	30,455
Clinton	35,415	16,432	716	59	138	25,572	7,387	24,202	1,788	18,838
Columbiana	108,276	50,697	1,409	174	219	98,920	59,247	68,590	40,508	33,621
Coshocton	35,427	13,405	415	68	112	31,141	11,675	29,337	0	25,674
Crawford	47,870	31,216	253	67	116	38,738	24,893	33,915	17,124	18,177
Cuyahoga	1,412,140	1,493,225	350,185	2,533	18,085	1,389,532	1,363,764	439,120	405,955	48,099
Darke	53,619	12,999	184	96	114	41,799	8,859	42,532	5,501	20,276
Defiance	39,350	20,739	493	80	121	25,925	13,894	26,387	10,099	6,966
Delaware	66,929	19,167	1,424	104	385	30,278	11,804	26,401	7,940	21,817
Erie	76,779	50,786	6,312	150	265	52,565	31,890	37,650	21,372	18,568
Fairfield	103,461	43,086	1,153	193	378	52,130	24,180	34,259	8,991	30,264
Fayette	27,466	12,682	662	50	102	22,554	10,560	21,725	5,751	12,726
Franklin	961,437	832,697	152,840	2,056	19,437	503,410	441,819	164,460	125,560	42,909
Fulton	38,498	15,746	93	62	137	25,580	3,494	22,801	2,148	7,781
Gallia	30,954	5,576	871	79	136	24,910	7,871	27,918	5,432	17,063
Geauga	81,129	11,367	1,056	83	312	26,646	0	14,744	0	17,827
Greene	136,731	106,133	9,611	398	2,133	58,892	33,030	31,613	8,696	21,946
Guernsey	39,024	16,145	616	70	141	38,452	14,739	34,425	8,241	30,438
Hamilton	866,228	840,243	181,145	1,204	9,198	723,952	669,807	409,479	349,573	156,844
Hancock	65,536	39,079	591	91	401	44,280	26,132	41,993	25,343	16,751
Hardin	31,111	14,274	236	66	115	28,573	12,115	31,187	15,051	8,251
Harrison	16,085	4,058	393	22	15	19,054	3,020	20,486	1,755	20,157
Henry	29,108	8,614	147	53	95	22,423	5,335	27,282	5,267	3,434
Highland	35,728	11,390	692	73	71	28,188	9,988	30,982	8,514	25,781
Hocking	25,533	6,557	234	55	25	19,520	5,972	24,398	3,480	14,119
Holmes	32,849	3,314	52	24	43	18,760	0	19,511	1,998	20,452
Huron	56,240	24,028	597	85	153	39,353	18,456	32,330	13,523	26,203
Jackson	30,230	12,691	218	53	39	27,767	12,195	34,248	14,342	12,719
Jefferson	80,298	51,393	4,488	167	266	96,495	47,589	44,357	20,829	29,133
Knox	47,473	14,323	381	93	195	35,287	12,185	27,768	6,633	28,872
Lake	215,499	190,681	3,528	250	1,447	75,979	43,049	21,680	8,850	14,654
Lawrence	61,834	33,353	1,559	57	75	49,115	20,431	39,534	11,868	15,246
Licking	128,300	62,155	2,217	247	475	70,645	36,928	47,070	18,157	38,846

	Total Population 1990	Urban Population 1980*	African-American 1990	Native American 1990	Asian 1990	Total Population 1950	Urban Population 1950	Total Population 1900	Urban Population 1900	Total Population 1850
Logan	42,310	11,888	804	58	240	31,329	10,232	30,420	6,649	19,162
Lorain	271,126	233,452	21,230	738	1,479	148,162	102,665	54,857	30,995	26,086
Lucas	462,361	443,454	68,456	1,164	4,981	395,551	353,218	153,559	133,678	12,363
Madison	37,068	11,406	2,764	96	157	22,300	5,222	20,590	3,511	10,015
Mahoning	264,806	240,295	39,681	444	985	257,629	213,327	70,134	44,885	23,735
Marion	64,274	37,040	2,707	148	285	49,959	33,817	28,678	11,862	12,618
Medina	122,354	62,409	850	172	684	40,417	13,063	21,958	3,996	24,441
Meigs	22,987	5,699	177	44	20	23,227	7,102	28,620	7,438	17,971
Mercer	39,443	13,357	14	85	100	28,311	5,703	28,021	2,815	7,712
Miami	93,182	51,890	1,779	158	606	61,309	31,412	43,105	21,547	24,999
Monroe	15,497	3,145	19	26	12	15,362	0	27,031	1,801	28,351
Montgomery	573,809	537,880	101,817	1,065	5,886	398,441	335,936	130,146	90,976	38,218
Morgan	14,194	0	570	64	12	12,836	0	17,905	1,825	28,585
Morrow	27,749	2,911	64	49	38	17,168	0	17,879	1,528	20,280
Muskingum	82,068	28,655	3,468	214	152	74,535	40,517	53,185	25,138	45,049
Noble	11,336	0	7	15	9	11,750	0	19,466	0	0
Ottawa	40,029	9,901	265	51	94	29,469	5,541	22,213	4,081	3,308
Paulding	20,488	2,754	236	54	20	15,047	0	27,528	2,080	1,766
Perry	31,557	7,945	57	46	21	28,999	7,193	31,841	4,003	20,775
Pickaway	48,255	11,700	3,036	127	95	29,352	8,723	27,016	6,991	21,006
Pike	24,249	4,603	327	72	41	14,607	0	18,172	1,854	10,953
Portage	142,585	72,083	3,906	292	1,191	63,954	28,394	29,246	8,544	24,419
Preble	40,113	6,839	147	53	65	27,081	4,242	23,713	3,155	21,736
Putnam	33,819	3,874	26	44	25	25,248	2,962	32,525	5,983	7,221
Richland	126,137	88,608	9,981	223	578	91,305	58,553	44,289	22,325	30,879
Ross	69,330	23,420	4,467	155	266	54,424	20,133	40,940	12,976	32,074
Sandusky	61,963	30,399	1,553	94	142	46,114	23,589	34,311	12,745	14,305
Scioto	80,327	41,371	2,458	409	126	82,910	44,165	40,981	17,870	18,428
Seneca	59,733	30,809	1,172	90	234	52,978	31,016	41,163	24,719	27,104
Shelby	44,915	17,657	615	49	393	28,488	11,491	24,625	5,688	13,958
Stark	367,585	279,790	25,052	950	1,529	283,194	201,772	94,747	51,585	39,878
Summit	514,990	477,342	61,185	1,065	4,989	410,032	352,196	71,715	50,268	27,485
Trumbull	227,813	172,176	15,221	341	973	158,915	98,611	46,501	18,567	30,490
Tuscarawas	84,090	42,179	623	138	187	70,320	38,360	53,751	22,639	31,761
Union	31,969	7,414	1,168	57	132	20,687	4,256	22,342	4,688	12,204
Van Wert	30,464	14,365	193	31	78	26,971	13,166	30,394	8,650	4,792
Vinton	11,098	0	4	16	3	10,759	0	15,330	0	9,353
Warren	113,909	52,860	2,415	231	627	38,505	10,006	25,584	5,591	25,560
Washington	62,254	26,368	774	111	185	44,407	16,006	48,245	13,348	29,540
Wayne	101,461	35,443	1,557	130	535	58,716	22,968	37,870	7,964	32,981
Williams	36,956	22,310	23	46	127	26,202	10,232	24,953	5,000	8,018
Wood	113,269	61,667	1,168	197	1,028	59,605	25,902	51,555	13,955	9,157
Wyandott	22,254	9,641	20	20	65	19,785	7,657	21,125	5,171	11,194
Ohio Total	10,847,115	8,332,659	1,154,826	20,358	91,179	7,946,527	5,578,274	4,157,455	2,098,136	1,980,328

* 1990 information not available.

The Governors of Ohio

1803 - Under the First Constitution, representatives to the General Assembly were elected to one-year terms on the second Tuesday of October. Senators were elected for two-year terms with one-half the positions filled every year. Governors were elected to two-year terms, with the terms beginning on the first Monday in December of the year of election.

Name	Took Office	Left Office	Number of Terms	National Offices
Edward Tiffin	1803	1807	2-	US Senator 1807-1809
Thomas Kirker	1807	1808	Completed Tiffin's 2nd term.	
Samuel Huntington	1808	1810	1	
Return J. Meigs	1810	1813	2-	US Senator 1808-1810, Postmaster General of US 1814-1823
Othniel Looker	1813	1814	Completed Meigs's second term.	
Thomas Worthington	1814	1818	2	US Senator 1803-1807 and 1810-1814
Ethan Allen Brown	1818	1821	2-	US Senator 1822-1825
Allen Trimble	1821	1822		
Jeremiah Morrow	1822	1826	2	US Senator 1813-1819
Allen Trimble	1826	1830	2	
Duncan McArthur	1830	1832	1	
Robert Lucas	1832	1836	2	
Joseph Vance	1836	1838	1	
Wilson Shannon	1838	1840	1	
Thomas Corwin	1840	1842	1	US Senator 1845-1850, Secretary of Treasury 1850-1853
Wilson Shannon	1842	1843	1- Re-elected but did not complete 2nd term.	
Thomas Bartley	1843	1844	Completed Shannon's 2nd term.	
Mordecai Bartley	1844	1846	1	
William Bebb	1846	1848	1	
Seabury Ford	1848	1850	1	
Reuben Wood	1850	1853	1+ Resigned during 2nd term.	

Name	Took Office	Left Office	Number of Terms	National Offices
William Medill	1853	1856	1+ Completed Wood's term and then elected.	

1851 - The Second Constitution included the same election and installation dates as the ammended First Constitution.

Salmon P. Chase	1856	1860	2	US Senator 1849-1855, Secretary of Treasury 1861-1864, Chief Justice of US Supreme Court 1864-1866
William Dennison	1860	1862	1	
David Tod	1862	1864	1	
John Brough	1864	1865	1- Died in office.	
Charles Anderson	1865	1866	1- Completed Brough's term.	
Jacob D. Cox	1866	1868	1	US Senator 1869-1870.
Rutherford B. Hayes	1868	1872	2	
Edward F. Noyes	1872	1874	1	
Willaim Allen	1874	1876	1	
Rutherford B. Hayes	1876	1877	1-	Resigned from second term to serve as President of the US 1877-1881
Thomas L. Young	1877	1877	Completed Hayes 2nd term.	
Richard M. Bishop	1878	1880	1	
Charles Foster	1880	1884	2	US Secretary of Treasury 1891-1893.
George Hoadly	1884	1886	1	

In 1885 the Constitution was amended to hold elections on the first Tuesday after the first Monday in November.

Joseph B. Foraker	1886	1890	2	US Senator 1897-1909
James E. Campbell	1890	1892	1	
William McKinley	1892	1896	2	President of the US 1897-1901.
Asa Bushnell	1896	1900	2	
George K. Nash	1900	1904	2	
Myron T. Herrick	1904	1906	1	
John M. Pattison	1906	1906		Few days Died in office.

In 1906 the Constitution was amended to have officials take office on the second Monday of the following January. Therefore, terms of office shifted to odd-numbered years.

| Andrew L. Harris | 1906 | 1909 | 1 | |

388

Name	Took Office	Left Office	Number of Terms	National Offices
Judson Harmon	1909	1913	2	US Attorney General 1895-1897
James M. Cox	1913	1915	1	
Frank B. Willis	1915	1917	1	US Senator 1919-1928
James M. Cox (2nd)	1917	1921	2	Candidate for US Presidnet 1920.
Harry L. Davis	1921	1923	1	
A. Victor Donahey	1923	1929	3	
Myers Y. Cooper	1929	1931	1	
George White	1931	1935	1	
Martin L. Davey	1935	1939	2	
John W. Bricker	1939	1945	3	
Frank J. Laushe	1945	1947	1	
Thomas J. Herbert	1947	1949	1	
Frank J. Lausche (2nd)	1949	1957	4-	Resigned to serve as US Senator 1957-1969
John W. Brown	1957	1957	Served a few days to complete Lausche's term.	
C. William O'Neill	1957	1959	1	
Michael V. DiSalle	1959	1963	2	

In 1958 the Constitution was amended so that the governor and other executive officers would be elected to four-year terms. The governor was limited to two consecutive terms, but no limit was placed on the other offices.

Name	Took Office	Left Office	Number of Terms	National Offices
James A. Rhodes	1963	1971	2	
John J. Gilligan	1971	1975	1	
James A. Rhodes (2nd)	1975	1983	2	

In 1976 the Constitution was amended so the governors and lieutenant governors would be elected together.

Name	Took Office	Left Office	Number of Terms	National Offices
Richard F. Celeste	1983	1991	2	
George A. Voinovich	1991			

Glossary

abate to reduce, cut back, or diminish

abdicate to give up or deny assigned responsibility

abolish to put an end to

abominable very unpleasant or disagreeable

abridge to make smaller

academy a school, usually a private high school

accessible easily reached or obtained

acid rain a mixture of water vapor and oxides of sulphur and nitrogen that falls as rain or snow

AD Anno Domino, which is Latin for "year of our Lord"

Adena Hebrew word meaning "beautiful place"—the name of the home of the Worthington family in Ross County

adjacent along side of, touching

adjourn to officially end a legal meeting

aeronautical having to do with flying

aggregate total amount

aggregate sand and gravel used in making concrete

ambush surprise attack by a hidden enemy

amend to change a written document by adding, subtracting, or altering the wording

anarchist a person who tries to destroy the government

annex to add land to the area of a city or village

anthropologist a person who studies the life-styles of groups of people, especially prehistoric people

apportionment the process by which people of the state are assigned to voting districts so that each voter has equal influence in the General Assembly

archaic belonging to a very early period, prehistoric

archeologist a person who studies the remains of things created by ancient people

arterial important route of movement

article (law) a numbered, or lettered section of a set of laws

artifact anything made by a human being

assimilate to take in something and absorb it into the body

at large a system of voting in which everyone living in a large area elects candidates for public office

attorney general the chief lawyer of the state

auditor the official who checks on the accuracy of financial records

authority a group of people elected, or appointed, to manage a special aspect of government

ballot official printed form used for voting at elections

bankrupt unable to pay off what is owed to other people

barricade a protective fence, wall, or mound of earth

BC Before Christ or Before the Christian Era

bear (verb) to carry or endure

berm (or shoulder) level area along the side of a canal or highway

bid a proposal by a contractor to do a job for a price

bill (legislation) a proposed law

blacksmith a craftsman who works with iron

blimp an aircraft that floats in the air because of a large bag filled with very light gas

blubber the fat of a whale

board a group of people elected, or appointed, to manage a special aspect of government

bond a piece of paper that says a borrower owes the person who holds the paper a certain amount of money that will be repaid by a certain date with a certain rate of interest

booster person who supports and publicizes an organization

bottled gas a gas that is compressed to liquid form

boulder a rounded piece of hard rock more than three inches in diameter

bountiful filled with good things

bounty hunter a person who seeks a reward for performing a dangerous act, such as killing a dangerous animal

brine natural water that contains salt

British people who live in Great Britain, or The United Kingdom, which is made up of England, Scotland, Wales, and North Ireland

buckeye a tree which has nuts that look like the eye of a deer—the state tree of Ohio

burr stone a piece of natural rock used to grind grain

by-laws rules for operation of an organization

camp follower person who follows an army, but is not an official member of the military group

canal a waterway made by human beings to carry water from one place to another, or to move boats from one body of water to another

carburetor device used to mix air and fuel to produce energy in an internal combustion engine

cast iron iron made by melting pig iron and pouring it into a mold

Caucasian the scientific name for people whose skins are "white"

cave, cavern a natural opening in the earth large enough for a person to walk into

census a count of people or things of certain kinds

Central Business District the most important center of shopping, offices, and government of a town—in small towns, it is the only center of business, and in large cities, it is the largest center

ceramic material made by baking clay or sand at a very high temperature

chaos uncontrolled confusion

charcoal a form of carbon made by heating wood to remove all liquids and gases

charter a legal paper that defines the powers of an incorporated body

chauffeur a person who drives an automobile for someone else

chiropractor a person trained to adjust the internal relationships of the human body without use of medicine

circuit a path from a place of beginning, through an area, and back to the place of beginning

cistern a special hole in the ground used to store water

coax to encourage by gentle words

cogeneration the use of energy obtained from burning waste materials to heat buildings and/or generate electricity

coke a form of carbon made by heating coal to remove all liquids and gases

commission a group of people elected, or appointed, to manage a special aspect of government

common law rules of conduct that are enforced when no statutory law covers a situation

communal people living together in a group in such a way that the group owns and controls all of the resources

company town a town built by a company for use of its employees

competitor a person who is trying to win the same prize

compliance agreement with the rules and regulations

compromise an agreement between two or more groups to solve a problem that has several possible solutions

concrete a construction material made of stone, sand and a binding material

confederation agreement among equal bodies to work together

conglomerate ownership of several companies that provide a variety of unrelated goods and services

consequence result of an action or lack of action

conservancy district a geographic area defined by law to solve a problem related to natural resources

conservationist a person who works to save the natural resources of the Earth

conservative a person who likes the existing political situation and, therefore, resists changing it

consolidate to combine small parts into a larger whole

constitution basic framework of law that a group of people agree to adopt as the guide for their activities

constitutional law the process by which the meaning of words in the constitution are defined

contractor a person who signs an agreement (contract) to produce a particular service (such as building a bridge) in a certain length of time for a certain price

contribute to give money, time, and/

or talent to help a cause

convenience good something people must buy frequently

convert to change from one form to another

convince to satisfy a person that an idea is correct

coolant a special liquid-gas chemical used to cool a mechanical device

cordage rope, string, cord, twine, and similar products

coroner public official who decides cause of death

corporate raider a person, or organization, that gains control of a corporation against the desires of that corporation

corporation a legal body created by the state to carry out certain activities

county a legal subdivision of the state

courtesies friendly help

cross section a slice through an object to show what cannot be seen from the outside

cultivate to treat with special care so that a plant, or human relationship will develop in a healthy way

culture the way in which particular people live together in groups

cut stone a piece of rock that has been shaped to meet a human need

delegate (noun) a person chosen to represent a group, or another person, at an official meeting

denomination a religious group that has beliefs different from other religious groups

depression an economic situation in which many people are out of work and it is difficult to get money

deputy an assistant who is given the legal power to act for an elected official

diagonal if the corners of a square, or rectangle are numbered, in order, 1, 2, 3, and 4, a diagonal goes from 1 to 3, or from 2 to 4

dialect a special form of a major language

dirigible similar to a "blimp" except that it has a rigid frame inside the gas balloon

dissolve to melt a solid material in a special liquid

distilling to heating a liquid or solid material to remove lighter chemicals

district (voting) an area defined by law for the purpose of voting

divide (noun) the line joining the highest points of land lying between two streams

divine right power said to be given by God to a ruler

due north (south, east, west) true direction

dump an area in which solid wastes are "dumped" to get them out of the way

dynamo a machine used to generate electricity

economics the study of human activities involved in producing and distributing goods and services

economy the total way in which all goods and services are created, distributed, and used

efficient completing activities successfully with a minimum of time and effort

elector person who has the power to vote in an official election

eminent domain the highest right of ownership of land

emission the giving off of gasses by the process of burning

enterprise a business organization

entrepreneur a person who has the skill and determination to carry out activities that are of benefit to the public

epidemic a situation in which many people suddenly suffer from a particular type of illness

epoch the period of time during which a geological event took place

erosion the removal of a solid material by wind or flowing water over a period of time

esker a long, narrow hill of sand and gravel that was created by a glacier

essential anything absolutely necessary for carrying out an activity

excerpt a small portion of a written statement

excise (tax) a form of sales tax on particular products

executive a person responsible for carrying out policies set by a board of directors or a law-making body

exotic foreign, or of a different culture

expedient convenient to a particular purpose

expenditure an item of expense or cost

exploit to make use of

extract to take something out of a mixture of things

extravagant without regard for cost

faction a group of people who support a particular course of action

famine extreme shortage of food

Far East a general term used to represent the eastern half of the continent of Asia—it may, or may not, include India, Indonesia, and/or the peninsula of southeast Asia

fatigue physical or mental exhaustion

fervently with strong and sincere desire

Fiberglas brand name for insulating material made of glass fibers

fiscal having to do with money and/or finances

flammable catches fire easily

flatboat a raft that has sideboards to prevent water from washing across it, and some type of shelter for travellers

flax a plant from which linen and linseed oil can be made

flint a very hard mineral that has sharp edges when broken

flourish to grow rapidly and strongly

flushed (face) redness of face due to rush of blood

foment to stir up, as trouble

ford a place where you can cross a stream easily by walking

foresight ability of think and plan for the future

fossil the remains of a creature or plant that died long ago and turned into stone

franchise legal permission to operate a business for the benefit of the public under certain conditions

free enterprise economic system in which individuals can go into, and out of, business for themselves

friction resistance created when one surface slides across another

fugitive a person who has escaped and is hiding to avoid recapture

gauntlet two lines of people facing

each other with sticks to beat upon a person who runs between them

General Assembly the law-making body in the government of Ohio

general welfare the greatest good for the greatest number of people

genetic engineering methods of changing living cells to produce new types of life

geologist a person who studies the structure of the Earth

ghetto a part of a city in which only certain kinds of people live

glacier a large mass of ice that forms on the surface of the Earth over a long period of time, moves very slowly "down hill" or toward a warm area, and then melts slowly

glacial drift the soil, sand, and gravel dropped by a glacier as it melts

gypsum a soft white mineral used to make plaster for covering walls

harbor a place were boats can be tied or anchored and be safe from high waves

heathen people regarded has having incorrect religious beliefs

herbicide a chemical that will kill a certain type of plant life

heritage something passed down from those who lived earlier

history the record of human activity throughout the ages

hold (of ship) the part of a ship below the main deck

Hopewell the name given to prehistoric people who lived in the Ohio Country about one thousand years ago

hovel a very poor place to live

humor To go along with an idea to please another person

igneous rocks created by the slow cooling of material from the core of the Earth

illumination light, or understanding, in a place where needed

impartial making decisions in a fair and even manner

inauguration the ceremony of taking office in an organization

incinerator a building in which waste products are disposed of by burning

indentured to be under contract to perform a certain amount of work to repay financial help

Indian the name European explorers

assigned to the people they found living in North and South America

Indian Agent a person appointed by the government to work with the natives

industry production of goods and/or services

infrastructure the things that humans build to create a civilization, including roads, sewers, bridges, water systems

infringe to go beyond legal limits

ingenious having ability to solve difficult problems by new methods

inhabitant person who lives in a certain area

iniquitous wrong, evil, or sinful

initiative (law) the ability of voters to join together to ask the legislative body to adopt a specific law

insolent an attitude of dislike

intangible property official papers that represent wealth, such as stocks, bonds, and patents

interest (money) the fee, or "rent", a person who borrows money must pay for the temporary use of it

intensively with great concentration

internal combustion the burning of fuel inside a cylinder to create useful energy

interurban between cities and towns

intervention the ability to help to resolve a dispute

investment the putting money or effort into a project in the hope of gaining benefits

issues questions of public action

journal a written report of events made at the time they happen

justice alternate name for a judge of a supreme court

judicial relating to deciding whether or not people are obeying the law

kame a mound of sand and gravel created by a melting glacier

keelboat a simple boat that could be moved by wind, oars, or poles

kiln a special oven for heating materials to very high temperatures

laboratory a place to try possible ways to solve a problem

latitude the angle at the center of the Earth, northward or southward from the equator, to a particular point or line parallel to the equator

legend a story passed down by word-of-mouth from generation to generation about events that happened before there was writing

legislature any official body that has the power to make laws

legislative related to creating laws

liberal a person in favor of change in the political system

limestone the type of rock created from the shells of small animals and plants that lived in a warm ocean

linguist a person who studies the structure of languages

literary minded a person deeply interested in reading and/or writing

live stock farm animals such as cows, pigs, sheep, and goats

livelihood means of earning a living

loathsome very undesirable or unpleasant

lobbying the ability of voters to join together to encourage the legislative body to pass, or reject, a particular law

lock (canal) a structure that makes it possible for a boat to move up or down between two levels of water

locomotive an engine used to move trains over a railroad

loft a space up above main area of a building

longitude the angle at the center of the Earth from the meridian through **Greenwich, England**, to the east or west, to the meridian through a particular point

lot (land) a small, legally-defined area of land

lye a strong chemical obtained from wood ashes and used to make soap

lyric relating to the characteristics of a song

macadam a highway pavement made from broken stone

machine tool a machine used to make parts to build other machines

maize the original name for the grain we call "corn"

manufacture to make something

manufactured gas a gas, made by heating coal, that can be burned to produce light and/or heat

massacre the killing of people who are not able to defend themselves

mastodon a very large animal, similar to modern elephants, that lived before, or during the "Ice Age"

materiel all types of manufactured items, not including foodstuff

meager [or meagre] a very small amount

mercantile related to buying and selling goods

meridian a true north-south line on the surface of the Earth that passes through the north and south poles

metropolitan the entire region that is strongly influenced by a large city

mica a mineral that splits easily into flat, shining surfaces

migrant worker a person who moves from place to place during the year to do unskilled labor

migrate to move place of residence over a long distance

militia citizens who join together to defend themselves against an enemy

mobility the ability to move around

monopoly a single company that produces all available goods of a certain kind

monument a permanent marker set by a surveyor to identify a point on the surface of the Earth

moraine a large, long hill of sand and gravel created by a melting glacier

morass a great obstacle to progress, as in a swamp

mortar a cementing material used to hold bricks and/or stones together

mortgage a legal paper that gives a person who lends money a claim against land owned by a person who borrows money

mutilate to badly damage, especially a person

Native Americans people who lived in America before the first Europeans came

navigable a stream with enough water to permit boats to move along it

negotiate to try to settle an argument by talking and working together

neutral having no strong opinion on a subject

NIMBY an acronym representing "Not in my back yard"

normal school a college for training school teachers

Northwest Passage the water route across the northern limit of North America that connects the Atlantic Ocean and the Pacific Ocean

notwithstanding nevertheless

nursery (plants) a special place where plants are raised from seeds until they are strong enough to transplanted for final growth

obsidian a glass-like mineral created by a volcanic eruption

obsolete something that no longer meets present needs in the best way

Ohio pipe stone a soft rock that can be carved with simple tools

omnibus a form of public transportation that does not use electric motors

opened (a road) the process of clearing away trees and other obstacles so that wagons can move along a path

oppression the act of forcing another person to bear a physical, mental, or emotional burden

optimize to make a situation as good as possible

ordain to make a situation official by action of a government or church body

ordinance law

organic any material that contains the chemical element carbon

origin the place and/or time of the beginning of an event

paleo from a Greek word for "very old"

paleo-lithic a stone age group of people or events

palisade a fence made of tree trunks set upright in holes in the ground

panel (group) a group of people who meet to discuss a problem and perhaps suggest solutions

paramedic person trained to give high-quality emergency care

parcel (of land) a small area of land that has legal boundaries

parochial related to or supported by a religious group

passport the legal paper that allows a person to leave a country of citizenship and return to it

paternalism treating other people, especially employees, as children

penitentiary a large place in which the state keeps prisoners

persecute to harm someone because of a difference of opinion

perseverance the ability to carry out a project in spite of difficulties

personal property any object owned by a person, except items attached to the Earth

pesticide a chemical that will kill a certain type of insect

petition (verb) to ask for something in a formal way

petroleum a very useful liquid mineral made up of carbon and hydrogen—the term includes both oil and gas

pharmacist a person licensed by the state to sell medicines order by medical doctors

philosophy ideas relating to the meaning of life

photosynthesis the process used by green plants to change carbon dioxide of the air into oxygen

pig iron the crude form of iron obtained directly from natural iron ore

plaque an artistic wood or metal "sign" that tells something about the object to which it is attached

plunder to steal goods by force, or the items stolen by force

polio the popular name for poliomyelitis, which is also known as infantile paralysis

political boss a strong leader of a political party

politics the art of people living together in groups

polling place official voting place for a group of people

portage a path along which boats are carried from one body of water to another

Portland cement a fine dry powder that becomes very hard when mixed with water and allowed to redry

portrait a formal picture of a person

posterity people who will live in the future

preamble introduction to an important statement

preeminence of outstanding importance

prehistoric events that took place before humans were able to put their thoughts into written form

preserved saved for future use

produce (noun) fresh fruits and vegetables

prohibit to prevent in a legal way

prosperity time of high employment and general wellbeing

prosperous enjoying a good life

province (state) a subdivision of a nation similar to a state

province the activities for which a leader is responsible

provisions (food) the food and other supplies needed for a long trip

psychic mental power that is not learned through formal education

quarry a place where stone, or sand and gravel, are removed from the Earth for use by humans

raft a vehicle made by tying logs together for the purpose of travelling over water

raw material anything obtained from nature that can be used by humans

raze to tear down

real estate land and all forms of buildings erected on the land

real property similar to real estate

recess a short break in the schedule of meetings of an organization

recession a slow-down of economic activity

receptacle a container that holds small objects or liquids

reconstruction the period of American history following the Civil War when the South was controlled by the Union army

recruit to try to get helpers for a cause

rectangular system the basic method used in the United States to divide large areas of land for private ownership—another name for the Public Land Survey

redress to make up for bad treatment

referendum a public vote on an issue

refugee a person seeking a safe place to live

register (voting) the process by which a citizens proves that she/he has a right to vote in a particular area

relic an item left over from an earlier culture

repeal to cancel a law

repulse to drive back an attack

research the search for better understanding of something

resent to feel very unhappy about

reservation a place set aside for particular use

reservoir a lake created by human beings

resolution an official statement made by a legislative or executive body

respectively applying to each one in order

retaliate to "get back at" someone who does harm

revenue money received by an organization

right-of-way the right to move over land owned by someone else

rival (verb) to compete with

rivalry competition

ropewalk a factory in which rope is made

rural relating to an area where few people live

salt lick a place where salt (sodium chloride) can be found on the surface of the Earth

sandstone the type of rock created from sand under a large body of water

scale (map) the relationship of the distance between two points shown on a map and the same two points on the Earth

scalp to cut the skin and hair from the top of an enemy's head

scenario an outline of the story of a play, movie, or opera

scholar a person who has great knowledge about a particular subject

secretary of state the state official in charge of keeping all records relating to laws of the state and of voting

sedimentary (rock) rocks formed from material under water

self-conscious to be aware of one's self

self-sustained to keep going without help

sept a special, small group of natives

sewage human wastes in liquid form

sewerage a system of pipes to carry human wastes

shale sedimentary rock created from silt and clay

sharecropper a person who works on a farm for a share of the harvest

sheriff chief police officer of a county

shopping goods things that last a long time and/or cost large amounts of money

siege the surrounding of a place by an enemy so that the people inside cannot get away or receive help from the outside

silo a building (usually tall and round) for storing grain

slaughter to kill

slum an area where people live who do not take care of their homes

smelt to use high heat to obtain metals from their ores

soil the fine material on the surface of the Earth in which plants grow

sojourn to rest or live quietly

solicitor the official lawyer for a village of city

soot fine pieces of unburned carbon from coal or oil

spare (save) to let something live that might otherwise be killed

Sputnik the name of first USSR man-made satellite to circle the Earth

staple an important item of food in the diet of a region

statistic a number that represents a group of objects, for example, the average age of the children in a class

statutory law a law created by a legislative body for a particular purpose

steerage the lowest part of a ship that people can use for travel

steel a strong metal made by mixing iron with carbon and possibly other metals

stench a foul smell

stock (finance) pieces of paper sold by a company to spread ownership of the company—each piece says that the holder of the paper owns a certain number of shares of the company

Stone Age the period of time before people could work with metals

strip mine to obtain minerals by removing all earth and rocks that lie above the desired minerals

subdue to overcome

submerged to be under water

suburban relating to the area outside the central part of a city

suffrage the right to vote

summit the highest point

supplementary something added over and above meeting the basic requirements

supreme the highest or greatest

surplus an amount greater than presently needed

surveyor person who makes measurements to create legal lines on the surface of the Earth

survival the ability to continue to live

tallow material obtained by cooking animal fat

tanning the process of changing raw animal skins into leather

taxes money paid to support the activities of government

tariff a tax placed on goods brought into a nation from other countries

tarried stayed longer than expected

tedious slow and tiresome

temperance refusal to use too much of a harmful thing, especially alcohol

tenement a building in which many people live under crowded conditions

territory a large area of land

tetraethyl lead a chemical added to gasoline to improve the operation of an automobile engine

thence from this point onward

theology the study of religion

tillage the preparation of land for growing crops

tolerant the willingness to let other people have ideas that are different

toll the fee charged for use of a highway, bridge or tunnel

torrent an overwhelming rush of water

towpath the berm or shoulder of a canal on which animals walk to pull a boat

treasurer a person who receives all money for an organization, and pays all bills

tribe a group of people who live together and share common ancestors

tributary a less important person, or thing (as a river), that gives its resources to a more important person or thing

trustee the legal guardian of wealth for another person

tuberculosis a crippling disease of the lungs or bones

turbine a rotating machine for turning the energy of water or steam into useful work

turmoil troubles that interrupt peace and quiet

turnpike a highway that requires users to pay a fee

tyrant a ruler who governs without regard for the people ruled

urban an area in which many people live freely

vengeance the act of "getting even" with a person who causes harm

ventilation the movement of fresh air through a building

vested interest personal concern

veto the ability of the chief executive officer to reject a law passed by a legislative body

volley several guns fired at the same time

voyageurs from a French word meaning "travellers"

wampum patterns of beads sewn on leather made by the Native Americans to remember important events

ward (voting) a subdivision of a city or village used for purposes of voting

warded off avoided or turned aside

warehouse a place to store a large amount of something until it is needed

warrant (court order) a written order issued by a court

warrant (verb) to earn or deserve

warrant (land) a legal paper that says the owner is entitled to a certain amount of land

wealth material possessions that have value, riches

weathering the natural processes by which solid materials of the Earth are broken into small particles

wigwam (also wigewa) a building made from bent poles covered with skins or the bark of trees

wrought iron the form of iron obtained by heating and rolling, or hammering, pig iron

zebra mussel a small shell creature that clings to hard surfaces underwater and reproduces rapidly

zoning laws that control how land may be used

Illustrations Credits

Bibliography

Sources of Additional Information

There are many books relating to Ohio. Those listed below have been selected to include a wide range of interests.

Know Your Ohio Government Columbus, OH, League of Women Voters of Ohio, 6th Edition, 1987, 125 pages. This booklet is published every few years to keep the citizens of Ohio informed about our government.

Bailey, L. Scott, Publisher, *The American Car Since 1775* New York, Automobile Quarterly Inc., 1971, 504 pages A story of the successes and failures of inventors and manufacturers of American automobiles.

Boyd, T. A. Professional Amateur, *The Biography of Charles F. Kettering* New York, E.P. Dutton & Co., Inc., 1957, 242 pages Charles Kettering was one of the most creative scientists and engineers of our state.

Brewer, Priscilla J. *Shaker Communities, Shaker Lives* Hanover, NH, University Press of New England, 1986, 273 pages The religious group we call Shakers made many important contributions to American life.

Cheek, William *John Mercer Langston and the Fight for Black Freedom* Urbana, IL, University of Illinois Press, 1989, 478 pages Born into slavery in 1825, John Mercer Langston was on of the first African-Americans to graduate from Oberlin College. He went on to establish many other "firsts" for his people.

Clark, Edna Maria *Ohio Art and Artists* Richmond, VA, Garrett & Massie, Incorporated, 1932 [Republished by Gale Research Company, Detroit, 1975], 509 pages The story of Ohio artists and their works from the earliest days to the time of publication.

Condit, Carl W. *The Railroad and the City* Columbus, OH, Ohio State University Press, 1977, 335 pages The story of how Ohio was influenced by the building of railroads

Crouch, Tom D. *The Bishop's Boys A Life of Wilbur and Orville Wright* New York, W. W. Norton & Company, 1989, 606 pages The story of a very religious man and is famous children.

Dunbar, Paul Laurence *Lyrics by the Hearthside* New York, Dodd, Mead and Company, 1899, 277 pages This is one of several books about Paul Dunbar and his poetry.

Eckert, Allan W. *The Frontiersmen, A Narrative* (1967) and *Gateway to Empire* (1983) Boston, Little, Brown & Company, Allan Eckert, a resident of Ohio, has written several books dealing with the history of Ohio from the point of view of the Native Americans.

Auditor of State *Ohio Land Grants* Columbus, OH, na, 46 pages A brief history of how Ohio was divided for sale in early days.

Giffin, William Wayne *The Negro in Ohio, 1914-1939* Ann Arbor, MI, University Microfilms, Inc., 1969, 499 pages Based on articles from newspapers and magazines, this book reports on life as an African-American in Ohio during the years shown.

Goulder, Grace *Ohio Scenes and Citizens* Dayton, OH, Landfall Press, Inc., 1973, 253 pages A collection of stories about interesting people and places.

Hahn, Thomas F. Editor-in-Chief *The Best from American Canals* York, PA, The American Canal Society Incorporated, 1980, 88 pages A collection of short illustrated articles about all the canals built in North America.

Hochstetter, Nancy Editor *Travel Historic Ohio* Madison, WI, Guide Press Co., 1986, 168 pages A travel guide to interesting places in our state.

Hornung, Clarence P. *Wheels Across America* A.S. Barnes & Company, Inc., 1959, 341 pages A collection of pictures relating to land transportation in America from the earliest days.

Howe, Henry *Historical Collections of Ohio* in Two Volumes Norwalk, OH, The State of Ohio, 1898, V.1-992 p. V.2-911 p. Provides an interesting report on every county in 1846 and 1886.

Humphlett, Patricia E. *Astronauts and Cosmonauts Biographical and Statistical Data* Washington, Gov. Print. Off., 1985, 402 pages Full of facts about the space program and astronauts.

Jackson, James S. *The Colorful Era of The Ohio Canal* Akron, OH, The Summit County Historical Society, 1981, 24 pages A short history of the Ohio and Erie Canal.

Kunjufu, Jawanza *Lessons from History - A Celebration of Blackness* (Elem.Ed.) Chicago, IL, African-American Images A short history of African-American life in the United States.

Lafferty, Michael B. Editor-in-Chief *Ohio's Natural Heritage* Columbus, OH, The Ohio Academy of Science, 1979, 324 pages A nicely-illustrated book about how Nature influences us today.

Levin, Phyllis Lee *Abigail Adams: A Biography* New York, St. Martin's Press, 1987, 575 pages An interesting history of the "birth" and "childhood" of the United States.

Little, Charles E. Editor *Louis Bromfield at Malabar* Baltimore, The Johns Hopkins Press, 1988, 239 pages A collection of articles written by Bromfield about life in a rural part of Ohio.

Magill, Frank N. Editor *The American Presidents: The Office and the Men* Pasadena, CA, Salem Press, 1986, 869 pages Information about all of the Presidents of the United States.

Nabokov, Peter Editor *Native American Testimony An Anthology of Indian and White Relations* New York, Harper & Row, Publishers, 1978, 242 pages A collection of letters written, and statements made by Native Americans during the 19th century.

Rose, Albert C. *Historic American Roads* New York, Crown Publishers, Inc., 1976, 118 pages Short illustrated articles about the earliest highways of America.

Santmyer, Helen Hooven *"... and Ladies of the Club.."* New York, The Putnam Publishing Group, 1984, 1176 pages A novel that tells how life in a small city of Ohio changed from about 1860 to about 1930.

Schneider, Norris F. *The National Road, Main Street of America* Columbus, OH, The Ohio Historical Society, 1987, 37 pages A short history of the National Road across Ohio.

Siebert, Wilbur Henry *From Slavery to Freedom* New York, Macmillan, 1898, 478 pages A history of the struggle of African-Americans to gain freedom.

Siebert, Wilbur Henry *The Mysteries Of Ohio's Underground Railroad* Columbus, OH, Long's College Book Company, 1951, 330 p. The story of a "railroad" that had no stations or schedules.

Siedel, Frank *Out of the Midwest* (1953) and *The Ohio Story* (1950) Cleveland, OH, The World Publishing Company Two books of interesting stories about people and places of Ohio

Simmons, David A. *The Forts of Anthony Wayne* Fort Wayne, IN, Historic Fort Wayne, Inc., 1977, 26 pages A booklet about western Ohio from 1790 to 1815.

Stokes, Carl B. *Promises of Power* New York, Simon and Schuster, 1973, 288 pages The story of a poor African-American boy who began world famous in politics.

Thom, James Alexander *Panther in The Sky* (1989) and *Long Knife* New York, Ballantine Books Division of Random House, Inc. The stories of Tecumseh and George Rogers Clark, respectively.

Traylor, Jeff *Life in the Slow Lane Fifty Backroad Tours of Ohio* Columbus, OH, Backroad Chronicles, 1989, 217 pages A short guide to little-known historic places in Ohio.

Tunis, Edwin *Indians* Cleveland, OH, The World Publishing Company, 1959, 137 pages A well-illustrated book about the life-styles of Native Americans.

Vonada, Damaine *Matter of Fact* Wilmington, OH, Orange Frazer Press, 1987, 159 pages A collection of interesting facts about life in Ohio.

Waggoner, Madeline S. *The Long Haul West: The Great Canal Era* New York, G.P. Putnam's Sons, 1958, 320 pages An interesting history about how people moved from the East Coast to Ohio before 1850.

Waldman, Carl *Atlas of the North American Indian* New York, NY, Facts on File Publications, 1985, 276 pages A map history of the influence of white settlers on the Native Americans throughout the United States.

Woodward, Susan L. and McDonald, Jerry N. *Indian Mounds of The Middle Ohio Valley* Newark, OH, The McDonald & Woodward Publishing Company, 1986, 130 pages A guide to the remains of prehistoric people in Ohio.

WPA, Writers' Program of the Works Projects Administration *The Ohio Guide* New York, Oxford University Press, 1940, 634 pages Good information about all parts of Ohio as of 1939.

Zimmermann, George *Ohio: Off The Beaten Path* Charlotte, NC, East Woods Press, Fast & McMillan Publishers, Inc., 1985, 158 pages Information about interesting places outside the cities of Ohio.

Index